CW00553054

THE BUMPER BOOK OF WEYMOUTH

THE BUMPER BOOK OF WEYMOUTH

MAUREEN ATTWOOLL

HALSGROVE

First published in Great Britain in 2006

British Library Cataloguing-in-Publication Data
A CIP record for this title is available from the British Library

ISBN 1 871164 52 4
ISBN 978 1 871164 52 7

HALSGROVE
Halsgrove House
Lower Moor Way
Tiverton, Devon EX16 6SS
Tel: 01884 243242
Fax: 01884 243325
email: sales@halsgrove.com
website: www.halsgrove.com

Printed and bound by CPI Bath Press, Bath.

Introduction

A number of books have been published on the general history of Weymouth and even more on specific aspects of the town's past such as the harbour, shipping, architecture and transport. Others volumes have dealt with specific periods in Weymouth's history or with particular places, for the boundaries of the modern town include a number of villages which have very individual histories of their own. *The Bumper Book of Weymouth* looks at local history in a different way, by collecting together all kinds of information about the town and presenting it not in chronological order or by subject, but alphabetically to provide an A-Z guide to the people, the events, the buildings, the monuments and the occasional bit of folklore which are all part of the Weymouth story.

The choice of entries is a combination of my own quest to find answers to enquiries during the years I worked in Weymouth Library and the discussions I have had with others interested in local history. The entries in the book are necessarily brief and many of the topics are worthy of much more detailed study. A 19th century event summarised in a few lines in the book probably originally comprised many column inches in the local *Southern Times,* a weekly newspaper which I defy anyone to search with a specific item in mind without being sidetracked by all sorts of other fascinating and incredibly detailed local news. Is this compilation a complete guide? The answer has to be no, for it would take a multi-volume work and several lifetimes to compile such a work, which could never be completely up to date since history is made every day. I hope this is a book for anyone interested in Weymouth's past – to browse through and dip into and perhaps find something new.

Acknowledgements

I would like to thank Brian Jackson, Margaret Morris and Richard Samways who made a number of helpful suggestions regarding the text. Photographs of soon-to-be-demolished buildings were faithfully recorded by Brian Jackson, Bill Macey, Ted Tranter and Joe Ward. The rare photographs of the Suffragette Camp at Weymouth are reproduced by courtesy of Diana Spence. Other illustrations are from my own collection and Weymouth Library's Local Studies Collection and my thanks, as ever, to Nicola Brown and Weymouth Library staff for their help. Last, but by no means least, I thank my husband David Attwooll who has uncomplainingly had his life more than a little disrupted during the last few months while *The Bumper Book of Weymouth* was being compiled.

THE WEYMOUTH ENCYCLOPAEDIA

How to use this book

The Weymouth Encyclopaedia is arranged in A – Z format. If you are looking for a specific subject – a person, a building etc. look under the surname or building name. For example John Bagg will be listed under **BAGG, John** and Belfield House will be under **BELFIELD HOUSE**. If another entry relevant to the subject is mentioned in the entry you have looked up, it will be highlighted in **Bold Type**. There are also '*See*' and '*See also*' references to other entries which may provide more information. Rather than adding a bibliography at the end of the book, I have followed an entry with a 'Further reading' suggestion if a book has been published on that particular topic.

NOTE: Old street and terrace names have been identified, I hope accurately, from local maps, rate books, census returns and directories, but this is not an exact science and is complicated by factors such as proposed names which are not actually used, the duplication of names, the demolition of buildings and the occasional complete renumbering of streets. Any corrections or additions would be most welcome.

A1 Stores

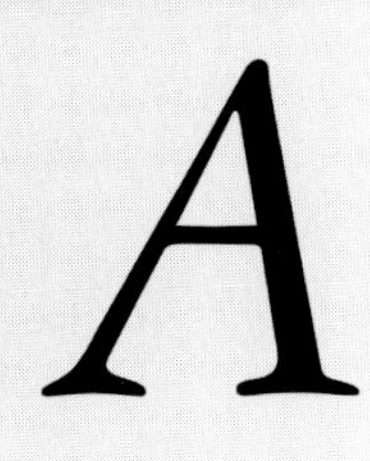

A1 STORES From 1936 until it closed in the mid-1980s, this large fruit and veg shop was at No.84a St Thomas Street, having previously occupied other town centre premises. When Comptons the Stationers single-storey shop at No.82 was demolished to allow the restoration of the once-hidden **'Old Rectory'**, the business moved into the former No.84a, renumbered as 83.

ABBOT'S COURT This was an 1890s mansion built and occupied by local builder **John Bagg**. It stood at the northern end of Radipole Lake, surrounded by extensive grounds. The road leading up to it was known as Abbot's Court Road until the 1920s when it was extended and renamed Ullswater Crescent, part of the housing development here which gave 'Lake District' names to its streets. John Bagg left Abbot's Court following his bankruptcy in 1910. For a time in the 1920s the occupant was **Thomas Burberry** of the clothing firm famous for its classic trench coat and 'Burberry Check' designs. The house was demolished in 1987, having been converted to flats around 1930. Apartments built on the site in 1988 have retained the 'Abbot's Court' name.

ABBOTSBURY ROAD In the early days before houses were built along it, this was known as Backwater Bridge Road. Although it heads towards Abbotsbury, the road probably takes its name from its connection with the Earls of Ilchester, once owners of much of the land in the Westham area, whose family seats are at Melbury and Abbotsbury.

ABERGAVENNY COTTAGE stood in **Dorset Place** (now **Newberry Road**). Timbers from the East-Indiaman ***Earl of Abergavenny*** wrecked off Weymouth in 1805 were used in its construction.

ABIGAIL is perhaps the best-known of the vessels which sailed from Weymouth to the New World in the 17th century. In June 1628 she left with **John Endicott** and other local emigrants, including three brothers from the Sprague family of Upwey, who settled in Massachusetts.

ABODE OF LOVE *see* AGAPEMONITES

ACT OF UNION 1571 This is commonly referred to as the 'Charter of Union' although it is not a Charter, but an Act of Parliament dated 2nd April 1571 and entitled *An Act for the incorporation and uniting of Weymouth and Melcombe Regis in the county of Dorset*. The exemplification document (an official copy of the original Act), dated 1st June 1571 is in the borough archives. *See also* DISPUTES

ACTS OF PARLIAMENT Probably the best known of the Acts of Parliament relating to Weymouth is the **Act of Union of 1571** which united the two separate and quarrelsome towns of Weymouth and Melcombe Regis into one borough. Over the centuries numerous Acts have been passed, most of them concerned with improving the town. Some were very specific – a 1760 Act dealt with repairing and widening local roads; one in 1820 authorised the building of a new town bridge. Many of the later ones were more general and wide-ranging, the first of these being the Corporation Act of 1887 which gave the Town Council power to create and issue Corporation Stock and thus raise the necessary funds for numerous improvements such as extensive harbour works, promenade lengthening and so on. Another in 1914 made provision for a number of harbour improvements, although years passed before some of them were implemented. One of the many clauses concerned with the 'good government' of the borough in the Weymouth and Melcombe Regis Corporation Act of 1935 empowered the council to acquire land and build a road along the western shore of Radipole Lake. This proposed road was then popularly referred to as the '**Parliamentary Road**'. WW2 put paid to this plan and it was the late 1980s before the present '**Weymouth Way**' opened, linking Westham and Radipole. Local authority Acts of Parliament are rare today, as most requirements are contained in more general legislation.

ACUTT, Douglas Gordon Weymouth-born, a teacher at **Melcombe Regis School** and a member of the **St John Ambulance Brigade**. In 1945 he published an account of his WW2 Civil Defence activities which includes details and illustrations of the numerous air raids on Weymouth.

Further reading : *Brigade in Action : the history of the origin and development of the St John Ambulance Brigade in Weymouth, and its co-operation with the Civil Defence Services during the War 1939-1945* by D.G.F. Acutt (published in Weymouth, 1946)

Doug Acutt stands alongside a Nazi plane which came down near the First Aid Depot at Cranford Avenue.

ADELAIDE ARMS HOTEL This pub was originally at No.4 Waverley Terrace, Westham, moving to a new building on the corner of Abbotsbury Road and Longcroft Road in 1902. Probably named after Queen Adelaide, wife of King William IV, after whom the Australian city was named, it pre-dates the Australian street names at Westham which commemorate the Anzac troops who were camped here in WW1. In 1928 the Adelaide Arms was renamed the **Royal Adelaide Hotel**, taking its new name from a vessel wrecked on Chesil Beach in 1872. It was the home of wartime Mayor **Joe Goddard**. Now, converted to housing, it is known as **Adelaide Court**.

ADELAIDE COURT, Abbotsbury Road is a late-20th century conversion to housing of the building previously known as the Adelaide Arms Hotel and Royal Adelaide Hotel. An earlier Adelaide Court, also known as Adelaide Place, was the final terrace on the east side of Queen Street, at its northern end. Demolished in 1936 under a slum clearance order.

ADMIRAL HARDY PUBLIC HOUSE Stands on Chickerell Road, opposite its junction with Abbotsbury Road. Opened on 15th December 1958, this was the first new public house built in Weymouth after WW2, the licence being transferred from the closed **'Lamb and Flag'** in Lower Bond Street. The name commemorates Portesham's Admiral Thomas Hardy of Battle of Trafalgar fame and was selected from entries in a competition run by brewers Eldridge, Pope and Co. Ltd.

ADMIRAL OF THE PORT This office was held by the Mayor of the Borough until 1828 when the Admiralty Courts were abolished.

AGAPEMONITES were members of a religious sect called the Agapemone or 'Abode of Love' whose licentious behaviour scandalised 19th century society. The sect's founders were Henry Prince and Samuel Starky, formerly the curate and rector respectively of a church in Somerset, and they actively recruited members in the Weymouth area. Meetings held at the Royal Hotel and a house in Wyke Road's Belfield Terrace brought in money and converts, many of whom, significantly, were women. A branch of the movement was established at Chalbury Lodge, Preston, the main 'Abode' being at Spaxton in Somerset. Prince's fondness for wealth and beautiful young women soon brought the sect into disrepute, with rumours of free love and strange rites abounding. Prince died in 1899 and a few years later his successor, another C. of E. cleric, was accused of immorality and unfrocked. The Agapemonite sect ceased to exist in the late 1920s.

'AGGIE WESTON'S' was the popular name for the Royal Sailors' Rests. Founded by Dame Agnes Weston, these were run on the lines of temperance clubs, with a Christian influence. Weymouth's Rest was in Lower Bond Street, in the converted former **Lamb and Flag** public house. It was first used in July 1961, and an official opening followed on 20th October that year. The Rest closed in May 1974, a new one opening at Portland a few months later. The building was used as a probation hostel for some years before being demolished in the late 1990s to make way for the New Bond Street shopping development.

AIRFIELDS *see* CHICKERELL AIRFIELD; LODMOOR AIRFIELD

ALBERT COTTAGES Four cottages which once stood in Lower Park Street (their site today is part of Wilkinson's store). The name was also used for the houses which are now Nos.58-64 Newstead Road.

ALBERT HOTEL, Park Street later became the Queen's Hotel.

ALBERT TERRACE became Nos.134-140 Abbotsbury Road.

ALBION CLUB This was a late-Victorian 'Gentleman's Club' which met in rooms above the **Royal Baths** in St Thomas Street.

ALBION INN This has been a popular pub name in Weymouth. One Albion Inn stood on the corner of Bath Street, adjacent to the present bus station in Commercial Road and is now a private house. Another, prior to WW2, was at No.61 Franchise Street, sometimes referred to as the Albion Jug and Bottle and also The Beehive. The third, at No.36 St Thomas Street is currently known as the 'Bar on the Corner'.

ALDERMAN COMBEN'S GARDEN, Rodwell Avenue is a little lawned area on the south side of Rodwell Avenue, presented to the town during his mayoralty 1915-1918 by **Robert Stone Comben**.

ALEXANDER, William Henry (1832-1905) A wealthy lawyer and philanthropist who contributed to many good causes. He donated the bulk of the funds necessary to provide a building to house the 1896 National Portrait Gallery in London, one condition being that he should select the architect, his choice being **Ewan Christian**. Locally, he donated funds towards the building of the **Princess Christian Hospital** and in 1891 he paid the entire cost of constructing the much-needed **Alexander Bridge** over the railway lines near Hanover Terrace, pedestrians in that area having previously risked life and limb to cross the tracks. W.H. Alexander died at No.6, Greenhill, on 26th April 1905 and is buried in Radipole churchyard

ALEXANDER BRIDGE This pedestrian bridge crosses the railway lines at the end of Hanover Road. The gift of **William Henry Alexander**, it opened in 1891 and was extended in March/April 1940 over railway tracks added since its original construction. The bridge, with a steep flight of steps at its western end, was taken down in April 2006, and its successor, put in place on the night of 5th/6th August 2006 and officially opened on 9th September, provides improved access.

The Alexander Bridge shortly before it was removed in April 2006.

ALEXANDRA GARDENS/ALEXANDRA GARDENS THEATRE Before Weymouth became a popular health and pleasure resort in the 18th century, the area of the seafront on which the gardens stand was considered to be the back of the town and the sands here were used as a dump for the town's rubbish. In the early 1800s, **Sir William Pulteney** put forward proposals to extend the Esplanade in a wide sweep at its southern end and on the resulting area of reclaimed land turfed enclosures were laid out, known as 'The Rings'. These were leased out, apparently for grazing. In 1867, George Robert Stephenson, one of Weymouth's wealthier visitors (related to the famous engineer) acquired the remainder of the lease and gave it to the town with the stipulation that the land should be laid out as public gardens. Weymouth lacked such a facility at this date, **Greenhill Gardens** and the **Nothe Gardens** not being developed until some years later. The gardens were duly planted and a tented awning erected in the centre to shelter bands playing there. Towards the end of the 19th century the Corporation introduced charges for entering the gardens, but these were fiercely disputed and by 1900 admission was largely free, except for occasional special events. The first use of the name 'Alexandra Gardens' comes in 1880, when the gardens were named in honour of Princess Alexandra, the popular 'Alix', who was betrothed to the Prince of Wales, later King Edward VII. In 1891 a traditional cast-iron bandstand was added, followed by classical statues and in 1904 thatched shelters, six in all, were erected around the perimeter of the gardens. These were removed in the 1960s and early 1970s. In 1913 the bandstand was enclosed within the shelter of a glass building known as the 'Kursaal', this being replaced in 1924 by the Alexandra Gardens Concert Hall, a venue with indoor and outdoor stages, which later became known as the Alexandra Gardens Theatre. The traditional Bandstand moved then to the Nothe Gardens, where it stayed until 1964. The Gardens were used for military purposes in WW1 and WW2. The Kursaal served as a reception centre in WWI for troops returning from the war fronts, many of them Australian soldiers injured in the fighting at Gallipoli. The early months of WW2 saw the Gardens and Theatre welcoming refugees from Europe and the Channel Islands, including almost the entire population of Alderney on 23rd June 1940. Some of the thatched shelters were bricked in for use as air raid shelters, and as the war progressed the whole area was taken over by the military. In 1942 the Alexandra Gardens Theatre became part of **HMS *Bee***, a working-up base for coastal forces and then, in October 1943, as preparations for the D-Day landings got under way, it became **HMS *Grasshopper***, later coming under the control of The United States Navy Advanced Amphibious Base (USNAAB) as USS *Grasshopper*. Post-war, the gardens re-opened to the public on 13th November 1945. In 1951 Britain celebrated the Festival of Britain at London's South Bank. One of the attractions there was the Guinness Clock, a whimsical automaton designed for the brewing company and this clock was a temporary attraction in the gardens in the summer of 1953. The Theatre closed in 1963, unable to compete with the new **Pavilion Theatre** of 1960 nearby and by May 1964 Charles Holland had converted it to house amusements, rides and coin-in-the-slot machines. In September 1993 the old theatre building burned down and it has since been replaced with a new amusements complex – the Electric Palace – on the site. The café block at the gardens' northern end was demolished and replaced by a refreshment kiosk in 1994.

An engraving of 1871 when the Alexandra Gardens were still known as the 'New Gardens'.

A summer evening, a good band, enchanting fairy lights – such a pleasant way to round off a day at the seaside in 1911, listening to Herr Meier's music in the Alexandra Gardens.

One of the thatched shelters in the Alexandra Gardens : a view from the 1950s.

Fire! The former Alexandra Gardens Theatre ablaze in September 1993.

ALEXANDRA TERRACE became Nos.1-10 Commercial Road. This was also the former name of Nos. 2-8, Franklin Road.

Alexandra Terrace, Commercial Road. All the water shown was infilled in the 1920s.

ALF'S FISH AND CHIPS is on the corner of Lynch Road and Chickerell Road. In the 1950s Alfonso Forte, of the famous hotel and restaurant owning **Forte family,** bought a farm site on the corner of the two roads and built shops around the old farmhouse, opening the prominent one on the corner as 'Alf's Fish and Chips' which was named after him and retains its name and business today. Alfonso Forte died in November 1962. *See also* IRON BOX DAIRY HOUSE

ALL SAINTS' CHURCH, Wyke Regis dates from 1455 and is thought to have replaced earlier churches on the site. It is the parish church of Wyke and was also the mother church of the parish of Weymouth, on the south side of the harbour, until the 1830s when **Holy Trinity Church** was built.

All Saints' Church, Wyke Regis in 1790, believed to be from a painting by Princess Sophia of Gloucester.

ALL SAINTS' CHURCH OF ENGLAND SCHOOL, Wyke Regis. The first turf on the school's site at Foord's Corner was cut on 28th April 1955. The foundation stone was laid in the following September and the school opened as All Saints' Church of England Secondary School on 1st May 1958. In the forty-plus years since it opened the buildings have been much extended.

ALLEN, Ralph (1694-1764) was a wealthy and regular visitor to Weymouth when the town was just beginning to realise that its future prosperity lay in the latest 'cure for everything' medical treatment of sea bathing. Allen's reorganisation of the postal system in his home town of Bath had made him a rich man, his methods later forming the basis for a countrywide postal service and his investment in the Bath stone quarries brought him even greater wealth. A mayor of Bath, he built Prior Park, his impressive home there. On Allen, Henry Fielding is believed to have based the character 'Squire Allworthy' in his novel *Tom Jones*. Ralph Allen's first summer in Weymouth was in 1750 and to his house at No.2 Trinity Road over the next decade came visitors from his influential circle of friends, and they no doubt spread the word about the benefits of bathing in (and even drinking) sea water, the 'fashionable liquor', at Weymouth. Allen's summer home still stands, now Nos.2 and 2A Trinity Road, with an extra storey added to the original building. Now converted to flats, in the late-18th century it was occupied by 'Mrs Hepburn's French and English Boarding School for young ladies' and in the early years of the twentieth century it was known as 'Winterslow House', a boarding house.

Ralph Allen's house in Trinity Road.

ALMA TERRACE was the former name of Nos.1-29 Alma Road. Probably takes its name from the Crimean War Battle of Alma, 1854.

ALMSHOUSES *see* DEVENISH HOMES; EDWARDS CHARITY; EDWARDS AVENUE; EDWARDSVILLE; and THORNHILL, Sir James.

ALPHA PLACE became Nos. 85-86 St Mary Street.

AMBULANCE STATION, Westwey Road Opened in September 1953 to replace the former station which was at the **Health Centre**, Westham Road. In the 1990s the station relocated to Souter Road, Radipole, the new building there being officially opened on 28th October 1998.

AMELIA, Princess (1783-1810) was the youngest daughter of King George III. She first visited Weymouth in 1792 and often accompanied the royal family until the King's visits ended in 1805. Always frail, she returned to Weymouth in September, 1809 but was too ill to accompany her sister Princess Mary and brother Adolphus, Duke of Cambridge, to the laying of the foundation stone of the King's Statue on 25th October. She died, aged 27, in 1810.

AMERICA'S CUP The 12 metre yachts *Sovereign* and *Sceptre* were in Weymouth in the 1958 and 1963 for trials to challenge for the America's Cup. When Sir Thomas Lipton's *Shamrocks* were here in 1903 preparing for the same challenge, *Shamrock III* was dismasted in Weymouth Bay during a sudden squall and one of those on board was drowned.

The huge mast of Sir Thomas Lipton's yacht Shamrock III *after her dismasting in Weymouth Bay on 17th April 1903.*

AMERICAN LINKS *see* ***ABIGAIL;*** AMERICAN MEMORIAL; *ASSURANCE*; ENDICOTT, John; HORDER, Edward Y; JENKINS, John

AMERICAN MEMORIAL, Esplanade was unveiled on 3rd December 1947, by Major General Clayton L. Bissell, DSC, DFC, US Military and Air Attaché. It bears a plaque presented to Weymouth by the 14th Major Port, US Army, commemorating the town's part in the embarkation of 517,816 troops and 144,093 vehicles from Weymouth and Portland Harbours on D-Day and during the months following. Portland's American Memorial bears a similarly inscribed plaque. In recent years additional plaques have been affixed to the Esplanade monument commemorating WW2 US losses in the area. The 20-foot high Portland stone column was designed by G.C.Wilkins, of the Borough Engineer's Department. A light atop the memorial is never switched off, and chimes mark the hours, the bell for which came from HM Launch 914, one of the invasion craft. A service is held here every year on Remembrance Sunday, following that at the town's main War Memorial nearby.

ANCHOR BEER HOUSE was in Lower St Mary Street, opposite the Guildhall.

ANCHORAGE, The, Park Street Cottages were pulled down in 1984 to make way for this warden-assisted development, which opened in 1986.

ANDERSON, Mark is Weymouth's current sand sculptor, successor to his grandfather, **Fred Darrington**.

ANDOVER TERRACE became Nos.4-12 Highland Road. Andover Road was the street name originally intended for Highland Road, which was also known as New Road in its early days.

ANTELOPE INN was on the east side of St Mary Street, south of Church Passage.

ANZAC MEMORIAL, Esplanade was unveiled in 2005, close to the War Memorial. It commemorates thousands of Australian and New Zealand troops who were encamped in the Weymouth and Portland area during WW1. A memorial to those who died here was erected in Melcombe Regis Cemetery, Newstead Road in 1925. *See also* AUSTRALIAN AND NEW ZEALAND TROOPS.

ARBUTHNOT FAMILY The Arbuthnots (sometimes spelt Arbuthnott) were prominent in local affairs in the 18th and early 19th centuries. John Arbuthnot, who was Mayor in 1789, the year of the first visit of King George III, was instrumental in the planning, construction and unveiling of the King's Statue. Admiral Marriott Arbuthnot (1711-1794) was a distinguished naval commander until he was ordered home after an unsuccessful action against the French in 1781 at Chesapeake Bay during the American War of Independence, after which he did not serve again. Related to the Penny and Taver families.

ARCADES *see* CLINTON ARCADE; MARKET HOUSE; ROYAL ARCADE; VICTORIA ARCADE

ARCADIA was attached to the Jubilee Hall. It was an outdoor venue for roller skating until enclosed as a hall in 1911 and used for dances and shows. Following alterations, it reopened as the Regent Dance Hall in 1926, was later used as a radio factory and then became a nightclub before demolition in the late 1980s. Arcadia was built on the site of what in the original 1880s plans was to have been swimming pool adjacent to the Jubilee Hall.

ARCH COTTAGES became Nos.30-34 Newstead Road

ARCHITECTURE Books containing a wealth of detail about local buildings are:-

Buildings of old Weymouth and Portland (4 vols) by Eric Ricketts (published in Weymouth in the 1970s, revised editions 1990s).

Revised list of buildings of special architectural or historic interest : Borough of Weymouth and Portland (Department for Culture Media and Sport, 1997).

An inventory of the historical monuments in the county of Dorset. Volume 2 South East (Part 2) (Royal Commission on Historical Monuments, 1970).

ARCHIVES The Borough archives contain historical records which date back centuries. Some original documents have been transferred to the Dorset History Centre at Dorchester but can be referred to on film at Weymouth Museum, along with much else of local interest. Today these records are preserved and cared for but this was not always the case and in the 19th century the town came perilously close to losing many rare and irreplaceable original documents – *see* 'SHERREN PAPERS' for further details.

Further reading : *Descriptive catalogue of the charters, minute books and other documents of the Borough of Weymouth and Melcombe Regis AD 1252-1800*, by H.J. Moule (Sherren & Son, Weymouth, 1883); *Weymouth and Melcombe Regis in the nineteenth century: abstracts from the minute books of the Weymouth Corporation, the Local Board of Health, the Urban Sanitary Authority and the Urban District Council, 1800-1899*, by Henry Wolff and Jack A.C. West (Weymouth Central Library, 1972).

ARCHWAY TAVERN, 28 Chickerell Road was rebuilt as the **Railway Arch Hotel**. The pub has now been converted to housing.

ARMADA *see* SPANISH ARMADA

'ARMADA CHEST' Two 16th century chests which are now in Weymouth Museum have both at various times been referred to as 'Armada Chests'.

One, an impressive chest with an intricate system of locks, is displayed in the 'Timewalk' and is reputed to have been taken from the captured Spanish Armada vessel ***San Salvador*** in 1588. Formerly kept in the Custom House, it was presented to the town in 1892.

A second, smaller chest came to Dorset a little earlier. It had been left in 1506 at Wolveton House, near Dorchester by royal visitors **Philip and Joanna**, King and Queen of Castile after they had been entertained there by Thomas Trenchard. In the 19th century the chest belonged to Colonel Pickard-Cambridge of Stanton Court, Greenhill, a descendant of the Trenchards. On his death, the chest was bought at auction by Weymouth Town Council and presented to **Sir Richard Nicholas Howard** who placed it in his home, Greenhill House. It was subsequently left by him to the Council in 1905 and is now in Weymouth Museum.

ARMISTICE SHELTER, Greenhill Gardens *see* BENNETT, Vilat Hackfath

ARMS *see* COAT OF ARMS

ARTHUR, Pierse Not a native of Weymouth, Arthur was a civil engineer. He designed the first Backwater Bridge (a timber road bridge on the site of today's **Westham Bridge**) and produced plans for the design of **Victoria Terrace**. He also published a fine map of the town in 1857, entitled Pierse Arthur's Trigonometrical Map of Weymouth and Melcombe Regis.

ARTS CENTRE *see* WEYMOUTH AND SOUTH DORSET ARTS CENTRE

ASDA took over the Newstead Road Gateway store in August 1989. Fine Fare originally planned to occupy this new supermarket built in 1988 on the former **Sidney Hall/Weymouth Football Club** site but Gateway took over before it was completed.

ASHLEY ROAD was the name in the early 20th century for Glen Avenue.

ASHLEY TERRACE became Nos.17-27 Cromwell Road

ASSEMBLY ROOMS Every fashionable spa and resort in the 18th century was expected to provide Assembly Rooms where society could congregate, socialise and be entertained. In the town's early days as a resort the 'Rooms' were in a building later to be known as the **'Old Rooms'** in Weymouth's Trinity Street. When society moved across the harbour in the 1770s to patronise Assembly Rooms in the new **Royal Hotel**, those in Trinity Street fell into disuse, becoming known as the 'Old Rooms' by 1785. Another fashionable venue in the Georgian period was **Harvey's Library and Card Assembly** on the Esplanade and there were also Assembly Rooms in the **King's Head Inn**.

Right: *In Georgian Weymouth the Assembly Rooms were the place to parade the latest fashions. These were in the first Royal Hotel.*

ASSURANCE was one of the vessels which sailed from Weymouth to America, arriving there on 8th July 1635. The leader of the party of Puritan emigrants was the Reverend Joseph Hull. His wife, children and three servants accompanied him and the *Assurance* carried 106 on board in all. These people settled in Wessagusset, which later became the town of **Weymouth, Massachusetts.**

ASTRID WAY was named after Weymouth's Tall Ship *Astrid*. The Astrid Trust was wound up in 1996. The Dutch firm who bought the ship put her up for sale again in October 1998 and Paul Compton, her former captain, launched an appeal to return the *Astrid* to Weymouth, but failed.

ATHELSTAN'S VENGEANCE The Saxon Chronicles relate that in AD 938 King Athelstan believed that his brother, Prince Edwin, was conspiring to dethrone him. He ordered that the prince be cast adrift in an open boat without oars or sails. Protesting his innocence, Prince Edwin threw himself into the sea and drowned. Athelstan, later overcome with remorse, was advised by monks to do penance by performing meritorious acts. He founded Milton Abbey, granting it *'All that water within the shore of Waymuth, and half the stream of that Waymuth out at sea; twelve acres for the support of the wear and its officer, three Thaynes and a saltern by the were, and sixty seven hides of land in its neighbourhood'.* Defining *'half the stream...'* may indicate that there was already some settlement on the Melcombe side of the harbour.

ATLANTIC COURT, Gloucester Mews is a late 20th century development on the site formerly occupied by fruit merchants Drake & Son, Ltd. and before that by A'Court's Garage.

ATTWOOLL, Jennings Alexander (1872-1961) A local councillor and Alderman, who led a personal crusade lasting more than forty years for the provision of a public library service in Weymouth. He was seventy six years old when he eventually turned a silver key in 1948 to open the town's first purpose-built library in a prefabricated building in Westwey Road. He was made a Freeman of the Borough that year. *See also* WEYMOUTH LIBRARY.

AUCKLAND TERRACE became Nos.1-19 Ilchester Road

AUGUSTA PLACE, Esplanade was built at the end of the eighteenth century and is probably named after Princess Augusta, second daughter of King George III and a regular visitor to Weymouth. It is now numbered 35-46, The Esplanade. An 'Augusta Place' of later date became Nos.27-29, Walpole Street and there was an 'Augusta Terrace' in Franchise Street in the 19th century.

AUSTRALIAN AND NEW ZEALAND TROOPS During WW1 there were huge numbers of Australian and New Zealand troops encamped in the Westham and Littlemoor areas, and also at Portland and Chickerell. The first arrivals were casualties of the unsuccessful 1915 Gallipoli campaign to gain control of the Dardanelles Straits, when thousands were wounded. They were sent to Montevideo Camp (No.2 Command Depot) at Chickerell to convalesce, the camp taking its name from Montevideo House, the large Georgian mansion there. The following year camps were opened at Westham and Littlemoor and in 1917 at Portland's Verne Citadel. They closed in 1919 and most of the troops who had remained here went home. On the former camps at Westham and Littlemoor houses have since been built, but the Anzac presence is remembered in street names such as Westham's Queensland Road, Sydney Street, Adelaide Crescent, Melbourne Street and Perth Street. At Littlemoor can be found Canberra Road and Crescent, Darwin Close, Brisbane Road, Geelong Close, etc. *See also* ANZAC MEMORIAL

AVENUE ROAD was formerly known as Langholme Street.

AVENUE VILLAS became Nos.39-48 Avenue Road

AVIATION *see* BALLOONING; BARNARD, C.D.; CHICKERELL AIRFIELD; COBHAM, Sir Alan; LODMOOR AIRFIELD; SAMSON, Lt. Charles; STAINFORTH, Wing Commander George Hedley; *THRASHER*

Further reading : *Wings over Weymouth*, by Colin Pomeroy (Dovecote Press, 2005)

AYLES FAMILY Several generations of the family were shipbuilders in Weymouth. Ayles Yard still exists today, on Nothe Parade (Hope Quay), but is now known as Nelson Wharf. The yard went out of the family's ownership in the 1880s, when it was sold to the GWR. It is a very picturesque spot, complete with late-18th century slip master's house and a section of roadway which could be lifted out for the slippage of vessels. Robert Andrews Ayles was appointed Weymouth Harbourmaster at the beginning of 1890, a post he held until 1914.

The racing yacht Conquest *built at Ayles Shipyard in 1844.*

Babbidge's Square

B

BABBIDGE'S SQUARE A long-lost place name. The square occupied an area close to the Quay at the lower end of St Thomas Street and St Mary Street. Any semblance of a square here was lost when property was demolished to allow approaches to a new Town Bridge in the early 1820s. The Babbidge surname occurs in 17th century deeds which also refer to *'a parcel of ground called Babbidges Key and sometimes Babbidges Square and sometimes Rowes Square...'*

BACKWATER/ BACK SEA A term used since very early times to describe the waters of the River Wey, from the sharp right-angled bend the river takes at the western end of today's North Quay up to Radipole. The terminology used to describe the Wey between the harbour mouth and Radipole has changed over the years and varies even today. Starting at the seaward end, the water as far as the Town Bridge is known as the 'Harbour' or 'Outer Harbour'. The stretch from the Town Bridge to Westham Bridge is known as the 'Backwater' or 'Inner Harbour' and, more recently, as 'Weymouth Marina'. Since the building of Westham Bridge in 1921, the water north of the bridge as far Radipole has usually been referred to as 'Radipole Lake' but the Backwater name is still used for this stretch and the rail bridge which crossed the lake was always known as the Backwater Rail Bridge or Backwater Viaduct.

BACKWATER RAIL BRIDGE (1863-1909) The first railway bridge to cross the Backwater/Radipole Lake was built in 1863 to carry the **Weymouth and Portland Railway** line. It was a timber structure and lasted until 1909, when it was replaced by a steel bridge.

BACKWATER RAIL BRIDGE (1909-1976) In 1909 a five-span lattice girder steel bridge replaced the timber bridge which carried the Weymouth and Portland Railway across the Backwater/Radipole Lake. Shortly after it came into use on 1st February 1909, a new station, Melcombe Regis, opened on embanked land opposite the end of King Street to serve the Portland line. In 1958 a gas main was attached to the bridge to take the gas supply across the Backwater and thence to Portland, the local gasworks having closed that year. The bridge became redundant when the Portland line closed to all traffic in 1965 (it had closed to passengers in 1952), although old rolling stock was stored on it until early 1966. Demolition of the bridge began in November, 1974 but it was problematic and the whole structure was not cleared until 1976. The present **Swannery Bridge**, a five-span concrete road bridge opened in April 1987, now crosses the water close to the line of the previous rail bridge.

The Backwater Rail Bridge of 1909 being demolished in 1974. Today's Swannery Bridge carries road traffic across the Backwater at almost the same spot.

BACKWATER ROAD BRIDGE (the first road bridge to Westham) *see* WESTHAM BRIDGE (1859-1921)

BACKWATER TUNNEL An unusual square stone structure which stood in the middle of Weymouth's Inner Harbour/Backwater prior to the development of the Marina complex in the 1990s always raised questions as to its purpose.

The timber bridge built in 1863 to carry the Weymouth and Portland Railway (opened 1865) across the Backwater. It was replaced by a steel viaduct in 1909.

It dated from 1836-7 and housed a vertical brick shaft leading down to a tunnel. This tunnel took gas supply pipes from the gasworks on Westwey Road under the harbour to Melcombe, pipes leading to the tunnel from the gasworks being laid directly under the harbour bed on the western side of the Backwater. A second shaft brought the mains up to near ground level close to the end of Coneygar Lane (Lower Bond Street). *See also* GAS SUPPLY

BAGG, John (1862-1923) Builder and builders' merchant, and a key figure in the development of Westham in the late 19th century. For some years John Bagg ran the largest building firm in Weymouth, owning several brickyards and with a branch in Dorchester. He built his own mansion, Abbot's Court, overlooking Radipole Lake in the 1890s. Three times Mayor, in 1900-1, 1901-2 and 1902-3, he was a popular man who lived extravagantly, entertained lavishly and over-reached himself financially, being declared bankrupt in 1910, having lived beyond his means for some years. Afterwards he moved to Boscombe and went into insurance. He died there in January 1923, aged 60, and his body was brought home for burial in Radipole churchyard.

John Bagg, three times Mayor of Weymouth in the early 1900s.

BAGGAGE SHED and LANDING STAGE, Weymouth Pier Built in 1889 by Weymouth Corporation when the GWR took over the cross-channel steamer service. Passenger landing facilities prior to this had been somewhat primitive. The baggage shed, a single-storey timber structure, was extended during the pier rebuild of the 1930s but was eventually demolished and replaced in 1967 by a two-storey block housing a passenger terminal, customs hall and offices.

BAILEY, Albert (1860-1916) Lived at Sutton Poyntz and was known as the 'Ploughman Poet', as he owned a market garden there. Author of poems and sonnets, his work was praised by Thomas Hardy.

BAILIFF Prior to the Union of Weymouth and Melcombe Regis in 1571, Weymouth did not elect a Mayor, but instead elected two bailiffs as its leading citizens. Following the Union two bailiffs continued to be elected to 'assist' the Mayor until 1835. Although the roles were not dissimilar, the term 'bailiff' indicates a form of manorial jurisdiction, the bailiff standing in for the manorial steward, usually an aristocratic royal appointee. The appointment of bailiffs dates back to the reign of King Henry I, who granted Weymouth to Swithun's Priory at Winchester. The Prior, in a Charter of 1252, granted Weymouth immunities and privileges similar to those of Southampton.

BAKER, Thomas (1837-1905) Art master at several schools in Weymouth from the 1870s until his death in June 1905. Frequent Royal Academy exhibitor who excelled in the painting of fruit pieces. His daughter Julia Baker was also an artist.

BAKER STREET, or BAKERES STREET was an ancient street in Melcombe, mentioned in 14th century documents, its location unknown today.

BALLAST QUAY or BALLAST WHARF was on the Weymouth side of the harbour and ran between the end of **Hope Quay** and the start of the **Stone Pier**.

BALLOONING The first known hot air balloon ascent from Weymouth was in August 1842 when Mr Green and Captain Currie, both experienced balloonists, ascended from the racecourse at Lodmoor in the *Royal Albion* balloon watched by a crowd of some 15,000. They came safely back to earth near Bere Regis. In the latter half of the 19th century there were a number of demonstration ascents, the intrepid airmen taking off from the Nothe area or Whitehead's field at Wyke Regis. A tragedy occurred in 1907 when a military balloon and its two occupants were swept out to sea – *see* ***THRASHER*** *for the details.*

Everyone stops to view the Royal Albion *balloon as it drifts over Weymouth in 1842. An engraving by Henry Burn.*

BALMORAL TERRACE became Nos.43-49 Abbotsbury Road.

BALMORAL VILLAS became Nos. 50-52 Abbotsbury Road.

BALTIC INN was on the east side of Park Street, almost opposite its junction with Wooperton Street. It was from the Baltic that sailing ships brought cargoes of timber into Weymouth and the pub was close to the timber yards and timber ponds along the Backwater shore.

BANDSTANDS There were once two decorative cast-iron bandstands on Weymouth seafront but, sadly, these elegant little structures around which an outdoor audience could enjoy brass band concerts, went out of fashion. At the southern end of the prom, one was installed in the Alexandra Gardens in 1891. It was moved to the Nothe Gardens in 1924, but was dismantled in 1964, having gone out of use and being too costly to maintain and repair. Opposite the Burdon Hotel (now the Prince Regent Hotel) a bandstand was erected in 1907, standing on the beach until Esplanade widening brought it onto the prom in the 1920s. This one disappeared in the late 1930s to make way for the **Pier Bandstand**, which bore no resemblance to a traditional bandstand at all.

BANK BUILDINGS is so called because at its southern end the largest building in the row was a bank in its early days. It later became, in turn, Mrs Voss's Boarding House, the Cherbourg Hotel, the Marine Hotel, the Edward Hotel and the Hotel Dumonts before being converted into Edward Court apartments in 1980. The building has undergone a great deal of alteration since it was erected and its original building date is uncertain. It appears in a painting by Thomas Girtin of late 1790s date and documentary evidence seems to suggest a completion date of around 1801. When the Baptist Church was extended in the 1920s two of the original houses in the terrace were demolished. Bank Buildings now comprises No.16, The Esplanade (the former Bank building), followed by Nos.17,18 and Bank Buildings Baptist Church.

BANK BUILDINGS BAPTIST CHURCH There was a Baptist minister in the town as early as 1715 and later in the century Baptists are thought to have met in a room in the building on the Quay then occupied by the seawater baths (where the Sailors Bethel, now headquarters of the Royal Dorset Yacht Club, was built in the 1860s). The Baptists have occupied the present site in Bank Buildings since 28th July 1814, their meeting place then comprising two houses at the end of the terrace, with a lease which forbade them from making any alterations to the façade of the buildings. In 1859 they were permitted to add the present fine colonnaded stone front to the church, and adjacent properties were replaced by the Baptist Hall in the 1920s. At the rear of the church there was once a small burial ground on which Sunday schools were later built.

This view of Bank Buildings in the mid-19th century shows the Baptist Chapel (right) before the present colonnaded front was added in 1859. The old bank is on the left.

BANK CHAMBERS, 63/63a St Thomas Street These were offices in the John Groves building on the corner of St Thomas Street and Lower St Alban Street, which was demolished in 1966. The Chambers took their name from the Weymouth Old Bank House, Groves' predecessor here. The site is now occupied by Tesco.

BAPTIST CHURCH *see* BANK BUILDINGS BAPTIST CHURCH

BARNARD, C.D. His 'World's first air circus' came to Weymouth in August 1931.

BARNARDO'S HOME A Dr Barnardo's Convalescent Home for Little Girls opened at No.9 Victoria Terrace in October, 1905.

BARNES, William (1801-1886) The Dorset poet, teacher and parson has a slightly tenuous link with Weymouth. He gave occasional lectures in the town and in 1861 became, for just a few months, the owner of No.13 Hope Street, a property he sold as executor of his son-in-law's will. As both he and his son-in-law were clerics, the house was named 'Parson's Pledge' in modern times.

BARNETT, Guy South Dorset's first Labour MP, elected 22nd November 1962. Angus Maude, representing the Conservative party, lost the seat by 704 votes, 5057 votes having been polled by the Anti-Common Market candidate Sir Piers Debenham. It was a shock result. The election had been called when Viscount Hinchingbrooke, South Dorset's Conservative MP for 21 years, succeeded to the title Earl of Sandwich on the death of his father and was elevated to the House of Lords. Guy Barnett lost the seat on October 15th 1964, when Evelyn King won it back for the Conservatives.

BARRACK STREET In 1872 the Council resolved that the High Street from 'Mr Ayles shop to Hope Square' was to be known as Barrack Street. (It led to the **Red Barracks**).

BARRACKS In the eighteenth century, when troops were required to be accommodated in English towns they were not usually housed in barracks, but billeted in inns and public houses, supplemented by tented camps. Since innkeepers had to pay to provision the soldiers, billeting was much resented. In the 1790s plans to build a number of barracks to house troops were put into operation and the first of these were still under construction when war with revolutionary France began in 1793. Three barracks were built at Weymouth during this period. *See* QUEEN'S BARRACKS; RADIPOLE BARRACKS; RED BARRACKS.

BARRACUDA BAR *see* OLD RECTORY

BARRETT, William Bowles (1833-1916) Born in Rodwell. A solicitor who held a number of public appointments. He was also a botanist, archaeologist and local historian. Realising the importance of oral history, in the 1860s he made notes of conversations held with his father and other elders of the town as they recalled the Weymouth of their younger days. He also transcribed extracts from the old Town Council Minute Books. He was a noted botanist who collected specimens and compiled a catalogue of the flora of the Weymouth area. His notebooks (4 in all), botanical notes and his large collection of rare local books are now in Weymouth Library's Local Studies Collection.

'BARROW BOYS' These were enterprising young lads who waited at Weymouth railway station in the 1950s and early 1960s with assorted trucks and barrows, offering to transport holidaymakers' luggage to their lodgings for a few pence. Their success became something of a contentious issue with local taxi drivers who soon realised they were losing fares!

BARTLETT, John Albion (1857-1934) Builder. Responsible for much of the development of Rodwell in the late 19th century, where he built **Springfield** and became the landlord of much property in the Chapelhay district. John Bartlett died at his home No.2 Bincleaves Road, in July 1934. A stone crane base bearing his name can be found on the quay wall just beyond the lifeboat house. Here, in 1896, he fitted a crane to lift the roadway at Cosens' No.2 slipway.

BASSO, Louis (1882-1962) Italian by birth and formerly a ship's engineer, Louis Basso came to Weymouth before WW1 to do diving and salvage work. He had a scrap metal store in High Street and was a partner in the firm which operated motor boats off Weymouth beach in the 1920s. He was employed to demolish Abbotsbury Castle in the 1930s, before returning to diving and salvaging. Well known for raising the sunken coal hulk *Haytian* in Portland Harbour in 1937.

BATH, KING'S A stone bath was made for King George III and installed at Gloucester Lodge in 1789, the intention being to acclimatise the King to the cold water of his first bathe in the sea by gently lowering the temperature of the water day by day during the first week of his stay. The bath, damaged during alterations to the Gloucester Hotel in 1988, was restored and is now in Weymouth Museum.

This rather uncomfortable-looking stone bath was intended to introduce King George III to the cold sea by lowering the water temperature each day in the week before he took his first bathe in Weymouth Bay.

BATH CHAIRS Bath Chairmen stationed themselves outside the main hotels on the sea front hoping for fares. Surprisingly, no local Bath Chair appears to have survived as a museum exhibit, although the chairmen were still plying for trade as late as 1929 when five were granted licences.

On the Esplanade in about 1900, three Bath Chairmen await fares.

Mr James Eaton Robens, in his nineties, is conveyed by Bath Chair to cast his vote in a local election. Today, this group would be standing outside Weymouth Library.

BATHING *see* BATH, KING'S; BATHING MACHINES; BATHS ON THE QUAY; MIXED BATHING; ROYAL BATHS; SEA BATHING

BATHING MACHINES The first mention of any kind of bathing machine or bathing hut in Weymouth comes in 1748 when R. Prowse had a 21-year lease granted *'of the room which is now made up of Timber and Boards on the North side of the Harbour Adjoining to his Land To be Used as a Bathing house and for no other purpose'*. Joseph Bennet was granted a similar lease. Once the visitors began to arrive, large octagonal bathing machines resembling wooden huts on wheels were placed on the sands and by 1785 some twenty or thirty were available for hire. Bathing in the 18th century was a cumbersome process. On the beach, the intending bather ascended the steps into the machine and closed its doors. A horse was then hitched to the seaward end of the machine and slowly began to trundle the machine and its occupant (who was disrobing in the privacy of the interior) towards the waves. Once in deep water, the horse was taken back to the shore, seaward-facing doors were opened, steps were let down and the bather was able to descend into the briny. 'Guides' or 'Dippers' were available for hire, usually strapping women who assisted an often timid and sometimes frail bather into the cold sea water, advertised as a cure for all the ills of a none-too-healthy age. When the bathe ended, the whole routine was repeated in reverse, the bather being dried, dressed and ready to step out by the time the machine was back on the sands. King George III first bathed from one of these octagonal machines, but once it was realised he would be a regular visitor to Weymouth much grander machines were built for the use of the royal family. These incorporated 'modesty hoods' which could be pulled down over the steps where the bather descended into the sea, thus providing a private, but rather clammy and claustrophobic 'bathing pool'. King George also had a floating bathing machine, with grilles which allowed sea water inside. When sea bathing became a popular pursuit in Victorian times, the 'dippers' were largely dispensed with, and soon it also seemed absurd to pay a man and a horse to pull a 'house on wheels' into the sea. Smaller machines came into use with small wheels enabling them to be easily moved off the beach in winter. In 1890 large Bathing Saloons containing individual cubicles were placed on the beach, with long ramps leading to the sea for bathers to walk along. There was, of course, no mixed bathing (this was not allowed until the early 1900s) and strict regulations were in force regarding the distance that the Ladies' Machine had to be situated from the Gentlemen's Machine. The machines were run as a commercial enterprise and the only free bathing allowed was at Greenhill where gentlemen were permitted to change behind screens erected by the Corporation. By this time, although some horse-drawn bathing machines were still in use, bathing huts and bathing tents for hire had appeared on the beach. As late as the 1920s and 1930s changing on the beach was still frowned on. A number of machines remained on the beach between the two World Wars, being used as changing huts but they were removed in 1939 and did not return, some being converted for use as garden sheds. In 1983 Weymouth Museum restored an octagonal bathing machine, donated in pieces by Mrs Clifford Chalker and once used as a summerhouse by her family. It is this one which is traditionally believed to have been used by King George III in 1789 and at some point in its history the royal coat of arms was added over the front door. New wheels were made for the machine and it is now in the Timewalk, Brewer's Quay.

Left: *'Royal Dipping' by John Nixon. As King George III takes his first bathe at Weymouth in 1789, a band stands by ready to play 'God Save Great George our King' as soon as the royal head goes under the water.*

Below: *An octagonal bathing machine believed to have been used by King George III, shown here on the sands around 1910. It is now in Weymouth Museum.*

Entitled 'Maids in their proper element' this view of the interior of the King's Floating Bathing Machine is believed to depict the three Princesses who were his eldest daughters.

A picture postcard of about 1910 which gives a good impression of the size of the individual bathing machines then in use.

BATHS ON THE QUAY, Melcombe side. Opened in the eighteenth century, these were on the site where the **Sailors' Bethel** was later built (now the HQ of the **Royal Dorset Yacht Club**). The baths were supplied with sea water, hot or cold, a contemporary guidebook stating that *'The Cold Bath is chiefly used by persons incapable of using the Bathing Machines either from lameness or very uncommon timidity'*. By the 1830s trade was falling off as the baths were not ideally situated, being amongst warehouses where steamers discharged their cargoes and adjacent to **Burdon's Coal Stores** where wagons were constantly loading dusty coal. The **Royal Baths** in St Thomas Street replaced them in 1842.

BAY TREE INN was on the Weymouth side of the harbour in the early 18th century. Location unknown.

BAZELL'S LANE was an early name for **St Leonard's Road**.

BEACON, The, 91 Wyke Road There have been two houses on this Wyke Road site, both deriving their name from the days when warning **beacons** were lit all along the south coast to warn of intending invaders sighted out at sea. One such a beacon once stood nearby. 'Beacon Hill', also known as 'The Beacon' was the home in the 1890s and early 1900s of **Captain Edwin Payne Gallwey** of the **Whitehead Torpedo Works**. His house was demolished and replaced in 1936 by the present large house, also called 'The Beacon', built for Sydney Renee Courtauld of the Courtauld textile family. She lived there until her death, aged 89, in February 1962 and in her will The Beacon was left to the National Trust. It was subsequently sold and converted into three dwellings. The nearby Courtauld Drive is named after her. She was the sister of **Catherine Dowman.**

BEACONS have long been used along the south coast as a warning that an enemy was in sight. A chain of them was set up within sight of each other and in times of danger a watch was kept at each one. Once one flared into life, the next would be fired and so on along the coast alerting the local defence forces to assemble. In this area, when the beacon was lit at Blackdown (where Hardy's Monument stands today) it alerted the watch at the Wyke Beacon above Wyke Road, whose lit beacon would then alert another on the Nothe headland, and so on. The local beacons, tall wooden towers with combustible material at the top, are illustrated on an intriguing 16th century map of the Dorset coast, now in the British Museum.

BEALE'S COURT was adjacent to No.27 Trinity Road, to the west of Holy Trinity Church.

BEAR HOTEL formerly the Bear Inn and thought to date back to the late 17th century, was at No.62 St Mary Street, and once had a large yard and stabling reaching back to St Thomas Street. The Bear ceased trading in 1929 and tailors Montague Burton built a new shop on the St Mary Street site.

BEATING THE BOUNDS This is an ancient custom derived from the annual blessing of crops and fields which often included a perambulation of parish boundaries. In the days before written records were kept it ensured that future generations would remember where the boundaries lay. Beating the Bounds was often a highly ceremonial event which usually took place in Rogation Week and sometimes on Ascension Day itself. A procession made its way slowly round the boundaries of the parish and at certain spots the elders of the village would 'beat' the boys on the seat of their pants, which was supposed to act as a painful reminder of the location of the boundary in later years. Weymouth has not always observed the traditional date, nor has there been a set interval of years between the perambulations. The 10 or 12 mile walk could be quite strenuous, entailing trips in rowing boats and the scaling of walls with ladders, although generous refreshments were usually provided

The ceremonial 'Beating of the Bounds' rarely takes place now. The long perambulation of the borough was an exhausting but quite jolly affair. This picture postcard showing a local lad being 'bumped' on one of the borough's boundary stones in 1909.

along the route. Town records make mention of perambulations of Melcombe Regis and Radipole in the 16th century. In later years some were proposed but not necessarily carried out. Definite Beatings of the Bounds took place in 1840, 1844, 1847, 1852, 1870 (on this occasion, to maintain authenticity, one of the party actually scaled and walked over the top of the old gasometer), 1896 (the boys were 'bumped' on new boundary stones erected to commemorate the extension of the borough in 1895), 1909 and 1933 (when more boundary stones were added, bearing Mayor Hamblin's name). In 1983 parties of children from Westhaven Junior School walked sections of the boundaries. *See also* BOUNDARIES

BEDFORD TERRACE became Nos.29-37 Cromwell Road.

***BEE,* HMS** The shore base was established at Weymouth in 1942 as a working up base for coastal forces and its craft occupied most of the northern side of Weymouth harbour from the Town Bridge to the Pavilion Theatre, which was used as a lecture hall. The Alexandra Gardens Theatre was used as the base's dining room and kitchen. In October 1943, when preparations for Operation Neptune and the D-Day landings got under way, the harbour was required to accommodate assault craft and HMS *Bee* left Weymouth (eventually moving to Holyhead). HMS *Grasshopper* took over the area to prepare for the 1944 invasion.

BEECHCROFT INFANT SCHOOL, Corporation Road opened in April 1991.

BEEHIVE PUBLIC HOUSE, No.61 Franchise Street was also known as The Albion. The area was cleared following WW2 air raid damage.

BELFIELD COTTAGE is on the east side of Gipsy Lane.

BELFIELD HOUSE was built around 1780 by Isaac Buxton for his wife Sarah and designed by John Crunden. It went out of the **Buxton family**'s ownership in 1855 and the thirteen-acre grounds which surrounded it were soon being seen as a development opportunity. There was, however, no reduction of the park until the 1870s when a portion of Belfield's grounds became the site of **Portmore**, a mansion entered via a long drive and entrance lodge in Cross Road. In the 1930s new roads and new houses were brought very close to Belfield, when the then owner sold off most of the remaining land. After military use in WW2, George Squibb became the new owner of Belfield in 1945 and he wrote a brief history of the house. Belfield was much restored by Captain and Mrs John Wright who bought the property in 1965, and it has had a number of owners since their deaths in 1980.

Further reading : *Belfield and the Buxtons* by G.W. Squibb (privately printed, 1954).

A view of Belfield House when it was surrounded by acres of parkland.

BELFIELD TERRACE became Nos. 4-14 Wyke Road.

BELGRAVE COTTAGES stood behind No.50 Dorchester Road (No.50 is the Dorset Cake Company's Belgrave Bakery). They were demolished, probably in the late 1960s, after lying derelict for many years.

BELLE VUE CINEMA, Belle Vue The cinema opened in a converted school building in December 1910 and closed on 29th September 1956. In 1958 the building was converted to become the present **Elim Church**. In the mid-19th century it housed a British Boys' School and in the late 19th and early 20th centuries the **Damons**, father and son, ran a museum-like warehouse on the ground floor where they dealt in skeletons, fossils and shells etc. The top floor was occupied by the Belle Vue Printing Company, which was later acquired by H.D. Warwick of 98 St Mary Street.

BELLE VUE COURT, Belle Vue Road was built in 1965.

BELVEDERE INN, High West Street was formerly known as the Netherbury Arms.

BELVIDERE, Esplanade Building commenced around 1818 but there were many delays before the terrace of 16 houses was finally completed in the early 1850s. Now Nos.116-131, The Esplanade.

BELVIDERE COTTAGE was on the corner where Crescent Street joins Victoria Street. Royal Crescent Surgery, built in 1986, now stands on the site.

BELVIDERE COTTAGES became Nos.27-32 Crescent Street.

BELVIDERE COURT was in Crescent Street.

BELVIDERE MEWS became Nos.18-26 Crescent Street.

BENNETT, Alfred John (died 1931) Architect, brother of **Vilat Hackfath Bennett**. Nephew of R.C. Bennett, designer of **Gloucester Street Congregational Church**, on whose death he took over the Weymouth architectural practice in 1904. The firm, at No.10 Gloucester Terrace, appears to have been run after his retirement by Arthur John Bennett.

BENNETT, Vilat Hackfath (1864-1948) Started a drapery business in Park Street in the early 1920s and went on to become the owner of the largest department store in the town, gradually buying up individual properties until his shop, V.H.Bennett, occupied a large site running through from St Thomas Street to St Mary Street at their junction with Bond Street. He was Mayor of Weymouth in the 'Peace Year' of 1918-1919. Disappointed that his own plans for a war memorial were not adopted, he instead presented the 'Armistice Shelter' to the town which still stands today in Greenhill Gardens. His home was 'Whitecross' on Buxton Road. The house was demolished in 2005 and apartments built on the site have retained the name of the old house.

Right: *Making good use of advertising space on the side of a local bus in the 1920s, V.H.Bennett publicised his store on the Portland-Upwey route.*

BENT PATH AVENUE was the former name of Melcombe Avenue.

BERESFORD, Admiral Lord Charles William de la Poer Commander of the Channel Fleet at Portland 1907-1909. He was originally offered the Freedom of the Borough in 1910 but at the time his duties prevented him from accepting it. He accepted the honour in 1913 but it was not until 12th May, 1914 that the ceremony took place (it had been planned for February that year, but was delayed due to the Admiral's illness).

BERESFORD LODGE became No.132 Abbotsbury Road.

BERESFORD VILLAS became Nos.7-9 Franklin Road.

BERNARD MITCHELL'S CHARITY *see* MITCHELL CHARITY

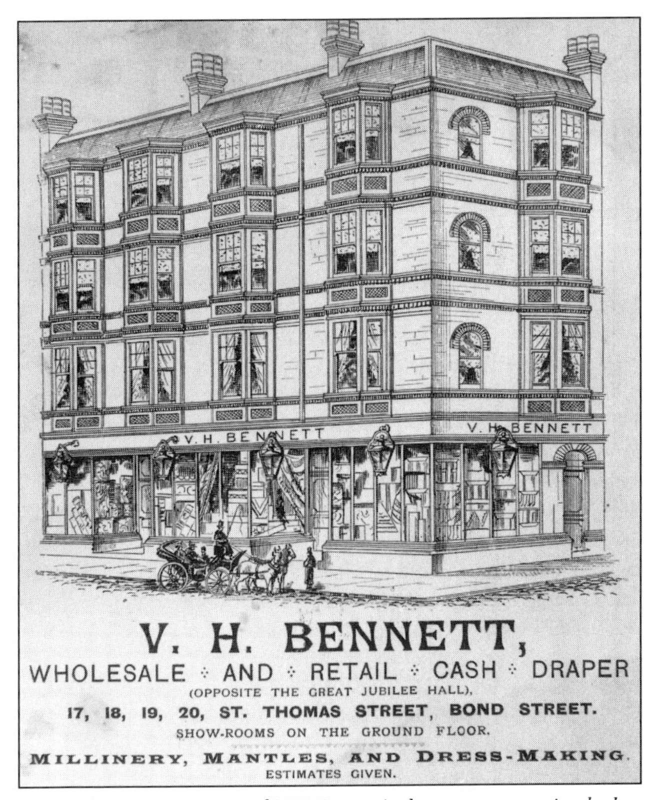

A St Thomas Street view of V.H.Bennett's department store in the late 19th century. The upper floors of the building are still very recognisable today.

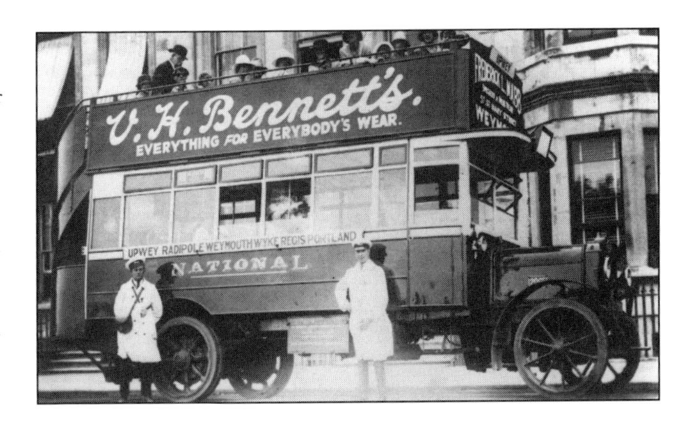

BESANT'S SHIPYARD was on Hope Quay (today's Nothe Parade). The last ship built there was the *Kate*, in 1863. The yard was later occupied by Cosens and Co (Cosens' No.1 slipway).

BETHANY HALL *see* GEORGE STREET HALL, Westham Road

BETTS TIMBER YARD and sawmills stood on the corner of Gloucester Street and Commercial Road (now the site of The Bridges Medical Centre). Their huge timber sheds extended along Commercial Road as far as Wooperton Street, and were built on reclaimed land, formerly a timber pond owned by **Philip Dodson**. Betts later became part of builders' merchants Webb, Major and Co. The timber sheds were demolished in the early 1980s and Park Street car park now fills the site.

BILES BROS. Wholesale and retail newsagents Shop at No.87 St Thomas Street opened in June 1958. The business had started 100 years previously in Lower Bond Street and later acquired wholesale premises in Great George Street. Two members of the family have been Mayors of the borough – Albert 'Bert' Biles in 1935-6, 1936-7, 1937-8 and his nephew Anthony Walden Biles in 1971-2.

BILLETING the compulsory billeting of soldiers and sailors on households was unpopular and became even more so in 1690 when it was transferred to innkeepers who had to provision the troops billeted on them without reimbursement. The problem was solved in the early 1790s with the erection of purpose-built **Barracks**.

BINCLEAVES/BINCLEAVES FARM This place name is thought to derive from 'within the cliffs' and was known in the mid-16th century. Bincleaves Farm (also known as Lovell's Farm) in today's Bincleaves Road area, was described as comprising some 50 acres when it went on the market in 1850 and housing developments began there in the 1860s. In May, 1891 a further one hundred plots of building land on the 'Bincleaves Estate' went up for auction.

BINCLEAVES BREAKWATERS Work commenced late in 1893 on the construction two additional breakwaters at Bincleaves to enclose Portland Harbour. The two original breakwaters at Portland, built between 1849 and 1872, did not provide an adequate defence against submarine and torpedo warfare. The Bincleaves Breakwaters were completed in 1905.

BINCLEAVES HOUSE General Penny was the first owner of Bincleaves House, which stood at the seaward end of Bincleaves Road and was the first of the houses built on the old **Bincleaves** farmland. In the 1890s it was the residence of George Eliot, of the **Weymouth Old Bank**, which crashed in 1897 and resulted in his bankruptcy. Bincleaves House was demolished in 1977, although its lodge still stands. The apartments of Dolphin Court and houses of Redcliff View have been built on the site of the old house. (An older house, referred to as Bincleaves Old Mansion House, is thought to have existed in the Hope Square area).

BINCOMBE The hamlet nestling below Ridgeway Hill is thought to take its name from the old words 'bean' (bean) and 'cumb' (valley) – the valley where beans are grown. Boundary extensions in 1933 brought a tiny portion of Bincombe into the modern borough, but the majority remains outside, making a large indentation on the borough's northern boundary. Parts of Holy Trinity Church date from the 12th century. In the churchyard two young German soldiers lie in unmarked graves, shot for desertion in 1801. They had attempted to sail away from their duty of guarding the town during the visits of King George III. Around this tragic incident Thomas Hardy based his story *The Melancholy Hussar*. Bincombe enjoyed a few minutes fame in the 1940s when a vast radio audience which awaited the Christmas Day message of King George VI heard the well-known Dorset broadcaster Ralph Wightman describe the celebration of Christmas in this village community before the King spoke.

BINCOMBE BUMPS On Bincombe Hill are the prominent Bronze Age round barrows known locally as 'Bincombe Bumps'. Here, in the Napoleonic era, King George III reviewed his troops and watched them participate in mock battles, ready to defend the coast against Bonaparte's invaders. The King's son, Frederick, Duke of York, was the Army's Commander in Chief and tradition has it that it was on Bincombe Hill that *'The Grand Old Duke of York, He had ten thousand men, He marched them up to the top of the hill, And he marched them down again'* although the location of the hill in the rhyme has never been positively identified.

BINCOMBE TUNNEL Construction of the railway tunnel which cuts through the chalk of Ridgeway Hill between Weymouth and Dorchester began late in 1846. It is 817 yards in length, Dorset's longest railway tunnel.

BIRD IN HAND PUBLIC HOUSE was at No.26 St Nicholas Street in the Victorian period *'opposite the new concert hall'*. This was formerly the 'Crown Tap' associated with the Crown Hotel.

BLACK DEATH In the 14th century rumours reached England of an epidemic raging in Asia, a deadly disease which killed within days, or even hours. It swept through the trade routes in the 1340s and once it reached Europe, it was not long before the bubonic plague, or 'Black Death' crossed the Channel, arriving in Melcombe Regis in the summer of 1348. The Grey Friars Chronicle states *'In this year 1348, in Melcombe, in the county of Dorset, a little before the Feast of St John the Baptist, two ships, one of them from Bristol, came alongside. One of the sailors had brought with him from Gascony the seeds of the terrible pestilence and through him, the men of that town of Melcombe were the first in England to be infected'*. A monk of Malmesbury wrote *'In the year of our Lord 1348, about the Feast of the Translation of St Thomas, the cruel pestilence, terrible to all future ages, came from parts over the sea to the south coast of England into a port called Melcombe, in Dorsetshire'*. By the end of that year the disease was at its height in Dorset and was spreading throughout the West Country and inland, decimating the population. It is estimated that between 30% and 50% of the people died in the 'Great Pestilence'. Bubonic plague is so called because it caused buboes or boils, inflamed swellings which turned black as the patient's condition worsened. There were further outbreaks in the 1300s and sporadic flare-ups until the 17th century. 'Black Death' was not a contemporary term and came into use in later centuries, possibly to distinguish it from the 'Great Plague' of 1665. One important outcome in 1348 was the virtual collapse of the old feudal system of labour as men began to realise their truth worth when there were too few left to work the land.

BLACK DOG HOTEL/INN St Mary Street is of early foundation, thought to have been built around 1600 and once known as 'The Dove Ale House'. 'The Dove' was the scene of an alleged murder in the 1640s (*see* **Chiles, John and Mary**) at which time it would have stood on the outskirts of the town. Legend has it that the inn's owner at a later date was the first person in Weymouth to own a black Labrador dog, brought into the port from Canada and the first of its breed to be seen in these parts. The pub became known as 'the inn with the black dog', which led to its change of name.

BLACK HOSPITAL was a popular name for the 1870s **Isolation Hospital** in **Rocks Terrace**. (Its exterior was painted with black tar).

BLACK ROCK AND BLACK ROCK FIELD From 1835 until 1895 the spot known as Black Rock denoted the northern boundary of the town. It is the high land at the western end of what is now Cassiobury Road and once directly overlooked the Backwater but now overlooks land infilled in the 19th and 20th centuries on which the railway and Radipole Park Drive and Gardens were built.

BLACKDOWN HOUSE, Buxton Road (former name **Claylands**) became a convalescent unit for patients from Herrison Hospital, in August 1948. It was opened by Miss L.M. Groves, daughter of the late Sir John and Lady Groves, whose home it had been from 1905 until WW2 when it was taken over by the War Department. When the health services ceased to use it the house was threatened with demolition in 2000, but it was saved and has since been converted into a Day Nursery. A housing development known as Churchill Gardens was built in the grounds in 2005.

BLOCKHOUSE LANE leads from St Mary Street to New Street. This was its original name, but in the 19th century it was known as 'Pope's Passage', reverting to Blockhouse Lane in 1880. The lane led to the site of a 16th century blockhouse fortification on the sea front. In 1960 the Woolworth store then on the southern side of Blockhouse Lane purchased Sargeants shop on the northern side and applied to close the lane with a view to expanding their store across it, but permission was refused.

BLOOMFIELD TERRACE, Rodwell Avenue Bloomfield Terrace achieved a certain brief and unjustified notoriety in 1865 when cholera was about in the south of England. A Mr Groombridge and his wife lodged there during a visit to Weymouth in 1865 and returned home to Epping, where he and eleven other people connected with his household contracted cholera, eight of them dying from the disease. To Weymouth came a medical man to ascertain if the disease had been contracted in the resort, but he found no trace of it. It subsequently transpired that Mr Groombridge had been feeling unwell for many months and had been advised to try a stay by the sea to improve his health – and, temporarily, no doubt it did, since tests on the water supply at his own home showed that the family's drinking water was taken from a well into which the contents of the house's cesspool had been leaking. The family continued to drink this impure water after their return home and quickly succumbed to the prevalent cholera. Bloomfield Terrace and Weymouth were in the clear.

BLYTON, Enid A number of books written by Enid Blyton were illustrated by local artist **Grace Lodge**.

BOARD OF GUARDIANS These Boards came into being under the Poor Law Amendment Act, 1834. The Board was the governing body of the local workhouse or 'union', a term used when several parishes grouped together to provide workhouse accommodation. Workhouses were renamed Poor Law Institutions in 1913. Boards of Guardians were abolished by the Local Government Act of 1929 and the final meeting of the Weymouth Board of Guardians was held on 25th March 1930. Responsibility for the Poor Law Institutions passed to the County Council and they became known as Public Assistance Institutions. *See also* WORKHOUSE

BOER WAR Local men who served in the Boer War 1899-1902 were granted the **Freedom of the Borough.**

BOGUE, Ida M. (1885-1972) Artist. Taught at the Convent of the Sacred Hearts in Carlton Road North. An unpublished children's book entitled *Child Hazel*, which she wrote and illustrated between 1912 and 1947, was highly praised when it was featured in the BBC-TV programme 'Antiques Roadshow' in 2004.

BOND STREET In earlier centuries Bond Street was known as Coneygar or Cunigar Ditch or Lane. It once marked the outskirts of Melcombe and was the place where earthen defence works were thrown up in time of war. Bond Street probably took its name from the Bond family, prominent in Dorset and the local community. In the late 1980s much of the area leading from St Thomas Street to the Inner Harbour and known as Lower Bond Street was boarded up prior to being demolished to make way for a new shopping development, which was much delayed. It finally opened in 2000, when this part of the street was renamed **'New Bond Street'**. 'Bond Street' now runs from the east side of St Thomas Street to the seafront, although in past years the stretch from St Thomas Street to St Mary Street was called 'Middle Bond Street', and from St Mary Street to the seafront 'Upper Bond Street'. Upper Bond Street in early documents is called 'the lane leading to the sea'.

BOND'S CHRONOLOGY Denis Bond of Lutton, who died in 1658, was an ancestor of the Bonds of Creech Grange. In his chronology he recorded many useful historical facts and anecdotes. His is the only surviving description of the first Weymouth Town Bridge of the 1590s.

BOOK OF REMEMBRANCE, ST MARY'S CHURCH Dedicated on 13th September 1950, the Book contains the names of all known residents of Weymouth and Melcombe Regis, military and civilian, who died in the two World Wars. A page of the Book is turned every week.

BOOT HILL today is part of Rodwell Road. In former times it was known as Boot Lane (presumably taking its name from the Boot Inn nearby) and before that as Leach Lane or Bucklers Lane. A plaque outside **Netherton House** records the generosity of **John Cree** who paid for road widening in 1851, and the road width was increased again in the 1890s.

BOOT INN, High Street dates from the mid-17th century and has been an inn at least since the early 1700s. Reputedly haunted and also the haunt of smugglers. In 1728 Customs man T. Parker was assaulted *'in the Boot Alehouse for going there to see for "runned goods"'.*

High Street's Boot Inn abounds with ghostly tales.

BOOTH, General William Of the Salvation Army. Visited Weymouth in November 1890 and spoke at the Jubilee Hall, and again in August 1906 when he was on a motor car tour of the country. On this occasion he received a civic welcome and spoke at the Sidney Hall.

BOROUGH STATUS Weymouth received its earliest surviving charter from St Swithun's Priory in 1252, the town having been granted to the Priory by King Henry I. This granted it status as a 'free borough' entitled to enjoy the privileges and immunities enjoyed by Southampton, but 'borough' and 'town' are terms rather loosely used in these early years. Although Weymouth is older of the two towns, no record exists of it having been officially incorporated as a borough, but, by having a common seal and a mace carried before the bailiffs it is referred to as a 'Corporation by Prescription'. Melcombe was granted borough status by King Edward I in a charter granted in 1280 and although this charter is lost, its terms are confirmed in ones of later date. In 1571 the separate towns became the single 'Borough of Weymouth and Melcombe Regis', the name of which changed to the 'Borough of Weymouth and Portland' in 1974, when local government reorganisation brought Portland within its new boundaries. *See also* WEYMOUTH; MELCOMBE REGIS.

BOSCAWEN Training ship and floating HQ for sea cadets until their hut at Bincleaves opened in 1964. It was moored alongside Westham Bridge and went to the breakers in April 1964. Earlier vessels of the same name had served at Portland as training ships for boys who joined the Royal Navy. The first *Boscawen* arrived in 1866 and was replaced in 1873. In 1907 this second *Boscawen* was replaced by *Sapphire* which was joined by two old battleships, renamed *Boscawen II* and *Boscawen III.* The shore-based training establishment at Portland was also known as *Boscawen.*

BOULTON VILLA *see* DOWMAN, Catherine

BOUNCING BOMBS The prototypes of the bouncing bombs designed by Barnes Wallis, which would eventually be used in the Dam Busters' raids on the Mohne and Eder dams in May 1943, were initially tested on the Chesil Beach Bombing Ranges in late 1942 and early 1943. Subsequent trials took place at Reculver in Kent. A prototype bomb recovered from The Fleet in 1992 is on display at Abbotsbury Swannery.

BOUNDARIES The inhabited limits of the two settlements of Weymouth and Melcombe Regis would not have stretched far beyond the harbourside in their early history. Both were originally contained within older settlements – Weymouth was part of Wyke Regis and Melcombe was part of Radipole. As they developed as ports in mediaeval times some agreement must have been reached as to their early boundaries. Weymouth's extended westwards to a point just south of the old gasworks site and included the beginning of Town Lane (today's Chickerell Road). Behind its harbourside houses the early boundary followed what is today St Leonard's Road, down around Hope Square and along today's Barrack Road. Beyond this line, all the land, including The Nothe, was part of Wyke Regis. Also belonging to Wyke was the whole area on the western shore of the Backwater, where the suburb of Westham would develop in the late-19th century. Melcombe's growth had begun at the harbour mouth, on the narrow sandspit leading down to the harbour. Its early boundary with neighbouring Radipole to the north was in the Greenhill vicinity but it was ill-defined and often the source of disagreements. **Clark's Hill**, part of **Melcombe Common**,

Dating from 1895 and bearing the name of T.H. Williams, Mayor of the newly-extended borough, a number of these boundary stones can still be found around the town.

for example, was described as being within Radipole in the early 1830s, but in 1617 there are references to this land being part of the borough and town of Weymouth and Melcombe Regis. These issues were resolved with the passing of the Municipal Corporations Act of 1835, which made the Borough boundary and the Parliamentary boundary one and the same. Thus the Borough's northern boundary was extended by the addition of a triangle of land formerly in Radipole, which included Clark's Hill and the Dorchester Road area as far as Lodmoor Hill, the boundary line being drawn east to west from the sluice on Preston Beach Road, across to Argyle Terrace and thence across to **'Black Rock'**, which, before infilling, overlooked the Backwater shoreline. On the Weymouth side in 1835 a tract of land behind Chapelhay was brought within the borough, taking in an area of Rodwell as far as Bincleaves and extending westwards to Cross Road, all formerly part of Wyke Regis. In 1895 the boundaries of the borough were extended again, encompassing the fast-developing suburb of Westham and also more of Radipole, including 'new' Radipole which was growing up in the Spa Road area between Dorchester Road and the old village. 1933 brought another major boundary change when parts of the parishes of Bincombe and Chickerell and the villages of Broadwey, Preston, Radipole, Upwey and Wyke Regis were added to the borough. The next major change came with the reorganisation of local government in 1974. The boundary was extended to include Portland and the borough took a new name – the 'Borough of Weymouth and Portland', replacing the former 'Borough of Weymouth and Melcombe Regis'. *See also* BEATING THE BOUNDS

BOUNDARY STONES *see* BEATING THE BOUNDS; BOUNDARIES

BOURNEMOUTH TERRACE Newstead Road became Nos.158-164 Newstead Road.

BOWLEAZE COVE *see* OVERCOMBE; RIVIERA HOTEL

BOWN, (Albert) George Was the first Mayor of the newly created 'Borough of Weymouth and Portland' in 1974.

BOYLE, Percy (1869-1953) Was the GWR's Traffic and Marine Agent at Weymouth Quay from 1915 until 1935. Alderman, Freeman of the Borough and Mayor in 1928-29 and 1929-30.

BOYS CLUB, Chickerell Road The YMCA Boys Club met originally in temporary premises in Holy Trinity Schools, Chapelhay. Fund raising for the purpose-built centre in Chickerell Road began in April 1960.

'BRACE OF WHITE GREYHOUNDS' was a pseudonym used by the author of a satirical work entitled *The Royal Tour to Weymouth and places adjacent in the year 1789* and reflects the custom of presenting King George III, whenever he passed through the New Forest, with a brace of white greyhounds in silver collars, led by a silken cord and coupled in a gold chain.

BREAKWATER or 'APRON' on the sands near the Alexandra Gardens was constructed in 1810 to protect the Esplanade wall which was being undermined at this spot. It was higher when first built, but later in the century it fell into

The remains of the Breakwater in 1910, one hundred years after it was built. It now lies beneath tons of sand which have built up at the southern end of the Esplanade.

decay and much of the stone was removed, leaving only the base. This still exists today, lost from view under many tons of sand which have since built up at this end of the beach.

BREWER'S QUAY opened on 30th June 1990. John Groves and Sons' handsome former brewery building and adjacent premises in Hope Square now house a shopping village, cafes, **Weymouth Museum**, **The Timewalk** and a Brewing Museum (with small-scale brewing). Adjacent former brewery buildings have been converted to apartments and houses now occupy much of the surrounding former brewery land.

BREWERIES In earlier centuries beer-brewing at home was quite usual and inns often had their own brew houses to supply their customers. The harbourside at 'Hope' was an ideal location for the establishment of a brewery, close to quays where barley cargoes (some coming down the River Wey from farms at Radipole) could be unloaded and in an area plentifully supplied with springs and wells – hence the derivation of such street names as Spring Gardens and Spring Lane, and **'Springfield'**, a fine house (now demolished) once owned by the head of the Devenish Brewery. Brewing has been carried on in the area for centuries and in Hope Square the two names of J.A. Devenish & Co., Ltd. and John Groves and Sons, Ltd. have long been associated with the brewing industry. William Devenish purchased an established brewery here in 1824 and Groves brewery was founded in 1840, the present large red brick brewery of John Groves and Sons being a Crickmay design of 1904. The rival firms temporarily united in WW2 when enemy bombs destroyed much of Devenish's premises, but it was 1960 when they officially merged, the Devenish name being used from then on. In 1985 brewing ceased locally when the company relocated to its other brewery in Cornwall. The buildings were converted to become the tourist attraction, shopping village and museum complex called **Brewer's Quay** in 1989-90. Still to be seen in the exterior brickwork of a number of the local pubs built by the companies are the initials of Devenish or Groves. *See also* DEVENISH, J.A.& Co., Ltd.; GROVES, John & Sons, Ltd.

BRICKYARDS Clay, the raw material required by the brick, tile and pottery industries is in plentiful supply in the Weymouth area. There was a building boom in the town following the visits of King George III and a number of brickyards must have been established to provide the local building trade with the bricks needed to keep pace with the demand for fashionable houses by the sea. Chickerell was to become the foremost supplier of bricks from the mid-19th century with two works at Putton Lane and Crook Hill, these not closing until 1965 and 1969 respectively. They also produced other wares required by the building trade – chimney pots, pipes, tiles etc. In the mid-late 19th century there are known to have been brickworks at Rodwell, (known as 'Middlehill' off today's Sudan Road), Wyke Road (Gypsy Lane area, known as Gulleshayes), the Nothe, Pye Hill, Greenhill, Radipole and Upwey. At Westham a brickworks dating from the early 19th century was taken over by F. W. Padgett of Poole in 1862 and was the largest in the Weymouth area. It underwent a number of name changes before going out of use in the early 1900s, by which time it was known as The Weymouth Brick, Tile and Pottery Company. The South Dorset Technical College (later Weymouth College) was built on the site in 1939 and when this establishment transferred all its departments to Cranford Avenue the site, accessed via Pottery Lane, was redeveloped as housing, the new street names commemorating some of the famous English pottery companies – Wedgwood, Aynsley, Goss etc.

BRIDGE/BRIGE is a lost place name. It is listed in the Domesday Survey of 1086 as having four fishermen, and centuries later there are mentions of 'Bridge', near Weymouth. It was possibly on the shores of The Fleet at Wyke Regis.

BRIDGE BUILDINGS, 233-241 Dorchester Road take their name from Skew Bridge over the railway at Radipole, as do Bridge Villa (No.231) and Bridge Terrace (Nos.243-249) close by.

BRIDGE BUILDINGS, Town Bridge (demolished) This was a handsome bow-fronted 3-storey terrace of shops with accommodation over, leading from Lower St Edmund Street to the Town Bridge, built by George Welsford following the construction of the 1824 **Town Bridge.** The terrace was demolished in 1928 when the present bridge was built and the site remained empty for years until an uninspiring office block, **Town Bridge House**, was built in the late 1950s. This in turn was reconstructed in 2005 in a style in keeping with adjacent old warehouses. It has kept the name 'Town Bridge House' and now contains a restaurant and apartments.

BRIDGE FURNISHING STORES *see* HAWKES, FREEMAN, Ltd.

BRIDGE INN, Melcombe was in **Bridge Buildings, Town Bridge**. Sometimes known as the Old Bridge Inn.

BRIDGE INN, Preston was much modernised internally in 1965 by brewers Devenish and its thatched roof was replaced by tiles.

BRIDGE INN, Radipole stood on the corner of Spa Road and Dorchester Road where there was formerly a pub called the 'Pig and Whistle'. The building is currently occupied by a Chinese takeaway.

BRIDGE TERRACE, see **Bridge Buildings, Dorchester Road.**

BRIDGING CAMP, WYKE REGIS was established on the shores of the Fleet in May 1928 to accommodate some 500 Royal Engineers personnel. The Corps of the Royal Engineers were granted the Freedom of the Borough in 1984.

BRIDPORT ARMS PUBLIC HOUSE was in St Thomas Street, opposite the Masonic Hall and is now The Duke of Edinburgh pub.

BRIGE *see* BRIDGE/BRIGE

BRISTOL TERRACE became Nos.1-6 Brownlow Street

BRITANNIA The newly-built Royal Yacht was here for trials early in 1954 and her first 'royal' voyage was later that year when she took the young Prince Charles and Princess Anne to rendezvous with the Queen and Prince Philip who were on a Commonwealth tour. *Britannia* was an occasional visitor over the years, but since her decommissioning in 1997 she has been on permanent display at the Scottish port of Leith.

BRITISH LEGION The foundation stone of the British Legion Club in Westwey Road was laid in March 1939 and it opened the following year, only to be destroyed in 1941 when German incendiary bombs razed it to the ground. After the war the Legion bought the former Eye Infirmary in King Street and opened their club there on 2nd May 1947. With membership falling and the lofty building costly to maintain, the club is seeking more suitable premises in 2006.

BROADLEY, Alexander Meyrick (1848-1916) was a much travelled barrister and a foreign correspondent for *The Times* until he settled at Bradpole and began amassing a vast collection of rare books, prints and maps, many of them Dorset items. He was particularly interested in 'Grangerizing', which was the addition of illustrative material such as maps, prints and letters to original book texts. His best-known 'Grangerized' work was the expansion of a copy of the second edition of **'John Hutchins'** *History and Antiquities of the County of Dorset* from four to fourteen volumes. This became known as the 'Extra Illustrated Edition' and is now in the Dorset History Centre. He also compiled a four-volume work entitled *Royal Weymouth*, a collection of text and illustrative material spanning the years of King George III's visits to the town. This work is in Weymouth Library's Local Studies Collection.

BROADWEY takes its name from its situation on the River Wey and although the spelling is now generally accepted as Broadwey, until the twentieth century 'Broadway' was still widely used.

BROADWEY MILL, Mill Street, Broadwey The watermill went out of use in the late 1950s and was converted to a private dwelling. The original 18th century flour mill buildings had been extended in 1846 and 1887.

BROWN, Alexander Jackson (1896-1972) Weymouth-born member of a long established family firm of local opticians. He was the author of a novel, the central character of which is his ancestor Admiral John Browne, a Weymouth merchant.

Further reading : *The Silk Admiral : a tale of old Melcombe 1585-1627*, by A. Jackson Brown (printed by Sherrens, Weymouth, 1968)

BROWN I. J. Nos.6-7 St Thomas Street Opticians, established in 1882. Until 2000 the business was at No.2 St Thomas Street.

'BROWN ROUTE' *see* RELIEF ROAD

BROWNE, John Herbert One of the leading figures in local politics in the Georgian period and a prime mover with John Arbuthnot in the planning and erection of the King's Statue, of which he laid the foundation stone in 1809. Mayor of Weymouth in 1780-81 and 1791-92.

BROWNE CHARITY Lady Browne in 1632 left £50, 20 shillings to aid repairs to the church annually and the balance to the poor of Weymouth.

BROWNLOW STREET probably takes its name either from Colonel Brownlow Knox, vice-chairman of the **Conservative Land Society**, which developed the Park District or Tory MP Adelbert Wellington who became the 3rd Earl Brownlow.

BRUNSWICK BUILDINGS built in 1828, was renamed Brunswick Terrace in October 1880.

BRUNSWICK PLACE also known as Brunswick Court was a terraced street (5 houses on each side) off the east side of Commercial Road, between the now demolished Nos.36 and 37.

BRUNSWICK TERRACE was known as Brunswick Buildings until December 1880.

Brunswick Terrace about 1910, in the days when the terrace overlooked one of the pretty cast iron and glass shelters erected along the Esplanade in 1889.

BRYANT, Rev. Arthur Sidney Rector of Upwey from 1924 until his death in August 1958. Keenly interested in art and music, and with a great knowledge of local history. Chairman of Weymouth Civic Society 1947-1952.

BUBONIC PLAGUE *see* BLACK DEATH

BUCKLAND RIPERS once belonged to the Framptons of Moreton. 'Boc-land' indicates land granted by charter; 'Ripers' is derived from a family name and dates back to the 13th century.

BUCKLER FAMILY of Causeway, Radipole In 1562 a stranger staying with the Bucklers died of the plague and by the following year the widow of Mr Buckler, two of her sons and a daughter as well as several other members of the household had died of the disease. A descendant of the Buckler family, **Sir John Hesketh Lethbridge**, erected a vault in the churchyard in the nineteenth century and a plaque on the monument is in memory of Sir Walter Buckler who lived at Causeway in the early 16th century.

BUCKLERS LANE is an old name for Boot Hill.

BUDMOUTH was the name for Weymouth in Thomas Hardy's Wessex novels.

BULL, John Photographer. Moved to Turton Villa in April, 1866 when he placed an advertisement in the local press stating that due to the move, he would be disposing of thousands of negatives made before Christmas, 1865. Were they local scenes? And what happened to them?

BULLEN, Admiral Sir Charles (1763-1853) Commander of HMS *Britannia* at the Battle of Trafalgar, 1805. Spent his childhood in Weymouth. His father, John Bullen, was related to Admiral Marriott **Arbuthnot**. Charles Bullen had a distinguished naval career before and after the battle. Knighted and made Admiral of the Blue in 1852, he moved to Southampton where he died and is buried.

BURBERRY, Thomas (1836-1926) Of the famous Burberry firm, designers of the classic trench coat and famous Burberry check pattern. Bought **Abbot's Court**, overlooking Radipole Lake around 1917. An active temperance advocate, staunch supporter of Sunday closing of public houses and donor to charitable causes in Weymouth. A native of Basingstoke, he died in 1926 at Hook, where he had a country residence.

BURDON, William Wharton (1795-1870) was a north country colliery owner. He built Weymouth Gasworks in 1834 and was its sole proprietor until 1866, and also owned coal stores on the quay. He was one of town's MPs from 1835 to 1837. Burdon may have had some financial interest in local building projects since **Wooperton Street** and **Hartford Terrace** were built in the 19th century and the Burdon family was from Hartford House and Wooperton in Northumberland. It appears that the **Burdon Hotel** was named after him. Oral evidence suggests that Burdon owned **Burdon's Buildings**, the former barracks, but his ownership has not been definitely established. He died in Newcastle upon Tyne.

BURDON HOTEL (now the PRINCE REGENT HOTEL), Esplanade When the hotel was being built early in 1855 and was as yet unnamed, it was informally referred to as the 'Railway Hotel', being close to the new railway station also then under construction. In May 1855 it was claimed that the hotel, which builder Philip Dodson was erecting in the centre of Victoria Terrace, was a larger and more superior structure than had been proposed in the approved plans, and this led to many arguments at council meetings about which plans had been agreed on originally-those of noted architect **Talbot Bury**, or later ones by **Pierse Arthur** (whose design was used). Dodson was a close business associate of William Wharton Burdon and the local newspaper *Southern Times* reported in December 1857 that *'We hear it was called the 'Burdon' hotel out of compliment to W.W. Burdon Esq. the proprietor of the Gas Works and Coal Stores in this town'* but it is not known if the gasworks owner had any financial stake in the hotel. The Burdon Hotel, also known as the Imperial Burdon Hotel, opened in August 1858. During World War I it was used as a military hospital. In 1954 there were proposals, fortunately not proceeded with, to convert the hotel on this prime seafront site into Municipal Offices. In 1971 the hotel changed both ownership and its name, becoming the Hotel Prince Regent. *See also* BURDON, William Wharton

Built in the Victorian period but in a style which complements the earlier Esplanade terraces, the Burdon Hotel is now known as the Prince Regent Hotel.

BURDON'S BUILDINGS, on the corner of Commercial Road and Lower Bond Street was a former malthouse and stores converted in the 1790s to become the Queen's Barracks. When the War Department had no further use for the barracks in the 1820s, they were converted back to stores and eventually to housing, known as Mechanics Lodging Houses, sometime in the mid-19th century. Oral evidence suggests that Burdon's Buildings, as the block became known, was owned by gasworks proprietor **William Wharton Burdon**. It was soon being referred to as a slum, its overcrowded and unsanitary conditions being blamed for an outbreak of smallpox cases in 1871. Nevertheless, poor families were housed here until the 1920s, by which time the building was in the ownership of Albany Ward Theatres Ltd. In 1925 the building was condemned as unfit for human habitation, and it was pulled down after the families living there were re-housed on the new council estate at Westham. A garage then occupied the site before Kennedy's builders merchants store was built. Along with other properties in Lower Bond Street the store was demolished in the 1990s to make way for the **New Bond Street** development.

BURDON'S COAL STORES, 10 Custom House Quay Owned by **William Wharton Burdon** and later by **Philip Dodson**. In 1860 Cosens and Co. took over the coal stores, converting them in 1884 by lining them with cork to store ice which the company began importing in large quantities. No.10 was Cosens' HQ from 1884 until 1962. (In later years the adjacent warehouse at No.9 Custom House Quay was owned by Burd<u>e</u>n's Transport – no connection with Burd<u>o</u>n).

BURN, Henry (1807?-1884) Artist. Born in Birmingham. Little is known of his early life and training. Between 1840 and 1852 he travelled extensively in England and produced lithographs on stone of topographical views. There are three of Weymouth- two which look south and north along the Esplanade, and a third which is an adaptation of his Esplanade view looking north and includes a hot air balloon ascent from Weymouth in 1842 – the only year he was here. In 1852 he sailed for Australia, settling in Melbourne, where he exhibited and published views of the city. He died there in 1884, having spent the last years of his life in Melbourne Benevolent Asylum.

Compare this view by Henry Burn of Weymouth Esplanade in 1842 with his view of the Albion *balloon (page 15). He obviously changed the details but not the background of this original picture to record the balloon ascent.*

BURNEY, Fanny (1752-1840) A successful popular novelist, Fanny Burney came to the attention of the royal family in 1786 and was offered the post of Keeper of the Robes to Queen Charlotte. Her job was not onerous, mainly assisting the Queen with her hair and her gowns (undergarments were left to lesser servants) and caring for Queen's favourite little dog. With time on her hands, she kept an entertaining diary of life at court during her time there from 1786 to 1791. She accompanied King George III and Queen Charlotte on their first visit to Weymouth in 1789 and made some interesting and humorous observations on the local scene. The King did not visit Weymouth in 1790 and by the time of his visit in 1791, Fanny had left the royal service. She married Alexandre D'Arblay, who had fled revolutionary France, in 1793.

Further reading : *Diary, 1778-1840 (Volume 4)* by Madame D'Arblay. (Macmillan, 1905)

BURNING CLIFF, HOLWORTH An odd phenomenon which became something of a tourist attraction in 1826-7 was the spontaneous ignition of the shale cliffs at Holworth, to the east of Weymouth, which burned for some considerable time and provided extra income for the boatmen who took parties out to view the spectacle from the sea.

The Burning Cliff at Holworth was a tourist attraction in 1827 and should have been left alone – when locals started digging in the cliffs to find the reason for the spontaneous fire, it went out!

BURY, Talbot (1811-1877) Noted architect who worked with Sir Charles Barry and Augustus Pugin on details of the design for the Houses of Parliament. In Weymouth he designed Holy Trinity Schools at Chapelhay (1853, now demolished) St John's Church (1854), the Market House (1855, now demolished) Fish Market (1855) and made the original drawings for Victoria Terrace on the Esplanade in the 1850s, although these were replaced by the designs of Pierse Arthur. Some sources attribute the design of Weymouth Guildhall (built 1836-7) to him.

BURY STREET led to a burial ground belonging to the parish of St Mary. The street was demolished in April 1975 along with some buildings in Lower Bond Street, including a Methodist Chapel. The site was redeveloped initially as a supermarket and multi-storey car park, but the store later made way for the present Cineworld cinema (opened as the Multiplex). The Bury Street burial ground had been emptied in 1974 and all the remains were re-interred in Melcombe Regis cemetery. The gravestone of **Thomas Knight**, murdered by smugglers in 1832, was transferred to Weymouth Museum.

BUS SERVICES Eventually replacing the old horse buses, the first motorbuses were introduced in the town in late June 1905, run by the GWR. The service was not without its problems and it ceased in 1909. Motor buses returned briefly in 1911, a service run by Motor Coaches Ltd., but in 1912 the GWR returned, running a joint service with the LSWR, which was somewhat disrupted during the WW1 years. In the 1920s other companies appeared on the scene and competition increased, but by the late '20s the larger companies were taking over, the GWR taking a 50% interest in what was to become the Southern National Omnibus Company in Weymouth, which eventually took over the service in its entirety, the last GWR bus running in 1933. Today, as First Southern National, the company runs the majority of local bus services with independent operator Surebus operating on some routes.

Further reading : *Isle of Portland Railways. Volume Three : Railway, associated and other bus services* by B.L.Jackson (Oakwood Press, 2000).

BUS SHELTER, Esplanade This stood directly in front of the King's Statue and was erected in 1930/1931. It was removed in 1954 when work began on the construction of the present large traffic island at the Statue.

BUS STATION, Edward Street/Commercial Road The original bus station was built in 1929. On 21st October 1940 a single enemy plane dropped one oil and three high explosive bombs on the area, demolishing the garage and eight houses (a further nineteen were so badly damaged they had to be pulled down) and killing five people. Rebuilding of the bus station, by Bird and Cox, contractors for the original garage, commenced in January, 1955.

BUSHBY, Dorothy (1900-1985) of Portland House, Belle Vue Road. Staunch supporter of the Scout movement, her father being a friend of Lord Baden-Powell. Bequeathed her home to the National Trust.

BUSSELL, Ernest (1878-1967) Owner of an extensive and very fine collection of early paintings and prints of Weymouth which were donated to Weymouth Library by his widow. Known as the 'Bussell Collection', these are now in Weymouth Museum. His ironmongery business was in St Mary Street, the family formerly having run ships' chandlery stores. His father

In Bury Street, mansard roofed cottages and a little graveyard shaded by trees have all gone and the entire street no longer exists. A painting by Eric Ricketts.

was Captain Charles Bussell who sailed the locally-built *Kate* from Weymouth to the U.S. in the 1860s and 1870s.

BUSSELL, Peter (1774-1850) Weymouth man, captain of the sloop *Dove* which was captured by a French privateer when on voyage Weymouth-London in 1806. Bussell spent eight years in a French gaol before returning home in 1814. He had kept a detailed diary of his experiences in France, which was later published by his great-grandson. The *Dove* was retaken by an English ship in 1810 and was eventually wrecked on Chesil Beach during severe storms at the end of November, 1838, her master then being Captain P. Bussell, presumably her original owner.

Further reading : *The Diary of Peter Bussell 1806-1814*, edited by his great grandson (Peter Davies, 1931)

BUTCHERS ARMS INN (now demolished) was in West Street, the area being redeveloped in 2003. The pub probably took its name from a number of slaughterhouses which were once in the vicinity, the pub being built on part of a slaughter-house site.

The whole of the west side of West Street has been redeveloped and the Butchers Arms is no more.

BUTLIN, Billy Billy Butlin began negotiations with Weymouth Council to develop **Lodmoor** as a Butlin Holiday Camp in 1962, talks continuing into 1963 as rental terms could not be agreed. A Public Inquiry into planning permission started 1st October 1963 and Government approval for the holiday camp was given in February 1964. Work was due to start in March 1964 but there were further disagreements over the infilling and drainage of the site, which were settled in June 1964. Butlin's announced a target date of June 1966 for the opening of the camp, but more delays and disagreements put the estimated opening date to 1968. With issues still unresolved and doubts over economic feasibility, the announcement that Butlins would not, after all, be coming to Weymouth, was made in October 1966.

BUTTS LANE was an early name for **St Leonard's Road.**

BUXTON FAMILY Isaac Buxton was a wealthy London merchant who built **Belfield House** as a country seat around 1780. Belfield lies on the way to Wyke Regis between Wyke Road and **Buxton Road**, to which the family gave its name. Buxton's widow, in her will, left the property to her grandson, Thomas Fowell Buxton, who leased it to his uncle, Charles Buxton. Thomas Fowell Buxton (1786-1845) was MP for Weymouth from 1818 to 1837 and is best known, with Wilberforce, as a great advocate for the abolition of slavery and the slave trade in the 1820s and 1830s. He was created a baronet in 1840 and there is a monument to him in Westminster Abbey. Buxton was a partner in Truman, Hanbury & Co's brewery.

BUXTON ROAD takes its name from the **Buxton Family** of Belfield House. The road has had several alternative names - Buxton's Lane, Sweete Lane, Lower Road and Lower Wyke Road (Wyke Road being Higher Wyke Road). Buxton's Lane continued as today's Cross Road forming the eastern boundary of the Buxton property. Used now as a main thoroughfare to Portland, Buxton Road was simply a lane in the 18th century and traffic used the turnpike road which went along the beach from what is today Old Castle Road to Smallmouth. Here a ferry took foot passengers to Portland and horses and vehicular traffic were able to cross at low water in the days before the first Ferrybridge was built.

'BUY BRITISH' VAN This advertising stunt was a van with slogans on its front and sides illuminated with 3000 flashing lights, exhorting those who saw it to buy British and Empire goods. It toured the country and was in Weymouth on two occasions – in 1935 and 1936.

BYNG, Colonel John, 5th Viscount Torrington The 'Torrington Diaries' are accounts of his journeys through England. He visited Weymouth in August, 1782 and although he found little to approve of in the resort, his descriptions of the seaside and its social life are both entertaining and informative.

Further reading : *The Torrington Diaries*, by John Byng (Eyre and Spottiswoode, 1954)

CABMEN'S SHELTER *see* TEA CABIN

CALAIS, SIEGE OF, 1347 In times of war ports were required to provide ships and men to supplement England's naval forces and it is some indication of Weymouth and Melcombe's growing importance in mediaeval times that they were able to supply 20 ships and 264 men (the figures are approximate and vary in different accounts) to aid King Edward III's eventual capture of Calais following the long siege in 1347.

CAMBRIDGE ARMS PUBLIC HOUSE was at 31 St Mary Street. Closed 1903.

CAMBRIDGE TERRACE became Nos.6-8 Lennox Street

CAMDEN, William (1551-1623) The first version of his survey of England was published in 1586 and is known as 'Camden's Britannia'. In it, his reference to Weymouth is brief, but a later edition gives a little more detail about the town which had *'Growen very much greater and goodlier in buildings by sea adventurers than heeretofore'*.

CAMDEN TERRACE became Nos.26-50 St Leonard's Road. Nos.1-2 Camden Villas became Nos.22-24 St Leonard's Road. There was also a Camden Terrace in Wyke village.

CAMERA OBSCURA The camera obscura was a darkened room where a mirror was used to project a picture of the surrounding landscape through a lens to be viewed inside, where it could be sketched or merely enjoyed. Early-19th century guidebooks mention Weymouth's Camera Obscura which stood on the Nothe promontory.

CAMERON, Verney Lovett (1844-1894) Born at Radipole. Naval officer and explorer. In 1873 when he was sent to Africa on an expedition to relieve Livingstone (who had in fact died), Cameron became the first European to cross equatorial Africa. His account of the journey, *Across Africa* was published in 1877. He later accompanied Sir Richard Burton to the Gold Coast. Cameron was also prominent in the suppression of the East African slave trade. He wrote a number of books dealing with his time in Africa as well as adventure stories for boys.

CANDLE AUCTIONS An old country custom used for the sale or letting of land. At Broadwey candle auctions for the annual letting of a piece of land known as Parish Mead or Parish Meadow continued into the first half of the 20th century. The gift of William Gould, the annual produce from the land was to be used to exempt the poor from statute labour on the highways. On the termination of the year of the previous tenant, an auction was held at which an inch of candle was lit and bidding commenced, continuing until the candle burnt out. Whoever had the bid as it was extinguished had the land for that year. Occasionally in the 17th century the Town Marsh was let for pasture by candle auction and the petty customs were let to the highest bidder in the same manner.

CANDLE FACTORY *see* SNOOK'S CANDLE FACTORY

CARAVANS Tented camping and caravanning began in the Preston area in the 1920s. By the late 1940s and the 1950s the growth of the sites and the lack of a main drainage system was a cause for concern, overcome in the late 1950s when a new sewerage system for the area also served the caravan sites.

CARGO STAGE A small wooden cargo stage, with a steam crane, was built at Custom House Quay in 1877 and extended in 1880. It was completely reconstructed between 1948 and 1951.

CARNEGIE, Andrew (1835-1919) Wealthy Scottish-born industrialist, who made his fortune in the USA and established many cultural and scientific institutions, including numerous public libraries. In 1903 he offered Weymouth £5000 to build a free library and his offer was accepted, conditional on a site being found. Unfortunately, time went by, no site was decided on and the opportunity was lost as Mr Carnegie, the benefactor of libraries in many UK towns, withdrew the offer.

CARNIVAL Weymouth's earliest 'Carnival Processions' were not summer events but were held on or around November 5th to celebrate Guy Fawkes night. In November 1882, after a lapse of a few years, Weymouth held a grand torchlight procession which made its way from North Quay to Greenhill, complete with bands, some 300 people in fancy dress, tableaux, sailors and the lifeboat crew. The evening ended with a monster bonfire and fireworks at Greenhill. Heavy rain drenched the procession, as it did the following year and in 1884 the whole event had to be postponed for a day as the November weather was so bad. This brought forth the suggestion that a summer carnival might be more appropriate. Enthusiasm for the November 5th celebrations waned and by 1893 the winter procession had become short and straggly and was abandoned altogether in 1894. Meanwhile, in 1890 a number of local friendly societies had joined together and decided to hold a parade and open air concert in August and this seems to have been the foundation of the summer carnival, raising funds for the local hospitals. It was not held every year, but the August procession seems to have become more of a permanent fixture around 1910. The carnival went ahead in August 1939 just prior to the outbreak of WW2 but was then not held again until 13th August 1952. 'Carnival Day' is now a hugely popular event, raising money for local charities and is usually held on the third Wednesday in August. A regatta was a regular event in the same month until the 1960s.

CARS *see* MOTOR RACING

CARSWELL CHARITY of 1741 gave land, the interest on which was to benefit the town's Dissenting minister. Should there at any time be no such minister in Weymouth and Melcombe Regis, the interest was to be given to four poor widows.

CARTER'S COTTAGES, Turton Street These cottages were built in 1835 and are described in the RCHM as 'Carter's Almshouses'. A stone on the front of the building is inscribed 'S & M.C. 1835'. On some maps they are shown as 'Cotter's Cottages'.

CASCADE AT THE NOTHE The water cascade in the Nothe Gardens was installed to celebrate the wedding on 1st September 1982 of the Prince and Princess of Wales.

CASE, John and Co. Cabinet Makers, Upholsterers, Undertakers and House Furnishers, established around 1850. Their 'Cabinet Warehouse' occupied a rather fine building, now in use as a shoe shop, at Nos. 8-9 Bond Street.

CASINO Weymouth's first Casino opened at Lodmoor House in the 1960s.

CASTLE INN, Horsford Street was described in 1866 as being *'near the barracks and Spring Lane where a number of houses were being built'*. Closed in the early 1900s.

CATHOLIC CHURCHES *see* CHURCH OF THE HOLY FAMILY; ST AUGUSTINE'S CHURCH; ST CHARLES' CHURCH; ST JOSEPH'S CHURCH

CEMETERIES Until the middle of the nineteenth century churchyards traditionally provided the 'last resting place' but in many towns these were becoming overcrowded. The problem was particularly acute in Melcombe Regis where there were three small graveyards – one adjacent to St Mary's Church, another in Bury Street, and a third adjacent to Bank Buildings Baptist Church (the latter two have now been built over). Legislation was required and in the early 1850s the Burial Acts came into force, enabling local authorities to acquire land for the provision of municipal cemeteries, these to be managed by Burial Boards. It was decided to establish a cemetery at Westham, and Melcombe Regis Cemetery opened on 31st March 1856, off what is now Newstead Road. This was some years before the development of the suburb of Westham and the surrounding area was open ground at this time. London architect W.J. Pinch designed two chapels for the cemetery, Presbyterian and Non-Conformist. An additional piece of land adjacent to the cemetery was acquired in the early 1890s and sometime in the early years of the 20th century the Non-Conformist chapel was taken down and rebuilt in the new extension, both chapels then serving all denominations, although they are not used now. Weymouth's cemetery overcrowding problems were not so acute, most interments taking place at All Saints Church, Wyke Regis, and it was 1896 before the Weymouth Burial Board was set up, obtaining 5 acres of land off Abbotsbury Road for a cemetery. This opened in 1898. It had one chapel, for the use of CofE and Nonconformists. The Burial Boards ceased to exist on 31st March 1927 when they were taken by Weymouth Corporation. The Council is now responsible for the cemeteries at Westham and also at Wyke Regis. *See also* SOCIETY OF FRIENDS

CENSUS RETURNS are compiled every ten years. As population counts, they began in 1801 but the first detailed manuscript census returns date from 1841 and since then the only date missed was 1941, due to WW2. Although statistics are compiled from the Returns, all other information is kept secret for 100 years. 1901 is thus the most recent Census which can be consulted in full.

CETTI'S WARBLER this rare European bird began breeding at Radipole Lake in 1977.

CHAFEYS LAKE Goldcroft Road was extended across Chafeys Lake in 1961 to join Field Barn Drive and the new housing development at Southill. The road system here was altered in the 1980s when **Weymouth Way** was constructed.

CHALBURY HILL FORT at Preston dates to the Iron Age and was built around 300 B.C. It encloses about 10 acres and is about 380 feet above sea level at its highest point. Iron Age hut sites have been found within it, and pottery finds indicate its continued use in Roman times.

CHALBURY LODGE, Preston Road is an early 19th century house, once in the ownership of the Scutt family. It was converted to an old people's home in 1961, but this closed in the 1980s and the building has since been converted back to private housing.

CHALGROVE HOUSE became No.1 Walpole Street

CHALGROVE TERRACE became Nos.38-48 Ranelagh Road

CHAMBERLAINE, Reverend George Rector of Wyke Regis from 1809-1837. Chamberlaine Road is named after him. Concerned that his Weymouth parishioners had no church of their own, this charitable cleric paid the whole cost of building Holy Trinity Church beside the Town Bridge and he also established a trust fund in memory of his wife, Margaret, which enabled Wyke to replace its old Parish Room in Wyke Square with a new Memorial Hall in 1908.

CHANNEL ISLANDS Although Weymouth vessels would have been trading with the Channel Islands for centuries, the first regular sailings began in 1794 when the Post Office based its Mail Packets here, sailing initially once fortnightly, then twice weekly. Although this service was lost to Southampton in 1845, the opening of the railway to Weymouth in 1857 brought GWR interests strongly to the fore and since then, apart from a few short suspensions of the service, the longest being during WW2, Weymouth has maintained its links with the Channel Islands, albeit now with Wavepiercer craft carrying passengers in place of the traditional steamers. Weymouth was once the main port handling fresh flowers, tomatoes and other vegetables from the Channel Islands but competition from other ports and the increasing use of air freight brought about a decline in the cargo trade which ceased in the early 1970s. *See also* HARBOUR

Further reading : *Weymouth to the Channel Islands: a Great Western Railway shipping history*, by B.L. Jackson (Oakwood Press, 2002); *The Great Western at Weymouth: a railway and shipping history*, by J.H. Lucking (David and Charles, 1971)

CHANNEL SWIMMERS The Weymouth area has become well known for the success of its Channel swimmers who are:- Godfrey Chapman (1951); Greg Schofield (1964); Philip Gollop (1965-69); Mervyn Sharp (1967-74); Jacqui Hampson (1982); Lorraine Hopkins (1986-87); Manda Topp (1987); Chantal Hutchings (1991); Eddie Ette (1997); Laura Griffiths (1997); Kate Mason (2001); Lynn Ette (2002); Nick Ireland (2006). *See also* WATCH, Tom

CHANNING'S WALK is a lost Melcombe place name and may refer to a covered way which once led from the Golden Lion Inn to St Thomas Street.

CHAPEL ROW was a terrace of houses leading from No.17 Chapelhay Street. The houses were demolished following WW2 air raid damage.

CHAPELHAY is the district on the high land above Weymouth on the south side of the harbour. It takes its name from a little chapel of ease, dedicated to St Nicholas, which was erected here in mediaeval times when the parish church was two miles away at Wyke Regis. Hence the area became known as 'The Chapelry' or 'Chapelhay'. The chapel was converted to a fort during the Civil War fighting of 1645 and pretty much destroyed, after which the site became an open space and recreation area until Holy Trinity Schools were built on it in the 1850s. They, too, suffered war damage – from WW2 enemy bombs. The schools were pulled down in 1961, providing the site for the houses of Trinity Court. The whole of the densely populated area of Chapelhay was very badly damaged in WW2 air raids and much of the area was cleared and rebuilt in the 1950s. The flats of 'Chapelhay Heights' were built to replace the bombed terraced streets.

CHAPELHAY/CHAPELRY COURT was behind buildings to the west of Holy Trinity Church and it was purchased for demolition in 1884 to enable Chapelhay Steps to be built.

CHAPELHAY STEPS Prior to the construction of the present Chapelhay Steps in 1884, a steep flight of steps existed just to the west of them and these at one time led up to the old chapel at Chapelhay. Traces of this flight can be found today. It had been planned in the 1880s to build a road up to Chapelhay, but the idea was abandoned and the present flight of steps and connecting slopes was built instead. Houses alongside Holy Trinity Church were demolished to enable the work to go ahead.

CHAPELHAY STREET, Weymouth was known until 1872 as St Nicholas Street. Its name was changed to avoid confusion with St Nicholas Street in Melcombe, on the other side of the harbour.

CHAPELHAY TAVERN was originally two cottages and its use as a pub probably dates back to the 1830s or 1840s. It was taken over by Eldridge Pope in the early 1870s.

CHAPELRY is an alternative name for **CHAPELHAY**. The latter has been used in this book.

CHARABANCS Motor charabancs began operating in the years prior to WW1 and gradually took over the excursion trade from horse-drawn carriages and wagonettes, although two of these continued to run until 1939. Trips to the local beauty spots such as Upwey Wishing Well (cream tea) and Osmington (lobster tea) usually started at the King's Statue. The charabancs went further afield than the horse-drawn transport and in the 1920s and 1930s, when few families owned a car, 'chara' trips were very popular. They were a bit of an adventure – a bumpy ride on solid tyres, a hood to be drawn up if it rained and close fitting hats an essential accessory for the ladies whose hairstyles would otherwise be more than a little windblown by the end of the day.

Were they off to Lulworth Cove or booked for the circular tour? A trip on Victory Road Motors charabanc about 1920.

CHARITIES Over several centuries many small charities were set up, often by individuals who gave or left sums of money, the interest on which was to be distributed as specified – in many cases it was to be used for the relief of the poor. Those included in this volume are the older charities or those where a building was provided or a fund for a special purpose was set up. *See* BROWNE CHARITY; CARSWELL CHARITY; DE SELLA NOVA, Dr Arnold; EDWARDS CHARITY; MICO CHARITY; MIDDLETON CHARITY; MITCHELL CHARITY; SANDERSON WELLS, Dr Thomas Henry; TAYLOR CHARITY

CHARLES STREET This street is said to have been named after Father John Charles, priest at **St Augustine's Roman Catholic Church**, Dorchester Road in the latter half of the 19th century. *See also* FARWELL COTTAGES; SURREY TERRACE; SYDNEY TERRACE

CHARLES TERRACE became Nos.28-31 Hardwick Street.

CHARLOTTE, Princess (1766-1828) Princess Royal and eldest daughter of King George III. A frequent visitor during the period of Royal Weymouth 1789-1805.

CHARLOTTE, Princess of Wales (1796-1817) was the daughter of the Prince of Wales (later King George IV) and grand daughter of King George III. She visited Weymouth during the period of the King's visits 1789-1805 and also in 1814 and 1815. She married Leopold (later King of the Belgians) and died in childbirth in 1817.

CHARLOTTE, Queen (1744-1818) Wife of King George III. She accompanied the King on all his visits to Weymouth during the years 1789-1805.

CHARLOTTE ROW, Esplanade was built in the early 1800s and probably named after Queen Charlotte, wife of King George III. Now numbered as 47-51 The Esplanade.

CHARTER OF UNION 1571 is the term commonly used to describe the **Act of Union 1571**, although this was an Act of Parliament and not a Charter.

CHARTERS were written documents granted by the Crown or a manorial lord. They listed the town's rights, powers, liberties and privileges – such as the right to hold markets and fairs, elect mayors etc. – and they sometimes described boundaries. Charters laid down the basic structure of how the town was to be run in the days before there was any organised framework of local government. Towns would petition for new Charters when a new King or Queen came to the throne, in the hope of improving on their previous grant. All Charters became obsolete on the passing of the Municipal Corporations Act in 1835 which laid down the foundations of the modern system of democratic local government. The earliest Charter relating to the town which exists in the borough archives today dates from 1252 and was granted by the Prior of St Swithun's. It described the boundaries of Weymouth only (difficult to identify today) and granted the town the same privileges enjoyed by the port of Southampton. In 1516 Letters Patent replaced Charters as the form in which royal grants were made. Inspeximus Charters confirm that an existing document has been 'inspected' and confirmed. Exemplifications are official copies – attested copies of documents made under official seal. The town's last charter before the 1835 Act rendered them obsolete was granted by King George III in 1804.

The charters prior to 1800 are described in : *Descriptive catalogue of the charters, minute books and other documents of the Borough of Weymouth and Melcombe Regis AD 1252-1800* by H.J. Moule (Sherren & Son, Weymouth, 1883) The full text of the 1804 Charter can be found in pp. 49-80 of *The history of the borough and town of Weymouth and Melcombe Regis* by George A. Ellis (Weymouth, 1829).

CHEAM TERRACE became Nos.36-39 Derby Street.

CHELMSFORD STREET takes its name from Sir Frederic Thesiger, created 1st Baron Chelmsford in 1858. Attorney General in two Conservative governments. Most of the Park District streets, developed by the Conservative Land Society, are named after Tory politicians.

CHELMSFORD TERRACE became Nos.35-50 Chelmsford Street

CHEMICAL WORKS *see* SHALE WORKS

CHEQUERS INN location uncertain, possibly in the Hope Square area.

CHERBOURG HOTEL *see* BANK BUILDINGS

CHESIL BEACH But for the existence of the protecting arm of Chesil Beach, Weymouth would not exist at all and the sea would have eroded away the coastline, leaving Portland as an island and Ridgeway as a set of white cliffs. Chesil Beach extends some 18 miles from Bridport to Portland, is about 170 yards wide at Abbotsbury and 200 yards wide at Portland, with its visible pebbles increasing in size along its length and being constantly sorted by the sea, from the small shingle at Bridport to the large stones at the Portland end. Behind the beach between Abbotsbury and Portland lies the brackish lagoon known as The Fleet. The beach takes its name from the Saxon word *chesil* meaning shingle.

CHESTERFIELD PLACE, Esplanade was built in late 18th century and is one of the most altered of the Esplanade terraces. Originally comprising 9 houses, most of it was rebuilt in the 20th century as the Marks and Spencer store and Barclays Bank. It now comprises Nos.58 and 59 The Esplanade (Barclays Bank and the Seacroft Hotel). The other properties are numbered as St Mary Street. A terrace of the same name at Upwey.

CHICKERELL AIRFIELD was established in 1918 as a small aerodrome used by military aircraft operating in an anti-submarine role. When the RAF left at the end of WW1 the airfield was used briefly for flights run by civilian firms. In the late 1920s and 1930s Sir Alan Cobham was a visitor with his 'Flying Circus' tours, promoting aviation around the country and seeking suitable sites for municipal aerodromes. There were discussions in the '30s on the subject of a commercial airport for Weymouth but nothing came of them. Intermittent use by the military between the wars increased in the late 1930s when the Chesil Beach bombing ranges were established and the Air Ministry took over much of the airfield land. After WW2 activity the RAF remained until the airfield closed in October, 1959. The following month discussions were under way for the site's use as an industrial estate and early in 1962 the first firms moved units on the Granby Industrial Estate. *See* *also* BOUNCING BOMBS, COBHAM, Sir Alan, GRANBY INDUSTRIAL ESTATE

Further reading : *Wings over Weymouth*, by Colin Pomeroy (Dovecote Press, 2005)

CHICKERELL ROAD was formerly known as Town Lane, a name still in use in the mid-19th century.

CHILDREY, Joshua (1623-1670) Rector of Upwey from 1664 until his death. In the 1650s he published two small works on astrology but he is best known for his 'Britannia Baconica' on the curiosities of the natural history of England, Scotland and Wales, first published in 1660. He continued his observations in Weymouth, producing several volumes on the local weather and tides. These, which he intended to bequeath to the Royal Society, appear to have been lost, although letters he wrote during the same period do exist in the Society's archives. Childrey died on 26th August 1670 and is buried in the chancel of Upwey Church.

CHILES, John and Mary This was a curious case, dating from the 1640s during the Civil War years. Mary Chiles claimed her husband had murdered a man named William Courtney at the Chiles' inn and stolen gold and silver he carried in a canvas bag. She said she and Chiles threw the body into the sea, her husband assuring her that in time of war no-one would bother about another death. She confessed to the authorities many months later and her story must have been convincing as Chiles was arrested. He denied everything. The man Courtney was found to be still alive and he had been in Weymouth at the time, yet this odd case eventually went to the assizes where John Chiles must have been acquitted as he appears to have still been living in Weymouth at a much later date. Why did Mary Chiles put herself in a position where she might have been hanged? All this is supposed to have happened at the Dove Ale House, on the outskirts of the town, now known as the **Black Dog Inn**.

CHIPPERFIELD'S FUN FAIR Henry Chipperfield first brought his amusement park to Weymouth in 1952. Sited for many years near Westham coach park alongside Radipole Lake, the Chipperfields had to leave in 1984 when the land was cleared in preparation for the construction of **Weymouth Way**.

CHOLERA The worst cholera epidemic in Weymouth occurred in 1849 when 40 people died of it. *See also* BLOOMFIELD TERRACE

CHRISTCHURCH King Street was consecrated on 23rd July 1874. The architect was Ewan Christian and the builder Thomas Dodson. It was intended as a chapel of ease to St Mary's Church, to serve the growing population at the northern end of Melcombe. The name was chosen because Christchurch had been the original name of St Mary's Church in St Mary Street. **Sir Henry Edwards** presented the new church with a set of ten tubular bells. By the 1930s congregations had dwindled and the church closed in 1939. It saw use in WW2 as a Welcome Club for evacuees and a British Restaurant. The church was sold in 1955 and demolished in 1956-7, the work being carried out by local builder **Mr E.G. Coleman**. He presented the town with a seat made from the stone of the building, and this is now in Greenhill Gardens. The ten bells of the Edwards gift went to St Andrew's Church, Lincoln. From 1958 the site was used as a car park until **Garnet Court**, a block of flats and shops, was built on the site in 1977.

CHRISTIAN, Ewan (1814-1895) Architect of Christchurch, at the junction of King Street and Park Street (demolished 1956-7). Essentially an ecclesiastical architect, he was chosen by **William Henry Alexander** to design the National Portrait Gallery in London, but did not live to see its completion in 1896.

CHRISTIAN SCIENCE CHURCH, Melcombe Avenue Christian Science services began in Weymouth in 1924 and the church building in Melcombe Avenue opened in October, 1929. It was badly damaged in a 1944 air raid and rebuilt to the original design in 1950. Redundant in 2006, negotiations are under way for the site to be used by the congregation of **Maiden Street Methodist Church**, who lost their building in a disastrous fire in 2002.

CHRISTMAS DAY SWIM originated, probably in 1948, as a wager between Reggie Bugler, former landlord of the Duke of Cornwall pub, his successor there, R.S. Laker and Jim Stephens. Each bet against the other's ability to swim across the harbour on Christmas Day and so began the tradition of a Christmas Day swim. Cups were given by Mr and Mrs Edgar Wallis.

CHRISTMAS SHOP DRESSING *see* SHOWNIGHT

Christchurch and beyond it, the old Railway Station. An Edwardian view of Park Street.

Garnet Court, built on the site of Christchurch in 1977. The building took its name from Garnet Mahoney who for years ran a car park on the site of the demolished church.

CHURCH CONGRESS AND ECCLESIASTICAL ART EXHIBITION 1905 was held at Weymouth from 30th September-6th October, 1905. This was an important annual event in the Church of England calendar. 'The Guide to the Congress' (price 3d) ran to more than 300 pages, and described the numerous valuable ecclesiastical and municipal items loaned for the art exhibition held at the Sidney Hall.

CHURCH OF THE HOLY FAMILY (Roman Catholic), Chapel Lane, Upwey Opened 2nd May 1954.

CHURCH PASSAGE runs alongside St Mary's Church, linking St Mary Street and Maiden Street. On the St Mary Street corner once stood a house dating back to Tudor times, the home of Mayor John Pitt in the early 1600s. The building was pulled down in 1883 but some interesting fragments from it, including a 16th century door head with ancient carved figures supporting it, were incorporated in its replacement, No.45 St Mary Street.

The gentleman on the left has just walked by Church Passage and will shortly stroll past No.45 St Mary Street, a building of Tudor period which was pulled down in 1883.

CHURCHILL, Sir Winston (1620-1688) of Minterne Magna. The first Sir Winston Churchill, knighted in 1663, was MP for Weymouth in 1661. His son, Charles Churchill, represented the borough from 1701-1710.

CHURCHILL, Sir Winston (1874-1965) As First Lord of the Admiralty Churchill visited the Fleet at Portland in 1912, embarking at Weymouth Pier. He visited Portland in June, 1938 to see ASDIC at work and inspected the local coastal defences in 1939.

CHURCHILL GARDENS, Cross Road is a 2005 housing development in the grounds of **Blackdown House** (formerly Claylands)

CINEMAS *see* BELLE VUE; JUBILEE HALL (also for Gaumont, Regent); NEW BOND STREET (for Cineworld, Multiplex); ODEON (also for Cannon, Classic, Picturedrome); PALLADIUM; WESTHAM HALL CINEMA

CIRCUSES Some of best-known of the old circuses visited Weymouth. They included Lord George Sanger in 1897 (11th July), Barnum and Bailey in 1898 (19th August) and Buffalo Bill Cody in 1903 (4th August).

CITIZENS'ADVICE BUREAU opened on 7th September 1942 in the Bassett Café on the Esplanade near the present Criterion. It amalgamated with the Information Centre on the sea front in 1947 and moved on 2nd November 1959 to 26 Ranelagh Road, to No.72 The Esplanade (Royal Terrace) in the early 1960s and to rooms in The Guildhall at the end of the 1970s. New offices in Mulberry Terrace (part of Weymouth Library building) were opened on 8th November 1990 by Princess Anne.

CIVIL DEFENCE CORPS; AUXILIARY FIRE SERVICE; NATIONAL HOSPITAL SERVICE RESERVE AND SPECIAL CONSTABULARY Enrolment in these new services started in Weymouth on 15th November 1949.

CIVIL WAR (1642-1646) Although none of the major battles of the Civil War were fought in Dorset, Royalist and Parliamentary garrisons were present for over 3 years and there were constant skirmishes. Ports generally leaned towards Parliament, but Weymouth also had a strong Royalist party. Early in the war and with little fighting, Sir Walter Earle secured the town for the Parliamentarians and also took Portland Castle. Forts were set up at the Nothe and the chapel at Chapelhay and earthwork defences thrown up. Portland Castle was recaptured by the Royalists in August 1643 (Portland, being a Royal Manor, sided with the King) and Weymouth and Melcombe Regis also surrendered to the Royalists, who established a Mint locally, thought to have been at Sandsfoot Castle. In June 1644 Weymouth and Melcombe Regis and Sandsfoot Castle were once more in Parliamentary hands, captured by the Earl of Essex's forces, but Royalist plotters in Weymouth secretly liaised with Portland Royalists in a plan to retake the town from the Parliamentarians. A Royalist force was ferried from Portland, meeting up with the Weymouth King's men using the password 'Crabchurch'. Their attack on 5th February 1645 took the Parliamentarians by surprise and when Royalist reinforcements arrived the next day, Sir Lewis Dyve claimed the town for the King, but the battle was far from over. The supposedly defeated Parliamentarians fled into Melcombe and refused to surrender. They were led by Colonel William Sydenham, whose brother Major Francis Sydenham, had been killed in the fighting. Despite being bombarded by Royalists on the

Weymouth side, they dug in and awaited help, meanwhile counter-attacking by sending a fire ship into the Royalist ships in the bay and setting property alight. The fiercest fighting came later in February 1645 when Parliamentary reinforcements arrived and launched their attack, re-taking the town for Parliament, with Portland surrendering to Parliamentary forces the following year. The effects of the brief period of fierce fighting were disastrous for Weymouth and Melcombe Regis. Fire had spread rapidly through houses, many of them thatched. The bridge, quays and harbour had suffered major damage in the fighting and ships were diverting to other ports. The Civil War certainly hastened the decline of Weymouth as a port, although its harbour in the late-17th century was already too small to accommodate the larger ships then being built.

CLARE COTTAGES stood close to the railway line and overbridge in Newstead Road. They were demolished and replaced by modern bungalows in 1957.

CLARENCE BUILDINGS, Esplanade are named after William, Duke of Clarence and St Andrews (later King William IV), third son of King George III. Now numbered 19-30 The Esplanade.

CLARK, Captain Richard *see* CLARK AND ENDICOTT MEMORIAL

CLARK & ENDICOTT MEMORIAL This Portland stone column, with bronze plaque attached, was unveiled on 2nd June 1914. It originally stood outside the old Pavilion Theatre (later The Ritz) and commemorates two adventurers who sailed from Weymouth to the New World. Richard Clark set out from Weymouth on the *Delight* in 1583 to join Sir Humphrey Gilbert's expedition to Newfoundland. Although the *Delight* was shipwrecked, Clark was saved. Puritan John Endicott sailed from Weymouth in 1628 aboard the ***Abigail*** for New England, where he later became the first Governor of the state of Massachusetts. The monument was unveiled by Mrs Joseph Chamberlain, a descendant of Endicott. Following the Ritz Theatre fire in 1954, the column went into storage, but in the late 1960s it was re-erected in the Alexandra Gardens, albeit in a rather inconspicuous position. In March 2003, largely due to the efforts of Weymouth Civic Society, the Clark & Endicott memorial was moved to a more appropriate location on the harbourside, close to the Ferry Steps.

The Clark and Endicott Memorial is shown here in its original location, in front of the old Pavilion Theatre.

CLARK'S COURT/ROW was between Nos.13 and 14 East Street. Demolished under a slum clearance order in the 1930s.

CLARK'S HILL was the area of land on the west side of Dorchester Road extending approximately from William Street up to Radipole Barracks (today's Westbourne Road). It formed part of **Melcombe Common** and until the late 19th century its ownership was much disputed .

CLARKE, 'Tom' (William Daniel) was a craftsman blacksmith at No.8 Great George Street. He retired in 1957 and the premises were sold. Among many other works in wrought iron, he made a very intricate weathervane incorporating the Weymouth Coat of Arms for the **Reynolds Memorial Institute** at Broadwey, but this is no longer in place.

CLARKE, Victor In the late 1980s the Dorset Evening Echo ran a series of articles by Victor Clarke in which he reminisced on life in Weymouth in the 1920s and 1930s. A detailed and fascinating study of the town between the wars.

CLAYLANDS is a house on the corner of Buxton Road and Cross Road. It was built in the late 1860s by Edward Bayly, a local bank manager, and was bought in 1905 by the **Groves** brewing family who changed its name to **Blackdown House**. The last of the Groves family left the house in 1941 when it went over to war use and in 1948 it was converted by the local health authority for use in conjunction with Herrison Hospital at Dorchester.

CLEARMOUNT COURT, on the corner of Rodwell Road and New Close Gardens, replaced a garage block on the site in 1988.

CLEARMOUNT GARDENS became Nos.35-41 Buxton Road.

CLEARMOUNT VILLAS were early developments in Longfield Road.

CLEMO, Jack (1916-1994) Poet. Cornishman who settled in Weymouth later in life.

CLEVELAND HOUSE SCHOOL was a large private school at No.118 Dorchester Road. The house, much extended since it was first built, still stands.

CLIFTON HOTEL is now The Railway Tavern.

CLIFTON TERRACE became Nos.184-190 Newstead Road.

CLIFTON VILLA became No.42 Hardwick Street.

CLINTON ARCADE Often assumed to be a right of way, the Clinton Arcade, in the Clinton Building at the northern end of St Thomas Street and St Mary Street, was used by the public for 364 days a year, but closed on one day (usually Good Friday) to maintain the owner's private right of way. The arcade disappeared when Edwin Jones store took over the whole building and altered the ground floor, although people were still able to cut through the shop as it had entrances in St Thomas Street and St Mary Street. Today individual businesses occupy the site (Bella Italia and Mothercare) and it is no longer possible to take this short cut between the main streets. *See also* ROYAL BATHS

Like many other town centre buildings, much altered at ground floor level today, but very recognisable by its upper floors. This was the Clinton Arcade in St Thomas Street.

CLOVELLY, Belle Vue Road A magnificent Victorian house which overlooks Portland Harbour – a little too closely, as a series of landslips in the area has brought the cliff edge very close to the property. The first major slip here occurred in February 1904 and sent thousands of tons of soil and a large portion of the house's beautiful terraced gardens towards the seashore. Over one hundred years later, the cliffs here remain unstable and at the time of writing the popular **Underbarn Walk**, which runs below Clovelly, is closed.

CLUE, G. Leo Journalist on the Dorset Echo who was also a playwright and author. Lived in Fernhill Avenue in the 1940s. Died 1955 (not in Weymouth).

COACH PARK Moved from Westham to Lodmoor 1971.

COACH SERVICES In 1769 it took a day and a half to travel by road from London to Dorchester, by 1786 the same journey took 25 hours. Until 1800, passengers for Weymouth had to transfer to another coach at Dorchester. By 1810 the London to Weymouth run took 18 hours. After 1847 when the railway opened to Dorchester, the quickest route to London was by coach from Weymouth to Dorchester and then on by train. The railway extended to Weymouth in 1857.

COADE STONE is a ceramic artificial stone of great durability used for architectural ornaments which can be seen on buildings great and small all over the country. It was formulated at Mrs Eleanor Coade's Lambeth stoneware manufactory in the late 18th century. The **King's Statue** is made from it.

COAT OF ARMS was granted to the Borough of Weymouth and Melcombe Regis on 1st May 1592. The design incorporates many aspects of the borough's historic past. Its main feature is a gold three-masted ship with sails furled, on a blue sea. On its foremast is a banner bearing the three gold lions of England; on the mizzen mast is a banner bearing representations of a castle and a lion (Castile and Leon), a reminder of the town's mediaeval lord of the manor, Edward I and his Queen, Eleanor of Castile. The shield on the side of the ship bears the arms of Gilbert de Clare, Earl of Gloucester, who held the manor of Weymouth in the thirteenth century. After Portland became part of the new 'Borough of Weymouth and Portland' in 1974, new armorial bearings were granted in 1978 and the present coat of arms incorporates the 1592 design, surrounded by additional symbolic representations of Weymouth and Portland's history, including heraldic beasts supporting a block of Portland stone above a naval crown, and sea lions supporting a fishing net, cable and anchor.

This was the coat of arms granted to the Borough of Weymouth and Melcombe Regis in 1592.

Crested china bearing the town's coat of arms was always a popular souvenir to take home from the seaside.

COBHAM Sir Alan Aviator and showman Cobham landed at **Chickerell Airfield** in August 1929 in a ten-seater aeroplane during his Municipal Aerodrome Campaign of visiting 110 towns and meeting their mayors. Deputy Mayor Bartle Pye flew with him and he later gave free flights to local schoolchildren to stimulate their interest in flying. From 1932-1935 his legendary National Aviation Displays and Tours took place, visiting towns and cities all over the country in what became known as his 'Flying Circus', making several return visits to Weymouth during these years. He founded 'Flight Refuelling Ltd' at Tarrant Rushton, where he lived. 'Cobham Drive' in Weymouth, built on the site of Chickerell Airfield, commemorates his visits.

COFFEE TAVERN, Melcombe Regis at Nos. 9-10 St Thomas Street opened in May, 1881 and was known as The Three Cups. The building became the offices of the *Dorset County Post* later in the 1880s, and government offices (Labour/Employment Exchange/Job Centre) for much of the 20th century before being converted to the present Wimpy Bar.

COFFEE TAVERN, Weymouth The Weymouth Coffee Tavern dates from May 1879. It opened in a converted building formerly known as the **Good Templars Hall** in High Street. Serving tea and coffee, it was promoted by the temperance movement and aimed to be
A public house without the drink
Where men can read, converse, and think,
Then sober home return.
The building still stands, adjoining the Old Town Hall. In 1978 it became the meeting place of the Jehovah's Witnesses, and is now known as Kingdom Hall.

COKER'S SURVEY OF DORSET, published in 1732 was not Coker's work, but was actually written by **Thomas Gerard of Trent (1592-1634)** to whom Coker was related by marriage. Coker died c.1635 and the Survey was not published in his lifetime, but was posthumously attributed to him. Weymouth and Melcombe Regis is described briefly.

COLE, W T & Son, were pharmaceutical chemists at No.17 St Mary Street, founded in the first half of the 19th century. Some wonderful products included Messrs Cole & Sons Phosphated Nerve Tonic, Liver and Kidney Mixture, Mayblossom Dentifrice Cream and a Lily and Heliotrope Cream which ensured white hands and delicate complexions. The firm later moved to No.106 St Mary Street and remained in business until the 1990s, being taken over by a larger chain until 2003, when the shop ceased to be a chemist's.

COLEMAN, E. G. Weymouth building contractor in the 1950s and 1960s who took over the business of his father W.F. Coleman. Building works included the Redlands Estate, houses off Ullswater Crescent, Coombe Valley Estate, and St Charles RC Church, Wyke Regis.

COLLINGWOOD, Harry (1851-1922) (real name William Joseph Cosens Lancaster). Born in Weymouth. Author of adventure stories for boys, some with Weymouth settings.

COLWELL CENTRE *see* COLWELL HOUSE

COLWELL HOUSE, School Street was a Salvation Army hostel. It occupied the former **Weymouth Royal Hospital** building from 1921 and was originally for ex-servicemen and later the homeless. The name Colwell House was chosen in 1959 by Commissioner Culshaw, then in charge of Salvation Army Men's Social Work in Great Britain. His wife was formerly Eva Colwell Lord, Colwell being her mother's maiden name. The hostel closed in 1981, the building was demolished in 1983 and the Colwell Centre, an indoor shopping complex, was built on the site.

COMBEN, Robert Stone Mayor of Weymouth 1915-16, 1916-17, 1917-18. Presented Alderman Comben's Garden in Rodwell Avenue to the town during his mayoralty. Granted the Freedom of the Borough in 1952. Died in December 1957.

COMMERCIAL/PLEASURE PIER, at the southern end of the Esplanade. In the harbour's early days, its quays probably extended seawards on Melcombe side not much further than the site of today's George Inn. Extensions along the shoreline and out to sea were gradual and the whole of today's pier area is the result of extensive reclamation. Major infilling took place in the early 19th century to provide the land on which Devonshire and Pulteney Buildings and the Alexandra Gardens now stand, the pier being extended in piecemeal fashion as required. It was rebuilt in 1840. Known as the Pile Pier or Rubble Pier, it seems to have been of pretty rough construction. It was rebuilt and extended out to sea with a curved end in 1859, providing not only steamer berths but also a 'Marine Walk' for the visitors. Facilities added in 1889 included baggage warehouses and customs offices for the GWR Channel Islands traffic, and at the same time the Weymouth Harbour Tramway was extended from the end of Devonshire Buildings onto the pier. Although various minor alterations were made to it, the pier retained its 1859 outline until major reconstruction began in 1931 when work commenced on a new pier of reinforced concrete. Much wider, it followed the line of the old timber pier but continued another 300 feet out to sea and provided a promenade, shelters, dressing rooms for bathers and

The Esplanade and harbour in 1822, with a pier which extends only a short way out to sea.

a diving stage. Work was completed in 1933 and the new pier was declared open on 13th July by the Prince of Wales (later King Edward VIII and later again, the Duke of Windsor). The Pier was taken over by the military in WW2 (*see* ***BEE,*** **HMS*;*** ***GRASSHOPPER,*** **HMS***)* and played a major role in the embarkation of troops for the D-Day landings in Normandy. In 1972 a loading ramp and car handling facilities were constructed for a new roll on/roll off cross-channel service which commenced in 1974 and in 1977 it was decided to reclaim 4 acres from the sea to provide additional space for ro/ro facilities, Cherbourg traffic and imported cars. The Car Ferry Terminal extension opened on 7th May, 1980. The Anchor positioned at the entrance to the pier commemorates this occasion (it dates from the late 18th century and was dredged up off the Kent coast and restored at Weymouth). In 2006 major redevelopment of the whole pier, ferry terminal and Pavilion Theatre area is under consideration. *See also* HARBOUR

The Pier as extended in 1859, with Victorian visitors enjoying a marine walk in 1872. The newly-completed Nothe Fort is in the background.

In 1931 a massive rebuilding of Weymouth Pier began and the finished works were opened by the Prince of Wales (later King Edward VIII) in 1933.

COMMERCIAL ROAD In 1802 **Sir William Pulteney** put forward a proposal to embank more ground along the Backwater to form a 'commercial road', which would run from the turnpike on the Dorchester Road to the harbour bridge, forming a road or by-pass to carry commercial traffic away from the seafront and its wealthy visitors. The actual development of Commercial Road began in 1804, when lots along the shoreline westwards and the northwards from the Town Bridge to Coneygar Lane (now New Bond Street) were sold with the condition that the purchasers were to reclaim enough land not only to enlarge their own sites, but to provide sufficient ground to lay out a new road leading from the Quay to Coneygar Lane – this new road to be called Commercial Road. Progress on the final alignment of the road seems to have been particularly slow at this southern end. In the 1830s similar developments took place at the western end of School Street and the road was completed from here to King Street by 1857. The whole road must have been completed by 1872 as that year it was decided that Commercial Road would officially start at **Ferry's Corner**. Reclamation from the Backwater on Commercial Road's western side began in the 19th century and continued well into the 20th with the marina site (where Melcombe Regis School formerly stood) being infilled in 1904 and land for Melcombe Regis Gardens and Radipole Park Drive being reclaimed in the early 1920s.

Commercial Road before infilling in the 1920s left these houses overlooking Melcombe Regis Gardens instead of their previous view of the Backwater and its swans. The pub on the left is the Albion Inn and the Railway Tavern is on the right.

COMPASS INN, Weymouth. An 18th century inn, location unknown.

COMPREHENSIVE EDUCATION began in 1985. Broadwey Secondary School was renamed Wey Valley School. Portland Tophill School became Royal Manor School. Weymouth Grammar School and Westham Secondary School amalgamated to become Budmouth School.

CONCERT HALL, ST NICHOLAS STREET (also known as the New Concert Hall and the Music Hall). In the 1860s this was the name of the **Theatre Royal, St Nicholas Street**. Cosens and Company initially ran it as a music hall, but it was not a success and when a Drury Lane manager took it over he renamed it 'Theatre Royal'.

CONCORD PLACE was on the north side of St Leonard's Road between Queen's Place and Prospect Place. Some buildings had already been demolished prior to WW2 bombing, the rest were cleared after the war.

'CONCRETE ROAD' Built at Wyke Regis late in 1943 during the run-up to D-Day, this provided an alternative route to Portland in case Ferrybridge was damaged by enemy action. From Hillbourne Road it crossed the fields of Downclose (since covered with housing) linking with a concreted section alongside the line of the Weymouth and Portland Railway, thence to the rail bridge at Ferrybridge, which was fitted with timber decking to permit road vehicles to use it. The temporary road was never required but the section alongside the old railway line still exists.

CONEYGAR Until quite late in the eighteenth century there was little development on the western side of St Thomas Street beyond Coneygar Lane or Coneygar Ditch (old names for what is now Bond Street and New Bond Street), beyond which lay the 'Coneygar', stretching northwards. The ditch was a defensive boundary which ran from the sea to the Backwater. It was very offensive when left unemptied and was later filled in. 'Coney' is an old name for 'rabbit' and 'Coneygar' and 'Coneyland' imply ground so light and sandy as to be only fit for rabbits – an appropriate description since Melcombe Regis stands on a sandspit. The uninhabited land, or 'Warren of Conyes' at the northern end of Melcombe was let out in the 16th century, no doubt providing plenty of rabbits for the pot, as well as grazing for animals and land where the inhabitants were able *'to walk, bowle and shute'* and otherwise disport themselves. In the early 17th century a windmill was built on the Coneygar, where Gloucester Lodge stands today.

CONGREGATIONAL CHURCH, Dorchester Road was founded in 1802. The present building dates from 1880. In 1972 it became Upwey United Reformed Church and the last service took place in July 1992.

Left: *Viewed from Commercial Road, where Webb Major's building is now the site of the multi-storey car park. The telephone exchange beyond it replaced a row of terraced houses known as St Alban Terrace. The picture dates from 1971.*

CONGREGATIONAL CHURCH, Gloucester Street opened in 1864 replacing the chapel in West Street. The architect was R.C. Bennett. The church closed in 1971, services transferring to the United Reformed Church in Trinity Street. The building's foundations were unstable and the twin-spired church was demolished in 1980. The apartments of George Thorne House now stand on the site, named after one of the town's early non-conformist ministers.

An engraving made in 1871, a few years after the church opened.

CONGREGATIONAL CHURCH, Roman Road, Radipole The congregation first met in a room at the **Pig and Whistle** public house. A corrugated iron church building was opened in July 1906 and a new hall was built to the rear of it in 1954 – but it was the hall which began to be used as a church in the 1960s, a use which has continued to the present day. A new hall, with an entrance in Spa Road, opened in November 1962 and replaced the original 'tin chapel'. It is now the United Reformed Church.

CONGREGATIONAL CHURCH, Trinity Street The congregation initially rented a house in Hope Street, the first Hope Chapel being built in 1822 and enlarged in 1833. In 1861 a new chapel was built on the same site and dedicated in March 1862. No.11, St Leonard's Terrace was purchased in 1873 as a manse. In 1885 property adjoining the chapel in Herbert Place was purchased to build additional rooms and a lecture hall, which opened in April 1886. In 1971 the Congregationalists became part of the new United Reformed Church.

CONGREGATIONAL CHURCH, West Street Early Nonconformists who gathered in regular congregations as 'Protestant Dissenters' became known as Independents or Congregationalists, first meeting in some cottages in St Nicholas Street, on the site of which their first church, known as the 'Great Meeting' or 'Old Meeting House' was built. It was replaced by a new chapel on 20th May 1804, which closed in 1864 when Gloucester Street Congregational Church opened. The building then became successively a Concert/Music Hall/Theatre, a Foundry and a Cold Store before being demolished in 1968 to make way for a car park, part of which in the 1990s was redeveloped as flats. *See also* NONCONFORMITY; THORNE, Reverend George

CONNAUGHT HOUSE was built in the 1860s between Buxton Road and Wyke Road, on part of the extensive parkland fronting **Belfield House**. Connaught House was then known as 'Portmore' and was built by the Rev. Talbot Greaves, wealthy Rector of St Mary's Church, who preferred a house set in its own grounds to the church's Rectory in busy St Thomas Street (*see* Old Rectory). He left to take up a post in Bristol in 1881 and after further occupancy as a private house Portmore became a school in 1890. The school's head, John Richard Morgan, already ran a school in Connaught Road and when he moved to Portmore he renamed it Connaught House School. Various buildings were added around the house in the early 20th century. Connaught House School moved to Somerset on the outbreak of WW2 and did not return. During WW2 the building was taken over by the military and was used as a hospital for wounded Americans following the D-Day landings. In the post-war years accommodation was urgently needed for local authority schools and Weymouth Grammar School moved into the building in 1946, using it mainly for first-year forms. Pupils from Broadwey Secondary Modern School and Holy Trinity Junior School also shared Connaught House. Eventually local children were accommodated in purpose-built schools (including the post-WW2 Holy Trinity Schools, built in the grounds of Connaught House in the early 1950s) and the building then provided additional space for the South Dorset Technical College for some years. It was demolished in 1988 and the houses of Connaught Gardens now fill the site. The house's original Lodge still stands in Cross Road, at the entrance to the drive which led up to it.

Boarded up and nearing the end of its life in 1987, Connaught House was once a fine mansion. I suspect I was not the only 11-year old who spent a year at school there and failed to appreciate what a very beautiful house it had once been.

CONSERVATIVE LAND SOCIETY was responsible for the development of the Park District in the 1860s and 1870s, hence a number of the streets are named after Conservative politicians of the time- Ranalegh, Hardwicke, Walpole etc. The Society was formed in 1852 and bought up land in several

English towns hoping, by developing the areas with housing, to build up Tory strongholds.

CONSTABLE, John (1776-1837) The artist honeymooned in Osmington in 1816, when he painted 'Weymouth Bay', now in the National Gallery. His wife's family lived in the village and the couple were married in London by John Fisher, the vicar of Osmington. Constable also drew and painted other scenes at Weymouth, Preston and Osmington.

CONVENT OF MERCY, 74 Wyke Road Opened on Wyke Road in 1940. St Philomena's School (closed 1981) and the Holy Child Secondary School (closed 1967) were attached to the convent. Some of the convent lands were sold off for building in 1984.

CONVENT OF THE SACRED HEARTS, Carlton Road North The Sisters of the Sacred Hearts of Jesus and Mary Convent moved from Trowbridge to Weymouth in the 1890s and acquired a house in Carlton Road South which was used as a convent and small high school, referred to locally as the French Convent School. The foundation stone of the main Convent Boarding and Day School in Carlton Road North was laid in 1908 and the school opened in 1910. Later, more accommodation was required and Lodmoor House was leased from 1955 to 1960. In 1961 the school was also using a building in Glendinning Avenue that the convent had acquired some years before. The school closed in 1992 and the main building and its sports field have since been converted to housing. The Convent itself was used during WWI as a Red Cross Hospital from October 1914 until September 1917.

COODE, Sir John Eminent civil engineer of harbours, docks, rivers and drainage. In 1848 he worked under James Meadows Rendel on the Portland Breakwaters project, becoming engineer-in-chief on Rendel's death in 1858, a post he held until 1872 when the works were completed. He designed the first steel road bridge at Ferrybridge which replaced the old timber bridge to Portland in the 1890s. In Weymouth his scheme for the drainage of the town was partly adopted and he designed the **dam** (now demolished) which crossed the Inner Harbour just below Westham Bridge. His relations with the Town Council were at times somewhat fraught, largely due to the Council's reluctance to completely overhaul the towns almost non-existent sewage system.

COOMBE VALLEY ESTATE was built in the 1960s by local builder E.G. Coleman.

CO-OPERATIVE HALL, Caroline Place opened in 1936 and was later converted to the Co-op Bank. It is currently occupied by Weymouth and Portland Snooker Club.

CO-OPERATIVE SOCIETY The Co-op had extensive premises in the area. The first local shop opened in the 1860s in Park Street and branches were later established in other parts of the Park District, Chapelhay, Westham, Wyke Regis and the town centre, culminating in the opening of a purpose-built department store in Westham Road in 1926 which was extensively modernised between 1958 and 1961 (now Wilkinsons). As well as today's shops selling Grocery and Provisions, the Co-op once had fish shops and butcher's shops, its own bakery in Cromwell Road, a dairy in Franklin Road and a Coal depot at the station.

COOPER'S ARMS PUBLIC HOUSE Two pubs, now closed, on the east side of Maiden Street were the Old Cooper's Arms and the New Cooper's Arms.

CORNEY TERRACE became Nos.18-28 Newstead Road

CORNICK BROTHERS was a bakery business founded by brothers William and John Cornick in 1891, on the corner of Governor's Lane and East Street, moving in 1909 to the Belgrave Bakery on Dorchester Road at Lodmoor Hill. The Dorset Cake Company, run by former employees of the Cornicks, bought the Belgrave Bakery in 1961. *See also* BELGRAVE COTTAGES

CORNOPEAN INN was originally in Concord Place, St Leonard's Road (No.52). The area was cleared following WW2 air raid damage and the name and licence were transferred in post-war years to a converted house on the corner of Newstead Road and Granville Road which has since reverted to housing.

CORONATION ARCH of 1911, Esplanade. This was a dual-purpose temporary structure. It was erected on the Esplanade, opposite the Royal Hotel, in May 1911. The huge archway was covered with greenery and decorations and illuminated at night. It first bore inscriptions welcoming visitors to the prestigious **Royal Counties Agricultural Show** held at Lodmoor from June 13th-16th, 1911. Later in the month these banners were changed to 'Long live our King and Queen' to celebrate the Coronation of King George V and Queen Mary.

The 1911 Royal Counties Show and Coronation Arch on the Esplanade.

CORONER the Mayor was Coroner of the borough until superseded by the County Coroner when county councils were set up on the passing of the Local Government Act of 1888.

CORPORATION YARD, Westwey Road The Council depot moved from its yard at the Westham Bridge end of Westwey Road to a new base at Crook Hill, Chickerell and the site was cleared in 2003. The apartments of Harbour View have since been built on it.

COSENS AND COMPANY During the second half of the nineteenth century and throughout the twentieth, the influence of the firm of Cosens and Company was inextricably linked to the development of Weymouth Harbour and the fortunes of the town. Cosens built and serviced vessels, carried out both major and minor engineering jobs, ran the popular fleet of paddle steamers and sent their tugs out on salvage jobs at sea. The firm

was started in 1848 and went on to occupy slipways, offices and workshops all around the harbourside. Cosens No.1 slipway was formerly a shipyard owned by the **Besant family**, the No.2 slipway, now used by the Weymouth Sailing Club is also known as **Hooker's Dock.** Cosens and Co's head office from 1884 until 1962 was at No.10 Custom House Quay, after which they centralised the business at their premises in Commercial Road. Proposed redevelopment of this area brought about a move to Portland in 1987, but recession in the 1990s caused the decline of the company and it was sold in 1996, becoming Cosens Engineering Ltd for three years before being sold again in 1999. *See also* ICE HOUSES; THEATRE ROYAL, St Nicholas Street
Further reading : *Cosens of Weymouth 1848-1918* by Richard Clammer (Black Dwarf Publications, 2005) and *Cosens of Weymouth 1918-1996* by Richard Clammer (Twelveheads Press, 2001).

COSENS QUAY The area of the inner harbour opposite the site of the former **Cosens & Co**'s works in Commercial Road is now used as a yacht and car park. In 2006, it was named 'Cosens Quay' in commemoration of the firm's long and important association with the town. Where Cosens' workshops once stood there are now harbourside apartment buildings.

COTTER'S COTTAGES *see* CARTER'S COTTAGES

COUNTY COURT was at No.69 St Thomas Street in the years before WW2, the premises being later occupied by solicitors and then a bank. Its elaborate façade above street level is evidence of its former use. It is currently a shoe shop.

COURT LEET This was a manorial court dealing with minor offences and matters relating to the good government of the town such as street cleaning and maintenance and the granting of inn licences. Weymouth and Melcombe Regis each had a Court Leet and after their Union in 1571 these were presided over by the Mayor. Every male person able to bear arms was obliged to attend and absence without good reason incurred a fine of one penny. The majority of Courts Leet were abolished on the passing of the Municipal Reform Act in 1835 : some remain, including Portland's.

COURTAULD, Sydney Renee *see* **BEACON, The**

COVE INN, Cove Street closed in 1987 and is now converted to housing.

COVE RESTAURANT (now Perry's Restaurant), 4 Trinity Road In the 1960s an old carved stone dating back to the early 16th century was discovered set in a wall at the rear of this property. It depicted a tonsured monk, probably an abbot, holding a crozier. It is thought to have come from a monastic building, possibly the Friary in Melcombe Regis.

'CRABCHURCH' was the password used in the **Civil War** by Royalist plotters in Weymouth and Portland who carried out a surprise attack in February 1645 on the Parliamentary troops then controlling the town. *See also* CIVIL WAR

CRANE, Dr John The author (under the pseudonym 'J.C') of *Cursory Observations on Sea Bathing; the use of Sea-Water Internally, and the Advantages of a Maritime Situation, as conducing to Health and Longevity. To which is added A Concise History of Weymouth in Dorsetshire...* He was the Residing Physician at Weymouth c.1795 and also sketched Weymouth Esplanade.

CREE, John Once a resident of Weymouth, he later lived at Osmington, where he died in July 1853. A charitable man, he is mainly remembered in the town for his generosity in paying for **Boot Hill** to be widened, a plaque outside **Netherton House** recording this deed of 1851.

CREMATORIUM Adjoining the Weymouth Cemetery at Westham, the Crematorium was opened on 2nd June 1939 by Lord Horder, and has since been extended. Recalled at the time of its opening were memories of another Dorset crematorium- the first in England- which was built by Captain John Hanham in the grounds of his home, Manston House, near Blandford. At a time when only burials were permitted, Hanham sought to carry out the wishes of his late mother and his late wife who, before dying in the 1870s, had expressed a desire to be cremated. Having been refused permission by the Home Secretary, Hanham went ahead and built his own crematorium. The bodies, which had been lying in lead-lined coffins in a mausoleum, were thus reduced to ashes in 1882. When this became public knowledge, the legality of Captain Hanham's action was questioned, although no action was taken against him. The first public crematorium, at Woking, opened three years later, in 1885.

CRESCENT COURT was reached by an alleyway between Nos.8 and 9 Crescent Street.

CRESCENT STREET takes its name from its position behind 'Royal Crescent' (now Nos.101-115 The Esplanade), which was planned as a crescent of houses in the late 18th century, but was actually built as a straight row.

CRICKMAY AND SONS, Architects The firm was founded in Weymouth in the 1850s by George Rackstrow Crickmay and its success led to offices being opened in London where a second flourishing practice was established in 1882. Individual Crickmay buildings and whole estates were built in London and the south of England and even those built in the Weymouth area are too numerous to list here. They include churches, schools, business premises, hospitals, banks, halls, waterworks and private houses. The founder of the firm died in 1907 and the family's association with the practice ended with the death in 1978 of Hugh Crickmay, but the name lives on in the John Stark and Crickmay Partnership at Dorchester.

CRIME Under the Act of Union of 1571 the Mayor, assisted by the Borough Recorder and Bailiffs, was the chief justice of the peace for the town. He was able to hold regular courts called the Sessions of the Peace in which all kinds of crime committed in the town could be investigated and dealt with. Theft, violence,

Dr John Crane's view of Weymouth Esplanade in 1789 shows The Narrows where sea and Backwater met in rough weather.

drunkenness, profanity, etc. all came before him. The Mayor was also empowered to license local innkeepers. Serious crime such as murder could be investigated by the Mayor, but trial was usually left to the more august Assize Judges at Dorchester. On the passing of the Municipal Corporations Act in 1835, much of the work was transferred to the County Sessions. A local magistrates' or police court was set up in Weymouth which also had licensing powers. *See also* MURDERS

CROCKER'S FOLLY was a row of four cottages which stood on the east side of what is now Newstead Road, just south of where the 1860s bridge of the Weymouth and Portland Railway crossed it. They probably dated from the 1850s but the origin of the name is unknown. Were they built by a Mr Crocker? Was it folly to build dwellings behind the gasworks and its fumes?

CROMWELL ROAD INFANTS SCHOOL, Westham opened in 1906 and closed in 1991, to be replaced by Beechcroft Infant School.

CROMWELL ROAD SCHOOLS, Westham opened 10th January 1906, becoming Weymouth and Melcombe Regis Central School in 1921 and Westham County Secondary Modern School in 1948. The upper school moved to the Marquis site in 1969. On the introduction of comprehensive education in 1985 Westham School merged with Weymouth Grammar School on the Marquis site and took the name Budmouth School. Some of the Cromwell Road buildings remain, converted to other uses.

CROMWELL VILLAS became Nos.104-106 Abbotsbury Road

CROSS CHANNEL STEAMERS *see* CHANNEL ISLANDS; GREAT WESTERN RAILWAY; HARBOUR

CROSS KEYS INN, St Thomas Street later became the Jersey Hotel, then the **Jersey Tavern.**

CROSS ROAD was originally known as Buxton's Lane, as was Buxton Road.

CROWN FLOUR MILLS *see* TEMPLEMAN, Thomas John

CROWN HOTEL, St Thomas Street The present Victorian Crown Hotel replaced a much earlier Crown Inn on the same site. Only one sketch of the old inn is known, made by Samuel Grimm in 1790. The Crown Hotel was much enlarged at the time the Town Bridge was being rebuilt in the late 1920s, and the Victorian building in buff brick can clearly be seen between the newer red brick extensions on either side. Owners Devenish closed the hotel in 1974 but it was bought by hotelier Leslie King and re-opened in 1976.

CROWN AND SCEPTRE INN, Melcombe Regis existed in the early 18th century, location unknown.

CRUMP, Charles George Born in Weymouth. Assistant Keeper at the Public Record Office. Published books on historical research and a novel, *The Red King Dreams*, in 1931.

CULLIFORD TREE HUNDRED The Saxons developed the 'Shire' system from which the present Counties have evolved, the modern term 'sheriff' being derived from the Saxon 'Shire Reeve'. They further divided the shires into 'Hundreds' as units of local government, originally districts rated at a hundred taxable units. The area which is now Weymouth lay within the Hundred of Culliford Tree. The meeting place of the hundred is believed to be Culliford Tree Barrow (O/S6991/8547) on the Ridgeway above Preston.

CUMMING, H and W.H. (photographers) *see* DEBENHAM, E. & Co.

CUNIGER *see* CONEYGAR

CUSTOM HOUSE, Custom House Quay This fine waterfront building was used for many years as the Custom House and bears the Royal Arms in cast iron over its doorway. Today it is the headquarters of the Portland Coastguard. It was built about 1800, probably for one of the town's wealthier merchants. It has been suggested that it was built for **Nicholas Robilliard** of Alderney, who later went bankrupt. Its use as the Custom House dates from sometime in the first half of the 19th century- prior to this the building used as the Custom House was on the Quay at a spot close to where the flight of steps leads down from the Town Bridge today. It probably relocated when the 1824 Town Bridge was built. Across the harbour, Weymouth at one time also had a 'Customs Inspection House'.

CUSTOM HOUSE QUAY In 1872 'The Quay' was designated as the name for all the Quay from **Ferry's Corner** eastwards. Prior to this it had been known variously as The Quay, Custom House Quay and as West Quay west of the Town Bridge and South Quay east of it. Today 'The Quay' is known as Custom House Quay.

CUTTER HOTEL This public house, on the corner of East Street and St Alban Street, once extended through to Grosvenor Place on The Esplanade. In 1895 the part of the building on the seafront was converted to become the **Wordsworth Memorial Home of Rest.** In the 1880s the Cutter was a Temperance Hotel.

CUTTY SARK The famous tea clipper was presented by **Mrs Catherine Dowman** to the Thomas Nautical Training College for preservation in 1938, after the death of her husband Captain Wilfred Dowman, who had begun the restoration of the vessel. It was moved to Greenwich in 1954, where it is now on show. In 1956 Mrs Dowman launched the 3rd Wyke Regis Sea Scouts glass fibre sailing boat and named it *Cutty Sark.*

CYGNET COTTAGES became Nos.71-75 Abbotsbury Road.

Daisy Cottages

D

DAISY COTTAGES On the east side of Old Parish Lane, at its junction with Franklin Road.

DAM, Backwater/Inner Harbour The Dam was built in 1872. At that time the flow of water in the Backwater and Radipole Lake was tidal, as the first road bridge across to Westham was a timber structure which did not have the flow-controlling sluices of the present **Westham Bridge**. At low tide the sluggish water caused appalling health hazards and terrible smells as the town was depositing most of its raw sewage into the Backwater. The dam was intended to control the flow of the water and maintain a reasonable level in the upper reaches of the Lake and was part of a scheme designed by eminent civil engineer Sir John Coode. It was not a satisfactory solution and Sir John came in for criticism from the Town Council, but since the rest of his plan – for the erection of a pumping station and a sewage farm – had been abandoned, it was hardly his fault that the waters were still heavily polluted with sewage. Not until 1896 were proper measures taken to address the sewage problem. The stone-built Dam, redundant since the building of Westham Bridge in 1921, remained until 1995 when it was removed and the harbour dredged to allow the development of the present **Marina**. *See also* SEWERAGE

DAMON, Robert Born in Weymouth, where the family owned an outfitter's shop. He was a geologist and author of the *Handbook to the Geology of Weymouth and the Isle of Portland* first published in 1860. He ran a warehouse, known locally as a museum, in the building now occupied by the Elim Church in Belle Vue. It was crammed with fossils, corals, preserved snakes and insects, shells, minerals, antlers, sponges, skins, and skeletons, specimens of which he sent all over the world. His son Robert F. Damon carried on the business after his father's death.

DANIELL, William (1769-1837) Artist. Produced a collection of aquatints entitled *A Voyage round Great Britain* in 1823, which included a view of Weymouth.

D'ARBLAY, Madame was the married name of diarist **Fanny Burney.**

DARCH'S cycle and furniture shops, the Town Bridge Café and Swan Inn at the lower end of St Thomas Street were demolished in 1975. *See also* SWAN INN, St Thomas Street

DARRINGTON, Fred (1911-2002) Sand sculptor. Striking sand models made using only Weymouth sand and sea water have been a summer attraction on the beach since the 1920s and Fred Darrington's work could be seen from the early 1950s until his retirement in 1996. His eye-catching sculptures ranged from The Last Supper and a 90th birthday tribute portrait of the Queen Mother to Garfield and King Kong. His grandson Mark Anderson now continues this seaside tradition. In 1963 tons of Weymouth sand and seawater were transported to London where Mr Darrington sculpted exhibits at the Olympia Holiday Exhibition to publicise the resort.

DE SELLA NOVA, Dr. Arnold (died 1684) Surgeon. Son of **Peter De Sella Nova**. In 1684 he gave to the poor of Weymouth £5 and a leasehold shop, and £5 to the poor of Melcombe, the interest to be yearly divided. He was Mayor in 1668-69 and 1672-73 and owned **Francis Farm**.

The Dam stretches across the foreground of this photograph from the early 1880s. The first Westham Bridge, with central drawbridge, is in the background which also shows the twin spires of Gloucester Street Congregational Church and the tower of Christchurch.

DE SELLA NOVA, Peter (died 1654) Accounts vary as to how French Huguenot De Sella Nova came to be in Dorset but he arrived in 1623 and became a privateersman. He served as 'apothecary and surgeon-general' for various Parliamentary regiments under Sir William Sydenham and Sir Walter Earle during the Civil War. Owned an apothecary's shop in Melcombe Regis and other property. Died in 1654 and is buried in Jersey. Two sons, **Arnold** and Henry.

DEBENHAM, E. & CO, 88 St Thomas Street Portrait, marine and landscape photographers in the late 19th century. The business was taken over in 1898 by photographer Henry Cumming and he was succeeded by his son W.H. Cumming who later moved to Great George Street. The building then became the premises of William Whittle, florist, and is now occupied by an estate agent. The end wall of the building at the junction with School Street has always been boldly painted for advertising purposes and currently directs shoppers to the Colwell Shopping Centre a few doors away.

DEBENHAMS The department store took over the shops formerly occupied by Edwin Jones store (the firm which had succeeded VH Bennett) in 1973, but these were in four separate buildings and were not economically viable. Debenhams left the town early in 1982, but returned in October 1999 to occupy a new purpose-built store in the New Bond Street shopping complex.

DECONTAMINATION CENTRE, Westwey Road (at its junction with Westham Road). This was a gas cleansing station, set up to combat possible poison gas attacks during WW2. Fortunately not required for this purpose, the building was converted to a Children's Library in 1959, due to inadequate space in the prefabricated Public Library building on the same site. The two buildings were eventually linked by an extension in 1967, but were demolished when the new **Weymouth Library** in Great George Street opened in 1990. Harbour View apartments now fill the site.

DEFOE, Daniel (c.1660-1731) Writer on economic, social, political and historical matters and novelist. In 1724-6 he published his *Tour of the Whole Island of Great Britain* which ran to a number of editions, with many additions and amendments. His description of Weymouth in the first edition is brief and concentrates on the port trade, much more space being devoted to a near-shipwreck he witnessed during his visit. Defoe came to the attention of the Mayor when he was in Weymouth as being possibly involved in seditious activity.

DEHEER'S WAREHOUSE, No.9 Custom House Quay The firm of John Deheer, stevedores, ships chandlers and warehousemen arrived in Weymouth in 1951, handling imports and exports through the port. They occupied a mid-19th century harbourside warehouse (formerly occupied by Burden's Transport Ltd), which was converted to house bulk fertiliser in January 1963. Deheer's closed in February 1965, and the warehouse has been converted to the 'Deep Sea Adventure', a maritime-themed tourist attraction.

DELAMOTTE, William (1775-1863) Prolific painter of landscape and marine views, although only two are of Weymouth. He was the son of Peter Delamotte, whose library stood on Weymouth Esplanade. William's talent seems to have come to the notice of King George III, who arranged for him to be instructed in art. He was a frequent exhibitor at the Royal Academy from the 1790s to 1850. His Weymouth pictures are Esplanade views, looking north and south.

DENNIS ROAD takes its name from Dennis Farm, on the lands of which the houses of the Dennis Estate were built in the 1930s.

DERBY COTTAGES became Nos.1-3 Derby Street.

DERBY STREET takes its name from Edward Stanley, 14th Earl of Derby (1799-1869) an active Tory politician at the time when the Park District was being developed by the Conservative Land Society.

DERBY TERRACE became Nos.4-10 Derby Street.

DEVENISH, J. A. & Co., Ltd. In 1824 William Devenish took over premises in Hope Square owned by John Flew which had been used as a brewery at least since the early 18th century and may well have existed before that. The last of the family involved in the business was Major J.H.C. Devenish who lived at **Springfield** (now demolished) on Rodwell Road and died in 1953. On 11th August 1940 the Devenish Brewery suffered severe damage during an air raid, and the adjacent (and rival) brewers John Groves and Sons, Ltd. stepped in to assist with production. In 1960 Devenish took over the Groves Brewery and brewing continued until 1985 when it transferred to Redruth in Cornwall. Today the Devenish and Groves buildings, renamed 'Brewer's Quay' house the 'Timewalk'- a special effects walk through Weymouth's history, a pub, shops and Weymouth Museum, which includes a history of the local brewing industry and a small-scale brewery where the brewing process can be observed.

A nostalgic view of the Devenish Brewery dray horses.

DEVENISH GARDENS see DEVENISH HOMES

DEVENISH HOMES These homes for elderly and retired professional people were built under the terms of the will of Major John Herbert Clark Devenish (died 1953) who lived at **Springfield**, a fine house at Rodwell. Although the house has been demolished, its gate pillars and lodge can still be seen on Rodwell Road, almost opposite its junction with St Leonard's Road. Residential development now fills the site, on part of which stand eight 'Homes of Devenish' for the elderly, known as Devenish Gardens. More 'Devenish Homes' were built in Bincleaves Road and Belle Vue Road.

DEVENISH SQUARE sometimes known as Devenish Place, was on the north side of Governor's Lane between Nos. 8 and 9. The area was cleared in the early 1960s and is now Governor's Lane car park.

DEVON AND DORSET REGIMENT was granted the Freedom of the Borough on 12th May 1973.

DEVON COTTAGE became No.34 Walpole Street

DEVONSHIRE BUILDINGS were built sometime between 1812 and 1819 on land reclaimed from the sea. In 1819, Mr Welsford, the terrace's builder, agreed to take down the last house at the east end of Devonshire Buildings and make a circular finishing end, in keeping with the round houses at the top of St Mary and St Thomas Streets. Devonshire Buildings is now numbered 1-6 The Esplanade.

A view of Devonshire Buildings, probably dating from the early 1880s, before the Weymouth Harbour Tramway lines were extended onto the Pier.

DIAMOND TERRACE became Nos.100-128 Newstead Road

DIRECTORIES Many directories for Dorset and Weymouth have been published since the beginning of the 19th century but infrequently and by different publishers. The most regularly updated were KELLY'S DIRECTORIES.

DISPUTES the first recorded dispute between the two towns of Weymouth and Melcombe Regis over the harbour profits dates from 1284. By the 16th century the situation had worsened to such a degree that by Act of Parliament in 1571 the two towns were ordered to unite and become one borough, to be known as The Borough of Weymouth and Melcombe Regis.

Further reading : A summary of the disputes, by R.R.Sellman, can be found in *More Dorset Studies* by Maureen Weinstock (1960).

DISSENTERS' CHAPEL, West Street *see* CONGREGATIONAL CHURCH, West Street

DOCK ROAD was an alternative name for Newton's Road, leading to **Newton's Cove**.

DODINGTON, George Bubb, 1st Baron Melcombe of Melcombe Regis (1691-1762) Political manipulator and social climber Dodington was born George Bubb, the son of a Weymouth apothecary. He inherited immense wealth from his uncle George Dodington in 1720, took the name George Bubb Dodington and began planning his rise to fame and power, shrewdly buying property in Weymouth, which at that time was represented by four MPs in Parliament. In an age when only freeholders (property owners) could vote, Dodington was soon influencing elections, allying himself with Weymouth's powerful Tucker family in support of the Whig government of Sir Robert Walpole. The town became a 'pocket borough' its voting totally controlled by Dodington, who was also one of its MPs from 1754-1760. Dodington's 'wheeler-dealing' in politics was eventually his undoing, as he allied himself to too many opposing factions. He died in 1762 without heirs, a year after being created Lord Melcombe, so the barony died with him. Eastbury, a huge house near Tarrant Gunville designed by Vanbrugh, was only partly built when it was left to Dodington by his uncle. He spent years finishing it in extravagant style and entertained leading literary figures of the 'Eastbury Circle' there. After his death, Eastbury was pulled down as no one could be found to live in it and today only a tiny portion remains.

DODSON, Philip Weymouth's leading builder in the first half of the 19th century. He was also leader of the Liberal Party in the town and Mayor in 1855-56, 1857-58 and 1858-59. He was the original owner of the timber ponds and sawmills on Commercial Road which eventually became **Betts Timber Yard**. Among his building projects were the first Backwater Bridge, St John's Church, Holy Trinity Schools at Chapelhay, Weymouth Railway Station, Victoria Terrace and the Burdon Hotel. He was also the major shareholder in the Weymouth and Portland Steam Packet Company on its formation in 1851. His death, aged 59, on 10 July 1860, occurred when, according to the subsequent inquest, *'Labouring under the influence of temporary insanity, he took prussic acid and died'*.

DOMESDAY SURVEY 1086 There are a number of settlements named as Wai or Waia in Domesday but none has been positively identified as Weymouth. Melcombe is not listed and was probably included in the return for Radipole ('Retpola' in Domesday).

DOMINICAN FRIARY *see* FRIARY

DONKEY RIDES have been one of the attractions of seaside Weymouth since Victorian times, the main operators being the Downton Family. When John Downton and his donkeys retired in 2000, this traditional beach feature was missing from the sands for five years, but in 2005 a new company filled the gap.

DORCHESTER ROAD In 1872 it was decided *'that the Dorchester Road commence from Waterloo Place in the parish of Melcombe Regis and extend to the extremity of the borough in the direction of Dorchester'*, although there was no street numbering as such at this date. In 1897, two years after boundary extensions brought more of Radipole within the borough, Dorchester Road was renumbered in one sequence, having formerly comprised (West Side)- Henning Place, Belgrave Terrace, Hill

Dorchester Road in about 1925, showing the Royal Oak public house.

Terrace, Radipole Terrace, Union Place, Borough Villas, Argyle Terrace and (East Side) Wellington Terrace, Wellington Place, Belgrave Villas. In 1933 further boundary extensions took the numbering of houses on Dorchester Road out to Upwey.

DORSET DAILY ECHO The newspaper was founded on 28th May 1921 as the *Dorset Daily Echo and Weymouth Dispatch,* printed in Bournemouth in its early years. Initially it had a rival daily – the *Dorset Daily Press*, but this ceased publication in 1924 and the Echo took over its printing works in Weymouth's St Thomas Street. The works were destroyed in an air raid on 2nd April 1942, but not an issue was missed as printing continued at Bournemouth until the Weymouth offices were rebuilt and back in action in 1949. On 1st July 1958 there was a name change to *Dorset Evening Echo* and in 1999 the paper was renamed *Dorset Echo*. The St Thomas Street offices closed in 1999 when the printing works moved to the **Granby Industrial Estate** and are currently occupied by Yates wine bar. The *Echo* now has an office at No.56a St Mary Street.

DORSET INSTITUTE OF HIGHER EDUCATION was the name of Weymouth's teacher training college on Dorchester Road from 1976 until 1985. *See* WEYMOUTH TEACHERS' TRAINING COLLEGE

DORSET PLACE, Newberry Road comprises the west side of Newberry Road.

DORSET PLACE, Radipole was renamed Wellington Place in 1872.

DORSET TERRACE runs from Franchise Street to Chapelhay Street.

DOVE ALE HOUSE *see* BLACK DOG HOTEL/INN; CHILES, John and Mary

DOWMAN, Catherine (nee Courtauld) (1878-1972) Lived in Weymouth from the 1930s until her death. Married Captain Wilfred Dowman and is best known for her gift to the nation of the famous tea clipper ***Cutty Sark***. She also wrote children's books. Her home, Wyke Lodge, a mid-19th century house formerly known as Boulton Villa, has been demolished, but the housing development now on the site has kept the names 'Lodge Way' and 'Boulton Close'. Dowman Place, Harbour Point, Wyke Regis is named after Captain and Mrs Dowman. She was the sister of **Sydney Renee Courtauld**.

DOWNCLOSE ESTATE, Wyke Regis Council estate, developed in the early 1950s on lands known as Down Close.

DOWNCLOSE GOSPEL HALL, Doncaster Road, Wyke Regis opened 2nd July 1962. Closed 2006.

DOWNTON FAMILY *see* DONKEY RIDES

DRAINAGE *see* SEWERAGE

DREADNOUGHT HOAX was perpetrated on the Royal Navy in February 1910 by a group of six student friends, which included novelist Virginia Woolf. Having sent a telegram to the chief of the Home Fleet, then in Weymouth Bay, informing him to expect an official visit to his flagship HMS *Dreadnought* by the Emperor of Abyssinia accompanied by various dignitaries, the hoaxers donned exotic dress, darkened their skins with burnt cork and took the train to Weymouth (having demanded VIP treatment at Paddington Station). Met at Weymouth with suitable ceremony, they were then taken to the battleship and royally welcomed. On board they conversed in a ridiculous mumbo jumbo language, refused refreshments in case their make-up ran, yet got away undetected. On their return to London, the ringleader sent an account of their exploits plus a photograph to the *Daily Mirror* and it was some time before the Royal Navy was able to live down the visit of the six young people who had carried off what must be one of the most successful hoaxes of all time.

DREW, Joseph (1814-1883) Founded the Weymouth-based newspaper *Southern Times* in 1851 which he edited until 1862. Author and lecturer on religious and philosophical subjects, but probably best known for *The Poisoned Cup*, his novel about Sandsfoot Castle, which was published locally and ran to more than 20 editions between 1864 and 1963. Drew was a partner in Cosens and Co. from its early days and the company's chairman from 1874 until his death.

The Poisoned Cup : a tale of Weymouth and Sandsfoot Castle.

DRILL HALL, Lower St Alban Street The TA hall was built in 1891 for the Dorset Volunteer Artillery, Weymouth Battery which, after many name changes, became R' Battery of the 250 (Queen's Own Dorset and West Somerset Yeomanry) Medium Regiment, Royal Artillery, in 1957. The unit was disbanded in 1967 when the Territorial Army became the Territorial and Army Volunteer Reserve, and reformed as A Company The Dorset Territorials. From 1968 the Drill Hall was used as a store and it was demolished to make way for apartments which were built on the site in 2003.

A view of dilapidated and soon to be demolished buildings in Lower Bond Street taken in 2000. The apartment blocks of Beaufort Garden Mews and Martello Mews now fill the site. The TA premises and Drill Hall can be seen and, the building in the foreground was formerly occupied by Roberts Sweet Factory.

DUKE OF CORNWALL PUBLIC HOUSE, St Edmund Street was formerly known as the Duke of Cumberland.

DUKE OF CUMBERLAND PUBLIC HOUSE, St Edmund Street was the former name of the Duke of Cornwall pub.

DUKE OF EDINBURGH PUBLIC HOUSE, St Thomas Street was formerly the Bridport Arms.

DUMONT'S HOTEL/APARTMENTS *see* BANK BUILDINGS

DUNMARKLYN MANSIONS became No.70, Dorchester Road.

DUNN, Pat (1933-1999) was the first female football referee. Came to Weymouth with her family as an evacuee in 1939 and stayed. Began refereeing friendly matches in 1965, and, after a hard fought battle with the Football Association, became a qualified referee in 1967 – although the FA ruled that, as a woman, she was barred from officiating at matches. She went on fighting her cause and eventually, in 1976, the FA accepted that she could not be barred on account of her gender – backed up by the Sex Discrimination Act of 1973 – and she went on to referee matches for the next four years. Retiring from football refereeing in 1980, she took up cricket umpiring.

DWARFS WEDDING made the news in 1925 when Miss E.V. Walbridge and Mr A. Goodwin were married at Holy Trinity Church on 19th January. The couple appeared in circuses and at Blackpool Tower and were featured on picture postcards of the period.

E

EAGLE TAVERN, Trinity Road was pulled down in the 1860s.

EARL OF ABERGAVENNY The East Indiaman *Earl of Abergavenny* was lost on 5th February 1805 after striking The Shambles sandbank. Her captain, John Wordsworth, brother of poet William, attempted to run for the shelter of Weymouth, but the vessel was badly holed and sank less than two miles off Weymouth Esplanade, well within the sight of land. Her captain and more than two thirds of some 400 souls who had set out from Gravesend on the voyage to India and China were drowned. A memorial plaque can be found on the Stone Pier, unveiled on the 200th anniversary of the disaster.

Further reading : *The wreck of the Abergavenny* by Alethea Hayter (Macmillan, 2002)

Rescue came too late for many who clung to the rigging of the sunken East Indiaman Earl of Abergavenny. *By the time help arrived, many had tumbled into the sea and drowned in the freezing weather of February 1805.*

EARTHQUAKE SHOCKS a 'shock of earthquake' was felt in Wales and the West of England on 27th June 1906 – fortunately no-one was killed and damage reported was mainly toppled chimney stacks – but minor shocks were also reported in Weymouth that morning, where floors vibrated, furniture rattled and house bells were set a-ringing.

EAST CHICKERELL COURT AND FARM The farm covered some 300 acres between Radipole and Chickerell and was in the ownership of the Jesty family for many years. An early golf links was sited here and horseracing took place in the early 20th century. The farm went out of Jesty ownership in the late 1930s. In 1964 it was bought by local butcher Maurice Sapsworth but when the Central Electricity Generating Board named East Chickerell Court as the proposed site of a sub station to link up with its cross-country line of pylons the farmhouse and buildings were allowed to go to ruin and were eventually cleared. Nothing remains of East Chickerell Court and a transformer station now stands on the site. The Wessex Stadium and Police Divisional HQ also stand on former East Chickerell Court land.

EAST ROW and WEST ROW were terraces on the south side of Chapelhay Street. Lost to 1930s slum clearance and WW2 bombing raids. Two adjacent terraces bearing the same names stood on the north side of St Leonard's Road and suffered the same fate.

EBENEZER HALL, Abbotsbury Road Opened in June 1903. There was an earlier Gospel Hall, founded in 1884, on the opposite side of Abbotsbury Road, close to its junction with Old Parish Lane.

Further reading : *Ebenezer, Westham, Weymouth : a century of fellowship*, by David Mullen (Ebenezer Evangelical Church and D.P. Mullen, 2003)

EBENEZER PLACE became Nos.43-59 Franchise Street. Demolished following WW2 air raids.

EBENEZER VILLA was in Brownlow Street.

EDLIN, Robert The photograph of a handsome American soldier boarding a landing craft at Weymouth in June 1944 has become one of the iconic pictures of WW2. Lt. Bob Edlin served with A Company of the 2nd Ranger Battalion, one of the most elite units of the US Army. When he landed on Omaha Beach on D-Day he was shot in both legs and 31 of his 35 comrades were killed by machine-gun fire. He later returned to France and took the surrender of nearly 900 German troops. He was awarded the Distinguished Cross and the Texan Medal of Honour. Bob Edlin and other American survivors of the Omaha beach landings made several welcome returns to Weymouth on the anniversaries of D-Day. He died, aged 82, at his home in Corpus Christi, Texas, in 2005.

Further reading : *The Fool Lieutenant; a personal account of D-Day and WW2* by Marcia Moen and Margo Heinen (Meadlowlark Publishing Inc., Minnesota, 2000)

As he cheerfully boarded a landing craft in Weymouth Harbour on 5th June 1944, Lieutenant Robert Edlin and his fellow US soldiers were not to know that next day when they landed on Omaha Beach, it was to be the bloodiest of all the D-Day beaches where the American forces were to suffer huge losses.

EDMONDS, Frank Punch and Judy man on Weymouth sands every summer from 1925 to 1976, apart from the WW2 years. From a family of showmen, his father and grandfather were both Punch and Judy men. He worked at Weymouth with his uncle, Sidney Edmonds, who died in 1964.

EDWARD HOTEL/EDWARD COURT *see* BANK BUILDINGS

EDWARDS, Sir Henry (1820-1897) Wealthy merchant, not a native of Weymouth, who made his fortune in linseed oil, hence his nickname 'Linseed Edwards'. A Liberal, he was one of the town's two MP's from 1867 until 1885, the year he received his knighthood. He did not stand as an MP again, Weymouth in 1885 having become part of the South Dorset constituency. He was a great benefactor of the town, and his gifts included an annual dinner for the aged poor, almshouses on Boot Hill and Rodwell Avenue, a clock for the Old Town Hall, the works of the Jubilee Clock, bells for Christchurch and the Working Men's Club building in Mitchell Street. A statue of Sir Henry stands outside the Alexandra Gardens (the gardens were not one of his gifts, the site was chosen as being suitably prominent) and was unveiled by Sir Richard Nicholas Howard in January 1886. Sir Henry died 4th February 1897 and his ashes are buried in Melcombe Regis Cemetery, the spot marked by an impressive granite memorial. *See also* EDWARDS AVENUE; EDWARDSVILLE

Sir Henry Edwards, a great benefactor of Weymouth, whose statue stands outside the Alexandra Gardens. A 'Spy' cartoon.

EDWARDS AVENUE Ten houses in all, seven of which stand on the east side of Boot Hill and three at its junction with James Street (this corner formerly being known as Pastoral Place).The cottage homes were built by philanthropist Sir Henry Edwards in 1894 and bear a plaque of the arms of Sir Henry, as well as his crest, monogram and date of 1894 on each house.

EDWARDS CHARITY Property and lands given in 1716 by Jonathan Edwards and his wife Rebecca to provide for four poor widows dwelling on the Weymouth side of the harbour. Eventually, in 1829, enough funds had accumulated to build four almshouses on Wyke Road at its junction with Gypsy Lane, aided by a generous donation from the Rev. George Chamberlaine of Wyke Regis. These were demolished in 1957 and new bungalows in Rodwell Avenue replaced them.

EDWARDSVILLE, Rodwell Avenue Cottage homes for the elderly, opened early in 1897 and set back from the road with attractive gardens in front. They were a gift from Sir Henry Edwards to house the aged poor of the borough, originally providing accommodation for four married couples and twelve single old people. A statue of Sir Henry once stood in the grounds.

EGDON HALL, Lynch Lane was built in 1958 to house apprentices and junior scientific staff working at the United Kingdom Atomic Energy Authority establishment at Winfrith. The building is currently occupied by Weymouth and Portland Housing.

ELDON HOUSE became No. 1 Cromwell Road

ELDON TERRACE became Nos.3-9 Cromwell Road

ELDON VILLAS became Nos.40-42 Old Parish Lane.

ELECTIONS, PARLIAMENTARY The town's right to elect four MPs (*see* PARLIAMENTARY REPRESENTATION) caused its elections to be much prone to illegal vote rigging. Only freeholders could vote and a freeholder owning several properties could only vote once, so it was common practice to provide deeds (which were required as proof of the right to vote) to men who would vote for the prescribed candidate. On the return of the deeds after the election the alleged freeholder would be paid a fee. Secret ballots were unheard of, so it behoved the voter to vote in the way he had been directed. Close to the election, makeshift properties would be thrown up and deeds for these hastily drawn up to provide more 'freeholders' with the right to vote. It wasn't necessary for the prospective MP to visit or even know the town – his local agent 'bought' the votes with cash and plentiful supplies of beer. Elections tended to be rowdy and occasionally riotous affairs. The purchase of freeholds by those who could afford to buy property meant that a great deal of the town was owned by just a few men. One result was a 'property empire', handed down and increasing in size, which eventually became the **Johnstone Estate**. George Bubb Dodington was the best known political wheeler-dealer. He manipulated the voting in favour of Whig Prime Minister Robert Walpole in the first half of the 18th century aided by the Tuckers, a prominent local family. The history of the town's parliamentary representation is an involved and fascinating mix of deals, plots and personalities. The 1832 Reform Act reduced the town's MPs to two and in 1885 Weymouth became part of the South Dorset constituency. *See also* MEMBERS OF PARLIAMENT; PARLIAMENTARY REPRESENTATION

ELECTRICITY SUPPLY In the late-nineteenth century Weymouth was gas-lit, but gas was beginning to be rivalled by electricity. In 1897 Weymouth Corporation resolved to oppose the plans of two private companies who proposed to supply electricity for public and private purposes within the borough and to proceed with works themselves. A scheme was prepared and a site on the Backwater's western shore was purchased in 1901- this was 'Sunnybank' a house and grounds in Stavordale Road belonging to Mr J. B. Cole, one of the early developers of Westham. Builders J. and H. Bagg of Weymouth were awarded the contract for building the generating station which was completed in August, 1904, its tall chimney providing Weymouth with a new landmark. The DC power supply for public and private lighting began on 26th September 1904, the occasion suitably celebrated by a banquet at the Hotel Burdon. AC generators were installed in the 1920s and electricity showrooms were opened in Westham Road in December, 1933. Power was first taken from the National gride in 1932. Nationalisation on 1st April 1948 brought about the end of the Corporation's ownership of the Sunnybank generating station, but it continued in use. In August, 1966 the DC current was switched off for good and later that year the power station ceased operating, electricity then being supplied by Poole Power Station (since demolished) through the National Grid. Sunnybank was demolished in 1974, a laborious process as the proximity of the 200' high chimney to neighbouring houses meant it had to be taken down brick by brick. Much of the site has now been redeveloped as housing.

ELEPHANTS occasionally ambled through Weymouth, part of visiting circuses, until circuses featuring wild animals were banned from the town in 1987.

Circus elephants in Westham Road.

ELIM CHURCH, Belle Vue The church was formed in March 1958 and its congregation initially met in temporary accommodation in High Street before the purchase of the Belle Vue Cinema. The church opened in the converted cinema on 19th July 1958.

ELIOT, William (1794-1885) Head, at the time of his death in January 1885, of the banking firm Eliot, Pearce and Eliot. (*See* Eliot, Pearce & Co's Bank). His two sons Richard and George, took over the bank in 1885 and were responsible, with a third partner, for its failure in 1897.

ELIOT, PEARCE & CO's BANK (also known as the Weymouth Old Bank) Founded in Weymouth in the early 1790s, with other Dorset branches opening later. Best known for its failure in April 1897, the crash causing colossal financial distress in Weymouth, the surrounding district and beyond. Eliot's was highly respected; almost everyone banked there, and those who lost money ranged from Weymouth Corporation and most of the leading businesses in the town, to individuals with savings accounts and even schoolchildren. Although many small banks had failed in previous years and one or two larger Dorset banks collapsed earlier in the 19th century, no-one could quite comprehend that an institution such as Eliot's could crash. There had been hints a few months previously that all was not well when one of the partners, Sir Robert Pearce Edgcumbe, withdrew from Eliot's, but such was local confidence in the bank that its customers appeared to be untroubled by this warning. At the time of the failure, the two partners who filed for bankruptcy were George Edward Eliot and Richard ffolliott Eliot, but Sir Robert Pearce Edgcumbe (son of Edward Pearce, an earlier partner in the bank) was also called to account. The bankruptcy hearing proved that 'defective book keeping' by the partners over a number of years had shown the bank's finances to be in a healthy position when in fact the partners were investing funds in risky speculative ventures overseas and permitting huge overdrafts to builders who later went into liquidation. The bank was actually insolvent yet the Eliot brothers continued to trade and draw money to maintain their lifestyle as leading citizens of the town – Richard Eliot lived at Radipole Manor, his brother George, twice Mayor of Weymouth, at the now demolished Bincleaves House. Edgcumbe was a Dorchester man, his home being Somerleigh Court. Those creditors who had entrusted their funds to the bank received an initial payment of just 6s 8d in the £, the eventual settlement some six years later rising to 7s 11 ¼d.

ELIZABETHAN WAY, a walk on the Nothe headland, commemorates the Silver Jubilee in 1977 of the accession of Queen Elizabeth II.

ELLIS, George Alfred (died 1842) Author of *The history of the borough and town of Weymouth and Melcombe Regis*, published in 1829. He chaired a committee appointed to inspect the ancient documents in the possession of the town in 1839 (these had been entrusted to the Mayor during rebuilding of the Guildhall and storage in the new building was damp) but no action seems to have been taken over their care in later years as they fell into private hands. *See* 'SHERREN PAPERS'

ELLIS'S COURT was in the vicinity of Hope Street..

ELSIE VILLAS became Nos.26a and 26b Lennox Street

ELWELL is a place name dating back to the 13th century, and as the name derives from the old words 'haele' or 'haelu' for hale and healing and 'wella' for well, the location of the original Elwell (sometimes spelt as Hellwell) could be the spring which is the source of the present Wishing Well at Upwey.

ELWELL MANOR, Rodwell Road stands on the site of an old dairy house, rebuilt and lived in by **Robert Vining** and altered and extended in 1854.

EMBASSY HOTEL, Overcombe (now the Spyglass Inn) Built in the 1930s, the Embassy was known initially as 'The Nineteenth Cafe' as it was on the fringe of a miniature golf course at Overcombe. It accommodated high ranking officers of the US Army on and around D-Day and it is said that General Eisenhower dined here with General Omar Bradley. It re-opened in 1946 and was converted from a single storey building to two storeys in 1954.

EMMADALE COTTAGES became Nos.3-21 Emmadale Road.

EMMADALE ROAD is believed to be named after the granddaughter of Westham landowner **Emmanuel Knight**.

EMMADALE TERRACE became Nos.2-42 Emmadale Road

EMMANUEL CHURCH CENTRE, Field Barn Drive Church of England. Opened in April 1973 to serve the Southill area of Radipole.

EMPIRE DAY 24th May was instituted in 1902 after the end of the Boer War as a way of encouraging schoolchildren to be aware of their responsibilities as citizens of the British Empire. The date chosen was Queen Victoria's birthday. In the early years of the 20th century there were mass gatherings of children from the local schools at the King's Statue. Flags were flown, crowds turned out, hymns were sung, there were cheers for the monarch and the rest of the day was a holiday.

ENDERBY HOUSE, Clarence Buildings (Nos.27-28 The Esplanade) is now the Alexandra Hotel.

ENDICOTT, John *see* CLARK & ENDICOTT MEMORIAL

ENGLISH CIVIL WAR *see* CIVIL WAR (1642-1646)

ESPLANADE the name comes from the Latin word explanare, meaning to level out, and was often used in the military sense as an open levelled area of ground separating a fortress from a town, but it was later used to describe a levelled area intended to serve as a public promenade. The first use of the word Esplanade in Weymouth appears to be in 1785. It would then have been a bank of earth separating the sea from the roadway, probably faced with turf. A contract for walling the Esplanade was entered into on 17th March 1800 with Messrs. Hamilton and Vining. They were to build a wall 6 feet high and 2 feet thick commencing opposite the houses in Gloucester Row and continuing southwards in front of Gloucester Lodge and its gardens (known as 'The Shrubbery'). It was to be built partly at the expense of the proprietors of houses and lands facing the sea, who were invited to subscribe 13 shillings per running foot towards the cost. It was stipulated that the wall should be strong enough to withstand the force of the sea and effects of the weather for 10 years from the date of completion and that if the Corporation wanted to extend it, the builders would do so at the price agreed. Work began in April, 1800, but progress was slow. A second section was completed and a different contractor built a third section. Funds were low and Sir William Pulteney put forward a

1911 and schoolchildren line up in the vast open space in front of the King's Statue to celebrate Empire Day.

proposal in 1802 to embank more ground at the southern end of the Esplanade, taking it out in a wide curve. In 1804-5 this plan was adopted. Rubbish was tipped to infill the new site and a fine awaited those who tipped their rubbish anywhere else. The Esplanade wall was frequently knocked down or damaged in storms, and much of it was destroyed in the 'Great Gale' of 1824. A small stone breakwater was built out onto the sands in 1810 in an attempt to limit damage at its southern end – the base of this construction, which was later lowered, is now buried beneath more recent build up of sand. By 1827 the Esplanade wall and walkway, with posts and chains separating it from the roadway, was completed from Devonshire Buildings to Brunswick Buildings. Ten of these old stone posts can be seen opposite the Pier Bandstand; another, commemorating the Great Gale, is now mounted in the wall of a raised flowerbed at the opposite end of the prom. The wall was extended from Brunswick Buildings to the houses at Greenhill in 1839 and by 1891 it had joined Preston Beach Road, running along the front of Greenhill Gardens. Widening of the Esplanade seawards took place in the 1920s. The houses along the Esplanade, once numbered as individual terraces, are now consecutively numbered from 1 – 146 as follows:- 1-6 (Devonshire Buildings), 7-15 (Pulteney Buildings); 16-18 (Bank Buildings), 19-30 (Clarence Buildings), 31-34 (Grosvenor Place), 35-46 (Augusta Place), 47-51 (Charlotte Row), 52-57 (York Buildings), 58-59 (Chesterfield Place), 60-67 (Johnstone Row), 68-84 (Royal Terrace) 85-100 (Gloucester Row), 101-115 (Royal Crescent), 116-131 (Belvidere), 132-146 (Victoria Terrace). Features of the Esplanade such as the Jubilee Clock, War Memorial, etc. are listed separately.

ESPLANADE SHELTERS The attractive cast iron and glass shelters were installed along the Esplanade in 1889. When first built a number of them had balconies which directly overlooked the sands, but Esplanade widening in the 1920s has isolated most of them in the centre of the walkway. The larger shelter near the King's Statue was added in 1937.

ESPLANADE SUBWAY *see* SUBWAY, ESPLANADE

ESSEX VILLAS became Nos.5-12 Milton Road.

ETHEL TERRACE became Nos.31-33 Chelmsford Street

EVACUEES On 1st September 1939 hundreds of children from London, with some mothers and schoolteachers, arrived at Weymouth railway station. Weymouth and Portland had been designated a 'safe place', away from the expected enemy air raids on major cities. The evacuees stayed with local families and attended school on a part-time basis with local children, as classrooms were unable to cope with this sudden influx of around 6000 extra pupils. Locals suspected that the Weymouth and Portland area, with its large naval anchorage, might be anything but safe in wartime and they were proved right in 1940 when the air raids began. Many of the London children subsequently returned home.

EXCELSIOR TERRACE became Nos.72-98, Abbotsbury Road. It was built by the Excelsior Lodge of Odd Fellows.

EYE INFIRMARY *see* WEYMOUTH AND DORSET COUNTY ROYAL EYE INFIRMARY

John Upham's view of Weymouth Esplanade in 1812 shows the area reclaimed at its southern end. Devonshire and Pulteney Buildings have yet to be erected on this new ground.

The Esplanade looking very much the worse for wear in a very early photograph, probably taken around 1860. It is obviously a winter scene and there had been severe storms in the late 1850s which may account for the damage. The bow-fronted first Royal Hotel can be seen in the distance, on the right.

Faircross

F

FAIRCROSS An ancient cross was discovered in about 1880 in a ditch off Wyke Road, about half a mile from Weymouth. The field in which it lay was known as 'Faircross' which was perhaps the site of an ancient local fair, being on the road to Wyke Regis which had been granted fairs and markets in the 13th century. The stone was given to John Beale Vincent by Colonel Owen Swaffield, the owner of the land on which it was found, and placed in front of Vincent's new house 'Faircross'. John Vincent's son, also John, later inherited the house. He and his wife drowned in the *Empress of Ireland* tragedy in 1914. The house was demolished in 1973 but the cross was been re-sited in front of flats in Wilton Drive which were built on the site.

The mediaeval Faircross found close to Wyke Road in 1880, which is now placed outside flats in Wilton Drive, off Faircross Avenue.

FAIRCROSS ESTATE the first portion of this land – 8 plots opposite Belfield Park on Wyke Road – was sold for housing in 1896. It had been owned by the late Colonel Owen **Swaffield**.

FAIRFAX HOUSE became No.11 Cromwell Road

FAIRHAVEN *see* VICTORIA AND GREAT WESTERN HOTEL

FAIRS *see* PUTNIDGE FAIR; ST BOTOLPH'S FAIR

FAIRVIEW TERRACE became Nos.37-43 Walpole Street

FALKNER, John Meade (1858-1932) Author of *Moonfleet*, the famous tale of smuggling and shipwreck on the Dorset coast, first published in 1898 and much reprinted since. The son of a clergyman, he was born in Wiltshire in 1858, but lived in Dorset from an early age, moving to Weymouth in 1870 when his father was appointed curate of St Mary's Church. The family lived at the rectory, No.82 St Thomas Street (now a wine bar known as the Old Rectory until 2006 and now as The Barracuda Bar). Later in life Falkner became chairman of the armaments company Armstrong Whitworth.

FARWELL COTTAGES were on the north side Charles Street, between Nos.3 and 4.

FEATHERS PUBLIC HOUSE *see* GOLDEN LION INN

FENCHURCH STREET occasionally used in early documents, is another name for **Franchise Street**.

FERNERY, The The name in the early 20th century of No.83 St Thomas Street.

FERRIS, Vice Admiral Abel (1775-1858) Began his naval service in 1793 as a midshipman on board HMS *Thalia*, Captain **Richard Grindall**, and served under him as Lieutenant on HMS *Prince* at the Battle of Trafalgar in 1805. Retired to Weymouth, where he died in August 1858.

FERRY, HARBOUR Prior to the building of the first Harbour Bridge (later known as the Town Bridge) in the 1590s, the only means of crossing Weymouth Harbour was by ferry-boat. The ferry was sited just west of today's bridge and was described in Tudor antiquarian John Leland's description of the town in 1538 – *'The Townlet of Weymouth lieth straight against Melcombe on the other side of the haven, and at this place the Trajectus is by a boat and a rope, so that in the ferry boat they use no oars'.* Today, seaward of the Town Bridge, a ferry boat service still crosses the harbour in the summer months and is a favourite with both locals and visitors. For a few pence the ferryman rows his passengers from the Ferry Steps to the Nothe, collecting those for the return trip on the other side.

FERRY, SMALLMOUTH Prior to the building of the first Ferrybridge in 1839, a ferry took foot passengers across the

Looking towards Wyke Regis, this 1790 engraving shows the tethered ferry at Smallmouth and the Passage House, which were destroyed in the Great Gale of 1824. Wyke Church is in the background.

Fleet water known as 'Smallmouth' between Wyke Regis and Portland. It was a tethered ferry, and the ferryman pulled the boat across on a rope which passed through the boat and was attached to posts on the land on each side of the passage. Carriages and those on horseback were able to ford across at low water. In the **'Great Gale'** of 1824, massive seas widened the passage and re-activated earlier proposals for a bridge to be built at Smallmouth, although another fifteen years would pass before the first **Ferrybridge** was built in 1839.

FERRY'S CORNER is west of the Town Bridge, where Commercial Road and Custom House Quay meet. It was formerly a sharp right-angled bend, the angle of which was lessened in the 1860s when infilling of a section of the Backwater at this point allowed trains on the Weymouth Harbour Tramway to negotiate the corner. Problems arose when bogie stock was introduced in 1889, as trains could only round the bend by the use of special couplings. This was not remedied until 1939 when the quay was again widened at Ferry's Corner. The Corner takes its name from the workshops and yard of wheelwright James Ferry & Sons, which were sited here in the mid-19th century.

FERRYBRIDGE (RAIL) A 27-span timber viaduct was built in 1863 to carry the **Weymouth and Portland railway** line over the Fleet at **Smallmouth**. It was replaced by an steel bridge in 1902, built slightly seaward of the original. The line closed in 1965 and the steel bridge was demolished in 1971.

FERRYBRIDGE (ROAD) Three bridges have carried road traffic to Portland. The first opened in January 1839 and replaced the ferry at **Smallmouth**. It was a timber bridge built on trestles and was initially a toll bridge. In 1850 a permanent armed guard was established on the bridge to detain would-be escapees from Portland Prison, who were working in the quarries and on the construction of the breakwaters. Despite problems with the timbers which necessitated major repairs, this first bridge lasted over fifty years. It was replaced by a steel bridge in 1895, built to the designs of Sir John Coode. By the late 1970s this bridge was wearing out and the road across it was subsiding. Traffic flows were restricted as arguments raged over its replacement and finally, in 1982, following a scientific study and a public inquiry, the go-ahead was given for the present bridge. Its opponents had feared that the plans – to build the new bridge on land nearer Portland and then divert the Fleet water beneath it – would damage both Chesil Beach and the local fishing industry. The third 'Ferrybridge' opened on 10th October 1984; three weeks later the successfully diverted Smallmouth water flowed under it and the old channel was infilled.

FERRYBRIDGE COTTAGES Wyke Regis are numbered from Nos.19-37, the original Nos.1-18 having since been incorporated into the street numbering of Portland Road (Nos.203-237).

FERRYBRIDGE INN was formerly the Royal Victoria Hotel.

FESTIVAL OF LIGHT *see* SHOWNIGHT (modern) (this event was renamed Festival of Light in 2005).

FILMS WITH SCENES MADE ON LOCATION AT WEYMOUTH – a selection (dates given are when the film crews were in Weymouth, not necessarily the same as the year of release):- *Within the Maze* (1923), *Q Ships* (1928), *Down Channel* (1929), *Jack Ahoy* (1933), *Great Expectations* (1945)- not filmed locally, but Cosens paddle steamer *Empress* was hired and converted to resemble an 1830s cross channel packet for the film), *The Small Back Room* (1948), *The Gift Horse* (1951), *The Cruel Sea* (1952), *Seagulls over Sorrento* (1953), *You Know What Sailors Are* (1953), *Morning Departure* (1953), *The Ship that Died of Shame* (1954), *Above Us the Waves* (1954), *The Dam Busters* (1954), *The Man Who Never Was* (1955), *Moonfleet* (1955), *The Key* (1957)- title 'Stella' was used during filming. *The Feathered Wheel* (1956), *Further up the Creek* (1958), *S.O.S. Pacific* (1959), *The Bulldog Breed* (1959), *The Damned* (1961)-known as 'Children of Light' during filming, the title of the novel on which the film is based. *Petticoat Pirates* (1961), *Tom Jones* (1962), *The Heroes of Telemark* (1964)-the Weymouth GWR steamer *Roebuck* starred in disguise as the Norwegian coaster *Galtesund*. *Gordon of Khartoum* (1965), *Beau Geste* (1966), *Far from the Madding Crowd* (1966), *Remembrance* (1983), *The Thirty Nine Steps* (1987).

Cosens & Co.'s paddle steamer Empress, *hired to star in the 1945 film version of Charles Dickens 'Great Expectations' and suitably disguised as an 1830s cross-channel packet boat.*

FIRE BRIGADE Fire fighting equipment was provided for the town on a fairly haphazard basis until responsibility for fighting fires was handed over to the police in the mid-19th century. The formation of a volunteer fire brigade was mooted in the 1880s but it was 1895 before the first Volunteer Fire Brigade was established, captained by Mr W.E. Drake. The first Chief Officer, J.H.L.Courtenay was appointed in 1899 and by 1903 there were 2 officers, an engineer and 22 men, nine of whom received a quarterly retainer, the rest being volunteers. The service was funded by the Corporation, and prior to nationalisation in 1941 it remained a volunteer force. The National Fire Service was de-centralised in 1948 when the provision of local fire services became a county responsibility and the Dorset Fire Brigade established its HQ at the Weymouth Fire Station. In 1974 when the boundaries of Dorset were extended Weymouth became the divisional headquarters of 'A' division with another divisional HQ in the east of the county. Since 1988 the Dorset Fire and Rescue Service HQ has been based at Dorchester.

FIRE STATION The first building to house the town's fire fighting equipment was the 17th century **'house with the cannonball'** at the junction of St Edmund Street and Maiden Street and fire engines were housed here until November 1939, when the present Fire Station opened on North Quay. *See also* FIRE BRIGADE

FIRES Some of the major fires which have occurred in and around the town are the Alexandra Gardens Theatre 1993; Francis Farm 1923; Gloucester Hotel 1927; Gloucester Row 1934; Laundry, Queen's Road, Radipole 1910; Maiden Street Methodist Church 2002; Ritz Theatre 1954; Southdown Farm 1907; Sutton Poyntz 1908; Templeman's Flour Mills 1917; Town Fire 1666. Refer to the alphabetical listing for more details.

FIRST WORLD WAR *see* WORLD WAR 1

FISH MARKET, Custom House Quay The Fish Market opened just before Christmas, 1855. Within a few years there were complaints about the unsuitability of its position, close to quayside where ships were unloading cargoes of dusty coal which affected the quality of the fish, making it grey and gritty. Its previous location, on stalls in front of Bridge Buildings at the Town Bridge, had been even less suitable, the residents nearby complaining about *'an open gutter which brought an unhealthy fishy stench to within four feet of their houses, exacerbated by the intolerable smell from quantities of stale fish left lying about in hot weather'*. The Fish Market on Custom House Quay closed in 1868 and moved into the general **Market House**. It was used for storage until it reverted to its proper use in 1988, dirty and dusty cargoes no longer being unloaded on the harbourside.

FISHERMAN'S ARMS PUBLIC HOUSE High Street Badly damaged in 1940 air raids, the derelict pub was demolished in 1958. During the site clearance, a cash book dating back to the early 1880s was found. Kept by the landlord, it provided a colourful and interesting record of those who stayed there. His lodgers paid four pence a night, sometimes sharing a room with four or five others. Names were either not asked or not given, as his visitors are described as Watercress man, Tinker, One-arm man, Fur cap, Frame Maker, Happy Jack, and so on.

FISHING INDUSTRY Unlike the highly organised fishing industry in some other ports, Weymouth fishermen tended to sell their catches locally, although the number of fishing vessels has increased in recent years and fish is now transported out of the port by road. The 20th century saw a revival in oyster farming, with oysters being farmed in the waters of The Fleet and there is an annual **Oyster Festival** in Weymouth. Weymouth's **Fish Market** on Custom House Quay reverted to its proper use in 1988, having been used as a store for many years.

FLEET DRAINAGE Over the centuries the possibility of draining the Fleet has been considered and in 1630 a dam with sluices was actually built, although its site is unknown. The scheme failed due to the penetration of the sea through Chesil Beach at high tide.

FLETCHER, Hanslip (died 1955) Artist. He visited Weymouth in the late 1940s to produce illustrations of local scenes for the town's publicity department.

FLOODS 1955 On the night of 18/19th July 1955 a record 11 inches of rain fell at Martinstown and the following day the floods hit the villages of the River Wey. There was extensive destruction from Upwey down through Nottington, Broadwey and Radipole and water levels in Radipole Lake rose and overflowed into Radipole Park Drive, Commercial Road, Westham Road, Park Street and King Street. Swept down by the torrent, a huge mass of reeds and debris blocked the sluices of Westham Bridge. The Park District streets, always liable to flood in heavy rain, were already under water. There was further flooding in many areas of the town and beyond. Marsh Road residents had to be rescued from their homes by boat and the Marsh was flooded. At Preston and Sutton Poyntz homes and caravans were waterlogged. In Radipole village garden walls were flattened, houses were flooded and the river bridge severely damaged. There was deep water in houses at Nottington and Littlemead, Broadwey. In all this destruction, there were, sadly, two deaths. At Watery Lane, Broadwey no one realised that a hole scoured out by the waters was 12 feet deep and an 11-year old local boy, Robin Crump, drowned in it. At Sutton Poyntz, Mr B.E. Bailey was killed by lightning while sheltering under a tree.

FLORAL CLOCK, Greenhill Gardens Installed in 1936 by Messrs James Ritchie and Son of Edinburgh. Due to repeated vandalism, the hands of the clock have been removed.

FLORISSANT HOUSE became No.40 Brownlow Street

FLORISSANT TERRACE became Nos.12-16 Brownlow Street.

FLYING BOATS were occasionally anchored in Weymouth Bay in the late 1940s and 1950s, until the RAF's last flying boat squadron was disbanded in 1957.

FOORD'S CORNER, Wyke Regis takes its name from the local Foord family and is often incorrectly spelt Ford.

FOOTBALL *see* DUNN, Pat; FROWDE, Mark C; MARINDIN, Major Francis; WEYMOUTH FOOTBALL CLUB

FORESTERS' ARMS pub was in Great George Street and had also been known as The British Queen.

FORTE FAMILY of the hotel and restaurant empire. Italian Rocco Forte ran cafes in Scotland before moving south and opening cafes in south coast resorts, including Weymouth. His son Charles (later Sir Charles Forte) arrived to take charge of the Weymouth businesses in the late 1920s – there were two cafes, one in Brunswick Terrace (No.6, now Hamilton's restaurant) and a much larger establishment, Forte's Ice Cream Parlor, Soda and Milk Bar at No.1 Frederick Place (now a Hogshead pub). Charles Forte played for Weymouth Rugby Football Club and also played soccer in Weymouth. *See also* **Alf's Fish and Chips**, the business started by Alfonso Forte.

FORTS It is difficult to provide a list of forts in Weymouth as some were of a transient nature and sometimes merely earthworks thrown up and defended. The following are known of, but all the locations are by no means certain:- Blockhouse Fort (5 guns, with embrasures for 8), faced the sea, probably on the site of York Buildings; Cotton Fort (a rampart with 3 guns) was to the north of the town, probably intended to defend 'The Narrows'; Dock Fort (also known as Jetty Fort or New Fort) was in the vicinity of the harbour entrance, south side; the Lookout Fort was west of the Nothe; Mountjoy Fort, was a little to the north of Blockhouse Fort; North Fort, also known as Queen Elizabeth's Fort, was on the Nothe headland and Roundhouse Fort was on the seafront just north of Petticoat Lane (St Alban Street). In addition there were the Tudor castles at Sandsfoot and Portland, the temporary use of the chapel of St Nicholas at Chapelhay as a fort during the Civil War and the Victorian fortifications of the Nothe Fort, the Breakwaters (with their own forts) and the Verne Citadel at Portland.

FOUNDRY COTTAGES were Nos.1-2 West Street, close to Cosens & Co.'s foundry.

FOUNTAIN HOTEL, No.3 King Street Opened in January 1861. This was a rebuild by Crickmays of the former pub of the same name on the site. Now converted to shops.

4, NORTH QUAY *see* TUDOR HOUSE, No.4 North Quay

FOX, Charles Born in Weymouth. Well known broadcaster and author of books and articles about jazz. Also wrote a children's book *The Gale brought Adventure* under the pseudonym Richard Jeremy.

FOX INN, No.22 St Nicholas Street, Melcombe Stood on the east side of St Nicholas Street, almost opposite but just south of its junction with John Street. The pub was demolished in a WW2 air raid on 2nd April 1942. Landlord Tom Hewlett was injured and his son died in the raid. Mr Hewlett later ran a fruit and vegetable barrow near the Town Bridge and died in 1957. The adjacent Dorset Daily Echo offices were bombed in the same raid and when they were rebuilt after the war, the new building extended on to part of the Fox Inn site.

FOX INN, Weymouth existed in the early 1700s on the south side of the harbour, exact location unknown.

FOX-STRANGWAYS *see* ILCHESTER, EARLS OF

***FOYLEBANK,* HMS** The local area's first WW2 bombing raid came on 4th July 1940 when HMS *Foylebank* was attacked and sunk in Portland Harbour. More than 160 crew and 10 civilians were killed in the attack and **Leading Seaman Jack Mantle** was posthumously awarded the VC.

FRANCHISE STREET has also been known as Francis, Franches, Fanchurch and even Fenchurch Street. The derivation of the name is uncertain. It may stem from 'fraunchise', the district over which the privilege of a corporation extends or be taken from the Fraunceys/Fraunncheys family who were stewards of the royal manors of Weymouth and Wyke. Franchise Court was on the north side of it.

FRANCIS FARM was situated on open land below Markham House, between Wyke Road and Chickerell Road. The picturesque thatched farmhouse, then in the occupation of the Bazell family, burned down on 3rd June 1923. *See also* MARKHAM AND LITTLE FRANCIS

FRANKLIN VILLAS became Nos.11-13, Franklin Road.

FREEDOM OF THE BOROUGH Under the provisions of the Honorary Freedom of Boroughs Act 1885, the first person to be awarded the Freedom of the Borough on 30th October 1895 was the Headmaster of Weymouth College, the Reverend J.A. Miller. The names on the Roll of Honorary Freemen of the Borough to date are:-

1895 Rev. Dr John Aaron Miller
1900-1903 (Weymouth and Melcombe Regis granted the Freedom of the Borough to local men who had served in the Boer War: many other towns did the same). Harry Arnold; Charles Axe; Robert Baylis; Edwin Bower; William Brinsley; Tom Foot; James Forse; Henry Godden; Jesse Gosling; F.G.Horsey; Walter Knell; Henry Langford; George Lloyd; C.W. Lovell; M.C. McKean; H.Charles Marsh; Charles Mumford; W.G. Paul; John Pitman, William Potter; Herbert Pover; G.S. Read; C.E. Roberts; James Rowe; T.E. Stephenson; Alfred Symonds; H.G. Young.
1913 Admiral Lord Charles William de la Poer Beresford. Commander of the Channel Fleet at Portland 1907-1909 (ceremony May 1914).
1924 James Mcpherson Lawrie and Hubert Houssemane du Boulay. Medical men, awarded for their services to Weymouth hospitals.
1929 Alfred Dennis; Herbert John Groves; Sidny Spark Milledge; Bartle Pye, All the awards between 1929 and 1953 were to long-serving Councillors/Aldermen/Mayors.
1946 John Thomas Goddard.
1952 Robert Stone Comben.
1953 Francis Walter Henville Peaty; William Moggeridge; Jennings Alexander Attwooll; Percy Boyle; Albert Biles; Charles Henry James Kaile; Alfred Percy Burt; Arthur George England.
1955 Percy Smallman. Town Clerk of Weymouth from 1925/6 to 1956.
1958 Donald William Fry. Nuclear physicist.
1966 'R' Battery of the 250 (Queen's Own Dorset and West Somerset Yeomanry) Medium Regiment , Royal Artillery.
1973 Devonshire and Dorset Regiment.
1979 Captain, Officers and Ship's Company HMS *Osprey.*
1984 Royal Engineers.
1994 Eric Ricketts. Architect and local historian.
2002 Roy Gainey. Long serving councillor and twice Mayor.

FREEMAN OF THE BOROUGH Today, this is an honorary title conferred by the Council, usually on individuals who have given the town outstanding service or on a body of people who have a special association with the borough. *See* **Freedom of the Borough** for the roll of honorary freemen. To be a 'Freeman' in earlier centuries was very different, when only freemen were allowed to trade in the town and any 'foreigner' or non-freeman caught trading illegally was fined. Apprentices who had served their full term could apply to be admitted freemen at a nominal fee, as could the sons of freemen. A few men were elected as freemen without payment, usually MPs or others of some standing. For the rest, it was a case of paying for the privilege of practising their trades, and the fees varied, often depending on how well the applicant knew the Mayor and council, or if he was related to the town's leading citizens.

FREEMASONRY Dorset Freemasonry was founded in Weymouth in 1736, the first lodge being formed that year in the Three Crowns Inn, **Babbidges Square**, at the lower end of St Thomas Street. The Inn and buildings surrounding it were demolished in the 1820s to provide direct access to the new Town Bridge of 1824. The Inn gave its name to the masons' Three Crowns Lodge, which remained in existence until 1754. A Lodge formed in the town in 1770s closed in 1785. The present All Souls Lodge No. 170 originated in Devon, transferring to Weymouth in 1804 and meeting at the King's Head Inn and the Royal Hotel until the present Masonic Hall opened. The foundation stone of the Hall was laid in 1815 and it opened on 20th May 1816. A banqueting hall was added in 1876. A history of All Souls Lodge was written by Zillwood Milledge and published locally in 1896. A second Lodge, Trinity Lodge No 8025, was founded in 1965.

FREESTUN, Colonel William Lockyer Liberal MP for Weymouth 1847 to 1859, knighted in 1860. His grave in Melcombe Regis Cemetery is marked by an impressive granite obelisk.

FRESHFORD PARK, Grange Road was built in 2004.

FRIARY (sometimes referred to as the Priory) Dominican friars founded the Friary in Melcombe Regis in 1418, the last religious house to be founded in Dorset before the Reformation, and the last Dominican house to be founded in England. Its dedication is variously described as being to St Winfred or St Dominic. Due to their sombre habit, the brothers were known as the Black Friars. This was not a wealthy order, the friars originally relying on charity for support, but they worked in the community and arrived in Melcombe when the fortunes of the town were at a low ebb. The opening of the Friary was at first opposed by the Bishop of Sarum, but he relented when petitioners claimed 'there was no place dedicated to God in Melcombe' (there had been a 13th century chapel in Melcombe but it was either decayed or disused by 1418). The friars were not only concerned with the spiritual welfare of the inhabitants, they contributed to the prosperity and welfare of the town by building a jetty and a fort. Today Governor's Lane Car Park occupies the major part of the site of the old Friary. Its buildings stood on approximately an acre of ground, bounded by Upper St Alban Street, East Street, Maiden Street and Governor's Lane. In the 1530s King Henry VIII ordered the Dissolution of the Monasteries and in 1538 Melcombe Friary closed. Its buildings were put to various uses and it seems they gradually fell into ruin over the following centuries. A 1780s guidebook stated that much of the Friary ground and buildings were lying ruined, and those that remained were parcelled out into tenements, with the chapel having been converted to a malt house. In the 1850s some buildings still existed as the 1851 census confirms that 'the Friary and Little Friary' were occupied by poor families. The site in the 1860s was in the possession of the Johnstone Estate which cleared the buildings, the resulting open space being leased out for the erection of new properties. During demolitions in Governor's Lane in 1958 ancient walls, possibly those of the Friary, were found in cellars and an old doorway thought to have been of the Friary was demolished in the 1960s. There is in Weymouth Museum a chair known as the 'Prior's Chair', its back carved to represent a cardinal's hat and bearing the 'lion passant gardant' which was also carved above the Friary door. Said to be imbued with special powers, it is reputed to come from the Friary and to have been the gift of a visiting cardinal. The story goes that any person who died while sitting in the chair would gain automatic entry to paradise and it must have been a useful source of income for the friars. The chair's legendary powers were discounted after the Dissolution and in later years it was used to chair successful Parliamentary representatives. It disappeared altogether in the early 19th century but was rediscovered and, after the restoration of some missing carving, was presented back to the town. It was later used at mayor-choosing ceremonies, before finally taking its place as a museum exhibit. *See also* COVE RESTAURANT (site of a carved stone possibly from the Friary)

FRIARY LANE is an earlier name for Governor's Lane.

FRIEND The surname occurs locally in the 17th and 18th centuries and Friends were Mayors in 1691-92, 1695-96, 1712-13, 1737-38 and 1748-49.

FRIENDS' BURIAL GROUND, Barrack Road was established in 1713. Now a public open space, the burial ground has been cleared of headstones, although a few do remain close to the walls surrounding it. Until 1834 other Dissenters were interred here.

FRIENDS' CHAPEL was a converted building in St Thomas Street (probably No.45, at its southern end) which was demolished after 1858.

FRIENDSHIP INN was at No.30 Park Street and appears at some point to have been called the Jolly Sailor. As the Friendship Inn it closed in 1907.

FRITH, Francis (died 1898) Photographer. Not a local man, but there are many Frith views of the locality as Francis Frith and those who followed him in the Frith business travelled the country in the latter half of the 19th century and much of the 20th, endeavouring to photograph every city, town, village and scene of interest that they came across, many of the photographs being reproduced as picture postcards. The Frith archive contains more than a third of a million pictures.

FROWDE, Mark C (died December 1949) Joint manager of Cosens and Company from 1911 until 1942 and Managing Director 1925-1942. Much associated with local, county and national football and one-time Chairman of the Football Association and a life vice-president. Vice president of the Society of Dorset men. Lived at Stanton Court, Greenhill. One of the founders of Weymouth Football Club in 1890.

FRY, Donald (1910-1992) Weymouth-born Harwell physicist who led the team which discovered Zeta (Zero Energy Thermo-nuclear Assembly). Educated at St John's School and Weymouth Grammar School. On the day that he was awarded the Freedom of the Borough, 25th September 1958, it was announced that he would be Director of the new Winfrith Atomic Energy establishment, having previously been deputy director at Harwell. His wife, Jessie, was Mayor in 1978-79.

FURZY CLIFF *see* OVERCOMBE LANDSLIPS

GALLOWS were ordered to be erected at Greenhill in 1685 specifically for the execution of those sentenced to death following the Duke of **Monmouth's Rebellion**. None of those hanged were local men.

GALLWEY, Captain Edwin John Payne (1850-1906) of the Royal Navy. Manager and later Managing Director of Whitehead Torpedo Works at Wyke Regis from its opening in 1891 until his death in April 1906. Gallwey Road, constructed largely for employees of the factory, is named after him. He lived at Beacon Hill, Wyke Regis (the site of the present house 'The Beacon'). Buried at Thirkleby, Yorkshire, his family home.

GARDEN PLACE was the original name for the part of Gloucester Street which runs from Park Street to the Esplanade.

GARIBALDI, General Guiseppe Arrived in Weymouth by train in April 1864 and embarked at the pier to view the Channel Squadron and the breakwater works at Portland.

GARNET COURT is a block of flats and shops on the corner of King Street and Park Street. Following the demolition of **Christchurch** in 1956 this was for many years a car park managed by Garnet Mahoney and the apartment block built on it in 1977 was named after him. Illus. page 35.

GARTH, Major General Thomas An equerry to the royal family during the visits of King George III to Weymouth 1789-1805. He is reputed to be the lover of the King's daughter Princess Sophia and father of a baby born to her in Weymouth in 1800, the birth itself surrounded in secrecy and the story never confirmed or denied. Garth adopted the boy, 'Tommy Garth', and brought him up as his own son at Ilsington Manor, Puddletown. But was Garth protecting the royal family? It has been suggested that Ernest, Duke of Cumberland, Sophia's own brother, was the baby's real father. More than two hundred years on, the full facts will probably never be known. Tommy Garth turned out to be a bad lot and later tried clear his debts with an unsuccessful attempt at blackmailing the royal family, claiming he had papers in his possession which proved his true parentage.

GAS HOUSE LANE was original name of Newstead Road, at a time when there was little else but the Gasworks on the western side of the Backwater.

GAS SUPPLY As early as 1828 the Council was seeking a suitable site for William Wharton Burdon's proposed gasworks which were to light the town with gas. Burdon, a north country colliery owner built the gasworks in 1836 on the Backwater's western shore. To supply Melcombe, a gas main was laid under the Backwater running just below the harbour bed for about 100 feet to a square stone pier. This contained a vertical shaft by which the mains reached a tunnel which passed under the navigable part of the harbour for 420 feet to reach a second shaft in Melcombe's Commercial Road. The prominent shaft was visible in the Backwater until 1995, when it was removed. (*See* **Backwater Tunnel**). Burdon remained sole proprietor of the works until 1866, although in 1856 an Act of Parliament was obtained to form a company to be called The Weymouth and Melcombe Regis Gas Company. In the 1850s and 1860s his monopoly of the gas supply was a cause of great dissatisfaction in the town, not only due to the high price charged for the gas, but also for the inefficiency and quality of the supply -there were complaints about businesses being brought to a standstill due to the inadequacy of the gaslight. In 1867 a new Weymouth Consumers' Gas Company was set up and purchased the gas works from Mr Burdon – a seemingly amicable arrangement after protracted and difficult negotiations. The new company had offices at No.71 St Thomas Street. In 1928 the gasworks site was extended by the reclamation of three acres of mudlands along the western side of the Backwater (at the same time adjacent land was reclaimed on which Westwey Road was built) and the enlarged gasworks had an official opening in 1933. A frequent visitor was a tar boat, collecting, via a pipe under Westwey Road, the tar which was a by-product of the works. The gas industry was nationalised in 1948 and the Weymouth works became part of Southern Gas. The gasworks closed on 1st November 1958, after which the gas was pumped from the Southern Gas Board's

A view of the extensive gasworks site with Westwey Road in the foreground and the embankment of the Weymouth and Portland Railway top left, with the now-demolished bridge crossing Newstead Road.

Demolition of Weymouth Gasworks in 1962 ; Westwey House now stands on the site.

works at Poole. Demolition of the Weymouth works began in February 1962 and finished in July that year, two storage gasometers remaining. One of these was taken down in 1994 but the other, a rather rusty blot on the landscape, is still there in 2006. Conversion of the town to natural gas began in January, 1972.

GAUMONT CINEMA *see* JUBILEE HALL

GENERAL GORDON HOTEL The pub at Chapelhay was bought by the council from John Groves and Sons in 1956. It was demolished as part of the redevelopment of the area following WW2 bombing. The licence was transferred to **The Prospect,** its replacement in Franchise Street, which opened in 1959.

'GENERAL TOM THUMB' (i.e. Charles Sherwood Stratton) The diminutive American showman complete with Lilliputian coach, coachman and footman was in Weymouth briefly in September 1846.

GEOLOGY The complex geology of the local area is impossible to summarise but a number of books cover the subject in detail. Further reading : *The geology of the country around Weymouth, Swanage, Corfe and Lulworth*, by W.J.Arkell (HMSO,1947); *Weyland*, by Ronald Good (Longmans, Dorchester, 1946); *The Dorset Coast from Poole to Chesil Beach*, by Michael House (Geological Association Guide, Rev.ed. 1969)

GEORGE III, King (1738-1820) King George III first visited Weymouth in 1789, following his distressing illness of 1788 which became known as 'the madness of King George'. Modern medical research suggests that the King was actually suffering from a condition known as porphyria, a rare blood disease which causes bouts of spasms, convulsions, violent pain and agitated, often violent behaviour. When King George began to show signs of recovery early in 1789, convalescence was called for. His younger brother William Henry, Duke of Gloucester, had built a house at Weymouth, **'Gloucester Lodge'**, and it was here that the King, Queen Charlotte and their three eldest daughters stayed from June until September. It was the ideal spot for 'Farmer George' who could ride into the countryside and inspect agricultural methods as well as enjoying the benefits of sea bathing, the fashionable cure-all of the age. The King and Queen spent fourteen holidays at Weymouth between 1789 and 1805 and they were always accompanied by some of their thirteen surviving children, all of whom visited the town during the years of 'Royal Weymouth'. For the dates of the royal visits and the names and titles of the King's children *see* ROYAL VISITORS

The visits of King George III who spent fourteen holidays at Weymouth between 1789 and 1805 brought Weymouth fame as the country's leading health and pleasure resort.

GEORGE INN, Custom House Quay. The present George Inn of 1885 is the second on the site, the first having been demolished in 1884. The Corporation purchased the original George Inn, then in a dilapidated state, from the Mico Charity in 1882 to facilitate quayside improvements, setting back the new building to widen the quay. For details of the charities which derive income from the George Inn *see* MICO, Sir Samuel.

The old George Inn, property of Sir Samuel Mico, was replaced by the present pub of the same name in 1885.

GEORGE STREET HALL Westham Road, takes its name from 'Little George Street', Westham Road's name prior to December, 1922. It was built in 1888 for an assembly of Christians who do not take any denominational name and who had previously met in houses in the town. In Commercial Road, a plaque high on the wall of the building bears the inscription 'George Street Hall'. It is now known as Bethany Hall.

GEORGE THORNE HOUSE, Park Street An apartment block which stands on the site of the **Congregational Church, Gloucester Street,** demolished in 1980. It takes its name from the town's much persecuted 17th century non-conformist minister, the **Reverend George Thorne.**

GEORGES, Charles Edward (1870-1970) Artist. He was art master at Weymouth College, principal at Dorchester, Bridport and Weymouth Schools of Art and co-founder of the

South Dorset Arts Club. Died 16th January 1970 aged 100. Ninety of his works, mainly Dorset landscapes, were auctioned at Christie's in 1988.

GERARD, Thomas, of Trent (1592-1634) Gerard was the author of a work published in 1732, many years after it was written, under the title **Coker's Survey of Dorset**. It contains his description of Weymouth and Melcombe Regis around 1630 from which the following extract is taken:- '*Waymouth, as ytt now is, is but little, consisting of one street, which for a good space lieth open to the se, and on the back of it riseth an hill of such steepness, that they are forced to clymbe upp to their chappell by eighty steps of stone, from whence you have a fair prospect of the town and haven lying under it. From one side you may see Weeke {Wyke}, the mother church of Waymouth, and Melcombe on the other side, which much surpasseth the other for conveniency of scite, for this standing on a flat, affordeth roome for building, with a markett place, and convenient streets, and also yardes for their wares, by means whereof most of the merchants have chosen this for their habitations, which of late years is fairly new built.*'

GIANT POT PUBLIC HOUSE, Queen Street was formerly known as the Terminus Hotel.

GIEAR FAMILY (also spelt Geiar, Gear etc.) One of the prominent local merchant families of the 16th century, of sometimes doubtful honesty. They handled goods captured by local privateers on which they were adept at evading Customs duties. Thomas Giear, Mayor in 1618 and 1630 and one of the town's MPs, was found guilty of falsifying accounts for the same and was fined £2000, but it is doubtful if it was ever paid. He is thought to have built the fine house in Trinity Street (then part of High Street) which in the next century was converted to Assembly Rooms and today is known as the 'Old Rooms'.

GILDEA, Rev. William (1833-1925) Rector of Upwey, 1901-1922. During his time at Upwey, he purchased two ruined cottages at the top of Elwell Street, demolished them, and paid for road widening at the spot. A stone at the site is inscribed '*By the generosity and untiring efforts of the Rev. Canon William Gildea, M.A. (rector of this parish), this approach to Elwell-Street was widened and improved , entirely at his own expense. His fellow-members of the Weymouth Rural District Council desire thus to place on record their appreciation of the great interest he has always taken in this parish. October, 1917*'. He was also known for his wood-carving skills and presented the oak war memorial to Upwey Church.

GILL, Arthur M (1878-1951) Local historian and lecturer, formerly chief clerk of the GWR at Weymouth Quay. Many of his articles on Weymouth appeared in the local press. Secretary of the local branch of the Lifeboat Institution in his retirement.

GIRTIN, Thomas (1775-1802) Artist. Three views of Weymouth are known -*'Weymouth'* (a view looking across the harbour towards Melcombe, showing 'Bank House' with a ship-building yard alongside), *'Street in Weymouth'* (a view of Maiden Street) and *'Old Roofs, Weymouth'*.

GLEBE HOUSE stood in Cross Road and was once **Holy Trinity Church** vicarage. In the 1850s a vicarage had been partially built in Longfield Road, but funds ran out before it was completed and it was sold. A generous donation enabled Glebe House to be built but later incumbents found it to be too far from the church and moved back to Longfield Road. Glebe House in the 20th century was bought by developers and demolished, the houses of Glebe Close and Rectory Way filling the site.

GLEED'S SHIPYARD John Gleed's shipbuilding yard was in Melcombe, adjacent to Bank House, Bank Buildings in the late 18th/early 19th century. Tradition has it that here King George III around 1800 watched the launch of a ship called the *Yeoman*, the name of which was changed to *Royal Yeoman* at his command. She is said to have sunk on her first voyage, bad luck attaching to the change of a ship's name.

GLEN AVENUE was known in the early years of the 20th century as Ashley Road.

GLENTHORNE, Old Castle Road In the years following WW2, the house was converted to a British Legion Women's Section Rest Home, the use of which continued until the late 1980s. It is now private residence once more.

GLOBE INN, East Street During alterations to the pub in 1854 a large cannonball was discovered embedded in a wall, probably dating from the Civil War fighting of 1645 when another cannonball (which can still be seen today) lodged in the wall of a building in nearby Maiden Street. *See* 'HOUSE WITH THE CANNONBALL', Maiden Street

GLOUCESTER, William Henry, Duke of The younger brother of King George III. He was a frequent visitor to Southampton and the New Forest and in 1765 made a sea trip to Weymouth. He was obviously impressed with the resort, visiting it several times and around 1780 building himself a house on the seafront which became known as **'Gloucester Lodge'** or 'Royal Lodge'. This was where King George III stayed during all his visits to Weymouth, 1789-1805.

GLOUCESTER HOTEL The former royal residence **Gloucester Lodge** was sold in 1820 and was a private residence for some years. When it was sold again in 1859 it was converted into a 'first class family hotel' by Mr T.D. Luce, who also ran the adjacent Royal Hotel. In the 1860s a large new extension was built at its southern end, part of this new wing being occupied by members of the Weymouth and County Club. The main entrance to the building having formerly been in the side of the building, a new entrance was made at the front, between the two Venetian windows on the ground floor. Disaster struck on 3rd March 1927, when a huge fire ripped through the building and destroyed much of the interior,

The Gloucester Hotel, as the 1927 fire was brought under control. Note the blackened roof timbers.

although the façade was saved. Rebuilding added another storey to the original royal palace bringing the roofline almost level with that of the Victorian extension, and the hotel was back in business in April 1929. Various verandahs have been erected along the front of the building over the years. In the 1970s the hotel lost its 2-star rating and it was being used to house the homeless in the 1980s. It closed for good in 1985. The building was then converted to become business premises at ground floor level, with apartments above, opening in 1989. *See* GLOUCESTER LODGE for the building's earlier history.

GLOUCESTER LODGE was built for William Henry, Duke of Gloucester, younger brother of King George III. Having decided that sea air was beneficial to his health, he commenced the building of Gloucester Lodge, probably in 1780. Its architect is not known. **James Hamilton** is believed to have designed the northern end of Gloucester Row, but no documentary evidence exists to suggest he was also the architect of Gloucester's house, although it has been suggested that Nos.1-4 Gloucester Row pre-date the Lodge and may even have been leased by Gloucester while his house was being built (most sources date these four houses to the late 1780s). In the spring of 1781 the Duke's house was delayed by a lack of bricks, but it was probably finished soon after that. The Duke also leased the land south of the Lodge on which he laid out ornamental gardens called 'the Shrubbery', these separating his property from the town until 1815. It was to his brother's house that King George III came in 1789 to try sea-bathing as part of his convalescence following the episode of so-called madness that had so alarmed the country the previous year. The King, who visited Weymouth for long holidays almost every year between 1789 and 1805, eventually purchased Gloucester Lodge in 1801. After his last visit in 1805, other members of the royal family stayed at the Lodge intermittently but it was eventually sold, with its contents, in 1820. After some years in private ownership it became a hotel. *See* GLOUCESTER HOTEL for its later history. The marble bath at the Lodge, used by the King to acclimatise himself before plunging into the cold waters of Weymouth Bay, is now in Weymouth Museum.

The Duke of Gloucester's house as it appeared when King George III and the royal family stayed there. Note the side entrance, which was lost when a Victorian extension was added to the building.

GLOUCESTER MEWS A block of apartments with shops at ground-floor level built on the site of the **Odeon Cinema**. A plaque on the building's exterior commemorates its earlier use as the site of the stables and coach house of **Gloucester Lodge**. A window from the original Georgian building survives at the rear of the building.

GLOUCESTER ROW The Row comprises **Gloucester Lodge/Hotel**, Nos.1-4, the **Royal Hotel** (and adjacent **Royal Arcade**) and Nos.6-14 (the entire row is now numbered as 85-100, The Esplanade). No.3 Gloucester Row was once the home of Victorian naturalist **William Thompson**. By 1920 it was owned by **Dan Guy**, who had rebuilt the premises with a garage and petrol station on the ground floor, above which the family lived. On 14th November 1934 fire broke out and spread rapidly in the residence above the garage. Mr Guy lost his life in the fire after falling or jumping from a window and an elderly lady staying with the family also died. Fortunately the fire was confined to the upper floors, as hundreds of gallons of petrol were stored beneath the garage. No.3 was completely rebuilt following the fire to a 1930s art deco design in complete contrast to its Georgian neighbours at Nos. 1, 2 and 4.

GLOUCESTER STREET CONGREGATIONAL CHURCH *See* CONGREGATIONAL CHURCH, Gloucester Street

GLOUCESTER TERRACE became Nos.1-10 Gloucester Street.

GOAT CARTS Wicker carts pulled by goats took children for rides along the Esplanade and on short trips around the town. Popular in the 1920s and 1930s, one cart continued in use until the 1950s.

GODDARD, Joe (John Thomas Goddard) (1879-1946) Mayor from 1938-9 until 1944-5, Joe Goddard served the longest term ever as mayor of the town during the whole of the WW2 years. He was an ex-Regimental Sergeant Major, holder of the Military Cross, and a publican, landlord of the **Royal Adelaide Hotel**, Abbotsbury Road. On 1st November 1941 he had the misfortune to be bombed out of his own home. Recuperating from his injuries in a Weymouth nursing home, he was taken to the Guildhall 8 days later so that he could be sworn in again as mayor for the ensuing year! He recalled the air raid in a recorded message sent to the town of Weymouth, Massachusetts shortly afterwards. Joe Goddard was a popular and immensely hard-working Mayor who was awarded the OBE, but the war years took their toll. He died, aged 67 in 1946, just days before the ceremony which added his name to the roll of Honorary Freemen of the Borough. He inaugurated a fund named after him as a lasting memorial to all that the men and women of the district had done and suffered during the war. The balance of these funds was used for the complete renovation of the Weymouth and District Hospital's operating theatre in 1958, having earlier having paid for hospital equipment.

GOLDCROFT ESTATE was built in 1932.

GOLDCROFT FARM This farm does not appear to be of ancient date. Buildings are shown at Goldcroft on the 1864 Ordnance Survey maps but there is no indication that it was a farm. In 1932 an elderly Westham resident recalled that her family were the first residents of Westham, her father having moved to Goldcroft to farm in 1865. When the farm went up for auction in 1919, the sale catalogue described *'a modern and substantial farmhouse and recently-erected cottage'*.

GOLDCROFT TERRACE became Nos.166-182 Newstead Road.

GOLDEN EAGLE PUBLIC HOUSE, Lower Bond Street was demolished in 1998 to make way for the New Bond Street shopping development.

GOLDEN LION INN stands on the corner of St Edmund Street and St Mary Street. Although well-known as an eighteenth century coaching inn, it has earlier origins and was originally known as 'The Feathers'. Landlord in the 17th century was Gregory Babbidge and it is this family that gave its name to **'Babbidge's Square'** in this vicinity, a place-name long forgotten. Over the pub entrance stands a magnificent gilded sculpture of a lion, which in post-WW2 years sported a very straight broom-handle tail. In the 1944 run-up to D-Day American troops took the original curly tail back to camp as a souvenir and a broom handle (some say it was an axe handle) served as an emergency repair! Years later, Devenish's Brewery restored the lion's tail to its former curly glory. Richly carved panelling once on the interior walls of the pub was said to have come from the *Vera*, a steamship wrecked on Chesil Beach in 1889.

GOLF the first local golf course was laid out by William Jesty in 1894 in the grounds of his house, **East Chickerell Court**. Known as 'Weymouth Golf Links' and 'Weymouth Town Club' (no connection with today's club) it remained in use until the 1920s. Interestingly, Jesty claimed that golf had been played there for centuries and that it was the oldest golf links in England, but this claim has never been substantiated. The links which are the home of today's Weymouth Golf Club in Links Road were set up in 1910 by a private syndicate. Development was halted during the WW1 years and in 1921 the links were purchased by the Town Council.

GOOCH, Daniel (1816-1889) As a young man, Gooch was selected by Isambard Kingdom Brunel to be the first locomotive superintendent of the GWR. Following Brunel's death in 1859 he was appointed engineer of the steamship ***Great Eastern*** and in the years which followed he superintended her conversion to cable-laying. Prior to these voyages the ship was at Portland on several occasions and Gooch stayed in Weymouth to oversee the final preparations. His published diary contains a number of references to these visits and holiday trips he made to the town between 1869 and 1885.

Further reading : *Memoirs and diary*, by Sir Daniel Gooch (David & Charles, 1972)

GOOD TEMPLARS HALL The Good Templars organisation, with many similarities to the Masonic movement, was founded in the United States in 1851 to promote temperance, peace and brotherhood. By 1875 there were four Good Templars lodges meeting in Weymouth. The Good Templars Hall in High Street was built that year, opening early in 1876. It occupied a site adjoining the Old Town Hall and replaced a dilapidated building of probable Tudor date. The lodge had a separate coffee room, and was strongly supported by the temperance movement, drunkenness being a serious issue in Victorian Weymouth. The Good Templars movement later de-emphasised temperance and lost support over other rifts within the organisation and in 1879 the building was sold. It was promptly bought by temperance supporters who converted it to a **Coffee Tavern**. After various uses in the twentieth century, it was purchased in February 1978 by the Jehovah's Witnesses and, since extended, is now their meeting place, Kingdom Hall. The Good Templars still met locally at least until the 1930s.

'GOOSEBERRY GARDENS' were in Franchise Street. The 1864 O/S maps show extensive gardens on the northern side of Franchise Street, at its lower end.

GORDON CAFÉ became the Jubilee Fish and Chip café but it was demolished in 2006. The site on the corner of King Street and Crescent Street has been redeveloped as a café and flats.

GORDON CLUB General Charles Gordon's death at Khartoum in 1884 saw him elevated to hero status in England, commemorated by statues and the opening of 'Gordon Clubs' and 'Gordon Boys Clubs'. Richard Nicholas Howard opened one in Weymouth's High Street early in his mayoralty of 1885-6. An 1887 guidebook states that the Club was intended 'for the benefit of the artisan class'. It appears to have lasted until the early 1900s.

GORDON PLACE, Greenhill became Nos.28-30 Greenhill

GORDON ROW was a street on the north side of St Leonard's Road. Some houses were demolished under slum clearance orders during the 1930s, any that remained were demolished when the whole area was cleared following WW2 air raids. A street of post-war shops and houses has retained the name.

GORDON TERRACE, Westham became Nos.6-34 Melbury Road

GOSPEL HALL, George Street *see* GEORGE STREET HALL

GOSSE, Philip Henry (1810-1888) Naturalist. Author of many scientific works including *The Aquarium, an unveiling of the wonders of the deep sea*, published in 1854 in which *'The wood engravings by Messrs. Whymper represent the coast scenery in the vicinity of Weymouth'*. Gosse was a friend of **William Thompson**.

GOULD FAMILY of Upwey The last member of the Gould family in the UK sold the 512 acre family estate, including the Wishing Well, by auction in July 1964 as his sole heir, an American nephew, lived in the USA. The estate had been in the Gould family since 1872 and before that in another branch of the family – the Goodens of Fleet and Upwey – since the 1600s.

GOVERNOR'S LANE derives its name from a house which once stood here called 'The Governor's House', dating back to the days when Colonel Francis Sydenham was the Parliamentary Governor of the town in 17th century Civil War days. In earlier days when it marked the southern boundary of the **Friary**, the lane was known as Friary Lane. Practically the whole of the north side of Governor's Lane was demolished in the late 1950s, the remaining buildings being cleared in the 1960s. Now the site of Governor's Lane car park.

GRAHAM'S BAR, New Street Andrew Graham was a wine and spirit merchant who also manufactured aerated waters at his business in St Nicholas Street. His bar in New Street is perhaps best known for the murder there in 1902 of young barmaid **Hettie Stephens**.

GRANARY WHARF is the modern name for an early 19th century warehouse on Commercial Road, west of the Town Bridge, now converted to housing.

GRANBY INDUSTRIAL ESTATE stands on the site of the former **Chickerell Airfield.** The estate was developed in the 1960s, initially accommodating mainly light and precision engineering and building and distributive trades. The first firm moved in during February 1962. Initially the estate's street names were chosen from the titles of the sons of King George III – the Dukes of Cumberland, Cambridge, Kent etc., to which general 'county' street names were added later.

GRAND HOTEL, Greenhill This fine mansion, once known as Greenhill House, was built in about 1850, probably for John Trenchard, of the Warmwell family. It later became home to three Weymouth mayors – Sir Richard Nicholas Howard, Vere Oliver and Edgar Wallis. Following its requisitioning by the War Office during WW2, it was unoccupied for some years before being sold in 1959 to Edgar Wallis, who opened it as the Grand Hotel. In the late 1980s it was sold and now, as No.24 Greenhill, it is once more back in private ownership, converted to apartments.

GRANGE TERRACE became Nos.4-12 Grange Road

***GRASSHOPPER*, HMS** The shore base HMS *Grasshopper* in October 1943 took over the Weymouth harbour area formerly occupied by HMS *Bee*, to prepare for the D-Day invasion. In May 1944 the United States Navy Advanced Amphibious Base (USNAAB) was formally commissioned and took over *Grasshopper* which then became USS *Grasshopper*.

GREAT EASTERN Brunel's great steamship visited Portland in 1859, whilst on her acceptance trials in the Channel. This was a planned visit for coaling, but lasted rather longer than anticipated due to an explosion at sea which had blown out her forward funnel and killed several of her crew. Repairs were carried out in the shelter of the new breakwaters, then under construction. A section of the discarded funnel was taken to Sutton Poyntz where it was installed vertically as a strainer at the waterworks. It remained there until 2005, when, by now redundant, it was removed and taken to Bristol, to be restored and displayed at the *Great Britain* site. The *Great Eastern* made several more visits to Portland in the 1860s and 1870s prior to her transatlantic cable-laying voyages, superintended by **Sir Daniel Gooch.**

GREAT GALE OF 1824 On the night of 22nd/23rd November 1824, a storm which had been blowing all day rose in the darkness of the early hours to become a destructive hurricane which has gone down in history as the 'Great Gale', causing damage all along the coasts of Hampshire, Dorset, Devon and Cornwall. In the local area, Portland suffered severely, when the force of the sea knocked down houses close to Chesil Beach and drowned more than twenty people. The Ferry House at Smallmouth Ferry was destroyed and the passage rendered four times wider than before by the force of the sea. At Fleet, the little parish church was almost totally destroyed. In Weymouth, huge waves demolished most of the Esplanade and the basements of houses along the seafront were filled with seawater, sand and gravel. The piers were damaged and boats swept from their moorings floated down the town's main streets. At **The Narrows** sea and backwater joined across the roadway and swept a man to his death. In the days following the storm, tides threw up the bodies of those lost at sea in this huge and terrifying storm. The Esplanade's stone posts (more than 300) and some 5000 feet of chains which linked them were torn up. Two of these stones were inscribed before being replaced. One, *Esplanade destroyed by a tempest November 23rd 1824,* still exists and is now mounted in an Esplanade flowerbed wall, although barely readable today (a copy can be seen outside the Tourist Information Centre). The other, *'Rebuilt by R. Vining, builder, April 23rd 1825'* has been lost.

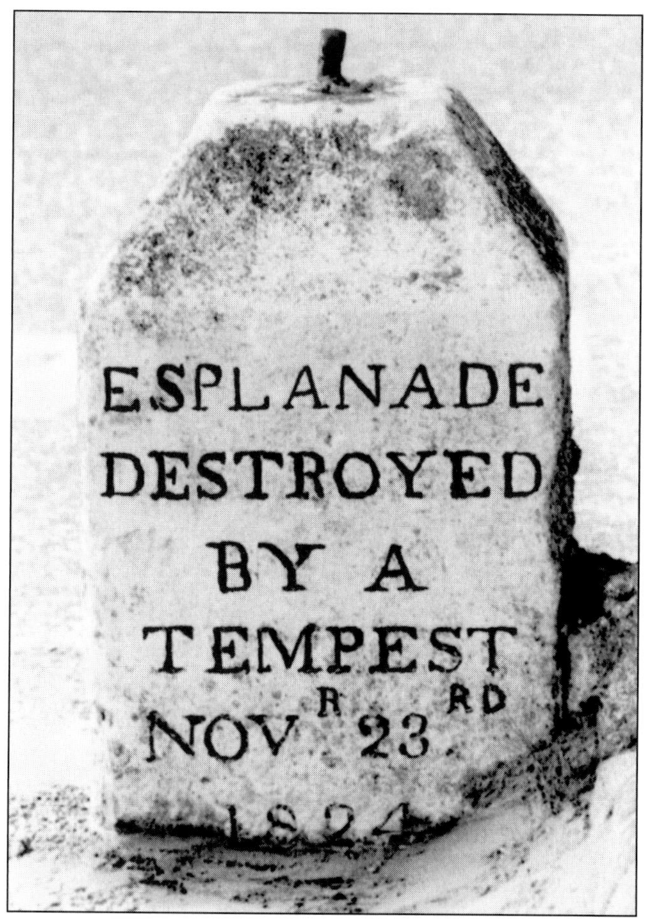

This little stone commemorates the catastrophic storm which occurred on 23rd November 1824. It was one of many linked by chains to define the Esplanade walkway and this one was inscribed to record the event before it was replaced on the seafront. Few of these survive today: this one has been set in a raised flowerbed wall at the southern end of the Esplanade.

GREAT WESTERN RAILWAY The GWR's long association with the town dates back to the opening of the railway to Weymouth on 20th January 1857, a joint GWR and LSWR undertaking. The company's interest in the steamer service to the Channel Islands began in April the same year, but it was the Weymouth and Channel Islands Steam Packet Company which ran the service , propped up by GWR money, until the railway company took over completely on 1st July 1889. Nationalisation of the railways and steamers in 1948 brought an end to the Great Western name, but the familiar vessels, bereft of GWR red paint on their funnels, continued in service at Weymouth for many years. *See also* HARBOUR; NEWTON'S COVE

Further reading : *Weymouth to the Channel Islands: a Great Western Railway shipping history*, by B.L. Jackson (Oakwood Press, 2002); *The Great Western at Weymouth: a railway and shipping history*, by J.H. Lucking (David and Charles, 1971)

GREAVES, Reverend Talbot Rector of St Mary's Church from 1855 until 1881, when he moved to a parish in Bristol. A wealthy man who chose not live in the church's Rectory at No.82 St Mary Street (this was for some years occupied by curates of the church). Greaves built himself a large mansion **'Portmore'**, between Buxton Road and Wyke Road which local residents will remember by its later name 'Connaught House'. Greaves died in 1898, at Stoke, Bristol, following a fall from his horse.

GREEN, Peter Legend has it that boatman Peter Green of Weymouth served with Nelson on board HMS *Victory* at the Battle of Trafalgar and that in old age when he rowed passengers across the harbour on the ferry boat he always wore his Trafalgar medal. A shame to dispel a good story, but no trace of Peter Green can be found in *Victory's* Muster Roll. It is perhaps more likely that Peter Green was at some point during his navy service on one of Nelson's ships. Those who served during the long years of conflict with Napoleon were awarded the naval general service medal and this may have been what the boatman wore. Interesting enough in itself, but the story was perhaps embroidered a little over the years to impress the visitors.

GREENHILL or **GREEN HILL** as a local place name goes back at least to the 15th century. *See also* GALLOWS

GREENHILL GARDENS In 1872 Greenhill Gardens were laid out and paid for by Sir Frederic Johnstone, but not dedicated to the public, although people had access to them. The Johnstones, who had long represented the town in Parliament, had apparently been reminded long before Sir Frederic Johnstone's time of a 'forgotten election promise' regarding the planting of Greenhill. Sir Frederic's ownership of the land was rowdily challenged in 1884 which led to a costly court case which Sir Frederic won in 1886 (*see* **Wallis, Thomas**). He presented the gardens to the town in 1902, the year King Edward VII and Queen Alexandra were crowned, as a Coronation gift. The gardens were extended in 1906 and their layout has altered over the years. Chalets were added in the mid and late 1920s. The gardens contain a variety of interesting structures and monuments – a WW1 'Armistice' shelter given by V.H. Bennett, a seat constructed from the stone of Christchurch and presented by builder E.G.Coleman, who demolished the church, the Stainforth Memorial; Floral Clock and a sundial presented by 1st Weymouth Company Girl Guides.

GREENHILL HOUSE *see* GRAND HOTEL, Greenhill

GREGORY'S CORNER was the southernmost corner at the junction of St Thomas Street and Lower Bond Street (now New Bond Street). Local chemist Gregory occupied Nos.75 and 76 St Thomas Street from the mid-19th century until the early 1900s, when he gave up part of the premises (No.76) to enable the Devon and Cornwall Bank to build a new bank on the corner, this later amalgamating with Lloyds. When Lloyds moved out the National Provincial Bank took over the building and in 1966 when the chemist moved out of No.75 the bank took it over, altering the façade to match their own (now NatWest).

GRESHAM TERRACE, Abbotsbury Road became Nos.64-70 Abbotsbury Road.

GREYHOUND PUBLIC HOUSE was in St Thomas Street.

GRIMM, Samuel Hieronymous (1733-1790) Artist. In the last year of his life this Swiss-born artist completed more than 200 pen and ink drawings of Dorset, many of which are of the Weymouth and Portland area. The collection is in the British Museum.

GRINDALL, Richard (1750-1820) Lived in Weymouth in the 1780s and 1790s and commanded HMS *Prince* at the Battle of Trafalgar in 1805. He was later knighted and became a Vice-Admiral in 1810. His son, Festing Horatio Grindall, born in Weymouth, was a midshipman on HMS *Victory* at Trafalgar. When commanding HMS *Thalia* in 1793 and seeking the endorsement of a press warrant, Richard Grindall obviously upset the Mayor (who had refused to endorse press warrants, not wanting to lose local seamen to the Navy) and it was resolved to send a letter to the Admiralty about his insolent behaviour.

GROCKLE A derogatory and unkind word originating in the West Country in the 1960s and used to describe the holidaymakers on whom resorts and holiday towns depend. Said to derive from Grock the clown, implying a person to be laughed at.

GROSVENOR HOTEL, on the corner of Greenhill and Westerhall. *See* PROVINCE OF NATAL HOTEL, its later name.

GROSVENOR PLACE is now Nos.31-34 The Esplanade.

GROVE, William Chafin (c.1731-1793) of Waddon Manor, Portesham. MP for Melcombe Regis 1774-1781. Waddon was originally owned by Bullen Reymes, MP for Melcombe Regis in the 17th century. His son, also Bullen, died in 1695 without issue and his widow married Harry Chafin. Through Chafin the property eventually devolved to William Chafin Grove. In 1774, the year he was elected MP for Melcombe, William Chafin Grove bought a great deal of property in the borough from the son of John Olmius, which would have secured him the necessary votes. He vacated the seat in 1781, and sold all his property to Gabriel Steward. (The c.1774 map of Weymouth which appeared in the first edition of John Hutchins' History and Antiquities of the County of Dorset' was drawn and engraved at the expense of William Chafin Grove and Gabriel Steward).

GROVE TERRACE is between Nos.27 and 29 Cromwell Road and was also known as Grove Cottages.

GROVES, Herbert John The eldest son of brewer **Sir John Groves**. He became a partner in the brewery firm in 1882. Mayor of Weymouth 1903-4.

GROVES, Sir John (1828-1905) of Rodwell Villa, Rodwell Road and Blackdown, Buxton Road. Chairman of Messrs. John Groves & Sons, brewers of Weymouth. Mayor of Weymouth in 1886-7, 1887-8 and 1888-9. Owned considerable property in the Rodwell/Chapelhay area including the whole of Rodwell Street and Upperton House. Gave to the parish of Holy Trinity the Sidney Groves Memorial Hall (always known as the **Sidney Hall**) which he built in memory of his youngest son Sidney, who died of pleurisy and pneumonia in July 1895, aged 26. Another son, Herbert John Groves was Mayor of Weymouth in 1903-4. Sir John, knighted in 1900, is said to be the last man knighted by Queen Victoria before her death. He died 2nd October 1905.

GROVES, John and Sons, Ltd. Brewers. The Hope Square business was founded by Mr Luckham in the early part of 19th century and taken over in 1840 by Levi Groves, who was succeeded by Mr John Groves in 1854. Hope Brewery was rebuilt in 1879 and extended in 1889. In 1896 the company became John Groves & Sons, Ltd. and soon afterwards purchased the Bank House and Garden at No. 63, St Thomas Street for office and warehouse use (the former occupier, the Weymouth Old Bank having crashed spectacularly in 1897). The present large brewery building in Hope Square was built in 1904. Groves and Devenish amalgamated in 1960, but local brewing ceased in 1985 and the Hope Square building now houses the Timewalk, Weymouth Museum and a shopping village as well as a brewery museum, where the brewing process can be followed. The St Thomas Street premises were demolished in 1966 and a Tesco store now fills the site.

The fine building erected by John Groves and Sons when the brewery bought the site of the Weymouth Old Bank House in St Thomas Street in 1897. It was demolished in 1966 and Tesco stands here now.

GROVES, Sidney *see* **GROVES, Sir John; SIDNEY HALL**

GUIDEBOOKS Today's colourful brochures have their origins in the 18th century when Peter Delamotte produced the first *Weymouth Guide* in 1785.

GUILD OF ST GEORGE The licence to found the Guild in St Nicholas Chapel at Chapelhay was granted by King Henry VI in 1442 and it was endowed with buildings and land in Weymouth, West Knighton, Wootton Glanville, Portland and Wyke Regis.

GUILDHALL The present Guildhall opened on 28th June 1838, the day of Queen Victoria's coronation, and is said to have been designed by Talbot Bury. It replaced a 17th century building on the same site, where an even earlier Town Hall may once have stood. The earlier building was often referred to as Melcombe Town Hall. (Weymouth had its own Town Hall, across the water, now known as the Old Town Hall). After the 1571 Act of Union, the local government of the combined town centred on the Guildhall where the Town Council met, magistrates held court, elections took place and the Mayor was chosen. It became the workplace of Corporation staff until 1904, when they moved to Clarence Buildings and ultimately to North Quay. Town Council meetings are still held at the Guildhall, which is licensed for weddings, having also in the past housed Weymouth Police Station and the Citizens' Advice Bureau.

The Guildhall which stood on the site of the present building prior to 1838. The King's Head Inn (demolished in the 1860s to provide the site for Maiden Street Methodist Church) can be seen in the background. One of John Upham's '1825 series' of local views.

GUINNESS CLOCK A summer attraction in 1953 *see* ALEXANDRA GARDENS

GULL, Cyril Arthur Edward Range Real name of novelist Guy Thorne. Not Weymouth-born, but he spent many years in the town. Author of more than 20 novels, some with Weymouth settings. Died in 1923, aged 46.

GUY, Dan Garage proprietor. In February 1921, Dan Guy's Gloucester Row garage was the first in Weymouth to supply petrol via a kerbside pump direct to the vehicle's petrol tank – prior to this drivers had to fill their tanks from two-gallon cans. (Dan Guy was to die in a fire at these premises in 1934 *see* Gloucester Row for details).

H

A picturesque view of Weymouth Harbour dating from 1790.

HALF MOON PUBLIC HOUSE stood on the north side of King Street, at its junction with Crescent Street. Now converted to shop premises.

HALL, Alice Author of *Will Hewling : a tale of Weymouth in the olden time* (its setting No.4 North Quay) and *A lodging house baby* and *Boys together* published in the 1890s/early 1900s.

HAMBRO ROOMS were in New Street.

HAMILTON, James (1748-1829) Architect and builder. Although Hamilton designed many of Weymouth's seafront buildings and is probably best-known for his design for the plinth on which the King's Statue stands (on which his name appears in large letters), little is known about his personal life. Buildings of his which can still be seen include St Mary's Church, some or perhaps most of Gloucester Row, Rodwell House, Hamilton House at Wyke Regis, Bridport Town Hall and the tall obelisk in memory of James Frampton which stands in the grounds of Moreton House. He worked with Robert Vining on the contract to wall the Esplanade in 1800, the promenade having previously only been banked up and turfed and open to damage from the sea. Hamilton is buried in Wyke Churchyard, there being *'a most respectable and numerous attendance'* at his Masonic funeral in 1829. His second wife, by whom he had five children, was left in straitened circumstances after his death and Masonic charity came to her aid. She outlived her husband by some thirty years.

HAMPDEN PLACE/HAMPDEN VILLAS became Nos.46-48 Abbotsbury Road.

HANOVER TERRACE is the north side of Hanover Road.

HA'PENNY BRIDGE *see* WESTHAM BRIDGE (1859-1921)

HARBOUR The harbour was the lifeblood of the two towns which grew up on each side of the mouth of the River Wey and the profits from it were a constant source of conflict between Weymouth and Melcombe Regis until their enforced **Union** in 1571. Over the years reclamation on both sides has slightly narrowed the harbour, but it has also been extended by the building of piers at its entrance. The Romans are thought to have sailed their galleys up the river to Radipole, unloading cargoes there for onward transmission to their new town Durnovaria (Dorchester) by road. The existence of a Roman villa in the Newstead Road area may indicate a landing place on the Weymouth side, possibly an inlet in the now-infilled Hope Cove area. Cross channel trade increased following the Norman conquest.Weymouth and Melcombe fared well exporting wool and importing wine, but there were times when regular raids by the French and catastrophic events such as the Black Death in 1348 wiped out trade and the inhabitants struggled to make ends meet. In 1433 Melcombe lost its wool staple to Poole and was reduced to the status of 'a creek'. Some prosperity must have returned as the towns were able to supply ships and men for the Siege of Calais in 1437 and mediaeval pilgrims embarked here for the shrine of St James of Compostella in Spain. In the 16th and 17th centuries Weymouth traded with other coastal towns and its ships voyaged to the Continent, the Mediterranean, the West Indies and the Newfoundland fisheries, with Puritan emigrants setting sail for the New World. Prosperity came to an abrupt end in 1645 when fierce fighting during the Civil War left the harbour silted up, its quays damaged and bridge in need of repair. Weymouth in the early 18th century survived but for a time its prosperous days were over. Its revival as a port coincided with the period of King George III's visits to the seaside when in 1794 it was chosen for the regular Post Office packet service sailings to the Channel Islands. The mails were lost to Southampton in 1845, but following the arrival of the railway in 1857, the Channel Islands Steam Packet Co. (subsidised by the GWR) and the LSWR (for a short time only) ran regular steamer services to the Channel Islands. The Weymouth Harbour Tramway, the link from the railway station to the Quay, opened in 1865. When the GWR took over the cross-channel service from the Steam Packet Company in 1889, three large new vessels arrived in Weymouth, necessitating the widening of the harbour at The Cove by the demolition of a number of houses in Hope Street, which backed onto the water. Facilities were improved and the Weymouth Harbour Tramway line, previously goods only, was extended along the Quay and carried passengers for the first time, taking them directly to a new landing stage and baggage hall on the pier. Weymouth's long association with the GWR passenger and cargo ships came to an end with nationalisation in 1948, although the familiar vessels stayed on under a different livery. A feature of the harbour in the first half of the 20th century was the arrival of the tall sailing ships from Baltic ports bringing in cargoes of timber and block ice. Although trade came to a standstill, WW2 brought a great deal of activity to the port as it welcomed thousands of refugees from Europe and the Channel Islands fleeing the Nazi Blitzkreig. **HMS *Bee*,** a harbourside shore establishment was established as a working up base for coastal forces and commandos training in the area carried out raids on the other side of the Channel in fast motor torpedo boats. 1943 saw HMS *Bee* converted to **HMS *Grasshopper*** as preparations for D-Day got under way with the eventual embarkation in June 1944 of American troops for the Normandy landings, almost half a million US military personnel leaving Weymouth on D-Day and during the months which followed. The Channel Islands service recommenced after the war and by 1960 Weymouth was the main Channel Islands port, although it would lose the cargo trade to competition from other ports and air freight by the end of the decade. Redevelopment in the early 1970s brought drive-on/ drive off car services to the Channel Islands and Cherbourg and a new car ferry terminal opened in 1974, much extended in 1980. In 1987 the Channel Islands service was taken over by British Channel Island Ferries, ending 130 years of railway involvement in shipping activities in the port of Weymouth. The traditional ferries were replaced in 1988 by Condor hydrofoils which had commenced operating in 1987 and today huge Wavepiercer craft, introduced in 1991, take passengers to the Channel Islands.

A classic view – 'Weymouth from the Nothe' – circa 1900.

HARBOUR POINT a housing development on the site of **WHITEHEAD TORPEDO WORKS, Ferrybridge, Wyke Regis**

HARBOUR TRAMWAY *see* WEYMOUTH HARBOUR TRAMWAY

HARBOURMASTER'S OFFICE is currently located in a mid-19th century warehouse, No.13 Custom House Quay.

HARDWICK COTTAGES became Nos.8-9 Hardwick Street.

HARDWICK ROW became Nos.34-38 Hardwick Street.

HARDWICK STREET is probably named after the 5th Earl of Hardwicke, who was Tory MP for Cambridge 1863-73, when the Park District was being developed by the Conservative Land Society. The street, over time, has lost the final 'e' of its name.

HARDWICK TERRACE became Nos.4-7 Hardwick Street.

HARDY, Thomas (1840-1928) Dorset's most famous author trained as an architect as a young man. He worked in London, but returned to Dorset to work for John Hicks whose business was later taken over by George Crickmay. Hardy was employed as an architect at No.77 St Thomas Street from 1869 until 1872 and he lodged at No.3 Wooperton Street. This was the period he was working on his first published novel *Desperate Remedies,* which appeared in 1871. He is thought to have worked on the designs of some of the houses at Greenhill in 1871 and several local schools, although he was also working on churches in Cornwall from 1870-1872. Hardy's name for Weymouth in his Wessex novels is Budmouth.

Further reading : *The architectural notebook of Thomas Hardy*, published by the Dorset Natural History and Archaeological Society (1966)

HARKER, Jarvis worked for the *Southern Times* in the 1870s. With Benjamin Sykes he was the author of *Sketches written in, round and about Weymouth* by 'H and B.S'. published in 1878, with a later edition.

HARMAN TERRACE became Nos.1-7, Highland Road.

HARMONY COURT/PLACE was a terraced street of 10 houses on the north side of Lower Bond Street.

HARTFORD TERRACE is a row of buildings adjacent to and including the Star Inn in Gloucester Street. Its name may have some association with **William Wharton Burdon**, proprietor of Weymouth Gasworks in the 19th century, whose family home in Northumberland was Hartford House.

***HARTLEPOOL,* SS** Following an E-boat torpedo attack on 4th July 1940, the ship sank near the entrance to Weymouth Harbour. Her forward part was raised and a new after-end built on, but the original after-end could not be raised and the wreckage was cleared in 1948.

HARTLEY TERRACE became Nos.2-8 Knightsdale Road.

HARVEY, John, Snr. John Harvey was one of the prominent figures in the Georgian social scene during the period of King George III's visits to the town. He ran 'Harvey's Library and Card Assembly' in Charlotte Row (a fine colonnaded building, now No.51, The Esplanade) which was probably second only to the main Assembly Rooms at the Royal Hotel. Harvey, an engineer, was also self-styled clock and watchmaker to King George III and in 1794 he was probably the first to advocate the enclosure of Portland Roads by the building of a breakwater. His '*Improved Weymouth Guide*' was published in 1800. He was also Weymouth's postmaster until his death in 1829 aged 71, and was, according to his obituary, *'one of the first projectors of Weymouth Waterworks, late civil engineer to Bootle waterworks, Liverpool and original projector of a breakwater for Portland Roads'.*

HARVEY, John, Jnr. (1786?-1856) Son of John Harvey (above). Followed his father as postmaster in Weymouth and maintained his enthusiasm for the breakwater project, although he died before the first phase was completed.

HARVEY'S LIBRARY AND CARD ASSEMBLY *see* HARVEY, John, Snr

HAVELOCK PLACE was a terrace of houses behind No.15 Chapelhay Street. Demolished following WW2 air raid damage.

HAWKES, FREEMAN, LTD. The business was started in Hope Square by Thomas Beer Hawkes around 1845, moving to premises at No.39 St Thomas Street, Lower St Alban Street and St Nicholas Street as 'The Dorset Furnishing Stores' in the 1860s. Hawkes had been joined in partnership by Charles Joseph Freeman, and in 1884, with Hawkes' sons Robert William Hawkes and Thomas Barling Hawkes, the firm commenced trading as Hawkes, Freeman, and Company, becoming Hawkes, Freeman Ltd. in 1900. In 1897 'The Bridge Furnishing Company' opened on the east side of the Town Bridge. 1908 saw another move when the Town Bridge building was sold to a cinema company (which opened the **Palladium Cinema** there four years later). Hawkes, Freeman built a new store in St Thomas Street which they expanded yet again in 1937 by building on the adjacent site formerly the **Bear Hotel** yard (the new building was used by the American Forces as a club during WW2). In May 1955 the company was acquired by Webb, Major & Co. Ltd. and the store was modernised, retaining its Hawkes, Freeman name. It closed in 1969.

HAWKSLEY, Thomas Eminent Victorian civil engineer who designed Weymouth's first pumped system of water supply and the waterworks buildings at Sutton Poyntz in 1856. Two water driven turbines pumped water from the chalk spring at Sutton Poyntz to Preston reservoir which gravitated through the town to Rodwell reservoir. He also submitted plans for the drainage of Weymouth in the 1860s but these were not implemented. *See* SEWERAGE; WATER SUPPLY

HAYWARD, A.A. Business man and estate developer. Originally ran nurseries in Spa Road, with shops in the town. Later turned to property development – hence Hayward's Avenue at Radipole. Died aged 89, in May 1953.

HAYWARD, Jack Weymouth's sand sculptor in the post-WW2 years and famous for his intricate models of cathedrals, made only from sand and sea water.

Sand modeller Jack Hayward at work on one of his cathedral sculptures.

HEALTH CENTRE, Westham Road Weymouth's public health offices opened on 4th July 1930, the day the present Town Bridge was declared open. The building was sited close to Westham Bridge, opposite St Joseph's RC Church. It was demolished in 2005 and apartment blocks now fill the site.

HELEN LANE Hutchins map of c.1774 names it as Hell or Healing Lane, Harvey's 1800 guidebook calls it Hellen Lane. There are references to a house called 'Hell' in the 17th century, said to be on the corner of East Street and Helen Lane.

HENNAH, Joseph Edward (1896-1963) Born in Newport. Painter in oil and watercolour. Exhibited at the Royal Academy. Came to Weymouth in 1939 and became Chairman of the South Dorset Arts Club. One of the founder members of the Weymouth and South Dorset Arts Centre. Died 20 March 1963. Lived at The Cottage, Nottington.

HENNING FAMILY Influential local family. The Hennings can be traced back to Tudor times and John was the builder of Poxwell House. Linked by marriage with the Trenchards of Wolveton since the 17th century. The family had property throughout Dorset, including Weymouth and Melcombe Regis. Henry Henning was one of Weymouth's MPs from 1679-1694. Edmund Henning was a banker in the Georgian period, whose bank failed. John Henning, son of Robert Henning of Alton Pancras, came to Weymouth, commenced in practice as a solicitor around 1800 and also founded **Radipole Spa**. He died 21st January 1860, aged 86 and left no surviving children.

HENNING PLACE, Dorchester Road, Radipole until 1872 was known as Prospect Place.

HENTY, George Alfred Born in 1832, he was a war correspondent and well-known novelist. Author of numerous popular adventure stories for boys. Not Weymouth-born, his local claim to fame is that he died here – aboard his yacht *Egret* in Weymouth Harbour, on 16th November 1902.

HERBERT, Graham Valentine (1911-1983) Award-winning commercial and portrait photographer. Took over the business at No.9 Coburg Place, St Thomas Street started by his father in the 1920s. Selections of his photographs have been published in *Weymouth: the golden years* and *Weymouth: more golden years* (Dorset Books, 2001, 2002).

HERBERT, Sidney John (died 1949) father of the above and founder of the photographic business 'Herbert of Weymouth' which he took over from the Waverley Studio in the early 1920s.

HIBBERD, Stuart (1893-1983) Dorset-born and educated at **Weymouth College** in the early years of the 20th century. Became well-known as the Chief Announcer of the BBC and was radio's 'Golden Voice' from 1924 until 1950.

HIGGINS, 'Professor' Guy Weymouth's Punch and Judy man entertained children on the sands from 1976 until his retirement in May, 2005.

HIGH STREET once extended all along the Weymouth side of the harbour from the Old Town Hall to The Cove. East of the Town Bridge it is now known as Trinity Road and Trinity Street, although this renaming did not immediately follow the building of Holy Trinity Church in the 1830s. High Street suffered damage in WW2 air raids and some derelict properties were demolished in the 1950s. The rest fell to the bulldozer in 1961 and 1965 and the town's Municipal Offices now fill much of the site. This had once been the heart of old Weymouth, an ancient narrow street which was a mix of large and small houses, shops and businesses, tiny cottages in alleys and the Weymouth Arms and the Fisherman's Arms pubs.

HIGH WEST STREET in Weymouth probably took its name to distinguish it from West Street across the harbour in Melcombe. Rather confusingly, old borough deeds describe High Street as 'also being known as West Street and High West Street'. High West Street Court was on its southern side, between Nos.27 and 28, and running parallel with Love Lane.

The distant Old Town Hall stands at the beginning of old High Street, much of which was cleared in the 1960s. The buildings shown on the right are in High West Street and are easily recognisable today.

HIGH WEST STREET TAVERN was close to the Old Town Hall.

HIGHLAND ROAD In the early stages of its development in the 1920s this was known as New Road and the original intention was to name it Andover Road.

HILL'S LANE is an older name for Hill Lane, running from Hope Square to the Nothe.

HOCKEY FESTIVAL was first held in 1963 (men's) and 1967 (ladies') and takes place annually over the Easter weekend at Redlands Sports Ground.

HODGES, Sir William Born in Weymouth. Became Chief Justice of the Cape of Good Hope. His *Law of Railways* published in the 1840s remained a standard work for many years.

HOLLAND ROAD, Westham takes it name from one of the family names of the Earl of Ilchester, once ground landlord of much of the land on which Westham is built.

HOLLAND VILLA became No.41 Hardwick Street.

HOLLAND'S AMUSEMENTS run the Amusements in the Alexandra Gardens and have done since the 1960s.

HOLLOWAY, William (1761-1854) Poet. Born near Blandford and moved to Weymouth when he began working as a printer for **John Love**, the town's well-known librarian and bookseller. In 1790, Love published a series of twelve engravings of scenes in and around Weymouth and Holloway contributed several of the descriptive verses which accompanied each individual plate. Of his work published in book form, *The Peasant's Fate* first published in 1802, was the best-known, and, like much of his work, described the rural Dorset of his youth. He also contributed poems to periodicals and his *On Their Majesties and the Princesses viewing the spot where the Halsewell was wrecked,* appeared in the Western County Magazine in October 1789. It commemorated the visit of King George III to the spot where the East Indiaman Halsewell was lost on the rocks below Worth Matravers in 1786, with great loss of life. His earliest known work *The Halsewell,* a poem, was published by John Love in 1788. Holloway left Dorset with his wife and family in 1798 to work in London and although he continued to write about the county of his youth, he never returned to live in it.

HOLLY TERRACE became Nos.1-5 Holly Road.

HOLMAN Lucie In 1943 Miss Holman was first Chief Librarian appointed in Weymouth, overseeing the 'Reference only' library service in 1944 and the opening of the Westwey Road public library in 1948. She left in 1949 and later moved to the United States. *See also* WEYMOUTH LIBRARY

HOLWORTH *see* BURNING CLIFF, Holworth

HOLY CHILD SECONDARY SCHOOL, No.74, Wyke Road was attached to the **Convent of the Sisters of Mercy**. The school closed in 1967.

HOLY TRINITY CHURCH Built on the site of some ancient properties, said to include an inn known as the White Hart, the foundation stone of Holy Trinity Church was laid on 1st September 1834 and the building was consecrated in 1836. It had been paid for by the Rev. George Chamberlaine of Wyke Regis, who felt that Weymouth townspeople should have a church of their own, their parish church until 1836 having been at Wyke Regis. Burials once took place in the extensive catacombs under the church, but these were closed later in the 19th century. The church was enlarged and re-oriented in the 1880s at the time Chapelhay Steps were being constructed. The crypt of the church was used in WW2 as an air raid shelter and ARP post. It was badly damaged in an enemy air raid in November 1940 and services were temporarily held in the Sidney Hall. *See also* ST NICHOLAS CHAPEL, Chapelhay; GLEBE HOUSE

Holy Trinity Church was newly built when this engraving was made in the 1830s. It also provides a good view of the 1824 Town Bridge.

HOLY TRINITY SCHOOLS, Chapelhay and Cross Road The foundation stone of the Chapelhay building, designed by Talbot Bury, was laid on 23rd May 1853. The school opened on Trinity Monday, 1854. Part of a pillar from the mediaeval chapel of St Nicholas which once stood on the site was built into one of the walls. The school was extended several times – an Infant School was added in 1858, and more buildings were added in the 1870s and 1890s. Enemy land mines which destroyed much of Chapelhay on 19th November 1940 severely damaged the schools and the children were dispersed to other accommodation in the town. The site was cleared in December 1961 as part of the post-war redevelopment of Chapelhay, although one wing of the school remained for a time, used by the South Dorset Youth Employment Bureau. The houses of Trinity Court now stand here. The old chapel pillar was transferred to Weymouth Museum. Post-WW2 replacement schools – Holy Trinity Church of England Infants and Junior Schools, designed by C. and H. Crickmay, opened in Cross Road on 1st September 1952 but in 2006 these are being replaced by new buildings on an adjacent site.

HOLYROOD COTTAGES became Nos.24-42 Holly Road.

HOLZEWICKEDE, Westphalia, Germany has been Weymouth's twin town since 1986.

HOMES OF DEVENISH *see* DEVENISH HOMES

HOOKER'S DOCK Nothing has been found concerning the derivation of this name (although 'hooker' is a colloquial name for a ship). This is the boatyard on Nothe Parade now used by Weymouth Sailing Club, which was formerly Cosens & Co.'s No. 2 slipway.

HOOPERNE VILLAS became Nos.110-112 Abbotsbury Road.

HOPE CONGREGATIONAL CHAPEL *see* CONGREGATIONAL CHURCH, Trinity Street

HOPE COVE Its name is thought to derive from an old word 'hop' meaning a small inlet. The Cove was not filled in until 1781 (today's Hope Square). Could this inlet have provided the Romans with a landing place on the Weymouth side of the harbour? The pavement of a fine Roman villa was discovered in nearby Newberry Terrace in 1902 and numerous scattered Roman remains have been found in the Rodwell and Wyke area.

HOPE QUAY (today's Nothe Parade) extended from The Cove to a point almost opposite today's Pavilion Theatre and from this point seawards it was known as the Ballast Quay.

HOPE SQUARE was redeveloped as a tourist attraction in the late 1980s. The centrepiece is **Brewer's Quay**, the big red brick former Groves brewery building containing **The Timewalk, Weymouth Museum**, a brewing museum and a shopping village and pub. Other brewery buildings were converted to apartments and new houses were built on brewery land off Rodwell Avenue. Hope Square was once a harbour inlet, known as The Hole or McSanders/Mcsaunders Hole and in 1781 the residents here were given permission to wall it across and fill in the area at their own expense, and this led to the development of Hope Square.

HOPE STREET Houses once stood opposite the present Nos.18-24 Hope Street and these backed directly onto the harbour. They were demolished in the late 1880s when the Cove was enlarged to allow GWR cross-channel vessels to swing in the harbour.

HOPE TAVERN was an Eldridge Pope pub at No.22 Hope Street, now a private house.

HORDER, Edward Y Millionaire founder of Horder's Inc. in Chicago, a vast wholesale stationery and office equipment store. Born in Weymouth in 1861 and attended St Mary's School. Worked in stores in London and went to the States for the first time in 1883. He returned in the late 1880s and subsequently built up the business which made him a millionaire. In 1929 he owned a new and impressive 7-storey building in Chicago.

HORSE LYNCH PLANTATION is north west of Southdown Farm and is also known as Teddy Bear Woods. Here, in May 1996, protestors against the 'Brown Route' relief road set up camp in protest at the possible loss of this wildlife habitat.

HORSE RACING Horse racing began at Lodmoor in 1821. It seems to have declined around 1860 but continued until the final meeting in 1882, when it was advertised in the Racing Calendar as Weymouth and Dorset County Races. Originally a three-day event, it went down to two days, usually at the end of August/beginning of September. Horse and pony races were usually held on the sands during **Yeomanry Weeks**, and in the early 20th century there was a racecourse at **East Chickerell Court**.

A lively scene at the Weymouth Races on Lodmoor in the 19th century.

HOSPITALS. WORLD WAR I The numbers of WW1 wounded coming into Weymouth necessitated the use of various buildings in and around the town as temporary hospitals and convalescent homes. Organised by the Red Cross were:-The Convent Hospital (The Convent of the Sacred Hearts, Carlton Road); G.F.S.Lodge (an unidentified house in Glendinning Avenue); Cassandra (a house at Greenhill); Ryme (a house in Old Castle Road); St John's Mission Hall, Chelmsford Street; Elwell Lea (a house at Upwey) and The Manor House, Buckland Ripers. The Sidney Hall and the Burdon Hotel were also converted for hospital use.

HOSPITALS *see also* ISOLATION HOSPITAL, Coldharbour; ISOLATION HOSPITAL, Radipole Lane; ISOLATION HOSPITAL, Rocks Terrace; MATERNITY HOSPITALS; PORT SANITARY HOSPITAL; PORTWEY HOSPITAL; PRINCESS CHRISTIAN HOSPITAL; WESTHAVEN HOSPITAL; WEYMOUTH & DISTRICT HOSPITAL; WEYMOUTH & DORSET COUNTY ROYAL EYE INFIRMARY; WEYMOUTH ROYAL HOSPITAL AND DISPENSARY; WEYMOUTH SANATORIUM.

HOUSE, Michael (1930-2002) Eminent geologist and author of a classic guide to the geology of the Dorset coast. Contributor to the successful bid for Unesco World Heritage status for the East Devon and Dorset coasts. Brought up in Weymouth and retired to the town.

Further reading : *The Dorset Coast from Poole to Chesil Beach*, by Michael House (Geological Association Guide, Rev.ed. 1969)

HOUSE NAMES In the 1920s when some streets in the borough were not yet numbered, house names were used to identify properties. A useful alphabetical list of these can be found in Sherrens *Directory of Weymouth* 1923, pages 53-63.

'HOUSE OF MUSICIANS' *see* HUGO, Victor

'HOUSE WITH THE CANNONBALL', Maiden Street Embedded in the wall of a 17th century building on the corner of Maiden Street and St Edmund Street can be seen a cannonball, thought to have been fired during the Civil War fighting of 1645. Another was found in the nearby Globe Inn but was not preserved. *See also* FIRE STATION

HOVERCRAFT Plans for a cross-channel hovercraft service in 1966 came to nothing. Its base was to have been Newton's Cove.

HOWARD, Sir Richard Nicholas (1832-1905) Solicitor. Hugely influential in the municipal life of Weymouth for more than 50 years. Mayor seven times- 1869-70, 1880-1, 1881-82, 1882-3 1883-4, 1885-6, 1893-4) and later Town Clerk. Had extensive business interests and owned land and property in Weymouth and places beyond – including Chickerell, Portland and West Lulworth. Knighted in 1886 for his services to the Liberal cause. Lived at **Greenhill House.** He was born in Devonshire, but the family had Weymouth connections and moved here when he was in his teens. Articled to John Tizard, solicitor, and on qualifying in the late 1850s, commenced in practice for himself. In the same period he was first elected as a councillor, becoming an Alderman in 1866. Aiming to secure the position of Town Clerk in 1879, on the death of Frederick Steggall, Howard resigned from the Aldermanic bench, only to withdraw his resignation when he discovered a motion being put forward by George Boulter Welsford, which would prohibit any agent for a parliamentary candidate from holding the post. (Howard was the agent for Liberal MP Henry Edwards). Tit-for-tat arguments followed and it appears that Welsford may also have had ambitions to become Town Clerk, but in the end, although both were to resign as aldermen, neither Howard nor Welsford was appointed and the post went to Pelly Hooper. Howard was soon back on the council. During his 1893-4, his final mayoral year, Town Clerk Pelly Hooper died suddenly and Sir Richard Howard achieved his ambition at last. Despite questions about the legality of their actions, the Council accepted Howard's resignation as Mayor and appointed him Town Clerk, a post he held for some ten years by which time he was in failing health and unable to fulfil his duties competently and retirement was more or less forced upon him. In his life-time Howard had been involved in numerous business projects and he was largely responsible for the building of the Jubilee Hall and was a major shareholder in Weymouth Gas Works. At Portland, he was held in less high regard being Clerk to the ineptly run Local Board of Health and owner of the loss-making Portland Gas Works, which he sold to Portland Council for a staggering £28,656. Unmarried, Sir Richard Nicholas Howard died on 25th November 1905 and is buried in Melcombe Regis Cemetery. His sister, Selina Aldridge, lived in Weymouth.

HOWARD PLACE became Nos.30-36 Walpole Street.

HOWGILL, John Stephen (1866-1950) Flute-player who became conductor of the Weymouth season band in 1903 and was musical director for 15 years at the first Pavilion Theatre. He is best known for his composition *'Weymouth Chimes'* which he wrote for tubular bells and dedicated to Weymouth's 1903-4 Mayoress, Mrs Herbert John Groves. The gavotte became enormously popular and was played to London audiences by, among others, Sousa's band. Sheet music was published by Chappell & Co. and when a gramophone record of *'Weymouth Chimes'* was produced, it sold in thousands. The flip side of the record was *'Christchurch Bells'.* John Howgill died on 15th September 1950. He lived at 185 Abbotsbury Road, where his daughter Elise taught piano for many years.

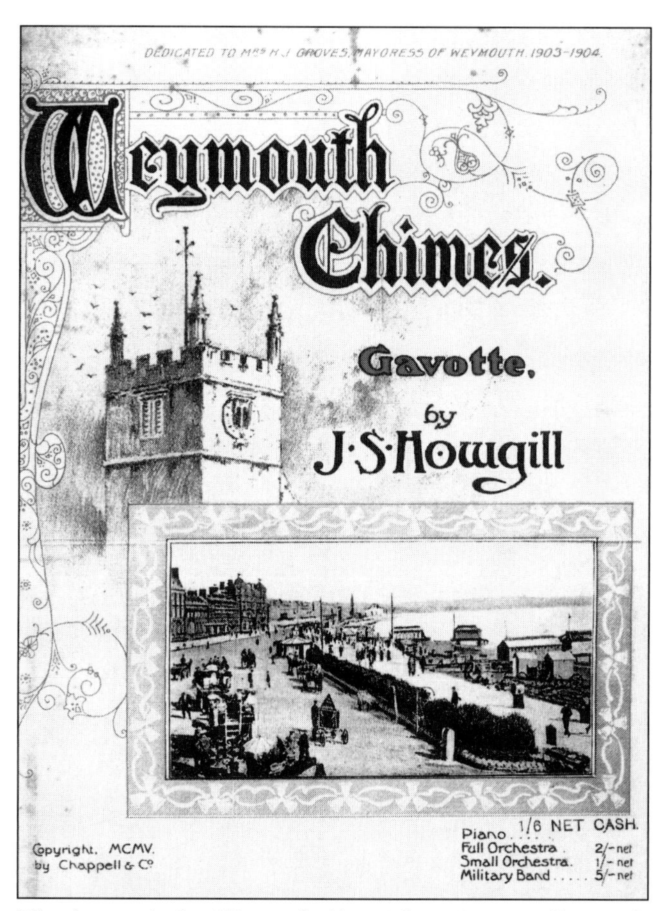

The sheet music for 'Weymouth Chimes' by J. S. Howgill. On the flip side of the gramophone record made of the tune was 'Christchurch Chimes'.

HOYOS, Countess Married to Austrian Count Georg Hoyos, she was Alice, daughter of Robert Whitehead of the Torpedo Works at Wyke Regis. On 11th April 1891 she laid the foundation stone of the works and it has been preserved at Harbour Point, the housing development since built on the site of the factory. Her name can also be found on the foundation stone of St Paul's Church at Westham.

HUGO, Victor and the 'HOUSE OF MUSICIANS' This is an unsolved mystery. In a letter written by Victor Hugo in 1864 he refers to Weymouth as follows *"La maison à statuettes de la rue Pierre-de-Blois est comparable à la précieuse maison des musiciens de Weymouth".* The house in La Rue Pierre-de-Blois is now known as La Maison des Acrobates in Blois and has a heavily carved façade which relates to no known building in Weymouth. The local coast features in Hugo's novel *L'homme qui rit.*

HUMPTY DUMPTY FIELD, Radipole Lane, west of St Ann's Church. This 6-acre field is probably the remains of the original mediaeval village settlement of Radipole, close to the 13th century church and old manor house.

HURDLE & Co. Butchers, provision and spirit merchants. William Hurdle founded the firm in the mid-19th century. Occupied various premises in the town and the shop at the junction of St Edmund Street and Maiden Street gave the name 'Hurdle's Corner' to this area.

HUTCHINS, John (1698-1773) Author of probably the best known, largest and most comprehensive history of Dorset ever published – *The History and Antiquities of the County of Dorset* – which appeared in three editions, none of which were published in John Hutchins' lifetime. He was a Dorset vicar who spent many years researching the history of the county, but died a few months before the publication of the first edition of his work. The editions (later editors expanded and revised Hutchins' original work) are as follows:-
1st edition 2 volumes. Published in 1774.
2nd edition 4 volumes. Published between 1796 and 1815.
3rd edition 4 volumes. Published as a 15-part work between 1861 and 1870. (A facsimile of this edition was published by EP Publishing Ltd and Dorset County Library in 1973).
Extra-illustrated edition. In the early 1900s a unique edition of the 2nd edition of Hutchins' was produced by Alexander Meyrick Broadley, a wealthy Bradpole collector of Dorsetiana, who 'Grangerized' the work -i.e. he took the original 4-volume text and added numerous original letters, paintings, autographs, engravings, maps and other rare items, expanding it to 14 magnificent volumes. This set was purchased at Sotheby's auction in July 1961 for Weymouth Library and is now in the Dorset History Centre, Dorchester.

HYDROFOIL Services to the Channel Islands commenced in 1987.

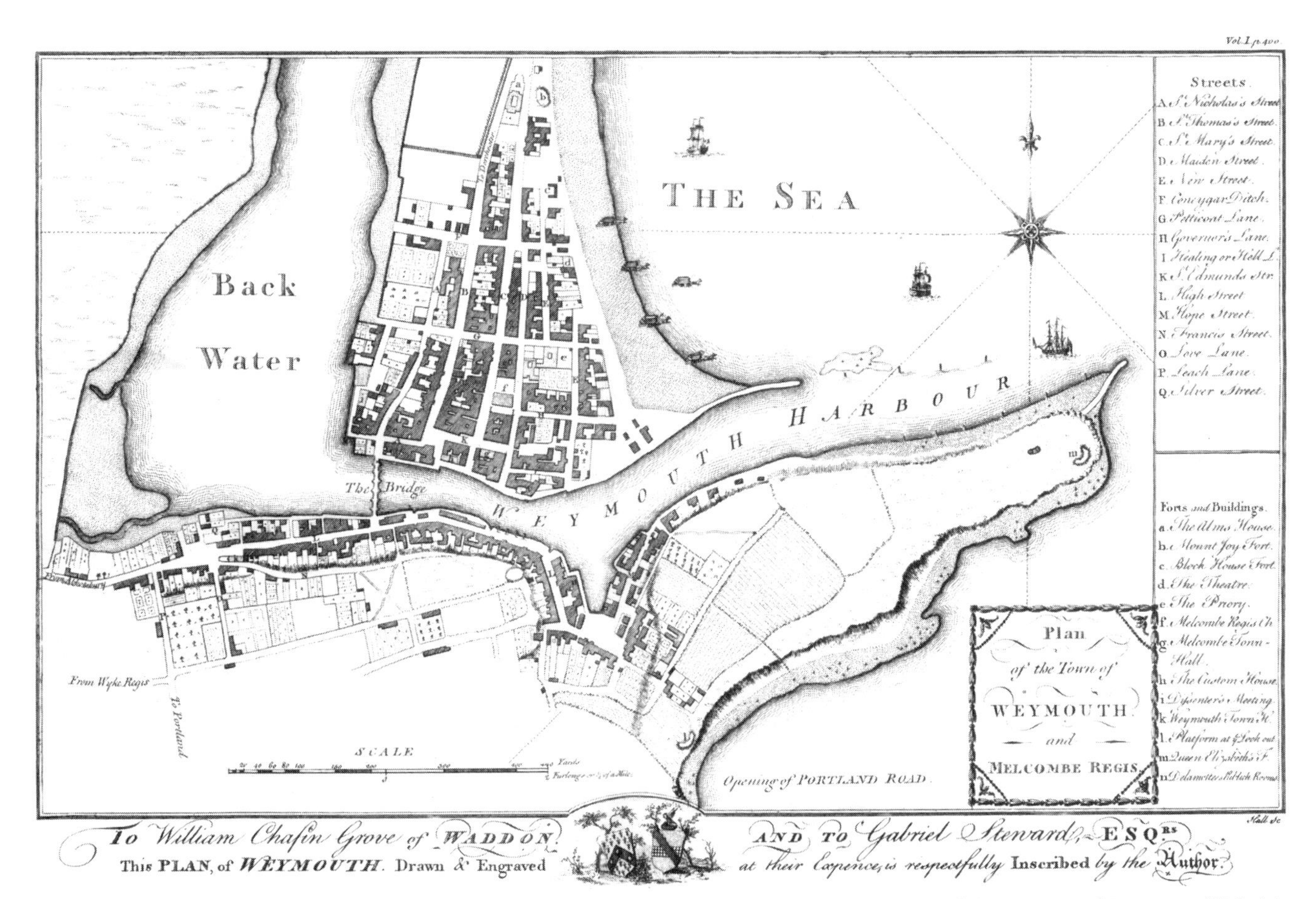

The map of Weymouth which appeared in the 1st edition of John Hutchins' History and Antiquities of the County of Dorset, *published in 1774. The 2nd edition contained a slightly revised map, but it was left out altogether when the 3rd edition appeared in the 1860s.*

Ice Houses

I

ICE HOUSES Cosens & Co. converted their coal stores at No.10 Custom House Quay to an ice well in the 1880s by lining the walls with cork. Block ice was brought in by sea from Norway and the Baltic and delivered around the town by horse and cart. The business expanded when refrigeration plant was installed in 1915 and manufactured ice was produced. This business relocated to the firm's West Street premises which were converted to ice-making and a cold store in 1925. There was also an ice house at the 1855 Fish Market on the Quay. Pierce Arthur's Weymouth map of 1857 shows an ice house 'in ruins' near the Sluice, Greenhill.

ILCHESTER, EARLS OF (family name Fox-Strangways) Possessors of large estates in Dorset (Melbury and Abbotsbury) and Somerset, the family seat being Holland House in London. Owned considerable property in Weymouth in the 19th century, including Littlefields on which much of the suburb of Westham was subsequently built. In the early 1890s the whole of the leasehold Littlefields Estate was purchased from the Earl and converted to freehold by local builder John Bagg and by 1896 171 houses had been built on it. Street names in the area commemorate the Ilchester family.

ILCHESTER ROAD takes its name from The Earl of Ilchester, once ground landlord of much of the land on which Westham is built.

ILCHESTER TERRACE became Nos.2-24 Ilchester Road.

ILCHESTER VILLAS became Nos.17-27 Abbotsbury Road.

***ILLUSTRIOUS*, HMS** The sinking of a liberty launch from the aircraft carrier HMS *Illustrious* in Portland Harbour was a great local tragedy of the post-WW2 years. 29 young men returning to their ship from shore leave in Weymouth lost their lives when the launch overturned in rough weather and sank just 60 yards from the aircraft carrier on 17th October 1948.

INDUSTRIOUS HAYMAKER An oft-quoted tale from the days of the visits of King George III. The King, known as 'Farmer George', liked to keep an eye on agricultural methods when he was in Dorset. Riding out near Upwey one day he spotted a lone woman working in a hayfield. He dismounted and asked her why she was on her own. One gentleman in riding gear looking much like another, she had no idea of the identity of her visitor and told him that all her colleagues had gone off to Weymouth to gawp at the King but she had better things to do. King George, far from being offended that she had failed to recognise him, rewarded the 'Industrious Haymaker' with a golden guinea.

King George III rewards the Industrious Haymaker at Upwey.

INTREPID BIRDMAN CONTEST first took place at Weymouth in 1983 and continued in the 1980s. Staged again on 29th May 2006 as part of Trawler Race Day.

IRON BOX DAIRY HOUSE In May 1955 when Alfonso Forte applied to build his fish and chip shop at Lanehouse 'an old stone and corrugated iron shed and advertisement hoarding' occupied part of the site and it was this structure which was known as Iron Box Dairy House, part of the former farm there.

ISOLATION HOSPITAL, Coldharbour (top of Coldharbour Hill, just past its junction to Nottington village) This corrugated iron structure was Weymouth Rural District's isolation hospital. It closed in 1933.

ISOLATION HOSPITAL, Radipole Lane Opened 22nd November 1902, with an adjacent smallpox hospital which opened a little earlier that year. Later became known as Westhaven Hospital.

ISOLATION HOSPITAL, Rocks Terrace, Newstead Road was a hospital hut hastily erected in 1871 for smallpox cases, there being an epidemic that year. It was known as the Black Hospital due to its tar-coated exterior. It went out of use in 1880/1881 when the new **Port Sanitary Hospital** was built at Wyke Regis. Rocks Terrace was built on the site.

IVY BANK, Chickerell Road was formerly Powell or Powell's Villa.

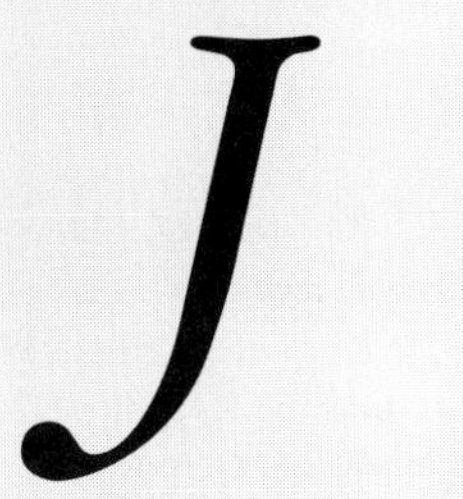

Jackson Family

JACKSON FAMILY Architects and surveyors The firm was founded by S.H.Jackson at York Buildings in the late 19th century. All five of his sons trained as architects and two carried on the Weymouth practice after his death.

JAMES'S COURT or JAMES COURT was off the east side of Park Street, between Nos.9 and 10, **West Parade**.

JEHOVAH'S WITNESSES meet in the former **Good Templars Hall/Coffee Tavern, High Street**

JENKINS, John James (1843-1911) Born in Weymouth in 1843. The family emigrated to the USA a few years later. As a member of the Wisconsin Volunteer Infantry, he saw action in the American Civil War. Later became, successively, City Attorney, County Judge, US District Attorney and was a Member of Congress for fourteen years. A speech he made in the House of Representatives in 1898 was printed by the Government Printing Office in Washington. Died in Wisconsin, June 1911.

JENNER COURT, Stavordale Road, opened in 1989 and was named after Honorary Alderman John Jenner.

JEREMY, Richard (pseudonym) **See FOX, Charles**

JERSEY TAVERN, 21 St Thomas Street A former pub on this site was known as the Cross Keys Inn. It was rebuilt by Eldridge Pope in 1890 as the Jersey Hotel, changing its name to the Jersey Tavern in 1979. In 2000 the premises were converted to a café.

So many local pubs have closed or changed their names. The Jersey Tavern in St Thomas Street is no more, the premises having been converted to a café in 2000.

JERVOISE, Edwyn Born in Weymouth. Wrote about England's famous bridges.

JOCKEY'S ROW ran parallel with and immediately below High West Street, within the area known as the 'Plains of Weymouth'. Said to have been named after a man known as 'Jockey' Bartlett. The houses, running up to the Boot Inn, were demolished under a slum clearance order in the 1930s. Now the site of Weymouth Fire Station, completed in 1939.

JOHN STREET ran between West Street and St Nicholas Street.

JOHN'S COURT was a street of terraced houses off the north side of Lower Bond Street. Most of the properties were demolished under a slum clearance order in the 1930s.

JOHNSTONE, Sir Frederic John William, 8th Baronet, of Westerhall in Dumfriesshire (1841-1913) Inherited enormous wealth when he was still a minor and owned a vast amount of land and property in Weymouth from which he derived considerable income in rentals (*see* JOHNSTONE ESTATE). Sir Frederic enjoyed the good life. He was a great horse-racing man, was a close friend of King Edward VII and by the end of his life had frittered away the whole of his fortune. By the time of his death in 1913 he was heavily in debt and had sold off his Westerhall estate in an attempt to avoid bankruptcy, leaving lawyers with a tangled financial web to disentangle, as it was disputed that he was sane at the time of the sale. Provision had to be made for him through the courts, Sir Frederic having signed away everything he owned including his bed and his clothes. He married, in 1899, a widow, Laura, Lady Wilton and the local property later transferred to her. Sir Frederic was Conservative MP for Weymouth from 1874-1884. He was generous with gifts and leases of building land for specific projects but rarely visited the town after a protracted and violent disagreement over the ownership of an area at the northern end of the town. Some townspeople felt that this land, on part of which Greenhill Gardens stand, was common land over which he had no rights. A local councillor, Thomas Wallis, acting as a private citizen, was involved in a lengthy court case which Sir Frederic won with costs, reducing Wallis to penury (*see also* **Greenhill Gardens; Wallis, Thomas**). Sir Frederic enjoyed cruising to distant parts in his luxury yacht *Zenaida*, and on a voyage to the island of Blanquilla off the Venezuelan coast, named a cove after his yacht and a black finch, *Eutheia johnstonei* (Johnstone's grassquit) after himself.

JOHNSTONE ESTATE The history of the land and property owning Johnstone Estate is a complex one and dates back to the first half of the eighteenth century when it appears that John Olmius, one of the town's MP's and not a local man, was buying up property to secure votes. This 'estate' in turn was purchased by others anxious to influence voting in this small town which at that time elected 4 MPs and had huge importance in politics. William Chafin Grove next owned the properties and land, followed by Gabriel Steward, related by marriage to the powerful Tuckers, from whom he had already inherited property. He in turn sold to Sir William Pulteney in 1790, whose name, before his marriage to a descendant of the Pulteneys, Earls of Bath, was Sir William Johnstone (for details of the Pulteney/Johnstone link and Johnstone genealogy, *see* PULTENEY, Sir William). Thus, on Pulteney's death in 1805, the estate passed down through various Johnstones and became known as the 'Johnstone Estate'. It was managed by a local agent, and there was a 'Johnstone Estate Office' at No.2, New Street. The ornate building still stands, now renumbered and converted to a food takeaway. After the death of Sir Frederic Johnstone's widow in 1916, the estate passed to her son by her previous marriage and took the name 'Wilton Estate'. It is only when investigating the history of individual buildings today that the full extent of the Johnstone Estate can be appreciated – many of Weymouth's well-known town centre buildings stand on land given by or purchased from it in Sir Frederic Johnstone's time. A big sale took place in August 1890 of Johnstone land off the Dorchester Road on which the streets of the Westerhall area were built. A further sale of business and private property was held in June 1933, followed by the disposal of more of the estate during the 20th century.

JOHNSTONE ROW was built c.1810 and takes its name from the Johnstones. The terrace is now numbered as 61-67 The Esplanade. *See* JOHNSTONE ESTATE.

JOLLIFFE, Sir Anthony, G.B.E. Accountant. Born in Weymouth in 1938 and spent his early school years here. Lord Mayor of London in 1982-1983. He invited Weymouth to take part in the Lord Mayor's Show in London and WPBC entered a float in the procession. President of the Society of Dorset Men.

JONATHAN & REBECCA EDWARDS CHARITY see EDWARDS CHARITY

JONATHAN TAYLOR'S CHARITY *see* TAYLOR CHARITY

JONES, Edwin John (Jack) Town Clerk of Weymouth from 1956 to 1979.

JORDAN HILL is the site of a Roman Temple at Preston, the remains of which can be seen today.

JUBILEE CLOCK was unveiled 31st October 1888 during the mayoralty of John Groves to commemorate the 1887 Golden Jubilee of Queen Victoria. The tower was paid for by public subscription, the clock was the gift of Sir Henry Edwards. The tower is 44 feet high. Its lower panels are decorated with medallion portraits of the Queen, those above with the borough coat of arms. Clock faces are each 4'8" in diameter, originally illuminated by gaslight at night. Rather drab in its early days, the clock tower was first painted in bright colours in the early 1920s. The clockwork mechanism was replaced by electrical works in 1960. When first erected the Jubilee Clock stood on a stone platform on the beach but in the early 1920s the Esplanade was widened out around it in a broad sweep.

The Jubilee Clock as first built, standing on a small promontory on the beach.

JUBILEE HALL was erected in 1887, the year of Queen Victoria's Golden Jubilee. Sir Richard Nicholas Howard was managing director of the company behind the initially grandiose scheme, which envisaged a galleried hall with lounges and a swimming pool, much of which never materialised. The huge hall was constructed, seating 2000-3000, but it was not a great success as its acoustic properties were poor. The immense space was extremely draughty and cold in the winter and there were calls for a smaller theatre to be built within it. As well as being used for theatricals, balls, exhibitions, public meetings, and music hall turns, the Jubilee Hall in 1909 was the first local entertainment venue to show moving pictures on a regular basis, calling itself 'The Royal Victoria Jubilee Hall and Picture Palace'. In a smaller area alongside, later enclosed and known as Arcadia, roller skating began in 1909. In 1926 the buildings were altered, re-opening as 'The Regent Theatre and Dance Hall' and in October, 1929 this was the first cinema in Weymouth to show 'talkies'. In 1951 it was renamed The Gaumont Cinema and Dance Hall, but the dance hall closed within months and the following year was taken over for light industrial use by the radio component manufacturing company Weyrad. The Gaumont cinema was modernised in 1959. Another name change – The Odeon – came in September 1968 and with its final name change in February 1976 it became the 'New Invicta', a combined cinema and Top Rank bingo hall. In less than a year, on 29th January 1977, the last film was shown and bingo prevailed. After a long campaign, spearheaded by Geoff Poole, to preserve the Victorian Jubilee Hall, it was demolished in 1989 to make way for a shopping precinct. Some of the structure is currently languishing in a Portland quarry, its future use uncertain.

JUBILEE RETAIL PARK opened in 1999. It stands on the site of the 1935 Jubilee railway sidings which were removed in 1987.

JUBILEE TERRACE became Nos.27-39 Newstead Road. Another terrace of the same name is on Dorchester Road at Broadwey.

JUBILEE WALK The Jubilee Walk at the Nothe commemorates Queen Victoria's Golden Jubilee, 1887.

JURASSIC COASTLINE World Heritage Site status was awarded by UNESCO in December 2001.

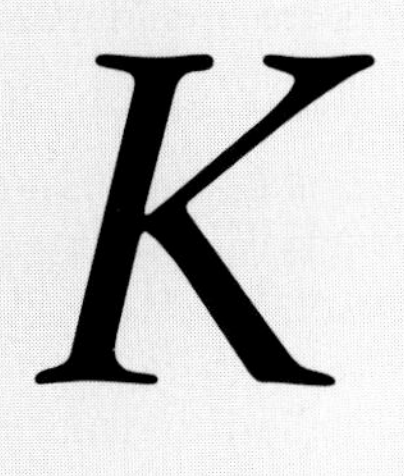

KELLAWAY'S COTTAGES became Nos.1-4 Kellaway Terrace and follow No.89 Newstead Road. May be a link with Thomas Kellaway, a retired businessman and prospective councillor for Westham in 1903.

KELLY'S DIRECTORIES The first Kelly's Directory for Dorset appeared in 1848. It was then published in 1855, 1859, 1867, 1880, 1885, 1889, 1895, 1898, 1903, 1907, 1915, 1920, 1923, 1927, 1931, 1935 and 1939. The entries for each place are confined to alphabetical lists of 'Gentry' and Traders so few private individuals are listed. Publication of much more detailed Kelly's Directories for Weymouth began in 1929, containing alphabetical listings by surname, street name, business name and trade. They were then published in 1930-31, 1932-33, 1934-5, 1936-7, 1938-39, 1940-41, 1948, 1951, 1955, 1958, 1960, 1963, 1965, 1967, 1969, 1971, 1972, 1973 and 1974.

KELSO TERRACE became Nos.87-101 Abbotsbury Road.

KERRIDGE, Benjamin (died 1887) Chief Clerk at John Groves Brewery. Drowned when the yacht *Laureate* was wrecked on the Breakwaters in October 1887.

KERRIDGE, John Benjamin (c.1831-1892) Born in Weymouth. Published several booklets of verse in the 1860s and a pamphlet on Dorset shipwrecks. Author of two unpublished works *Local Rakings* (1866) and *Weymouth and Melcombe Regis and its Environs* (1858) in which he recalls local events, people and places and reflects on *'the modernizing mania which has made rapid inroads upon its relics of bygone times'*. The manuscript volumes, with a modern transcription, are in Weymouth Library's Local Studies Collection.

KING, Dorothy B. Member of the National British Women's Abstinence League, who ran a 'home from home' centre for the forces at St John's Mission Hall in Chelmsford Street during WW2. She recalled the wartime years there in *Happy recollections* published by Henry Ling, Dorchester, 1946.

KING GEORGE III *see* GEORGE III, King

KING STREET King Street originally ran from the Esplanade and then headed north past the railway station. This section later became known as King Street West but in 1872 it was renamed Queen Street. King Street then ran straight from the Esplanade to Commercial Road.

KING STREET WEST was the original name of Queen Street. It was renamed in 1872.

KING'S COURT was an alley off Queen Street alongside the Terminus Hotel. It appears to have been renamed Queen Court when King Street West was renamed Queen Street in 1872.

KING'S HEAD INN, Maiden Street was demolished in 1866 to make way for **Maiden Street Methodist Church**. Probably the largest inn on the Melcombe side, it had Assembly Rooms in the early 19th century.

KING'S HEAD PUBLIC HOUSE, No.18 East Street took the licence of the Maiden Street **King's Head Inn** which was demolished in the 1860s to provide a site for Maiden Street Methodist Church.

KING'S STATUE Weymouth's John Herbert Browne received the King's approval for a life-size statue to be erected at the entrance to the town at the end of 1802. The finished statue, made of Coade Stone at the Lambeth Ornamental Stone Manufactory was ready for shipping to Weymouth in October 1804. What happened to it between then and the laying of the foundation stone in 1809 is not known. Due to the complex political situation at Weymouth there was some secrecy regarding the commissioning of the statue, Browne's opposition to **William Pulteney**, friend of the King and virtual controller of the borough's finances, being well known. Browne, John Arbuthnot and their supporters wanted to show their loyalty to the King without Pulteney's involvement or knowledge. The foundation stone was laid on 10th October 1809 in the presence of two of King George III's children, Adolphus, Duke of Cambridge and Princess Mary. By then Pulteney had died and the King's summer visits to Weymouth had ceased. The statue was unveiled on 25th October 1810. The lettering on its plinth, designed by James Hamilton, celebrates the fiftieth year of the King's reign. Although now Grade I listed, the statue has not always been popular and there were various proposals over the years to re-site it or even dispose of it altogether but the town eventually learned to live with its royal monument, which was first painted in heraldic colours in 1949. The great open space in front of the statue, where crowds once congregated to celebrate special occasions, has been whittled down. A large bus shelter was sited directly in front of the plinth in the 1930s and buses set off for their destinations from the area around it. When increasing traffic clogged up the whole road system at the statue,

Right: *The King's statue. A point of departure for horse-drawn carriages waiting to take visitors out for the day...*

the present traffic island was built and gardens laid out in 1955. Proposals for redevelopment in the 21st century suggest that this area may once more become an public open space watched over by King George III.

...for cyclists setting out on a ride...

...and meeting place for everyone when there was something to celebrate.

KINGDOM HALL *see* GOOD TEMPLARS HALL, High Street; COFFEE TAVERN, High Street

KITE FESTIVAL has been held annually in early May since 6th May 1991.

'KLONDYKERS' These Russian fish factory ships were a familiar site in Weymouth Bay in the winter months of the 1990s. They left Weymouth in October 1997.

KNACKER'S HOLE is an 18th century place name for the Redlands Farm area.

KNAPLOCK'S CORNER *see* NAPLOCK'S CORNER

KNIGHT, Emmanuel 'Manno' Knight was the owner of land and allotments known as Twelve Acres at Westham, and gave his name to Knightsdale Road. Wardcliffe Road and Emmadale Road are said to be named after his daughter and granddaughter.

KNIGHT, Lieutenant Thomas, RN Chief officer of the Lulworth coastguard, whose murder in June 1832 is one of the darkest episodes in the annals of local smuggling. He and another officer named Duke unexpectedly came across a gang of smugglers, who immediately attacked the Preventive Men and beat them senseless. Duke was left lying on the ground and subsequently recovered, but the badly injured Knight was thrown over the cliff and died. There was outrage over the affair as public opinion, which had long either supported or turned a blind eye to the smugglers' activities, was finally turning against their lawless behaviour. A procession of boats conveyed Lt. Knight's body from Lulworth to Weymouth for the funeral, attended by large crowds. The 42 year old officer left a widow and five children. His gravestone, from the former cemetery in Bury Street, is now in Weymouth Museum.

KURSAAL *see* ALEXANDRA GARDENS

Described in the local press of 1913 as 'a miniature Crystal Palace', the Kursaal lasted until 1924 when it was replaced by the Alexandra Gardens Theatre. The original bandstand of 1891 can be seen in the centre of the structure. See ALEXANDRA GARDENS/ALEXANDRA GARDENS THEATRE for more details.

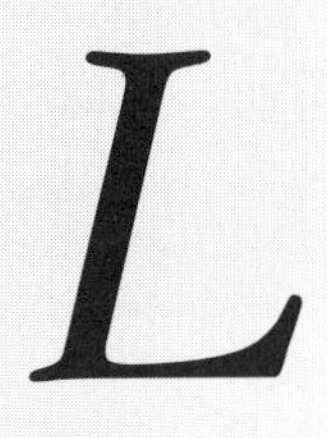

LABOUR EXCHANGE First one opened in Weymouth at Nos.9-10 St Thomas Street in June 1912.

LADY BROWNE'S CHARITY *see* BROWNE CHARITY

LAMB & FLAG PUBLIC HOUSE, Lower Bond Street was first leased by Eldridge Pope in 1851. Suffered some WW2 damage and closed for good in 1958, the licence being transferred to the new **Admiral Hardy** public house on Chickerell Road. The premises were purchased by the Royal Sailors' Rests in 1960 and converted to an **'Aggie Weston's'** Sailors' Home, later becoming a probation hostel. Demolished in the late 1990s to make way for the New Bond Street shopping development.

LANCASTER, Joseph (1778-1838) Quaker founder of the Lancasterian system of education. In 1805 King George III sent for him at Weymouth and promised Lancaster his patronage and support, concluding the interview with the words "It is my wish that every poor child in my dominions should be taught to read the Bible". A plaque bearing this inscription, once on the exterior wall of St Mary's Schools, is now displayed on the main staircase in Weymouth Library, Great George Street.

LANCASTER, William Joseph Cosens *see* COLLINGWOOD, Harry

LAND TRAIN, Esplanade was introduced in 1988 and runs during the season, taking passengers along the Esplanade to the Sluice Gardens at Greenhill.

The Esplanade land train has been a popular seafront attraction since 1988.

LANDALE TERRACE became Nos.21-35 Ilchester Road.

LANDMANN, Captain George Fortifications expert stationed in Weymouth to advise on coastal defences during the period of the visits of King George III. Apt to misjudge situations – he bumped into an 'old woman' on the Esplanade and discovered it was Queen Charlotte and tried to arrest Lord Hawkesbury as a petty thief. In the King's presence, his horse ran away with him over a cliff, fortunately landing on a ledge below.
Further reading : *Adventures and recollections, Vol.2*, by George T.Landmann (Colburn,1852)

LANE, Harriet Daughter of John Lane of Weymouth. Born 1852 and brought up in the town where her father was foreman of the Gas Works. In 1875 she was a hat maker living in London when she was killed and her body dismembered by her married lover Henry Wainwright, who was later hanged.

LANEHOUSE FARM The derelict farm off Lanehouse Rocks Road was redeveloped as housing in 2005. Stone from the old farmhouse was incorporated in some of the new properties.

LANEHOUSE ROCKS ROAD takes its name from quarries which were once on its west side.

LANGHOLME STREET was the original name for Avenue Road.

LARKWORTHY, Falconer (1833-1928) Born in Weymouth. Went to the Australian goldfields where he worked as a banker in the 1850s and 1860s. Later returned to England as an economist and banker. His reminiscences *Ninety-one years* were published in 1924.

LAST SUPPER, THE Painting by Sir James Thornhill above the altar in **St Mary's Church**. Presented by the artist in 1721 to the church formerly on the site. The painting practically filled the end wall of the old church and its arched top followed the old building's roofline.

LAUNDRY, No.77 Abbotsbury Road Opened 3rd May 1880. The building was designed by local architect Samuel Jackson. The laundry closed about 1970 and a garage was built on the site, replaced in 1990 by the flats of Swallow Court.

LAUNDRY, Queen's Road, Radipole was built c.1900 on the site of Radipole Spa and was rebuilt after being burnt down in a fire in 1910. It closed in March 1976 and the apartments of Jubilee Court now stand on the site.

LAURESTINE TERRACE became Nos.103-107 Abbotsbury Road.

LAWN COTTAGES, Chickerell Road stood almost opposite today's Tennyson Road.

LAWRENCE, Dan Butcher who farmed at Fairfield, Chickerell. Best remembered for his shop on the Town Bridge, which he converted from the former Palladium Cinema in 1933 (now The Rendezvous pub). He had a shop opposite in **Bridge Buildings**, until they were pulled down in 1928.

LAWRENCE, T.E. 'Lawrence of Arabia' His mother Sarah at some point lived at Brook House, Church Street,

Upwey. Thomas Robert Chapman took the surname Lawrence when he left his wife for Sarah Madden, the family's nursemaid. He and Sarah never married, but they had five sons, one of whom was T. E. Lawrence.

LAWRIE, Dr James Macpherson (1856-1937) Glasgow-born, came to Weymouth in 1883 to run **Weymouth Sanatorium**, Clarence Buildings. He was one of the founders of the **Princess Christian Hospital** at Greenhill and senior physician there. Left Weymouth soon after the amalgamation of the Princess Christian and Weymouth Royal Hospitals in 1921 (as **Weymouth & District Hospital**). Freeman of the Borough, 1924.

LEACH LANE is an early name for Boot Hill or Boot Lane (today numbered as Rodwell Road).

LEE, John 'the man they couldn't hang' or 'the Babbicombe murderer' Although strictly part of Portland's history, since he spent 23 years in prison there, John Lee's story is quoted locally from time to time. Found guilty of the brutal murder of an elderly Devon lady for whom he worked (a crime he strenuously denied), Lee was sentenced to death in 1885. He was taken to the scaffold three times and each time, although it had been checked, the trapdoor failed to work. Lee's sentence was commuted to life imprisonment and he was finally released in 1907.

LEGH, Iseult Involved in diverse and numerous social works in the town. The twinning of Weymouth and the French town of Louviers took place during her mayoral year 1958-59. Widowed in October 1944 when her husband Commander J.A.Pennington Legh, of the local coastguard, drowned when attempting to rescue the crew of a landing craft in mountainous seas at Chesil Cove.

LELAND, John (c.1502-1552) Tudor antiquarian and historian. In the 1530s he was given a royal order to travel throughout England to search out antiquities. His travels lasted some years and as well as noting the ancient remains, he also described the present state of each place he visited. *Leland's Itinerary,* as this work has come to be known, contains invaluable descriptions of Weymouth and Portland in Tudor times.

LENNOX STREET in the Park District probably takes its name from Lord Henry Gordon-Lennox who was a Tory MP and held posts in the Conservative government of the 1850s and 1860s. The Park District was developed by the **Conservative Land Society.**

LENNOX VILLA, 47 Lennox Street was known as Victoria Villa in the mid-19th century and appears to have had 'Hydrophatic Baths' attached.

LETHBRIDGE FAMILY Sir John Hesketh Lethbridge lived at Radipole. His ancestors, the **Bucklers**, lived at Causeway House. He erected a vault in Radipole churchyard to which he affixed a plaque in memory of Sir Walter Buckler who died in the 16th century, as well as a monumental tablet in St John's Church. In 1858 he presented the town with portraits of King George III and the Duke of Wellington. Sir John, who was also a local councillor, is buried in the vault he erected at Radipole.

LEWIS, Ernest Wamsley (1898-1977) Architect. Born in London, his family moved to Weymouth in the early 1900s. Worked in London, where he designed the New Victoria Cinema in 1930. Worked for Dorset County Council during WW2 and practised in Weymouth from 1946. Founded Weymouth Civic Society in 1944. Restored the **Trinity Street Cottages** and left them to Weymouth Civic Society.

LEWIS, William A gravestone in All Saints churchyard, Wyke Regis proclaims the innocence of William Lewis. Suspected of smuggling, he was killed in 1822 by a shot *'wantonly and maliciously fired'* from a naval schooner. The gravestone is close to the churchyard wall on Portland Road.

LIBRARIES The earliest libraries in Weymouth were the marine libraries which followed in the wake of sea bathing. Visitors required entertainment after their early morning dip in the briny and for a small subscription the reader could peruse the latest titles, look at a newspaper or journal, and view the all-important lists of who was in town. The libraries were a place to meet and socialise, play cards, drink coffee, or perhaps dash off a letter to those back at home on writing paper decorated with an engraving of a Weymouth scene. Some library proprietors published guidebooks, very like the holiday guides of today, listing hotels, boarding houses and places of interest, together with a little background local history. In Weymouth, Messrs Delamotte, Commins, Archer, Harvey, Love and others produced early guidebooks. *See also* WEYMOUTH LIBRARY

LIFEBOATS Weymouth's current lifeboat is the *Ernest and Mabel* named on 14th September 2002 after the parents of the prime donor, Miss Beryl Taylor. An inshore rescue boat, the *Phyl Clare III* is also stationed at Weymouth. Previously on station here were the lifeboats *Agnes Harriet* (1869-1887), *Friern Watch* (1887-1903), *Friern Watch* (1903-1924), *Samuel Oakes* (1924-1929), *Lady Kylsant* (1929-1930), *William and Clara Ryland* (1930-1957), *Frank Spiller Locke* (1957-1976), *Tony Vandervell* (1976-2002).

LINGDALE VILLAS became Nos.54-56 Abbotsbury Road.

LIPTON, Sir Thomas was in Weymouth with his America's Cup contenders *Shamrock I* and *Shamrock III* in April 1903. Shamrock III was dismasted in a sudden squall and one of the crew was swept overboard and drowned.

LISTED BUILDINGS *see* ARCHITECTURE

LITERARY INSTITUTION This was founded in the 1850s and was housed in rooms over the **Royal Baths** in St Thomas Street. It provided a series of lectures on various subjects during the winter months and a library. In conjunction with the Institution, a Museum was set up, mainly displaying relics from the local area.

LITTLE GEORGE STREET was the original name of Westham Road, which took its present name in December 1922.

LITTLEFIELD LEVEL CROSSING, Abbotsbury Road (just beyond Stavordale Road) was on the Weymouth and Portland Railway.

LITTLEFIELD VILLAS became Nos.2-8 Alma Road

LITTLEFIELDS ESTATE This is the land on which much of Westham is built. It originally belonged to the Earl of Ilchester. Local builder John Bagg initially acquired the leasehold but in 1896 he purchased the freehold from the Ilchester Estate, by which time almost ten acres were covered by buildings.

LITTLEMOOR The area now covered with housing was originally farmland with a few cottages and a pub- the New Inn. During WW1 a military camp was established here to accommodate some of the thousands of wounded Australian troops who came into Weymouth after the fighting at Gallipoli. Canberra Road, the first the street built at Littlemoor between the wars, commemorated their presence and the tradition has continued in the names of some of the streets built since. The real development of the Littlemoor Estate began in 1954 and the area's first school opened in 1961. Since then housing developments have continued and the large suburb now has its own church, shopping precinct and other facilities.

LITTLEMOOR ROAD In the days before there was any development along it, Littlemoor Road was known locally as Seven Gates Road.

LITTLEMOOR SCHOOL opened officially 8th November 1961.

LOBSTER HOUSE AND BEEFSTEAK HILL These extraordinarily-named large houses were said to have been built by Mr J.W.Lowman in the vicinity of the steam laundry, Abbotsbury Road.

LODGE, Grace (1893-1975) of Littlemoor Road. Author and illustrator of children's books. She also illustrated work by other authors, including a number of titles by Enid Blyton. Usually published work under her maiden name Grace Lodge: her married name was Grace Shelton.

LODMOOR In Victorian times the locals saw the Dorset Yeomanry in camp at Lodmoor in spring, enjoyed horse-racing in late summer and skated on Lodmoor in winter. Cricket and football grounds, a showground and even an airfield all appeared here in the early years of the 20th century, but Lodmoor has had a chequered history as plans for its development came and went. In the early 1890s Sir Frederic Johnstone offered 30 acres of the ground to the town for a Park and Recreation Ground, but the local council found the cost of infilling the ground was prohibitive and no action was taken. After Sir Frederic's death in 1913 the land was offered for sale to the council, but again declined. In 1925 the Weld Estate, owners of another large tract of land at Lodmoor, auctioned it off. The purchaser shortly afterwards bought the rest of Lodmoor from the Wilton Estate, (successor to the Johnstone Estate), selling it on in 1933. In 1948 the council was again considering the future of Lodmoor. By now the land belonged to Weymouth Bay Estate, a company which was building houses at Preston, and several individuals, including Mr A.E. Whettam, owner of a sizeable portion. In 1949 the council compulsorily purchased several hundred acres of Lodmoor for refuse tipping and car parking but did not proceed with proposals for a public park. Throughout the second half of the 20th century various proposals for recreational areas at Lodmoor were put forward – notable of those which fell by the wayside were **Billy Butlin's** plans for a holiday camp in the 1960s and a proposed Marina development in the 1970s. It was the 1980s before this formerly unattractive marshland was laid out as a country park and RSPB nature reserve with a Sea Life centre and other attractions and these, together with the new Preston Beach Wall of the 1990s, with its wide pedestrian walkway, have transformed this entrance into the town.

LODMOOR AIRFIELD An aviation ground with hangars was in use at Lodmoor by May, 1912. That year the first flight took place from a ship that was underway. A Short S38 hydroplane piloted by Lieutenant Charles Samson RN, was launched from HMS *Hibernia* and flew across the Weymouth Bay to land at the eastern end of Lodmoor. Famous aviation pioneers such as Claude Grahame-White and Benny Hucks flew from Lodmoor the same month. Lodmoor airfield continued in use until the early 1930s, although records of activity there are slight.

Further reading : *Wings over Weymouth*, by Colin Pomeroy. (Dovecote Press, 2005).

LODMOOR HIGH SCHOOL *see* LODMOOR HOUSE

LODMOOR HOUSE, Dorchester Road The Lodmoor House of today is a 1989 facsimile rebuild of a mid-19th century house which originally occupied the same site. (Before that, The Union Arms Inn stood here). Lodmoor House had become so dilapidated in the 1980s that it had to be demolished and replaced by the present residential home. The original Lodmoor House was used as a school for young ladies in the Victorian period and eventually became Lodmoor High School, the building being taken over as extra classroom space by the Convent of the Sacred Hearts in 1955. It was converted into flats in 1961 and a Casino operated here in the 60s.

LONDON AND SOUTH WESTERN RAILWAY When the railway to Weymouth opened in 1857 it was a joint LSWR (standard gauge) and GWR (broad gauge) venture. The LSWR ran a steamer service to Guernsey and Jersey in 1857 but it was short lived, their vessel *Express* being wrecked off Jersey in September 1859.

LONDON HOTEL, 5 Bond Street is now known as the Twenty Twelve Bar.

LONGHILL ROAD was the original name of **Rodwell Road** between Franchise Street and Bincleaves Road.

LONGHILL TERRACE Rodwell Road became Nos.38-44 Rodwell Road.

LOOKOUT, THE, Nothe This is the Belmont Terrace area.

LORD MAYOR OF LONDON *see* JOLLIFFE, Sir Anthony

LORD MELCOMBE REGIS Title, now extinct, awarded to **George Bubb Dodington**, wily wheeler-dealer in 18th century local politics, who died unmarried and without heirs.

LORD WEYMOUTH Title held by the Thynne family, Earls of Bath, of Longleat in Wiltshire.

LOUVIERS Weymouth was officially twinned with the French town of Louviers in Normandy on 4th April 1959.

LOVE, John (1752-1793) Artist, publisher, bookseller, librarian. Publisher of *The New Waymouth Guide* c.1788 and of a series of engravings by different artists in 1790, entitled *A collection of prints of the picturesque views of Weymouth, Portland, Lullworth and Corfe,* which he dedicated to The Duke of Gloucester. A second series was begun, but John Love died before it was completed. These prints are easily identifiable by their oval format. Although remarkably thin as a youth, on his death in 1793, aged 41, he was said to be *'...the most remarkable Man in all England for his Weight and Corpulence'.* The coffin containing his 26-stone body weighed about a ton and was lowered from a window at his home by ropes on two pieces of timber.

LOWER BOND STREET *see* BOND STREET; NEW BOND STREET

LYNCH LANE INDUSTRIAL ESTATE The first firms moved into the estate in late 1948.

LYONS HEAD INN Location unknown.

Right: *John Love, the Weymouth bookseller and publisher of a series of views of the town and surrounding area in 1790.*

Below: *John Love's 1790 view of Weymouth Esplanade, looking north.*

MACE, William (1809-1898) Talented amateur artist, lived at Spring Gardens until c.1890, died at Shaftesbury. Only known work is his 'Personal Sketch Book' of original small watercolours now in Weymouth Library's Local Studies Collection.

MACES The council maces, carried before the mayor on ceremonial occasions, are a curious throwback to the days when a club was carried as a weapon of war. When used by the bodyguards of royalty or other important dignitaries, the holding end of the club would be decorated with gold or silver and it is from these clubs that the modern mace is derived. The decorated holding end is now held aloft, and the mace is really an upside-down club. Weymouth's current silver gilt maces date from the 17th century. They were presented to the council by a former mayor in 1824, replacing two of much plainer design.

MACSANDERS or MACSAUNDERS HOLE or sometimes just 'The Hole'. In September 1781 permission was given to the inhabitants near the Cove to wall it across and fill it up at their own cost. This is now Hope Square.

MAGISTRATES COURT, Westwey Road Officially opened by the Duchess of Kent on 13th March 1978.

MAIDEN STREET METHODIST CHURCH The foundation stone of the Wesleyan Methodist Church, designed by James Wilson, was laid on 28th June 1866, on the site of the demolished **King's Head Inn**. It replaced a smaller chapel in Lower Bond Street. Fire destroyed the church on 17th January 2002 and it is now an empty shell. In March 2006 the burnt-out church was put up for sale, any developer being required to restore the façade of the starred Grade II listed building to its original state, including the rose window, which was blown out in the fire. The Methodists hope to build a new church on the site of the redundant **Christian Science Church** in Melcombe Avenue.

MALTHOUSES In Weymouth there are four in and around Hope Square, built for Devenish and Groves in the latter half of the 19th century. All have now been converted to housing.

MAN IN THE IRON MASK Harry Bensly in the early 1900s accepted a wager that he could travel the world disguised in an iron mask. He visited Weymouth during his travels.

MANNING, Rosemary (1911-1972) Born in Weymouth. Headmistress of a girls' school in Hampstead. Author of children's books and novels for adults, some published under the pseudonym Mary Voyle.

MANTLE, Leading Seaman Jack Foreman He was posthumously awarded the Victoria Cross for his bravery during the air attack on **HMS *Foylebank*** in Portland Harbour on 4th July 1940. German Stukas dive-bombed the ship but Leading Seaman Mantle, his left leg shattered in the blast, stayed at his gun firing at the enemy aircraft until he collapsed and died. He is buried in the Naval Cemetery at Portland. A summerhouse at Portland Hospital, erected in his memory in 1956, had to be demolished due to subsidence in the 1980s.

MAPS Listed below are the best-known historical maps of Weymouth which are of sufficiently large scale to provide details of streets and buildings.

1500s *Plan of Waymouth and Melcomb Regis in the reign of Henry VIII* Modern copies of this map are frequently reproduced. It is reputedly based on an original in the British Museum which has never been traced. It does, though, appear to be an accurate representation of the town at this date.

1774 A *Plan of the town of Weymouth and Melcombe Regis* was published in the 1st edition of John Hutchins' *History and Antiquities of the County of Dorset* and paid for by two Weymouth men, William Chafin Grove and Gabriel Steward. It is detailed, although it goes no further than the northern end of St Thomas and St Mary Streets, there being very little development along the Esplanade at this date. A key lists the main streets, forts and buildings and five bathing machines indicate the growing popularity of the town as a health and pleasure resort. A slightly updated version of the map appears in the 2nd edition of Hutchins', published in 1805. This shows a planned 'road' on the west side of the town, but fails to include some of the major building and reclamation projects which had taken place since the 1774 edition. When the 3rd edition of Hutchins was published in the 1860s, the Weymouth plan was omitted. *See* illustration p.75.

1800 *Harvey's Map*. Published as the frontispiece of Harvey's *Improved Weymouth Guide* in 1800. Shows the early development of the Esplanade, including Gloucester Lodge and its extensive shrubbery.

1840s *Tithe Maps and Apportionments* provide names of owners and occupiers of land and buildings, use of land, field names, place names.

1857 *Pierse Arthur's Trigonometrical Map of Weymouth and Melcombe Regis* Civil engineer Pierse Arthur designed the first timber road bridge across the Backwater and this beautifully detailed map shows it as 'the site of Arthur's proposed bridge'. Pier extensions are dismissed with the comment 'ill erected pier'. Scale is approximately 1:2500 and streets and buildings are clearly named.

1864 *Ordnance Survey*. The first large-scale maps produced by the Ordnance Survey. Those of the town centre at 1:500 (10.56 inches = 1 mile) scale provide invaluable detail. A much larger area is covered by the 1:2500 O/S maps of the same date.

20th/21st Century *Ordnance Survey*. The 1864 O/S was followed by that of 1902 and there were further editions in the 1920s and 1930s. WW2 halted a 1940s survey; instead, the RAF carried out a photographic aerial survey in 1946 – useful, as WW2 bomb damage can be seen. The 1950s saw the introduction of 1:1250 O/S maps for urban areas and since then there have been regular revisions.

MARCEL COURT, Abbotsbury Road was built in 1988 and named after Marcel Gaillard who once ran the shop which was pulled down to make way for the development. He was a former footballer who played for Weymouth FC before moving on to manage Dorchester. He died in 1976.

MARGARET OF ANJOU, Consort of King Henry VI landed at Weymouth 14th April 1471 having been in her native France trying to raise support for the Lancastrian cause.

MARINA The first pontoons were installed in the inner harbour in 1970. In the 1990s the Marina was developed following the removal of the dam, extensive dredging and positioning of many more pontoons. The Marina building stands on the site of **Melcombe Regis School**.

MARINDIN, Major Francis Born in Weymouth 1st May 1838. Keen footballer throughout his army career. In 1871 he attended a Football Association meeting to consider the establishment of a Challenge Cup, for which all clubs should be invited to compete – thus the FA Cup was born. Marindin subsequently played in two FA Cup Finals and refereed nine.

MARINE HOTEL *see* BANK BUILDINGS

MARINE LIBRARIES *see* LIBRARIES

MARKET DAYS A Charter of 1280, confirmed in 1318, granted Melcombe a Monday market in addition to the usual Tuesday one. By the 18th century market days were Tuesday and Friday. Before the present Guildhall was built in 1838, the market was held beneath a covered way which ran along the old Guildhall building. After 1838, long rows of stalls were set up in the same general area but some felt the straggly appearance of these and the noise and bustle which accompanied them were not quite the thing for a fashionable watering place. The covered Market House replaced them in 1855. Today the weekly market is held on the Swannery car park on Thursday, with an additional Monday market in summer.

MARKET HOUSE The Market House stood in St Mary Street, adjacent to St Mary's churchyard. Designed by architect Talbot Bury, it was an unusually elegant and ornate building for a market house. Bury also designed the Fish Market on Custom House Quay and both buildings were opened on the same day – 18th December 1855. The Market House opening was not an unqualified success as there were complaints from stallholders about the charges levied on them by the council. The building had already had a bad press due to arguments between the council, the architect and the contractor over the standard of building work. The interior was remodelled in the 1890s, but use of the Market House declined in the twentieth century and by the 1930s only a handful of stalls were occupied. Despite the beauty of the building (which it was difficult to stand back and appreciate due to the narrowness of the street) the decision was taken to demolish it and it was pulled down in 1939, to be replaced by a block of shops with flats above. The new, unadorned and strictly functional building with an arcade through to Maiden Street retained the Market House name until it was remodelled in the late 1990s. It was then renamed Brenda Dench House in memory of Weymouth's Mayor, who died during her year of office in 1995.

The Market House, a handsome building in St Mary Street, was demolished in 1939. The end wall shown on the far right was retained and can be seen today in the building's replacement, originally also called the Market House but now renamed Brenda Dench House.

MARKET STREET The present Market Street dates from 1870 and stands on the site of the old **Friary** buildings. Earlier references to 'Market Street' simply indicate streets where the market was held-*i.e.* St Mary Street and St Edmund Street.

MARKHAM AND LITTLE FRANCIS 40 acres of green space between Wyke Road and Chickerell Road officially designated a town green in June 2001, which local supporters feel is under threat from possible development. The land separates the built-up areas of Wyke and Westham. The site has been turned down for housing since the 1950s.

MARKS AND SPENCER first opened in Weymouth in 1932. The store was extended in 1955.

MARQUIS OF GRANBY PUBLIC HOUSE, Chickerell Road Stands just outside the borough boundary and is not the first pub of that name on the site. The original, a Devenish building of 1878, stood on what is the present pub's garden. It was replaced in 1978. The chalet-style design of the new pub led to it being renamed 'Swiss Cottage' for a time, but it sensibly reverted to its traditional name in the 1990s since generations of locals have always referred to the area as 'The Marquis'.

MARSH, THE This low-lying area of mudflats on the south side of the harbour was washed by the tides until attempts were made early in the 17th century to wall part of it and let the land for grazing. The Marsh covered a substantial area- the Sidney Hall and Football Ground (now the site of Asda and its car park), Marsh Road, the railway embankment and the playing fields and athletics facilities all stand on the former Marsh, the sports ground having been infilled by tipping in the first half of the twentieth century.

MASONIC HALL *see* FREEMASONRY

MASSANDRA, No.9 Greenhill A private house used as a Red Cross Hospital during WW1 and as the Weymouth and Dorset County Royal Eye Infirmary from 1934-1989. Now the Trimar Hospice.

MASTER OF CEREMONIES was the Georgian equivalent of an Entertainments Manager, responsible for regulating the resort's social scene and keeping the visitors amused. Mr Rodber, who held the post from 1783 to 1819, drew up a list of do's and don'ts for those attending dances at the Assembly Rooms and these 'Rules for the Balls' make entertaining reading in the 21st century. The post lapsed around 1830.

MATERNITY HOMES The best remembered, apart from **Portwey Hospital**, was a maternity home run at No.10 Victoria Terrace (now No.142 The Esplanade), in conjunction with The Victoria Nursing Home at No.9. It probably went out of existence soon after Portwey opened as a maternity hospital in 1948. A temporary WW2 maternity hospital for evacuee expectant mothers was at Nos.13 and 13a, Greenhill.

MAYORS In the days when Weymouth and Melcombe were two separate towns, Melcombe elected a Mayor and Weymouth elected two Bailiffs, although their roles were basically the same. Melcombe's Mayors are known to date back to the 14th century, although there is no specific mention in any existing Charter of the town being granted any such right. Following the Union of 1571 one Mayor was elected to represent the whole borough and since then well over 400 mayors have been elected. From the 16th century Mayor choosing took place on St Matthew's Day, 21st September but on the passing of the Municipal Corporations Act in 1835 the mayor was elected in November – on the 9th unless that day was a Sunday. In 1948, on the passing of the Representation of the People Act, the date was changed to May. No Mayor was chosen on 9th November 1948, the election being held over until May 1949. The town's first woman mayor was Charlotte Wootton, in 1956-7. *See also* BAILIFF

Further reading : *The Borough of Weymouth and Portland : a mayoral history*, by Maureen Attwooll (D. Hollings, Weymouth, 2004)

MAYPOLE is traditionally thought to have stood at the junction of St Mary Street and Bond Street, and in 1989 the spot was marked by a plaque set in the roadway.

MEDHURST, James Antiquarian and Manufacturer of Tunbridge Ware. Mr Medhurst is credited with discovering the remains of the Roman Temple at Jordan Hill, Preston in 1843 and the tessellated pavement at Preston (now covered over) together with numerous other Roman artefacts. Many of his discoveries were displayed (and on sale!) in his Museum of Antiquities on the Esplanade. On his death the entire collection, some 200 'Archaeological and Ethnological Articles' was put up for sale by C.T.Jefferies & Sons, Bristol. *See also* TUNBRIDGE WARE

MEDIAEVAL WEYMOUTH AND MELCOMBE REGIS Very little remains of the mediaeval towns apart from the grid layout of the streets of the town centre on Melcombe side. Many old buildings would have been of timber construction, much prone to damage by fire and war.

MELBURY ROAD, Westham takes its name from Melbury Sampford, ancestral home of the Earls of Ilchester, once ground landlords of much of the land on which Westham is built.

MELCOMBE COMMON This is the land to the north of Melcombe Regis on which the houses of Greenhill (and Greenhill Gardens) Westerhall, Carlton Road, Kirtleton Avenue, Glendinning Avenue etc. stand. The ownership of this land was disputed as early as the 17th century when it was claimed by both Melcombe Regis and Radipole and in the 19th century when it was in the hands of the **Johnstone Estate** and alleged to be town property. *See* BOUNDARIES; CLARK'S HILL; WALLIS, Thomas Samuel

MELCOMBE HOUSE, King Street was demolished October 1963. It stood between Terminus Street and Upway Street. The name is now used for the building which was formerly the **Portland Railway Hotel** in King Street.

MELCOMBE PLACE which links Lennox Street and William Street is one of the few places in the town where the name 'Melcombe' can be seen. Another street, of more recent origin, is Melcombe Avenue.

MELCOMBE REGIS From its early foundation until the enforced Union with Weymouth on the south side of the harbour in 1571, Melcombe was a quite separate town on the north side of the harbour. Since 1571 the use of the word 'Weymouth' is usually taken to indicate the whole of the town. There are two schools of thought regarding the derivation of Melcombe's name. One suggests it is from the old words meoluc (milk) and cumb (valley), thus 'valley where milk was got', a fertile valley. An alternative derivation stems from mele, (a mill), and combe (a vale or flat). If so, this would be a very early reference to mills. Melcombe is not listed in Domesday, probably then such a small settlement it would have been included as part of Radipole. As 'Melecumbe' it is first found in the early 1100's when the port, with Weymouth, was granted by King Henry I to the Prior and Monks of St Swithun at Winchester. Its 'Regis' suffix denotes royal ownership and Melcombe came into the possession of Prince Edward (later King Edward I) in 1254 when it was given as a marriage gift to his bride, Eleanor of Castile. The use of the name 'Melcombe Regis' is first found in 1336. *See also* DISPUTES; HARBOUR; WEYMOUTH

MELCOMBE REGIS CEMETERY *see* CEMETERIES

MELCOMBE REGIS GARDENS date from the 1920s and are on infilled ground reclaimed from the Backwater. The bowling green pavilion is a replacement of an earlier building and tennis courts and a rose walk have been replaced by a car park.

Tennis in Melcombe Regis Gardens in the 1930s. The Gasworks buildings and Gasometer in the background have now disappeared from the scene (the current gasometer is a 1950s structure) as have the tall chimney and associated buildings of the electricity generating station. The tennis courts are the site of today's Melcombe Regis car park.

MELCOMBE REGIS SCHOOL There have been two schools with this name. The first, a private school, originally occupied what is now the Arts Centre Building in Commercial

Road during the mid-late 19th century. *See* Weymouth Middle School (its original name). Melcombe Regis School, a state school, occupied a site on the corner of Commercial Road and Westham Bridge. It opened in 1912 and closed in 1970, the buildings becoming home to Weymouth Museum from 1972 until 1989, when the Museum relocated to Brewer's Quay. The old school was then demolished and Weymouth Marina building now stands on the site.

Melcombe Regis School, Westham Road, after its conversion to Weymouth Museum. The Weymouth Marina building now stands on this site.

MELCOMBE REGIS STATION, on the Weymouth and Portland Railway. Opened in April, 1909, on a site opposite today's Bus Station. Prior to its construction, passengers had boarded the trains for Portland at Weymouth Railway Station. Melcombe Regis station remained in use as a relief platform after March 1952 when the Portland line closed to passengers. The buildings were demolished in 1966 and the last traces of its platforms disappeared in June 2000 when 'Swannery Court' housing was built on the site.

MELROSE VILLAS became Nos.100-102 Abbotsbury Road.

MEMBERS OF PARLIAMENT Weymouth, which once had 4 MPs, became part of the South Dorset Parliamentary Constituency in 1885. MPs since that date are:-1885-1886 Henry Sturgis (Liberal); 1886-1891 Colonel Hambro (Conservative); 1891-1906 Major Brymer (Conservative); 1906-1910 Tom Scarisbrick (Liberal); 1910-1922 Angus Hambro (Unionist); 1922-1929 Major Yerburgh (Conservative); 1929-1941 Viscount Cranborne (Conservative); 1941-1962 Viscount Hinchingbrooke (Conservative); 1962-1964 Guy Barnett (Labour); 1964-1974 Evelyn King (Conservative); 1974-1987 Viscount Cranborne (Conservative); 1987-2001 Ian Bruce (Conservative); 2001-to date Jim Knight (Labour).

METHODIST CHAPEL, Broadwey Erected in The Grove, 1838, closed in 1928 when the present church on Dorchester Road replaced it.

METHODIST CHAPEL, Caroline Place Opened 1869 as the United Free Methodist Chapel. Later used by the Salvation Army until the Citadel opened in Westham Road in 1903. The building then became the printing works for the *Weymouth Telegram.*

METHODIST CHAPEL, Derby Street Founded in 1871, the Wesleyan Methodists' chapel building opened in October 1902. Closed in 1980 and now used as the premises of a dance studio.

METHODIST CHAPEL Hope Square The congregation of Primitive Methodists first met in houses in the Hope Square area in the 1830s. In 1841 the chapel in Hope Square was built and it was used until 1876 when a new chapel was built in St Leonard's Road.

Melcombe Regis Station at the town end of the Backwater rail viaduct. The water shown here has long since been filled in and no trace of the station now remains – Swannery Court apartments stand on the site.

METHODIST CHAPEL, Lower Bond Street The Wesleyan Methodists had formerly met in the St Thomas Street Meeting House vacated by the Quakers. The Wesleyan chapel was built in 1805, becoming redundant in the 1860s when **Maiden Street Methodist Church** opened. Used in the twentieth century as a store by the local building firm of Webb, Major & Co. Ltd., it was demolished in 1975 to make way for a supermarket and multi-storey car park. (The supermarket has since been replaced by a multi-screen cinema).

METHODIST CHAPEL, Lynch Lane Opened 27th April 1968 and replaced a temporary building of 1949.

METHODIST CHAPEL, Maiden Street *See* MAIDEN STREET METHODIST CHURCH

METHODIST CHAPEL, Newstead Road Wesleyan Methodists established a mission in Westham in 1895 meeting in a room at the Rock Hotel. The chapel opened in November, 1902, and was bombed on the eve of Good Friday, 2nd April 1942, a particularly bad air raid on Weymouth with heavy casualties. The present Westham Methodist Church opened 16th April 1955 on the same site.

METHODIST CHAPEL, Preston Tiny chapel built in 1816 and no longer in use. (The grandfather of John Wesley lived at Manor Cottage, Preston.) *See also* WESLEY FAMILY

METHODIST CHAPEL, St Leonard's Road Built in 1876 for the Primitive Methodists. Damaged in WW2. Remained in use until 1966 when it was sold and rebuilt as private houses.

METHODIST CHAPEL, Church Street, Upwey Erected in Church Street in 1809 for 'Dissenting Protestants' it was known as the Independent Chapel and was later used by the Primitive Methodists. It closed around 1932 and is now converted to a house.

METHODIST CHAPEL, Wyke Regis The Wesleyan Chapel opened in Collins Lane in 1842 and was converted to a bakery after being replaced by the Portland Road Chapel in 1903.

METHODIST CHAPEL, Wyke Regis The Primitive Methodists chapel opened in Gallwey Road in 1900. Following the amalgamation of the Wesleyan and Primitive Methodists in 1932, services were concentrated on the Portland Road chapel.

METHODIST CHAPEL, Wyke Regis The Wesleyan chapel on Portland Road opened in 1903 and replaced the chapel in Collins Lane.

MICO, Sir Samuel A wealthy and important 17th century London merchant and shipowner who found Weymouth a good port for his extensive import and export business. His premises on the Quay later became the George Inn (not the present Inn, which was built to replace it in 1885). Mico was knighted in 1645 and died in 1665. In his will he did not forget the part Weymouth had played in his fortunes and he left his house (the George) on the Quay to provide for the apprenticeships of 'three poor children yearly' and a sum of £500 to invest in land at Osmington. Once a year, the profits from this were to pay 20 shillings to 'some good divine' to preach a sermon at St Mary's Church on the Friday before Palm Sunday. The balance was to be distributed on that day to 'ten poor decayed seamen of the age of three score years and upwards'- with the proviso that they must, if able, attend the sermon, along with the apprentices. More than 300 years on, the trust set up to administer the Mico Charity still distributes annually the income from investments.

MICO CHARITY see MICO, Sir Samuel

MIDDLE SCHOOL *see* WEYMOUTH MIDDLE SCHOOL

MIDDLETON CHARITY In the late-16th century Robert Middleton gave £100 to be lent to young merchants from time to time to assist their business. The young merchants however, were apt to give the trustees the slip and by the mid-19th century only £25 remained! The interest on it went to the poor.

MIGHTY HOOD was the name of the Rodwell Hotel for some years in the 1980s.

MILITARY AND VETERANS FESTIVAL has been held annually in June at Weymouth since 1996.

MILITARY ARMS PUBLIC HOUSE, Barrack Road was taken over by the Royal Naval Association in 1973 as the Anchor Club, which closed in 1987.

MILLENNIUM STONE commemorates the opening of Weymouth's New Bond Street shopping centre on 25th May 2000 – it is set in the paving outside Debenhams store.

MILLER, Glenn Controversy has always surrounded the disappearance of Glenn Miller on an air journey in 1944 and similar controversy surrounds an appearance in Weymouth - although there is no documentation of the event, many say he played with the Glenn Miller Orchestra here during WW2.

MILLS, E. Nurseryman and florist. It was on the site of his gardens at Westham that **St Joseph's RC Church** was built.

MILLS Two windmills are known to have existed in Melcombe Regis in the 17th century. One stood on open ground close to the site of the present Gloucester Lodge. There was at least one early windmill in Weymouth, possibly on the **Springfield** site. *See also* BROADWEY MILL; NOTTINGTON MILL; PRESTON MILL; RADIPOLE MILLS (2); SUTTON MILL, SUTTON POYNTZ; UPPER MILL, SUTTON POYNTZ; UPWEY MILL (all watermills)

MILN(E)THORPE AVENUE/ROAD in the 1920s was the stretch of road from Ullswater Crescent to Radipole Park Drive and it became part of Radipole Park Drive in the early 1930s.

MILTON ARMS, St Alban Street A former inn sometimes known as Milton House. A building of late 16th or early 17th century date, it was restored in 1980.

MILTON TERRACE There have been three terraces with this name – in Milton Road, Salisbury Road (south west side) and Dorchester Road (between Nos. 179 and 181)

MINIATURE RAILWAY, Westham Coach Park Opened 1947, dismantled 1982.

MINSON'S COURT, St Thomas Street appears to have been between Nos.6 and 7 St Thomas Street. It is presumably the same as Minsing/Mincing Court.

MINT It is believed that a Royalist mint was in operation at Sandsfoot Castle in the English Civil War, during the period August 1643 to June 1644.

MISS DORSET speed boat for pleasure trips in the Bay, arrived 1929.

MISS WEYMOUTH speed boat for pleasure trips in the Bay, arrived 1929.

MISS WEYMOUTH BEAUTY CONTEST was first held in 1947 and won by Miss Betty Roffe (although Nancy Crewe in 1934 seems to have been an unofficial 'Miss Weymouth' when she wore a costume borrowed from a London pantomime in which an actress portrayed 'Miss Weymouth'). The contest has not been held since 1980.

MISS WORLD Winner in November 1965 was Lesley Langley (Lesley Hill) of Preston, Weymouth. The town held a civic reception for her on 27th January 1966. (Miss World 1964 was another Dorset girl, Ann Sidney, from Poole).

MITCHELL CHARITY Bernard Mitchell by will dated 1646 left money for the distribution of coal to six poor widows in Melcombe Regis.

MITCHELL STREET dates from 1873 and stands on the site of the old **Friary** buildings. In the 16th century the 'Michells' were leading merchants in the town with premises in the East Street/ Helen Lane area, so this may have influenced the choice of name.

MIXED BATHING was not permitted in Weymouth until the early 1900s. It was definitely allowed by 1908 when the Weymouth press was commenting on the fuss being made at other resorts who were trying to introduce it.

MIXEN, The The Mixen rocks are off the Nothe.

MOGG, Ronald P.L. Born in Weymouth. Worked for the Dorset Daily Echo. His first book of poems *'For This Alone'*, written in a German prisoner of war camp in 1943 was published in 1944 and reprinted in 1945.

MONMOUTH REBELLION All the action took place further west and Weymouth had no direct involvement in the attempt by the Duke of Monmouth (illegitimate son of King Charles II) and his supporters to retake the English throne in 1685. However, there were grim reminders in the town of the severe sentences meted out by the notorious Judge Jeffreys at Dorchester's 'Bloody Assizes'.The Mayor was ordered to erect a gallows at Greenhill where twelve rebels were executed and their grisly remains had to be displayed for all to see. In the borough *'six quarters and one head at the grand pier, two quarters at Weymouth town's end, four quarters and one head near the windmill; two quarters at Weymouth town hall; one quarter and two heads on the bridge; one quarter and two heads at Melcomb town hall'*. Those lucky enough to escape with their lives were sentenced to years of slavery on the sugar plantations of Jamaica and Barbados and two of the overcrowded vessels carrying them sailed out of Weymouth in 1685. These were the *Betty* and the *Happy Return*. *See also* WISEMAN, William

MOONFLEET *see* FALKNER, John Meade

MOORHEAD, Paul Ex-Weymouth Grammar School pupil won the Digital Schneider Trophy air race in June 1984.

MORGAN, Ffloyd (correctly, MORGAN, Thomas Lloyd) In St Mary's Church, there is a headstone, reset as paving in the nave, which bears the following inscription:-
This stone was erected in remembrance of the cruel murder committed on the body of Ffloyd Morgan (who lies here) on the 27th April 1792 aged 22
Here mingling with my fellow clay,
I wait the awful judgement day:
And there my murdrers shall appear
Although escaped from justice here
Poor Thomas Lloyd Morgan, an engraver from Herefordshire, who was found dead on the Town Bridge at Weymouth. He was supposed, according to the local paper, *'to have spent the preceding night in a house of ill fame and to have met with his death there'*. The coroner recorded a verdict of *'Wilful murder by some person or persons unknown'*. Two men and two women were arrested and charged with murder, but were acquitted despite one of their number turning King's Evidence against her supposed accomplices. Who paid for this memorial stone- and felt so strongly that the guilty had escaped?

MORRIS, Eric (died 1964) Artist and Sculptor. Sculpted the Wyverns at the entrance to County Hall, Dorchester, the massive Portland stone figures 'Erst' and 'Forthward' over the main entrance to Winfrith Atomic Energy Research Establishment and his work can also be found in Dorset schools and churches. He painted the King's Statue in heraldic colours for the first time in 1949. Lived at Sutton Poyntz and took an active interest in the village, especially the moves in the 1950s to restore the then tumbledown cottages beside the duck pond.

MOSELEY, Henry Gwyn Jeffreys (1887-1915) Born in Weymouth. Famous for his pioneering research in nuclear physics and for his discovery of atomic numbers. Published papers in scientific journals and seemed destined to become one of the country's most eminent scientists, but he was killed, aged 27, at Gallipoli in 1915. Moseley has a crater on the far side of the moon named after him.

MOTOR RACING Dorset Automobile Club's annual race meeting and speed trials on Weymouth sands took place for a few years prior to WW1 – 1914 was the last occasion. As well as the cars (a feast of names- Bugatti, Hispano-Suiza, Berliet and Sunbeam among others) there were also motor cycle races.

MOUNT PLEASANT FARM The 117-acre farm has long since disappeared. On its site off the Dorchester Road now stands Morrison's supermarket and Mercery Road, originally the New Look store's distribution depot.

MOUNTBATTEN, Lord Louis and Lady Edwina Were in Weymouth at the end of March 1957 – he was at sea in HMS *Salisbury*, she visited various naval and civilian organisations including the St John Ambulance Brigade. He was also here in 1958 as First Sea Lord, addressing scientific workers at the Admiralty, Portland.

MULBERRY HARBOURS Today, two huge concrete structures can be seen in Portland Harbour. They are more than 200' long and weigh over 7½ thousand tons apiece. Dating from WW2 they are 'Phoenix Caissons', specially designed prefabricated components which were towed across the Channel in 1944 and then sunk to provide temporary 'Mulberry Harbours' for the British and American troops who landed on the French beaches on D-Day. During the following weeks, although the US Mulberry Harbour was badly damaged in storms, the British Mulberry served its purpose well, enabling troops, vehicles and supplies to be landed successfully. After the war, the Royal Navy required extra berthing facilities at Portland and eight of these huge Phoenix units were put in place to provide additional shelter within the harbour. Following devastating floods in Holland in 1953, six of them were released to provide sea defences for the Dutch. The two that remain at Portland (the only ones left in the UK) have listed building status due to their historic role in the Allied invasion. There is some doubt as to whether these units were actually brought back from France but they were certainly built for the invasion force.

The massive Phoenix caissons of the WW2 Mulberry Harbours which were towed across the Channel on D-Day to form temporary harbours on the French coast.

MULBERRY TERRACE included Mulberry Cottage and was once a terrace of houses off School Street, but these were demolished in the 1980s prior to the redevelopment of the New Bond Street area. Today this is a pedestrian way linking School Street and Commercial Road.

MULTI-STOREY CAR PARK Weymouth's only multi-storey car park in Commercial Road was completed in 1978.

MUNDY, Peter Travelled in Dorset in 1635 and described snails falling from the skies like rain:- *'When I came over to Weymouth side, I found there on the grass a multitude of small coulord shell snailes, ½ as bigg as pease. The people report they dropp out of the Ayre, finding them on their hatts as they walke the fields. The like is reported of the raineing of small froggs on the Isle of Jersey (where I had formerly bene)'* He also described the lobster boats which brought lobsters from Cornwall to Weymouth – 100 dozen on a boat, arriving at Weymouth in 48 hours for onward road travel to London where *'they are near one third part dead on arrival and sell at low prices'.*

MUNICIPAL OFFICES The local government of the joint borough was originally administered from the Guildhall. In October 1904 it transferred to the former **Weymouth Sanatorium** in Clarence Buildings until new buildings on North Quay were opened by Princess Anne on 1st June 1971 as part of the Quatercentenary celebrations of the 400th anniversary of the Union of Weymouth and Melcombe Regis.

MUNTZ, Elizabeth (1894-1977) Sculptor. Canadian-born. Lived and worked at Chaldon Herring from 1938. Examples of her work can be found in the Weymouth area and include carved decorative panels at Wey Valley School.

MURDER (up to the early 20th century) *see* PARMITER, Robert stabbed in an alehouse row in 1619; CHILES, John & Mary Alleged murderers, unproven, 1645; WILLIAMS, Winston murdered August 1701; MORGAN, Ffloyd (John Lloyd Morgan) murdered 1792; KNIGHT, Thomas murdered 1832; PUCKETT, Dr Adam Stapleton murdered 1862; LANE, Harriet murdered in London 1875; STEPHENS, Hettie murdered 1902

MUSEUM *see* WEYMOUTH MUSEUM

MUSEUM OF COASTAL DEFENCE *see* NOTHE FORT

MUSEUM OF WATER SUPPLY *see* WATER SUPPLY

MUSIC HALL *see* THEATRE ROYAL, St Nicholas Street

MUSIC HALL TAVERN was at No.12 St Nicholas Street in the 1890s and was also known as The New Concert Hall.

MYRTLE COTTAGE became No.118 Abbotsbury Road

MYRTLE COTTAGES are part of Marsh Road.

MYRTLE TERRACE is now Nos.1-27 Marsh Road

MYRTLE VILLA became No.24 Lennox Street

MYRTLE VILLAS became Nos.15-16, Milton Road

NAG'S HEAD INN is now No.3 New Street.

NANGLE, Henry (1834-1896) of Radipole House. Came to Weymouth in 1872 when he was appointed as Sir Frederic Johnstone's agent in the town, a post he held until his death in November 1896. 'Nangle's Farm', the old farmhouse now within the Weymouth College housing development off Dorchester Road, presumably has some link with him as this was a Johnstone Estate property.

NAPLOCK'S CORNER/KNAPLOCK'S CORNER is a lost Melcombe place name. It was the extreme southwest corner of Lower St Edmund Street.

NARROWS, The This was the area north of today's King's Statue where the sandspit on which the town of Melcombe was built narrowed sharply and became a thin strip of land between the sea and the Backwater, widening out again at Greenhill. Across The Narrows in rough weather sea and backwater frequently joined forces. In 1770 the builder of the first Royal Hotel proposed that he should take a lease on part of the Narrows *'commonly called the Town's End'* for a hotel. The largest infill on the western side of The Narrows began in 1834 when land was reclaimed for a proposed public park, which never materialised. Instead, part of the reclaimed land was used for railway lines and station and the rest was filled with the houses of the **Park District**.

NATIONAL SCHOOLS were Church of England schools. The name derives from the National Society for the Education of the Poor in the Principles of the Established Church, founded in 1811.

***NAUTILUS,* USS** The world's first nuclear powered submarine arrived at Portland 12th August 1958, her first port of call since leaving Pearl Harbour on 23rd July, after a pioneering sea passage under the North Pole ice cap. The crew were given a civic reception at Weymouth.

NAVY TAVERN *see* OLD ROOMS, Trinity Street

NELSON WHARF, Nothe Parade occupies the site of the former **Ayles Family** shipyard.

NETHERBURY ARMS was the former name of the Belvedere Inn, High West Street.

NETHERTON HOUSE, Rodwell Road was built c.1720 and is sometimes called Weymouth Old Manor House. From 1766 it was leased to Taylor Penny, mayor in 1773 and 1785. On his death in 1786 it appears to have remained in the family until 1863 when it became the property of Sir Frederic Johnstone. For a short time in the 1880s it served as Holy Trinity vicarage and in the early 1900s the Misses Tizard ran Netherton House School, until moving in 1910 to Enderby School, 10 Clarence Buildings. After 20th century use as The Netherton Hotel, Netherton House opened as a nursing home in 1990, but this has since closed and the house has reverted to private accommodation. *See also* SNOOK, Dr Samuel Penny-.

Netherton House at Boot Hill's junction with Chickerell Road. Houses now fill the site beyond the house where the old wall stood.

NEW ARRIVAL PUBLIC HOUSE was in Park Street in 1870 but it is unclear where.

NEW BOND STREET was the eventual plan adopted for a new town centre shopping complex, after several developers had put forward plans and then pulled out. The Jubilee Hall was demolished in 1989 in anticipation of a new development but it was 1998 before boarded-up shops in Lower Bond Street were removed and work commenced. The developers were the Shearer Property Group and Hill Samuel. The scheme brought Debenhams and Woolworths back into the town plus other popular shops and the Cineworld (formerly Multiplex) cinema around a 'square' which includes the ancient White Hart Inn and provides a blend of old and new. Outside Debenhams is the Millennium Stone, set into the walkway, which commemorates New Bond Street's official opening on 25th May 2000.

NEW BRIDGE HOTEL/PUBLIC HOUSE, Commercial Road Stood on the corner of Westham Road, opposite Westham Bridge. Demolished in 2003 and replaced by an apartment block with shops at ground floor level.

NEW CONCERT HALL PUB *see* MUSIC HALL TAVERN

NEW COOPER'S ARMS *see* COOPER'S ARMS

NEW COURT was a terrace of houses between Nos.14 and 15 West Street.

NEW ROOMS, Cove Row was built around 1840 as the New Rooms Inn but is currently in use as a coffee house.

NEWBERRY ROAD Each side of the street had its own name at one time – the east side was known as Newberry Terrace and the west side as Dorset Place. The whole street is now numbered as Newberry Road.

NEWBERRY TERRACE *see* NEWBERRY ROAD

NEWFOUNDLAND TRADE Weymouth vessels probably began sailing to the Newfoundland cod fishing grounds in the late 16th century, taking out mixed cargoes and returning with salted cod, train oil and other products such as furs and skins. The voyages were long and hazardous but many Newfoundland traders prospered. For Weymouth the most profitable period of the Newfoundland trade was in the first half of the 17th century, before the Civil War. The trade revived in the early 1700s, the town fitting up twenty ships for Newfoundland in 1711 and eighty in 1732, although this must have been an exceptional year. Poole was the main port for the Newfoundland trade.

NEWSPAPERS The earliest local newspaper is the *Sherborne Mercury and Western Flying Post* which first appeared in 1736 and went on to become today's Western Gazette. In the eighteenth century the *Mercury* was more of a national newspaper, with local news usually reported briefly, if at all. The *Dorset County Chronicle*, published in Dorchester from 1821 is a useful source, but it was 1851 when publication of the *Southern Times* commenced in Weymouth that local news really came into its own. Its pages are packed with detail and a joy to read. Other weeklies were published in the late 19th and early 20th centuries but the *Southern Times* had the longest run, publication ceasing in 1963. Publication of the town's current daily newspaper, the Dorset Echo, began in 1921.

NEWSTEAD ROAD In the days when there was little on the western shore of the Backwater apart from the gasworks, Newstead Road was known as Gas House Lane. Parts of it were also referred to as Portland Road and Cemetery Road. The decision to call the whole section from the gasworks to Goldcroft Farm 'Newstead Road' was taken early in 1904. The road was once crossed by the overbridge of the Weymouth and Portland Railway but this was taken down at the beginning of 1987.

NEWSTEAD VILLAS became Nos.93-101 Newstead Road.

NEWTON'S COVE In the early 18th century Robert Newton was a brewer in this area, with lands on the south side of Hope Street so it is possible he gave his name to Newton's Cove. The GWR proposed building a port here in the 1890s and some preliminary work was carried out, including the building of a wooden bridge over Newton's Road (replaced by the present concrete one in 1934) and the naming of a pub – the Railway Dock Hotel – in anticipation of the scheme proceeding. Newton's Road was also known as Dock Road. The whole GWR port idea was eventually abandoned in 1913. Landslips have always been a problem in the Newton's Cove/Nothe Gardens area and impressive sea defence works were completed in August 2003. *See also* HOVERCRAFT; RAILWAY DOCK HOTEL

NEWTOWN PLACE became Nos.69-73 Franchise Street. Bombed during WW2. The entire area was cleared and redeveloped.

NICHOLAS STREET *see* ST NICHOLAS STREET

NIGHTINGALE COURT on the corner of Hardwick Street and Victoria Street was built on the site of **Tilley's Garage** in 1984.

NILE, Battle of the News of Nelson's victory over the French at Aboukir Bay on 1st August 1798 was brought to King George III at Weymouth where great celebrations took place.

'NINETEENTH, THE' *see* EMBASSY HOTEL

NIXON, John (1760-1818) Artist. Frequent exhibitor at the Royal Academy 1784-1815. Produced a number of views of Weymouth and its surroundings and 'Royal Dipping', the famous cartoon of King George III's first bathe in the sea at Weymouth in 1789 is attributed to him.

NOAH'S ARK A non-floating ark built on a concrete base in Radipole Lake was designed as an aquarium and opened on 25th May 1966. It is currently a restaurant.

NON-CONFORMITY Weymouth has a long tradition of non-conformist religion. Dissenters, those who did not conform to the beliefs of the established Anglican church in the 17th century, were numerous in Weymouth. They met in private houses and were frequently persecuted. The real history of non-conformity in this area dates from the expulsion of the Reverend George Thorne on the passing of the Act of Uniformity in 1662, he being one of some two thousand ministers ejected from their livings for refusing to use the Book of Common Prayer as ordered by the Act. George Thorne is the best known of those persecuted but among many others were Edward Dammer of Wyke, John Light and John Wesley (grandfather of John Wesley, the founder of Methodism) of Preston and Sutton Poyntz. There was trouble in Weymouth in 1664 when the anniversary of the death of King Charles I was ordered to be kept as a solemn religious occasion but non-conformists refused to observe it. They opened their businesses as usual and troops were called in to close the shops. The 1672 Declaration of Indulgence granted religious liberty to Romanists and Dissenters and Thorne returned but in 1673 persecution began again and non-conformist ministers had to conduct meetings in secret until the Act of Toleration in 1689. *See also* CONGREGATIONAL CHURCH, West Street; THORNE, Reverend George

NORTH COUNTRY SAILOR PUBLIC HOUSE was in Maiden Street

NORTH QUAY The old houses of North Quay once directly overlooked the harbour, separated from the water by only a pathway until 1840 when a new quay wall was built, allowing a road to be built in front of them, with further improvements in 1871 and 1883. The naming of North Quay is often considered to be illogical, but this is the north-facing shore of the old town of Weymouth. The names 'West Quay' and 'South Quay' were already in use for the quays on the Melcombe side of the harbour although these were later to be known as Custom House Quay. Maps are not always accurate- Pierce Arthur's town map of 1857 names North Quay as West Quay, with a North Quay (actually West Quay) in Melcombe. Buildings on North Quay and in High Street were demolished in 1961 and 1965. Among those to go was the **Tudor House, No.4 North Quay**. In their place was built the present Municipal Offices, opened in 1971.

NOTHE The name is usually taken to mean 'North' although 'Nose' is also suggested. Halfway along the stretch of quayside between the Nothe Steps and the Stone Pier can be found a flight of steps leading up to the top of the Nothe, with railway lines mounted on the sides. These were used to take stores and ammunition up to the **Nothe Fort**, after they had been unloaded at a small jetty opposite their base, which was removed in the 1930s.

NOTHE FORT The fort was built between 1860 and 1872 on its commanding site overlooking the waters of Weymouth and Portland. This had long been a traditional site for a gun emplacement (*see* FORTS). The Nothe Fort was part of a series of defences to protect the south coast from possible attack at a time when the French were displaying aggressive tendencies by strengthening their Navy and fortifying the port of Cherbourg almost opposite Weymouth across the English Channel. The local defence scheme also included the building of the two breakwaters extending out from Portland for the protection of shipping in Portland Roads, the Verne Citadel and various gun batteries at Portland. Manned in both World Wars, the Nothe fort was used by the military until 1956 and it was sold to the Borough Council in 1961. No immediate use was found for it and the buildings fell prey to vandals until 1979 when Weymouth Civic Society undertook to restore the site and open it to the public. Today the Nothe Fort is a premier tourist attraction and houses the Museum of Coastal Defence.

NOTHE GARDENS were first laid out in 1889. Around the perimeter is the Jubilee Walk (Queen Victoria's Golden Jubilee 1887). In the gardens are Elizabethan Way (Queen Elizabeth II's Silver Jubilee 1977) and the Royal Wedding Cascade (Wedding of Prince and Princess of Wales, 1982). Parts of the sea wall were demolished over time by landslips, one of which, in January, 1988 destroyed a WW2 pillbox. *See also* NEWTON'S COVE

NOTHE PARADE *see* HOPE QUAY

NOTTINGTON The derivation of the place name is uncertain. 'tun' (ton) is an Old English word for farm and it is thought that this could refer to 'Hnott's Farm'. The place name is first recorded in the 12th century.

NOTTINGTON COURT *see* NOTTINGTON HOUSE

NOTTINGTON HOUSE, Nottington Lane was built in 1817 for Richard Tucker Steward and it remained in the family until about 1930, when it was sold. In 1941, during WW2 it became an Anti-Aircraft Gun Operations Centre with responsibility for the west of the county. After the war the huts which had been erected in the grounds for the use of the military were taken over to provide much needed accommodation and they housed local families until the early 1960s. Nottington House was demolished in 1967. Flats built in the grounds close to the old house's site are known as Nottington Court.

NOTTINGTON MILL The watermill has been converted to a private dwelling known as 'The Old Mill House'.

NOTTINGTON SPA The foundation stone of the octagonal spa building, designed by local man **Robert Vining,** was laid in April 1830, although the health giving spring had been discovered more than a century before. The sulphurous water smells revolting but is very pure and it is said that if you drink the Nottington water you will never grow old! For those unable to afford to stay at the spa, this water with its healing properties could be bought and consumed off the premises. It was claimed to cure every condition from ringworm and rheumatism to chronic gout and nervous affectations, all for two pence a pint! The spa must have gone out of use by 1876 as by that date a hand laundry was being run there. For much of the 20th century the Gordon-Steward family owned the Spa, but it was sold in the 1960s and has had several owners since.

NUNEHAM TERRACE became Nos.50-54 Ranelagh Road.

The Nothe Gardens in the 1940s. The Bandstand was removed in 1964.

The octagonal spa building at Nottington. A view from around 1910.

OAKLEY PLACE The original Oakley Place, which ran between St Leonard's Road and Rodwell Avenue, no longer exists. It was badly hit during WW2 air raids and all the houses were later demolished as part of the Chapelhay rebuilding programme. The present Oakley Place, a cul-de-sac, was built in the 1950s.

OCEAN COURT is a housing development at Overcombe Corner which features a 'lighthouse tower' and was built in 2003.

ODEON CINEMA, Gloucester Street was built on the site of Spivey's Garage, motor coach proprietors. In the late-18th/early-19th century this had been the stable block belonging to the royal residence, Gloucester Lodge. A window from the Georgian era still exists and has been incorporated into the 'Gloucester Mews' apartments built here in 2005. The Odeon opened on 2nd June 1933 (Odeon standing for '**O**scar **D**eutsch **E**ntertains **O**ur **N**ation'). It changed its name in December 1967 to the Classic Cinema, in 1985 to the Cannon and in 1994 to The Picturedrome, before finally closing at the end of October 1999.

ODEON CINEMA, St Thomas Street *see* JUBILEE HALL

OLD BOROUGH ARMS, Chickerell Road was built in 1897 and closed as a pub in 1978. It is now the HQ of the local Moose Lodge.

OLD BRIDGE INN/BRIDGE INN was in **Bridge Buildings** at the Town Bridge.

OLD CASTLE PUBLIC HOUSE, Sudan Road was built in 1926, a Crickmay design. Takes its name from the nearby **Sandsfoot Castle**.

OLD COOPERS ARMS *see* COOPER'S ARMS

OLD MANOR HOUSE, Melcombe Regis is believed to have been in St Thomas Street.

OLD MANOR HOUSE, Weymouth *see* NETHERTON HOUSE

OLD PARISH LANE for most of its length follows the line of the borough boundary as extended in 1895 to include Westham. At one time the part of the street which runs from Cromwell Road to Abbotsbury Road was known as Parish Lane.

OLD RECTORY, Nos.81 and 82, St Thomas Street Now a wine bar, this building (actually a pair of fine late-18th century houses) was set back from the street and concealed for most of the twentieth century by shops constructed in front of it. These were removed in the 1980s and by 1999 the houses had been magnificently restored. No.82 was at one time the rectory of St Mary's Church, but in Victorian times the wealthy Rector chose not to live there, building for himself a mansion out of town called Portmore. The rectory was then occupied in the 1870s by St Mary's curate, Thomas Falkner, father of John Meade Falkner whose famous novel *Moonfleet* is a tale of shipwreck and smuggling on the Dorset coast. No.81 was the home in the 1870s and 1880s of another well-known local family when architect George Crickmay lived there. The Old Rectory wine bar was renamed The Barracuda Bar in the summer of 2006.

OLD ROOMS, Trinity Street This 17th century house is believed to have been built for merchant Thomas Giear, mayor in the 1600s and one of the town's influential citizens. Having later become the Navy Tavern, it was converted to become the resort's first Assembly Rooms and by 1768 a large extension had been added to the original building to accommodate the growing social scene (this is now the 'Old Rooms Inn'). When new 'Rooms' opened on the Esplanade, those in Trinity Street fell into disuse and by 1785 were known as the 'Old Rooms'. In the twentieth century, after use by a local undertaker, brewers Devenish & Co. took the building over as offices.

OLD ROOMS INN now occupies the extension to the original **Old Rooms**.

OLD TOWN HALL, High Street The Old Town Hall was the building from where the local government of Weymouth was administered prior to its Union with Melcombe Regis in 1571. Just how much of the original building remains is uncertain, as it was extensively rebuilt in the 1770s and altered again in 1896. It has had a variety of uses over the years, as stables, polling station, school and HQ of the local Girl Guides. A building adjoining the rear of the Old Town Hall was of Tudor date, but in 1875 it was pulled down to provide a site for the **Good Templars Hall** (later becoming the **Coffee Tavern** and now Kingdom Hall, the meeting place of the Jehovah's Witnesses). In 2006 the Old Town Hall lies empty, damp and decaying, and no-one seems to know what its fate will be.

OLDMEADOW, Katherine L. Author. Not Weymouth-born but she set her 1934 children's novel *When George III was King* in Weymouth.

OLIVER, Vere Langford (1861-1942) Noted local historian and Mayor 1921-22. Lived at **Greenhill House.**

OLMIUS, John (1711-1762) A most intriguing figure in Weymouth's history. A wealthy London merchant of Dutch origin, he purchased a large amount of property in Weymouth to ensure a seat in Parliament, representing the town from 1737-41 and 1761-62. His main aim seems to have been to secure an English peerage, but he failed and only close the end of his life was he granted an Irish title, becoming Baron Waltham of Phillipstown. His son Drigue Billiers Olmius, Baron Waltham, was MP for Weymouth from 1768-1774. The family seat was at New Hall, Boreham, Essex and Drigue Olmius gave up his interest in Weymouth in 1774 and stood instead for an Essex constituency. He sold all his Weymouth property to **William Chafin Grove** and this eventually became the nucleus of the **Johnstone Estate.**

OLYMPICS 2012 It was announced in July 2005 that Weymouth and Portland will host the sailing events of the 2012 London Olympics. Weymouth and Portland sailors were medallists in the 2004 Athens Olympics:- Sarah Ayton (gold), Nick Dempsey (bronze), Simon Hiscocks (bronze) and Chris Draper (bronze).

OPERA HOUSE, Derby Street was built in 2004. Photographers Photomasters previously occupied the site.

'ORANGE ROUTE' *see* RELIEF ROAD

OSBOURNE TERRACE became Nos.26-35 Brownlow Street

***OSPREY,* HMS** Granted the Freedom of the Borough in March 1979.

OVERCOMBE 20 acres of land known as Overcombe Golf Links between the Embassy Hotel (today's Spyglass) and Bowleaze was presented to the town for use as a public open space in September 1955 by Mr and Mrs A.J. Mayne.

OVERCOMBE COURT was built in 1965.

OVERCOMBE LANDSLIPS Frequent landslips at Furzy Cliff, Overcombe in the 1960s and 1970s brought the cliff edge too close to six former coastguard cottages which stood here and they were reduced to two. Extensive reinforcement work was undertaken in the 1982-84 to stop the erosion at this spot.

OVERDALE TERRACE became Nos.14-22 Holly Road.

OXFORD TERRACE became Nos.120-130 Abbotsbury Road. Another of the same name became Nos.60-65 Walpole Street.

OYSTER FESTIVAL is an annual event, first held in July 2001.

Granting the Freedom of the Borough to the Captain, officers and ship's company of HMS *Osprey in 1979. Weymouth and Portland's Mayor that year was Jessie Fry.*

Paddle Steamers

P

PADDLE STEAMERS The paddle steamer fleet of Cosens & Co. provided pleasure trips for countless thousands of holiday makers and locals from the mid-19th century until 1967 when the last paddler, the *Embassy,* left the port. They also served as liberty boats in the days when sailors of the Royal Navy thronged the town on shore leave, went on war service in WW2 and acted as salvage vessels when ships were in trouble in local waters. Too many to list by name here, their history and that of the company is documented in a two-volume work by Richard Clammer.

Further reading : *Cosens of Weymouth 1848-1918* by Richard Clammer (Black Dwarf Publications, 2005) and *Cosens of Weymouth 1918-1996* by Richard Clammer (Twelveheads Press, 2001).

PADGETT, F.W. of Padgett's Pottery. *See* BRICKYARDS

PALLADIUM CINEMA, Town Bridge Opened in July 1912, in premises which were a major rebuild of the former Town Bridge furnishing stores of **Hawkes, Freeman, Ltd.**, the company having moved to bigger shop in St Thomas Street. The Palladium closed in January 1931 and was converted to a butcher's shop in 1933 by Dan Lawrence. The building saw WW2 use as a Forces Club and from the 1940s-1960s was Pankhurst's Motor Cycle Showrooms. Latterly a nightclub and pub which has undergone several name changes, currently 'The Rendezvous'.

PANSY TERRACE became the east side of Prospect Place, Chapelhay.

PARAGON BUILDINGS became Nos.1-4 St Alban Street.

PARISH CHURCH, MELCOMBE REGIS *see* ST MARY'S CHURCH

PARISH CHURCH, WEYMOUTH *see* HOLY TRINITY CHURCH

PARISH LANE *see* OLD PARISH LANE

PARK COTTAGES became Nos.39-40 Hardwick Street

PARK DISTRICT The decision to reclaim a large area of marshland from the Backwater resulted in the laying of the foundation stone of the Park Wall on 4th June 1834. Difficulties early on resulted in the wall having to be raised two feet as it was not high enough to prevent the Backwater overflowing. On the infilled land a fashionable park with walks and drives and two handsome entrance lodges was to be laid out, but the Royal Victoria Park never materialised and the land was let out for grazing. Within a few years the park became the subject of a financial scandal when details of its planned sale became public knowledge and proved that certain of the town's civic leaders were hoping to buy the land for a ridiculously low price and line their own pockets from the profits of any future development or re-sale. Luckily, one councillor not involved in the 'plot' realised what was going on and alerted the ratepayers to full awareness of what was happening. After much publicity and the commencement of a suit in chancery the sale was stopped and the land was eventually sold for £5,000. After the GWR and LSWR opened the line to Weymouth in 1857 on the Park land, the Conservative Land Society purchased the rest of it in 1858 for housing, the first house of the 'Park District' going up in 1861. The Society named many of the streets after Tory politicians of the time.

In 1834 the foundation stone of the Park Wall was laid. The crowd which has gathered to witness the event stands on Black Rock (at the end of today's Cassiobury Road) and all the water shown in the foreground has since been infilled.

PARK MALT HOUSE public house was in Park Street.

PARK STREET should have led to a grand public park, which was never built (*See* PARK DISTRICT). South of its junction with Gloucester Street, Park Street was known as West Parade until the mid-1930s.

PARK TAVERN stood at the junction of Carlton Road South and Dorchester Road. Not to be confused with the later Park Hotel in Grange Road.

PARK TERRACE became Nos.1-4 Melcombe Place.

PARK VILLA became No.25 Lennox Street.

PARK VILLAS, Alexandra Road were part of **Radipole Barracks** and have been demolished.

PARLIAMENTARY REPRESENTATION From 1571 until 1832, apart from a short time during the Commonwealth when the town had just one MP, the Borough of Weymouth and Melcombe Regis was entitled to send 4 representatives to Parliament, a privilege possessed by no other town except London. This anomaly dated back to the early 14th century, when, as two separate boroughs, Weymouth and Melcombe Regis elected 2 MPs each. When the towns were forced to unite and become one borough by Act of Parliament in 1571, no adjustment was made to their parliamentary representation. This made the town a very attractive vote-catching proposition and its elections much prone to illegal vote rigging. Only on the passing of the 1832 Reform Act was the borough deprived of two of its four MPs and when the Redistribution Act became law in 1885, Weymouth lost both its Members, the borough becoming part of the electoral division of South Dorset. *See also* ELECTIONS, PARLIAMENTARY; MEMBERS OF PARLIAMENT

'PARLIAMENTARY ROAD' This was the popular name for a road planned in the late 1920s which was to run along the western shore of Radipole Lake from Westham to Radipole. It was part of a plan to reclaim a large area of the Lake and develop it with leisure facilities. An Act of Parliament sanctioned the road in 1935 and during the years it was talked about but never built, it became known as the 'Parliamentary Road'. WW2 and post-war economies put an end to the original plans. 'Weymouth Way' along the Lake's western shore opened in 1987, deviating slightly from the route of the road planned more than 50 years before. *See also* RADIPOLE LAKE.

PASSAGE HOUSE Before the first Ferrybridge was built to cross Smallmouth in 1839, a tethered ferryboat took foot passengers across to Portland from Wyke Regis. They waited in a shelter on the mainland known as the 'Passage House'.

PASTORAL PLACE *see* EDWARDS AVENUE

PAVILION THEATRE (1908-1954) The Pavilion, built by the Town Council, stood on a piece of reclaimed land adjoining the pier and was opened by the Earl of Shaftesbury on 21st December 1908. A roller skating rink at the rear of the building opened the following year, this later becoming the site of the 'Royal Palm Court' and dance hall. Live shows predominated at the theatre although films, only occasionally screened in the early days, became a regular feature in the 1930s. Taken over by the military in WW2, this use continued for some months after the war ended when the theatre served as a Royal Navy parcels department of the GPO. When the Pavilion re-opened in 1950 it was under a new name 'The Ritz', where films and live shows alternated until the building was destroyed by fire on 13th April 1954. It was replaced by the present Pavilion Theatre in 1960. *See* next entry for the history of the present Pavilion Theatre. *See also* RITZ THEATRE

PAVILION THEATRE (1960 – to date) Following the fire of 1954 which destroyed the Ritz Theatre, there was a great deal of litigation which delayed its replacement and the first pile of the present Pavilion Theatre was not driven until September 1958. The architects were Verity and Beverley of London and it was opened by Mayor Edgar Wallis on 15th July 1960, the first show being 'Let's make a night of it' starring Benny Hill with Cyril Stapleton and his Band. Artistic shell and pebble mosaics depicting mermaids once decorated the front outer walls of the theatre, but these suffered from weathering and were later removed. A brightly painted portico erected at the front of the building in 1983 became known as the 'Noddy' entrance. In 2006, plans for the extensive redevelopment of the theatre and ferry terminal are under discussion.

PEACOCK, Thomas Love (1785-1866) Author of satirical works. Born in Weymouth 18th October 1785, but the family was here for a very short time and their address in the town is not known.

PENGOVER HOUSE, Bincleaves Road was built in 2004.

PENMAN PLACE became Nos.16-20 Hardwick Street

PENN, Admiral Sir William (1621-1670) MP for Weymouth in 1665. His son William Penn founded the state of Pennsylvania in the 1680s. Sir William's great-grandson John Penn was Governor of Portland from 1805 to 1834 and built Pennsylvania Castle.

The delightful seaside Pavilion Theatre opened in 1908. It was a largely wooden structure, and succumbed to fire in 1954, less than four years after reopening under its new name 'The Ritz', following wartime use.

PENNY FAMILY Captain Taylor Penny, RN leased Netherton House from 1763 until his death in 1786. His son was Taver Penny, RN (1770-1841). A two day sale of property in September 1850 contained much of the **Taver/Arbuthnot**/Penny inherited property, all of which, apart from one Lot, was on the south side of the harbour. May have given their name to **Penny Street** in the Park District. *See also* NETHERTON HOUSE; SNOOK, Dr Penny-

PENNY STREET in the **Park District** does not appear to have been in the development as originally planned. It was built on what was intended to be one of the lanes which run along the backs of the rear yards of houses in adjoining streets but, unlike them, does not continue through to Ranelagh Road. Unlike many of the Park District street names Penny Street does not appear to have taken on the name of a Conservative politician. May be named after the **Penny Family**.

PEST HOUSE An early isolation unit, outside the town, where any person suspected of suffering from the plague could be confined. There are references to a Pest House at **Clark's Hill** but it appears to have gone out of use by 1668, by which time fears of an local outbreak of the 'Great Plague' of 1665 had presumably passed.

PETTICOAT LANE until 1872 was the name of Lower and Middle St Alban Street, St Alban's Row being the name of Upper St Alban Street. Today Lower St Alban Street leads from Commercial Road to St Thomas Street, and the rest of the street is known as St Alban Street.

PETTY CUSTOMS were quite separate from the King's Customs, which had to be paid to the Crown. The Petty Customs were charges levied on practically everything which came in through the port and the income from them was used for the benefit of the town.

PHILIP and JOANNA Archduke Philip of Austria and Queen Joanna of Castile made an unscheduled visit to Weymouth in January 1506 when their fleet, returning home to Spain from the Netherlands was hit by violent storms in the Channel and sought the calmer waters of Weymouth Bay. The appearance of foreign ships initially caused some consternation locally, but once it was realised that this was a peaceful 'invasion' the royal visitors were welcomed and taken to Sir Thomas Trenchard's home, Wolveton House, near Dorchester, before journeying to the court of King Henry VII in London. Language was a problem, and a Spanish speaking interpreter was required. John Russell of Swyre, a relative of Trenchard, had travelled in Spain, knew the language and accompanied the party. Their visit resulted in a lucrative trade treaty and honours for John Russell who eventually became the first Earl of Bedford. A chest left by the royal visitors at Wolveton House was later owned by Colonel Pickard-Cambridge, a descendant of the Trenchards. Sold to Weymouth Town Council, it was presented to Sir Richard Nicholas Howard who left it back to the council in his will in 1905.

PHOENIX INN location unknown

PHOENIX MINERAL WATER MANUFACTORY was on North Quay in the mid-late 19th century and gave its name to 'Phoenix House' demolished as part of the site clearance here in 1965.

PICKET HOUSE, St Edmund Street (i.e. the former **Fire Station**). The Admiralty leased part of the building from 1906 to 1938 as a Picket House and re-occupied it in 1948.

PICKFORDS, Lower St Alban Street opened in June 1960 and was built on the site of Hawkes, Freeman's furniture repository, bombed in WW2. The premises are currently occupied by a furniture showroom.

PIER Weymouth has had a number of piers over the centuries, all altered, extended, demolished (or not built at all!) *See* COMMERCIAL/PLEASURE PIER (at the southern end of the Esplanade); PIER BANDSTAND (at the northern end of the Esplanade); PROPOSED PIER (in the centre of the Bay); STONE PIER (at the Nothe); TEMPORARY WW2 TRAIN FERRY TERMINAL (Weymouth Harbour); WHITEHEAD TORPEDO WORKS (which had its own pier in Portland Harbour).

PIER BANDSTAND This was a controversial structure which opened on 25th May 1939. Its open deck area was supported on a short pier comprised of angled piles which gave the structure a tumbledown appearance, although the art deco structure above, with stage and spacious dance floor/seating area, was strikingly modern. Many felt the Pier Bandstand spoilt the long continuous sweep of Weymouth Bay, some felt it was impractical, being open to the weather (plans in the 1950s to erect a sliding roof over it came to nothing) and there were even proposals to conceal the piles with a 'skirt' around base of the structure. It was a popular venue for all manner of entertainments such as beauty contests, music competitions, wrestling and summer evening dancing. The building fronting onto the Esplanade was extended in the 1950s and 1960s and remains today, but on 5th May 1986 the 'pier' section , being too costly to repair, was demolished.

Under construction in 1939, this photograph shows the oddly angled piles on which the Pier Bandstand stood.

The Pier Bandstand's entrance, sun deck and stage made it an attractive summer venue, but its critics felt it spoilt the long sweep of Weymouth Bay.

PIER TOLL HOUSE The attractive pier toll house survived the **Ritz Theatre** fire in 1954 and stayed in place until after the present **Pavilion Theatre** opened in July 1960, but it was demolished in November 1960 to improve access to the Pavilion Ballroom.

PIG & WHISTLE PUBLIC HOUSE was on the corner of Dorchester Road and Spa Road. Now a Chinese takeaway.

PILGRIM HOUSE, Hope Square Also known as the White House. A 17th century house, rebuilt in the late 18th century. Derelict when taken over by Weymouth Rotary Club for conversion to a senior citizens' day centre, which opened on 25th September 1962.

PILGRIMAGES From the 15th century pilgrims left Weymouth for the shrine of St James of Compostella in north-west Spain, usually on vessels carrying between 30 and 120 passengers.

PILGRIMS WAY, leading from The Esplanade to Custom House Quay was named in 1994 to commemorate 17th century emigrants who sailed from Weymouth to the New World.

PINDAR, Peter (1738-1819) was the pen name of Devon-born doctor John Wolcot, the author of gossipy and derisive satirical verse in the Georgian period, much of it about George III. *A Royal Tour and Weymouth Amusements; a solemn and reprimanding epistle to the Laureat...* was published in 1789.

PINEAPPLE GATEWAY Two stone pillars topped with pineapples welcoming visitors to Weymouth were unveiled on either side of the A354 on Ridgeway in October 2005. Erected by Weymouth Rotary Club.

PIRATES In the 16th and 17th centuries pirates harassed shipping in the English Channel. Although Weymouth complained bitterly about raids by foreign pirates and the dangers to local shipping, many Dorset sailors served as crew on pirate vessels and local merchants victualled and fitted out pirate ships.

Further reading : *Dorset Elizabethans*, by Maureen Weinstock (John Murray, 1967)

PLACE NAMES This is a huge subject and multi-volume works have been written on the derivation of Dorset place names. There is only space to include some of Weymouth's lost and more unusual ones in this volume. A very comprehensive work which lists field, place, street and building names and their derivations is *The Place Names of Dorset, Part 1* by A.D.Mills (English Place Name Society, 1977).

PLAGUE Melcombe has a dubious claim to fame as the port of entry into England of the worst ever plague – the **Black Death** – in 1348 but this was not the only plague year. In 1562 a stranger staying with the Buckler family at Radipole died of the plague and by the following year the widow of Mr Buckler, two of her sons and a daughter as well as several other members of the household had died of the disease. There were plague outbreaks in 1604-7, 1624-25, 1636-38. At the time of the Great Plague of 1665 it was ordered that *'a very good watch shall be kept day and night by the Townspeople until further order... to prevent those that come from infectious places from entering into this Towne'*. Two watchmen were appointed to watch the north end of Melcombe and two to watch the west end of Weymouth. *See also* PEST HOUSE

PLAINS OF WEYMOUTH is an old name for the low-lying area below High West Street (i.e. the western section of North Quay), continuing westward below Chickerell Road to the start of Newstead Road.

PLEY, George (Senior) was a ship owner, merchant, agent to the Admiralty for the supply of stores, dealer in foreign merchandise and brewer who supplied the Royal Navy. He was a friend of Samuel Pepys. Pley served Cromwell well in the Civil War, supplying vessels and he was MP for Weymouth in 1659. Both he and his son, also George, were Mayors of the borough several times in the 17th century.

PLUME OF FEATHERS pub was in Little George Street (Westham Road).

POISONED CUP, The A novel by **Joseph Drew**, set in the Tudor period and featuring Sandsfoot Castle. First published in 1864, it was still being reprinted in the 1960s.

POLICE Policing of the borough until the early 19th century was largely carried out by the constables (appointed by the Court Leet) and watchmen. The Municipal Corporations Act of 1835 enabled town councils to appoint Watch Committees and establish police forces. Weymouth had a Day and Night Watch, but it was considered insufficient for the town and in 1846 a police force consisting of an Inspector and eight police constables was appointed, increasing in manpower later in the century. From 1890 until the setting up of the Volunteer Fire Brigade in 1895, the police also dealt with fires in the town. The Borough Police Force became part of the county police in 1921.

POLICE STATION The town's main police station occupied cramped and unsuitable accommodation in the Guildhall for more than 100 years. On 1st July 1955 a new police station opened on Dorchester Road between Lodmoor Hill and the Spa. This was closed when a new police station for east Weymouth opened on an adjacent site in 2002, and the original site is being redeveloped as housing. Princess Anne opened the new Dorset Police Divisional Headquarters near the Wessex Stadium on 22nd February 2002, with a new police station for west Weymouth nearby.

PONTIN, Fred *See* RIVIERA HOTEL. Fred Pontin died in October 2000.

POOLE AND YOUNG A firm which toured with exhibitions described as 'Panoramic Dioramic and Phonoscope Entertainments'. In 1871 they were displaying scenes from the Franco Prussian war to audiences at the Burdon Hotel. They also put on shows at the Jubilee Hall.

POOR HOUSE, junction of Lower St Alban Street and Commercial Road Melcombe's Poor House became redundant on the building of the **Workhouse** on Wyke Road in 1836. It was let out to poor families in the nineteenth century and eventually became the premises of a boat builder. It has since been demolished.

POOR HOUSE, Wyke Road Weymouth's Poor House stood just west of the **Workhouse** which replaced it on Wyke Road in 1836.

POPE'S PASSAGE was an alternative name used in the 19th century for Blockhouse Lane. It was officially changed to Blockhouse Lane in 1880.

POPULATION Although Weymouth and Melcombe Regis are described as 'towns' in their early history, they were very small places and their populations are difficult to estimate but at the time of their Union in 1571, it has been estimated that there were probably fewer than a thousand inhabitants. When the first official population count took place in 1801 Weymouth and Melcombe Regis had 3617 inhabitants. In 1811, 4732; in 1821, 6622; in 1831, 7655. In each case the number of inhabitants on the Melcombe side of the harbour was almost double that of the Weymouth side. From this date onwards it is difficult to compare population figures on each side of the harbour as they begin to be influenced by many factors such as boundary extensions, reclamation, and the continued growth of the seaside which centred on the Melcombe side of the harbour. In 1835 boundaries were slightly extended and by the time the first detailed Census was carried out in 1841 the borough's population was 7708. In 1851, 8230; in 1861 10013; in 1871, 11361; in 1881, 11550; in 1891, 11217. By the next Census in 1901, when the population was 19843, boundaries had again been extended, bringing areas of Westham and Radipole within the borough. 1911, 22324; 1921, 24556; 1931, 22188. The boundaries were extended again in 1933 bringing the surrounding villages into the borough and a corresponding population increase. Due to WW2, no Census was taken in 1941. In 1951 the extended borough had a population of 37099, in 1961, 41045; in 1971, 42349. In 1974 Portland came within the borough but the figures given here for 1981, 1991 and 2001 exclude those for Portland. Population in 1981 was 46260; in 1991, 48360 and in 2001, 50868.

PORT SANITARY HOSPITAL, Ferrybridge, Wyke Regis Opened in October 1880. Intended for sailors and seafarers but was also used by local patients. Infectious diseases being rife, by 1901 it was overcrowded and plans were in hand for a new isolation hospital at **Westhaven**. The Ferrybridge building was later used as a technical school, but since the 1950s, surrounded by chalets, it has been part of a holiday camp.

PORTER'S ARMS PUBLIC HOUSE was at the rear of the Guildhall, on the corner of Lower St Mary Street and Custom House Quay.

PORTLAND Although Portland became part of the Borough in 1974, it has a diverse and fascinating history all of its own which is not included in this work, apart from references necessary to enlarge on or complement aspects of Weymouth's history.

PORTLAND, Battle of British Admiral Robert Blake engaged the Dutch fleet under Admiral Van Tromp in battle off Portland in February 1653. Fighting lasted three days, and the Dutch were heavily defeated.

PORTLAND ARMS PUBLIC HOUSE was on the east side of Maiden Street, and was taken down when Mitchell Street was built in the 1870s. Now the site of an extension to the Working Men's Club.

PORTLAND BREAKWATERS and the enclosure of Portland Harbour The colossal civil engineering project comprises four breakwaters built between 1848 and 1905. The first stage was the construction of two breakwaters at Portland between 1849 and 1872. Designer James Meadows Rendel, died during their construction, and the work was then overseen by John Coode, who was knighted when the breakwaters were completed in 1872. The two breakwaters stretching out from Bincleaves were built between 1893 and 1905. Millions of tons of waste Portland stone was used in the entire project, together with quantities of finishing stone and Cornish granite.

Further reading : *The Royal Navy at Portland since 1845*, by Geoffrey Carter (Maritime Books, 1987); *Portland; an illustrated history*, by Stuart Morris (Dovecote, 1985)

PORTLAND BUILDINGS became Nos.15-19 Custom House Quay.

PORTLAND PLACE (1) a terrace of four houses plus Victoria Villa which were on the north side of Lennox Street between Melcombe Place and Victoria Street. (2) a terrace of 6 houses which stood on the west side of Boot Hill, at its junction with Wyke Road.

Left: *The Port Sanitary Hospital opened in 1880 at Ferrybridge.*

PORTLAND RAILWAY HOTEL, No.20 King Street, was renamed The Dog House for a short time at the end of the 20th century and is now converted to housing, known as Melcombe House.

PORTLAND ROAD runs from its junction with Wyke Road near Wyke Church down to Ferrybridge, but in the 19th century a section of Newstead Road was also known as Portland Road.

PORTLAND ROADS was the term used to describe what is today Portland Harbour before **Portland Breakwaters** were built to enclose it.

PORTMORE was a mansion built off Cross Road, on land once part of the Belfield estate. It was built by Rev. Talbot Greaves, Rector of St Mary's Church from 1856 until 1881. He had originally taken up residence in the church's Rectory in St Thomas Street, but on the completion of his new house in the late 1860s, the rectory was occupied by the curate of the church. At Portmore his family motto *Aquila non captat muscas* (an eagle does not bother to catch flies) was carved over the front entrance. He left to take up a post in Bristol in 1881 and after further occupancy as a private house Portmore became Connaught House School in 1890, this being the name of a school the headmaster, John Richard Morgan, already ran in Connaught Road. For the building's later history *see* Connaught House. The building was demolished in 1988 and the houses of Connaught Gardens now fill the site. The original Lodge still stands in Cross Road at the entrance to the drive which once led to the house.

PORTWEY HOSPITAL occupied the former **Workhouse** on Wyke Road. It served as an emergency hospital during WW2 and was converted to become Portwey Maternity Hospital in 1948. The last baby born there before it closed on 7th September 1987 was Joseph Paul Rookes. The building was put up for sale and there were concerns that it might be demolished but in the 1992-3 it was very successfully converted to housing known as 'Union Court'.

POST OFFICE The present Post Office opened in March 1907, having previously occupied other premises in St Thomas Street. The building was extended in 1921/22.

POULTON, 'Professor' Mark Weymouth's 'Punch & Judy' man since Summer 2005.

POWELLS VILLA on Chickerell Road has been renamed Ivy Bank.

POWER STATION (proposed), Portland Harbour Test drilling was carried out on the beach between Sandsfoot and Ferrybridge in February 1966 when Portland Harbour was being considered as a possible site for a power station. Fortunately the proposals went no further.

POWYS, Llewelyn His delightful essay *Weymouth in the Three Eights* recalls childhood holidays in Victorian seaside Weymouth. It can be found in his *Somerset and Dorset Essays* (Macdonald, 1957).

POYNTZ FAMILY gave its name to **Sutton Poyntz**.

PREFABS were allocated by the Ministry of Health to towns suffering from post-WW2 housing shortages. Local sites included Westhill Road, West Bay Crescent and Bohay's Drive, Wyke Regis; Littlemoor Road, adjoining the railway; Radipole Lane/Chickerell Road close to Fiveways junction.

The government supplied temporary prefabricated buildings to cope with the post-war housing shortage. These prefabs (on the right) were in the Camp Road area of Wyke Regis.

PREHISTORIC SETTLEMENT Evidence of Stone Age occupation in the local area is sparse and scattered, but Mesolithic sites at Portland and along the Fleet and stone circles and enclosures on the Ridgeway indicate that man was living here in these early times. In Weymouth evidence of early settlement came in 1921 when a Bronze Age sword was dredged up in the Backwater, where two more swords of the same period were found in the 1930s and a Bronze Age barrow was discovered alongside the main Dorchester road at Redlands. The beginning of the Iron Age around 450 BC brings an increase in evidence of early occupation and the Iron Age hill fort at **Chalbury** is one of some twenty in Dorset, Maiden Castle being the largest.

PRESS GANGS The impressment of men for service in the Royal Navy was a common method of recruitment in time of war and busy ports dreaded the arrival of the Press Gang, whose attempts to take men for naval service were frequently hindered and sometimes ended in violence. Rioting broke out in 1706 when the *Pembroke* galley's press gang visited Weymouth, resulting in two of the press gang and two locals being wounded. The most famous local incident occurred in 1803 and is Portland's story, where a young girl was shot dead, along with three local men, as an angry mob faced the crew of the frigate *L'Aigle*, intent on signing-up men for the 'King's shilling' and a riot ensued. *See also* GRINDALL, Richard

PRESTON was brought within the borough in 1933. The name is a version of the Old English 'preost' (priest) and 'tun' (farm), priest's farm, it once being a prebend to Salisbury Cathedral.

PRESTON BEACH ROAD Prior to the construction of the present Preston Beach Wall the A353 Preston Beach Road was subject to frequent flooding in stormy weather, the force of the sea dumping thousands of tons of pebbles on the roadway and causing severe traffic congestion. Various solutions had been tried over the years to prevent the shingle spilling over onto the road. Groynes were erected on the beach to prevent shingle drift but they became worn. Large stone blocks placed on the beach to add protection were instead thought to increase the problems. The old sea wall was frequently damaged as seas poured over it. Work on a new scheme of sea defences began in January 1995 and included the replacement of thousands of tons of lost shingle and the construction of a rock groyne at the Weymouth end of the beach to retain drifting shingle. A massive new sea wall was constructed, incorporating a broad walkway which has extended the Esplanade from Overcombe to the harbourside. The scheme was officially declared complete by the Duke of York on 7th September 1996.

PRESTON MILL, Mill Lane, Preston Watermill on the River Jordan. Mill Cottage, part of the old mill, remains.

PRESTON ROAD as a street name did not come into use until the late 1930s. Prior to this house names were used and developments at the end of the beach road used 'Overcombe' as an address. Preston Road was sometimes referred to as the 'Weymouth-Bournemouth Road' or the 'Bournemouth Road'.

PRESTON TOLL HOUSE dated back to the days of the Turnpike Trusts. The toll gate on Preston Beach Road once stood a little closer to the town. In 1853 the gate and toll house were moved to a new location on the Lodmoor side of the road, about 150 yards north of the present waste-disposal site entrance. Redundant when the turnpike roads were taken over by local authorities towards the end of the 19th century, the toll house became a private house, best remembered as the home of local character **'Sugar-em' Shorey**'. It was demolished in 1959.

With the toll gate still in place, this photograph of Preston Toll House probably dates from the 1880s, shortly before the Turnpike Trusts were abolished.

PRIDHAM, Hubert Llewellyn (died 1960) Born in Weymouth. GP, journalist and author of children's adventure stories. Best known children's book *Purbeck Marble*. Produced, with photographer Edwin Kestin, *The Dorset Coastline*, published in 1954.

PRINCE ALBERT PUBLIC HOUSE, Westham Road was rebuilt in half-timbered style by brewers Devenish in 1939. Changed its name several times at the end of the 20th century and is now known as Finns.

PRINCE REGENT HOTEL was formerly the Burdon Hotel. It was renamed in 1971.

PRINCESS CHRISTIAN HOSPITAL AND SANATORIUM This was the original name of **Weymouth and District Hospital** in Melcombe Avenue. It was named after Princess Helena, fifth daughter of Queen Victoria and wife of Prince Christian of Schleswig Holstein. She was much involved with nursing and the training of nurses. A Crickmay-designed building, the hospital stood on land leased from Sir Frederic Johnstone and was opened by the Countess of Ilchester on 19th November 1902. A nearby building, Moffatt House, was purchased as a Nursing Home for nurses and private patients. In 1921 the hospital amalgamated with the **Weymouth Royal Hospital** in School Street and was renamed **Weymouth and District Hospital**. The buildings were much extended throughout the 20th century. For the hospital's history since 1921, and the derivation of its ward names *see* WEYMOUTH AND DISTRICT HOSPITAL.

PRINCESS DIANA MEMORIAL GARDENS Following the death of the Princess of Wales in 1997, Radipole Park Gardens were renamed in her memory in November 1998.

PRIOR'S CHAIR *see* FRIARY

PRIORY *see* FRIARY

PRIVATEERS Privateers were merchant ships fitted out, armed and commanded by local men sailing under 'letters of marque', a licence giving them legal authority to capture enemy ships, from which they profited handsomely. 'Enemy' did not necessarily England was at war with a country, as it included the vessels of foreign powers which attacked local ships – a common occurrence when pirates prowled the seas. Privateering was lucrative – a percentage had to be handed over to the authorities but the rest of the profits were divided up between the captain and crew. It was also dangerous, with the risk of being killed, wounded or captured and imprisoned in a foreign prison. Many Weymouth merchants were engaged in privateering in the 17th and 18th centuries. Privateering ceased in 1856 when European countries agreed to end it.

PROBATION HOSTEL, Westwey Road was built in 1988 to replace a building in Lower Bond Street which was demolished as part of the redevelopment of the area.

PROPOSED PIER (in the centre of the Bay) A number of proposals were put forward in the late nineteenth century to build a pier out into the Bay from a central point on the Esplanade, such as the Gloucester Hotel or Jubilee Clock. None of these were proceeded with and the long sweep of the Bay remained uninterrupted until the **Pier Bandstand** was built in 1939.

PROSPECT, The, Franchise Street. The Prospect public house opened 1st May 1959, part of the post-WW2 redevelopment of Chapelhay. It took on the licence of the war- damaged General Gordon pub nearby, which was demolished.

PROSPECT PLACE, Chapelhay was partly destroyed in WW2 air raids. This is a popular street name. Prospect Place (Radipole) was renamed Henning Place in 1872. There is also a Prospect Place off the Dorchester Road at Upwey and Prospect Terrace, Westham became Nos.1-27 Melbury Road.

PROVINCE OF NATAL HOTEL On the corner of Greenhill and Westerhall, this was originally the Grosvenor

Hotel. It was purchased in 1948 by King George's Fund for Sailors with money raised by the people of Natal in a 'Salute to Britain' appeal. It re-opened on 7th May 1949 as the Royal Naval Hotel, providing holiday accommodation for the families of naval men serving in the local area. When the RN presence in the area declined it reverted to use as a civilian hotel but its 'Province of Natal Hotel' name retained the South African link. The hotel closed in the early years of the 21st century and was converted to apartments in 2005, under a new name-'Number Five', Greenhill.

PUBLIC HEALTH ACT 1848 was designed to improve the sanitary conditions in Great Britain by providing a central Board of Health with powers to create local boards to oversee water supply, sewerage systems, refuse collection etc. Some local authorities resented what they saw as government interference in local matters and those on the Weymouth side of the harbour wanted nothing to do with the *Preliminary Inquiry into the sewerage, drainage and supply of water and the sanitary condition of the inhabitants of the parish of Melcombe Regis* which took place under the terms of the Act in 1849. This inspection resulted in a damning report on sanitary conditions in the town and was followed by almost fifty years of wrangling and ineffective half-measures before work began on a proper sewerage system in 1896. The Local Board of Health (later the Urban District Council) was set up in 1851, the Weymouth Rural District Council being responsible for the outlying parishes until boundary reorganisation in 1933.

PUBLIC LIBRARY *see* WEYMOUTH LIBRARY

PUCKETT, Dr Adam Stapleton A kindly physician from Broadwey, Dr Puckett was much concerned with the poorer people in the villages he served. On July 8th 1862 he and Zachariah White, the relieving officer, rode out to Preston, where John Cox lived with his elderly and infirm parents. John Cox was locally thought to be mad, and many felt he should be confined in an asylum. Puckett and White, knowing the harshness of the asylum, thought a fortnight in the Workhouse would be enough to calm John Cox and enable him to return home. John Cox was having none of it and he beat Dr Puckett to death with part of a bedpost, having chased him outside. Neighbours cowered, terrified, as Cox returned to the scene with a saw and hacked off parts of the doctor's body. Meanwhile, Zachariah White returned from the Ship Inn, where he had gone to procure a cart to convey Cox to Weymouth workhouse. He came across the mutilated body of Dr Puckett and, fearing for his life, fled back to the Ship, where waterworks company engineman John Ford bravely went to the scene and collected up the body parts. He then rode to the Plough Inn at Osmington, where he found John Cox quiet and fearful. He was arrested and taken to Dorchester Gaol. At his trial he was judged to be insane and he was taken to the asylum, the very place that his victim Dr Puckett had tried to save him from.

PUDDING STONES although not geologically identical, this seems to be an alternative name used locally for **Turtle Stones**.

PULLINGER'S RESTAURANT was on the first floor of the **Pier Bandstand**. The Pullingers retired in 1981 and the premises are currently occupied by a Chinese restaurant.

PULTENEY, Sir William (1729-1805) He was formerly Sir William Johnstone, of Westerhall, Dumfriesshire and changed his name in 1767 when his wife, who was a descendant of the Pulteneys, Earls of Bath, inherited a fortune. He became very influential in 18th century local politics and was Mayor of Weymouth in 1796-7. Extremely rich, he purchased a substantial amount of Weymouth property formerly owned by the Tucker/Steward families and increased his fortune by lending money to the Corporation for improvements, much to his own advantage as the value of his own property in the town increased. On his death his Weymouth estate passed to his nephew Sir John Lowther Johnstone and was owned by successive Johnstones. The numerous properties brought in tidy sums in ground rents for the 'Johnstone Estate', which later became the 'Wilton Estate'. Pulteney's virtual monopoly of the Corporation was opposed by two local men, John Arbuthnot and John Herbert Browne. Action for a new charter against Pulteney resulted in a massive bill- and Pulteney, the victor, lent the Corporation the money to pay it, with interest, leaving the town ever more under his influence.

PULTENEY BUILDINGS, Esplanade Now numbered 7-15 The Esplanade. Named after **Sir William Pulteney** who put forward proposals to reclaim the land at the southern end of the Esplanade on which the buildings stand.

PUMP HOUSE outside St John's Church. This small octagonal building contained the pumping station for the old waterworks. It was removed soon after the church was built as it was not required by the new waterworks company set up in 1855.

PUMPS, WATER The public water supply for those on the Weymouth side of the harbour was originally obtained from two pumps, which supplemented the wells and springs in the area. One, erected in the 1770s, stood on land below High West Street. When the present Weymouth Fire Station was erected in 1939 it remained in position but was almost out of sight behind the building, until 1990 when it was removed and re-erected in Hope Square. Another pump of mid-19th century date which stood on the west side of Rodwell Road, outside the grounds of Springfield, has been lost. *See also* WATER SUPPLY

A photo showing the location of the Weymouth water pump. The houses of Silver Street and Jockey's Row beyond it were demolished in the 1930s and on this site the Fire Station was built in 1939. The pump has since been re-erected close to Hope Square.

PUNCH & JUDY entertainers on Weymouth sands:- Mark Edmonds, from 1926-1976, 'Professor' Guy Higgins from 1976-May 2005 and from 2005 to date 'Professor' Mark Poulton.

'PURPLE ROUTE' *see* RELIEF ROAD

PURSER, Thomas A feared Dorset pirate of the 16th century who threatened the town with 'spoil and fire' when he was prevented from taking a French ship near Weymouth.

PUTNIDGE FAIR John Hutchins, writing in the late 18th century, was told of a week-long fair called 'Putnidge Fair' possibly dating from mediaeval times, which was once held in the town, selling goods from various places in France. This seems to be the only reference to it and its location was not known.

PYE, Bartle (died 1932) An oil cake merchant in the first quarter of the 20th century. His firm occupied a large warehouse at No.13 Custom House Quay, currently the Harbour Master's office. He was Mayor in 1911-12 and 1927-28.

PYE, William (1853-1934) Artist. Born in Blackburn, Lancs. Resident in Weymouth from the 1880s until his death in 1934 aged 79. Lived at Dunmore, Longfield Road. Painted local landscape and harbour scenes in oils and produced numerous etchings of scenes in and around Weymouth.

PYLONS, Electricity A public inquiry in the fight to stop them being erected in the Broadwey and Upwey area began on 17th November 1964 and the Minister of Power gave the go-ahead in September 1965. The new High Voltage Grid crossed Weymouth in 1968.

One of Will Pye's engravings from 1913, showing the Tudor cottages in Trinity Street, with a glimpse of the harbour beyond.

QUAKERS *see* SOCIETY OF FRIENDS

QUATERCENTENARY was the 400th anniversary (1571-1971) of the Union of Weymouth and Melcombe Regis. Two weeks of celebratory events were held 1st-14th June 1971. The Local History Exhibition in Melcombe Regis School set up to commemorate the Quatercentenary was the foundation of **Weymouth Museum**.

QUEBEC PLACE is off the west side of Park Street, behind the Star Inn. In the 19th century there was an iron foundry opposite the houses.

QUEEN COURT is off Queen Street, adjacent to the Terminus Hotel. Appears to have been King's Court prior to the renaming of King Street West as Queen Street in 1872.

QUEEN STREET was formerly known as King Street West. It was renamed in 1872.

QUEEN VICTORIA STATUE stands in front of St John's Church, Greenhill. Queen Victoria had no connection with Weymouth. She visited the town only twice – in 1833 as a 14-year old Princess on a countrywide tour being groomed by her mother the Duchess of Kent, for her future role and an unscheduled visit as Queen in 1846 when she and Prince Albert suffered from seasickness aboard the royal yacht *Victoria and Albert* and put into Weymouth briefly to recover – they went straight to the Earl of Ilchester's residence at Abbotsbury. The bronze statue on its Portland stone plinth was erected as a mark of respect for her long reign (from 1837-1901) and it was unveiled by her youngest daughter Beatrice, Princess Henry of Battenberg on 20th October 1902. The sculptor was George Simonds.

QUEEN VICTORIA'S GOLDEN (1887) AND DIAMOND (1897) JUBILEES were celebrated in fine style locally with decorations, dinners, processions, bands, fireworks and special fare for the workhouse inmates. The **Jubilee Clock** and **Jubilee Hall** commemorated the 1887 Jubilee.

QUEEN'S BARRACKS This was a Cavalry Barracks, probably dating from 1803 and situated on the corner of Coneygar Lane (later known as Lower Bond Street), which at that time overlooked the Backwater. Named after Queen Charlotte, wife of King George III. A building already on the site was rented and converted to barrack use. By the 1820s the barracks was redundant and later in the century it became known as 'Burdon's Buildings', a tenement block housing many families, which was notorious by the 1870s for its unsanitary and overcrowded conditions which continued into the 20th century. The building was closed in the late 1920s, the families living there being re-housed on the new Westham council estate. The site was then occupied by the Regent Garage until 1955, when Kennedy's Builders' Merchants built a new shop there. Now redeveloped, Debenhams new store of the 1990s stands on the site. *See also* BURDON'S BUILDINGS

QUEEN'S HALL is the ballroom of the Royal Hotel.

QUEEN'S HEAD PUBLIC HOUSE existed in the 18th century. Location unknown.

QUEEN'S HOTEL (originally known as the Albert Hotel) stands on the corner of King Street and Park Street. It was a three storey Victorian building, but with the prospect of an extended railway station being built in the 1930s, it was decided to pull the old 'Queen's' down and the present red brick hotel went up in its place, ready to cater for increasing numbers of visitors. WW2 scuppered the railway plans and the proposed expansion was much reduced. It was 1986 before a new station was built, a basic, small-scale structure.

QUEEN'S OWN REGIMENT OF DORSET YEOMANRY CAVALRY were in camp in Weymouth during the late-19th and early-20th centuries, usually for one week in May. *See* YEOMANRY WEEKS

QUEEN'S PLACE linked Franchise Street and St Leonard's Road. It was demolished in 1955 following WW2 air raid damage.

QUEEN'S ROW was a terrace of houses, Nos.15-31, on the south side of St Leonard's Road. Partially rebuilt following WW2 air raid damage.

QUIBO COTTAGE/ QUIBO LANE This most unusual house and street name is a bit of a mystery. The cottage was owned by local shipbuilder Mr Besant in the mid-19th century. Was he perhaps a seafarer who had visited Coiba Island (formerly known as Quibo Island) off the coast of Panama?

QUIET PLACE was a tiny side street between Nos.17 and 18 East Street, leading to a pair of cottages.

R

RAF CHICKERELL *see* CHICKERELL AIRFIELD

RADIPOLE The ancient settlement now within the modern borough is thought to take its name from the old word 'hreod' meaning reeds or rushes and 'pol'; a pool, hence 'reedy pool'. An alternative suggestion takes the 'Rad' or 'Red' of the name to suggest the colour – possibly a red dye. Radipole is listed in the Domesday Survey of 1086, but its neighbour Melcombe is not, indicating that Radipole was the more important settlement at this time.

RADIPOLE BARRACKS This was a Cavalry Barracks housing some 400 men and 400 horses built in 1798 on the southwest side of Dorchester Road. It occupied a site now enclosed by Westbourne Road and Alexandra Road. Radipole Terrace and York Villa were originally barrack buildings. The barracks was enlarged in 1804-5, more than doubling its original capacity and it was here that the Hanoverian troops of the King's German Legion were based. Once the threat of a French invasion ended, the barracks was reduced in size, and by the 1820s was declared redundant and sold off.

RADIPOLE CHURCH *see* ST ANN'S CHURCH, RADIPOLE

RADIPOLE COURT *see* RADIPOLE HOUSE

RADIPOLE FARM of some six hundred acres was up for auction in October, 1802. It had two farm houses- one, known as the 'old farmhouse' was at the Spa. The 'new brick farmhouse' of 1802 still stands, off Dorchester Road. It was used by Weymouth College for some years prior to the College selling off its older buildings and constructing new buildings on the Cranford Avenue site in 2004. Known at one time as Wadsworth's Farm, it was also known as Nangle's Farm

RADIPOLE HALT on the Dorchester-Weymouth railway line opened in July, 1905 and closed at the end of 1983. It was demolished early in 1984 and few traces remain.

RADIPOLE HOUSE stood on Dorchester Road at Lodmoor Hill. In the late 19th century it was the home of Henry Nangle, local agent for the Johnstone Estate. The house received a direct hit during an air raid on 15th April 1941, killing four soldiers billeted there. Radipole Court, homes for the elderly, was built on the site in 1965.

RADIPOLE LAKE was a real lake with islands until Westham Bridge was built in 1921, since when the flow of water in the lake has been controlled by sluices. It became a freshwater lake and the reeds spread to cover large areas. An ambitious scheme in 1933 to reclaim 70 acres of the Lake and develop it with leisure facilities (3 football pitches, cricket ground, hockey ground, bandstand, tea gardens etc. plus a new road along the Backwater's western shore) did not materialise although some preliminary works were carried out, interrupted by WW2. Tipping in the 1950s provided the Swannery car park but the rest of the scheme faded away, largely due to the increase in costs since it was envisaged more than 20 years before. Today the Lake is an RSPB Nature Reserve. *See also* BACKWATER; 'PARLIAMENTARY ROAD'

RADIPOLE LAUNDRY, Queen's Road *see* LAUNDRY, Queen's Road, Radipole

RADIPOLE MANOR (also known as West Mead) is a large house set in extensive grounds off Radipole Lane, probably dating from the late 1860s. The house made the news in May 2005 when it was put up for sale. Its owner, the late Miss K. H. de Burgh Hayes, had lived in the property for 85 years and although much of the building had been uninhabited and had fallen into disrepair, its total lack of modernisation recalled a time of gracious living long gone. In the latter half of the 19th century it was the home of Richard ffolliot Eliot *(see* next entry). *See also* RADIPOLE OLD MANOR, Radipole Lane

RADIPOLE MANOR HOUSE ESTATE The first sale of building land on which 'new' Radipole developed took place in May 1890 and comprised plots on both sides of Spa Road and on Dorchester Road south of Radipole Lane. The land belonged to the Eliot brothers of the Weymouth Old Bank, who unbeknownst to everyone else, were heading for bankruptcy. The sale included the site for the Spa Hotel. More land was sold in a second auction held in July the same year. *See also* ELIOT, PEARCE & CO's BANK

RADIPOLE MILLS There were once two watermills at Radipole. Upper Radipole Mill is now a private dwelling. The Lower Mill was demolished but Mill Cottage remains.

RADIPOLE OLD MANOR, Radipole Lane stands next to the church. It was rebuilt in the 16th century by Richard Watkins and incorporates parts of an earlier structure, possibly once belonging to the monks of Cerne Abbey.

RADIPOLE PARK DRIVE was built in the 1920s on land reclaimed from the Backwater.

RADIPOLE PARK GARDENS of the 1930s stand on infilled land between Radipole Park Drive and the railway lines. The Gardens were renamed Princess Diana Memorial Gardens in November 1998.

RADIPOLE PRIMARY SCHOOL, Radipole Lane officially opened 1st April 1966, although it had been in use since January 1965. Temporary buildings on the site had housed infants since 1953. Replaced **Radipole School**.

RADIPOLE SCHOOL The village school of 1854 opposite St Ann's Church closed in 1964.

RADIPOLE SPA A sulphuretted hydrogen spring was discovered at Radipole in 1830, although it had probably been known about in earlier times. A pump room was erected and the spa, owned by John **Henning**, was soon in business. It seems to have gone out of use by 1875, when all the spa's fixtures and fittings were offered for sale, although in 1898 when the Spa buildings were sold the medicinal springs were still much to the fore in the sale publicity. By 1905 the site had been built over by the Steam **Laundry**, and a plan to re-establish the spa that year fell through.

RADIPOLE TERRACE *see* RADIPOLE BARRACKS.

RADIPOLE TOLL HOUSE dated from the days of the Turnpike Trusts. The turnpike gate originally stood on Dorchester Road opposite the northern end of Brunswick Terrace but it was moved in 1853 to a spot on Dorchester Road, almost opposite its junction with Spa Road. The Trusts ended in the late 19th century and the building was later converted to housing. It projected across the pavement and increasing road traffic made life hazardous for both its occupants and passing pedestrians. The toll house was demolished in 1972.

RAIL BRIDGE across the A354 on Ridgeway Hill dates from 1954 and replaced an earlier structure of 1900.

RAIL BRIDGES across the Backwater/Radipole Lake. *See* BACKWATER RAIL BRIDGE (1863-1909); BACKWATER RAIL BRIDGE (1909-1976)

RAIL BRIDGES across Smallmouth. *See* FERRYBRIDGE (RAIL)

RAILWAY The opening of the railway to Weymouth on 20th January 1857 assured the town's future as a popular holiday resort. It was initially a joint GWR (broad gauge) and LSWR (standard gauge) undertaking, the GWR's line from Yeovil joining the LSWR's line from Southampton at Dorchester, the track then being mixed gauge to Weymouth until 1874 when it became standard gauge only. GWR trains ran to Paddington and LSWR trains to Waterloo and dual service continued until 1961 when it became Waterloo only. Diesels were introduced in the 1960s and the last regular steam passenger train out of Weymouth ran on 9th July 1967. The railway engine sheds were cleared in the early 1970s. Electrification of the main line in May 1988 brought about the demise of the **Weymouth Harbour Tramway** – Weymouth's 'railway through the streets'. *See also* WEYMOUTH RAILWAY STATION

RAILWAY ARCH HOTEL, 28 Chickerell Road was a rebuild of the former Archway Tavern and was converted to housing in 1985.

RAILWAY DOCK HOTEL, Rodwell Avenue Opened 1902. The pub took its name from the new harbour the GWR was planning to build in **Newton's Cove**, a scheme which was finally abandoned in 1913. The pub's first licensee was James Underwood and it stayed in same family for almost seventy years. Demolished in June 1989.

RAILWAY HOTEL, 64 (but originally numbered 28) **Park Street** appears in the 1851 Census (although the railway did not reach Weymouth until 1857!). It became a Devenish pub in the 1880s but closed the following decade, probably in 1897. It was between Clifton Place and Albert Street.

RAILWAY STATION *see* WEYMOUTH RAILWAY STATION

RAILWAY TAVERN was on the corner of Commercial Road and Wesley Street.

RALPH ALLEN'S HOUSE, Nos.2 and 2a Trinity Road *see* ALLEN, Ralph

RANELAGH HOTEL, Ranelagh Road Closed as a pub in January 1968. Served as HQ of the Conservative Club for some years.

RANELAGH ROAD was formerly known as Ranelagh Terrace (when only Nos.1-8 had been built) and then Ranelagh Street. It takes its name from Viscount Ranelagh, chairman in 1854 of the **Conservative Land Society**, which developed the Park District.

'REC', Newstead Road The Recreation Ground, Newstead Road was Weymouth Football Club's Ground behind the **Sidney Hall**. The Club moved to the new Wessex Stadium in 1987 when the ground and the adjacent Sidney Hall were sold for redevelopment as a supermarket. **Asda** now stands on the site. *See also* WESSEX STADIUM; WEYMOUTH FOOTBALL CLUB

RECLAMATION Just how much of the modern town of Weymouth stands on reclaimed land has to be one of the most fascinating aspects of its history. Development of the original town of Weymouth on the south side of the harbour was restricted by the high ground of Chapelhay behind the town. Melcombe, opposite, grew up on a very narrow sandbar. As both towns increased in size, reclamation of land from both sea and Backwater was inevitable. On the south side of the harbour probably the earliest attempts at gaining additional ground came with attempts to wall part of the Marsh in the 17th century. Further east McSaunders Hole was infilled in 1781, providing today's Hope Square area. Over the centuries the harbour has been made slightly narrower by the building of quays and port facilities on both sides, but it has been enlarged seawards by the construction and extension of piers at the harbour entrance. The Commercial Pier which had seen little alteration since Victorian times, was reconstructed in the early 1930s and enlarged for the roll on/roll off ferry services introduced in the 1970s. The tipping of thousands of tons of waste Portland stone in the late 1970s on the pier's bay side completely altered its shape and these works were officially opened in 1980. The Backwater was once considerably wider. Its eastern shore originally followed a line slightly inland of today's Commercial Road, widening out towards the sea at a place called The Narrows (the site of today's Prince Regent Hotel) where sea and Backwater frequently met in stormy weather. The first scheme for reclamation on the Backwater's Melcombe shore began in 1804 when ground began to be infilled westward along the quay from the Town Bridge, continuing northwards along the Backwater to today's New Bond Street, this eventually linking with further infilling to the north to become today's Commercial Road. More land was gained when infilling took place west of Commercial Road, where timber ponds gave way to the solid ground on which the present Marina, car parks and harbour walk have been built, this reclamation commencing in the early 1900s and continuing through the 20th century. Following the construction of the present Westham Bridge in 1921 yet more land was gained to the north, providing the sites for Melcombe Regis Gardens, Radipole Park Drive and Radipole Park Gardens. The Swannery Car Park stands on land infilled in the 1950s. Along the Backwater's western shore, Westwey Road came into being in 1932, following extensive reclamation in the late 1920s to enlarge the gasworks site and provide a road between the Sidney Hall and Westham Bridge. North of the bridge, tipping provided a new shore for the site of car and coach parks and a funfair, which stood here prior to the building of the sewage pumping station in 1982 and the construction of Weymouth Way, the relief road which since 1987 has linked Westham to the Dorchester Road at Radipole. 'The Narrows' ceased to exist when a large area of the Backwater behind the Esplanade was infilled for a proposed park, this reclamation commencing in 1834 when the foundation stone of the Park Wall was laid. The park never materialised and the railway and the houses of the Park District fill this land today. Even the Esplanade itself has advanced seawards, being extended in a sweeping curve at its southern end in 1805 and widened in the 1920s which included the extension around the Jubilee Clock.

RED BARRACKS (also known as Weymouth Barracks), The Nothe This was originally a Cavalry Barracks, completed in 1796-97. It burned down in 1798 and in 1801 a start was made on rebuilding, this time for Infantry units, but the work was not completed until early in 1803. Once the threat of a French invasion ended, the Red Barracks was converted back for use by the cavalry. It was used by the military until the second half of the 20th century, after which it was occupied by a department of the Post Office until 1975. Saved from the demolition gangs, it was converted to housing in 1984 and is now known as Wellington Court.

RED LION INN, Hope Square was renamed 'Dorset Brewers Ale House' in the 1990s but has now reverted to its former name.

RED WAREHOUSE, Custom House Quay This early 19th century red brick building, extended later in the century, stood on the corner of Lower St Mary Street and Custom House Quay. Demolition began in October 1958. An extension to the Ship Inn now fills the site, which for some years was used as a car park.

The big 'Red Warehouse' on Custom House Quay, built in the early 19th century and later extended, was pulled down in 1958. An extension to the Ship Inn now fills the site.

RED WHITE AND BLUE PUBLIC HOUSE was in Governor's Lane.

REDLANDS takes its name from Redlands Farm and opinions vary as to the derivation of 'Red' in the name – it may possibly be the colour red, or derive from the ancient form of 'reed' as in Radipole ('reedy pool') Lake. A slightly less picturesque name for the Redlands area on early maps is 'Knacker's Hole' – a pit used by a knacker.

REDLANDS ESTATE Work began in 1958 and to the new houses were added three shops at the junction of Greenway Road and Blenheim Road. The building contractor was E.G. Coleman of Weymouth.

REFUSE DESTRUCTOR installed at the Corporation yard in Westwey Road was first used 25th January 1904.

REGATTA Regattas have been held in Weymouth at least since the 1840s. Until the 1960s it was customary to hold the Carnival and the Regatta in August, on separate days.

REGENT CINEMA/THEATRE & DANCE HALL *See* JUBILEE HALL

RELIABLE DRIVE was the former name of Waverley Road.

RELIEF ROAD (proposed) Plans to relieve congestion on the A354 (Dorchester Road) and the A353 (Preston Road) by the construction of a relief road have been under discussion for many years. In the early 1990s three schemes were under consideration, known as the Brown, Orange and Purple Routes. The 'Purple Route', with proposals to cut through the countryside to the west of Weymouth, was not popular. The 'Brown Route', as originally proposed, would have supplied a dual carriageway from Manor Roundabout, skirting Littlemoor in a wide loop before turning northwards to Ridgeway, with a short link road to Preston. This option seemed all set to be realised (although with only a single carriageway) in 2000, after years of lengthy discussions and a public inquiry. However government funding did not materialise and planning consent lapsed. In the 21st century the proposals have been reconsidered and the Orange Route is now favoured – this had been Weymouth's preferred option in the 1990s, when county planners supported the Brown Route. The Orange Route, a single carriageway road, takes a more direct line from Manor Roundabout to Littlemoor, with a new road through Littlemoor and a longer link road to Preston. Both Brown and Orange routes climb Ridgeway following the line of the present A 354, but running below it via a series cuttings and embankments to avoid the present road's hairpin bend before rejoining it at the top of the hill. These are the proposals awaiting government sanction in 2006, fourteen years after the first alternative route proposals were put forward and more than half a century after it was first realised that the increasing use of motor vehicles would inevitably create huge problems in accessing the town.

REST AND WELCOME PUBLIC HOUSE was on the east side of Boot Hill (now the site of Edwards Avenue).

REX, George (of Knysna, South Africa) Several books published in the 19th and early 20th centuries set out to prove that George Rex was the rightful heir to King George

III. He was said to have been the son of a secret early marriage between the future king and a Quaker girl, Hannah Lightfoot. Much of the evidence produced was based on hearsay rather than fact and extensive archives not available to the authors at that time have since disproved any link between George Rex and King George III.

REYMES, Colonel Bullen (1613-1672) A soldier in the King's Army during the Civil War, Reymes suffered financially under the Commonwealth, but was back in favour following the Restoration. He owned Waddon Manor, Portesham, his wife having inherited the property from her father, Thomas Gerard. Reymes also owned property in Melcombe and was MP for the town from 1660 until 1672. In the late 1660s, at the request of the mayor, he obtained 300 tons of stone from the King's quarries to build a new Town Bridge in Weymouth, but the new bridge did not materialise and there is no record of what happened to the stone.

REYNOLDS MEMORIAL INSTITUTE, BROADWEY Opened 13th May 1933. Frank Reynolds of Broadwey left money for the building of the institute, specifying that there should be no political meetings held there and no intoxicating liquor sold or consumed and no gambling. Post-WW2 it had a variety of uses but is now a social club. The building once sported a rather fine weathervane bearing the borough coat of arms, designed by local blacksmith **Tom Clarke**.

RICHMOND TERRACE became Nos.10-13 King Street and **RICHMOND TERRACE EAST** became Nos.7-9 King Street.

RICKETTS, Eric James (1913-2002) Architect, Local Historian, Artist, Conservationist and Freeman of the Borough. Weymouth-born, a man who loved his town and cared passionately about conserving its past for future generations. His enthusiasm was conveyed not only in his talks and books about Weymouth's buildings and their history but in his superb drawings of the town, which recreated scenes of long ago with meticulous attention to detail. An inscribed stone seat in his memory stands on Weymouth harbourside, close to the Ferry Steps. It was erected by Weymouth Civic Society, of which he was a Life President. Ricketts Close, a development on the former Weymouth College site off Dorchester Road, is named after him.

Further reading : *Buildings of old Weymouth and Portland (4 vols)* by Eric Ricketts (1970s, some revision 1990s).

RIDGEWAY The hairpin bend on the A354 at Ridgeway dates from the cutting of a new road to replace the steep old 'Roman Road' over the hill in 1824.

RIDGEWAY HILL BUNKER was built in the 1950s as the anti-aircraft gun control room for the defence of Portland Harbour. It was never used operationally and in latter years it was the Royal Navy's map and chart store.

RINGS, THE *see* ALEXANDRA GARDENS

RINGSTEAD Two 148 feet high dish-shaped wireless aerials which dominated the scene at Ringstead for twelve years were communication links built in 1961 for the USAF Tropposcatter Station, which was operational from 1963 to 1972. They were dismantled in 1973.

RISING SUN INN, Prospect Place was purchased by the Council from Groves brewery in 1956 and demolished during the post-WW2 redevelopment of Chapelhay.

RITZ THEATRE This was the new name given to the Pavilion Theatre of 1908 when it was handed back to the town council by the military in 1947 following WW2 use. It re-

13th April 1954 saw the Ritz Theatre destroyed by fire.

opened as the 'Ritz Theatre' on 19th May 1950, having been closed as an entertainment venue for more than 10 years. Films were shown out-of-season, with a live show during July, August and September. The film chosen for the theatre's opening night was 'The Forsyte Saga' in Technicolor. Four years later, on 13th April 1954, the Ritz caught fire whilst it was being refurbished for the coming summer season. The fire gained a rapid hold in the largely timber building and within an hour it was almost completely gutted. Only the front of the theatre and the Palm Court ballroom at the rear remained standing, the auditorium and stage being totally destroyed. Crowds watched the fire, which was visible for miles around, their numbers swelled by local schoolchildren, home from school for the Easter holidays. Demolition work began in April 1955. A Big Top was erected on the site in 1956 and that summer an ice show performed inside it. *See also* PAVILION THEATRE

RIVER JORDAN, Preston (alternative spelling JORDON) The river has two sources, the major one rising in the springs north of Sutton Poyntz, the other to the east of the village. They join in the village and flow south to the sea at Bowleaze Cove. There were once three mills on the Jordan – one at Preston and two in Sutton Poyntz.

RIVER WEY Some four miles long, the River Wey is the reason for the town's existence. The towns of Weymouth and Melcombe Regis developed as trading ports at the river mouth. The Wey rises at Upwey just beyond the spring known as the Wishing Well and flows though Upwey, Broadwey Nottington and Radipole (once serving the mills in each of these villages) before broadening out into Radipole Lake then narrowing again as it flows through Weymouth Harbour, joining the sea through the channel between the pier and the Nothe.

RIVIERA HOTEL, Bowleaze Coveway A striking hotel of modernist design built of reinforced concrete and completed in 1937. It was designed by Lionel Stewart-Smith of Weymouth, an architect then in practice at No.9 Royal Terrace. The later addition of an extra storey, very much in keeping with the original design, is almost undetectable. Unfortunately the original luxury hotel did not open as planned, as its owner was declared bankrupt before the building was completed. It provided accommodation for disabled evacuee children during the Second World War and in 1958 became part of Fred Pontin's holiday camp empire. In 2000, the Riviera was taken over and extensively refurbished by Hollybush Hotels and has since been sold again. In 1997 the art-deco hotel gained listed building status as an important architectural example of its time.

ROBENS, James Eaton (1814-1910) Set up in business in 1834 as a tailor and outfitter and eventually went into partnership with his son-in-law as Robens and Mace, in St Mary Street. A Liberal councillor very active in the political life of Weymouth. He worked closely with Sir Henry Edwards in setting up the latter's philanthropic works in the town. In his nineties he recalled the Weymouth of his youth in a delightful little book published a few years after his death.

Further reading : *Recollections of a nonagenarian* by James Eaton Robens (Weymouth, 1914)

ROBERTS SWEET SHOPS AND FACTORY were begun in the 1840s by Herbert Roberts, a pastry cook who moved to Weymouth and started making boiled sweets. The firm had premises in Park Street and Commercial Road before moving in the early years of the 20th century to a factory in Lower St Alban Street, with shops in St Thomas Street and St Mary Street. In 1960 the firm was taken over by Walter J Rugg and Co. Ltd, wholesalers, confectioners and tobacconists.

ROBILLIARD, Nicolas An Alderney man with shipping interests in Weymouth in the early-19th century. He ran the *Alert*, a packet boat to the Channel Islands, which became a successful rival to the official Post Office packets, prompting the Post Office to introduce an extra boat on the service. Robilliard lost trade to this new augmented PO service and the *Alert* went out of business in 1810, taking her owner with her, for he went bankrupt in the same year. There is a local tradition that Nicolas Robilliard built the fine house on Custom House Quay which later became the **Custom House**, but there seems to be no record of him owning it.

ROCK COTTAGES became Nos.43-45 Newstead Road

ROCK FACTORY, Caroline Place turned out mile after pepperminty mile of pink and white seaside rock with 'Weymouth' running through it. The business started up in 1950 and was owned by Messrs. Alfred Miles Ltd. Production ceased in 1970. The premises are currently occupied by a printing business.

ROCK HOTEL opened in 1881, Westham's first public house.

ROCKLAND HOUSE became No.65 Abbotsbury Road.

ROCKLAND VILLAS became Nos.57-59 Abbotsbury Road.

ROCKLANDS was suggested when names were being sought in the early 1880s for the new suburb which became known as Westham.

ROCKS or ROCK TERRACE became Nos.47-89 Newstead Road This was one of the earliest developments in what would become the large suburb of Westham.

RODWELL as a place name dates back to the 17th century and is thought to indicate 'a reedy spring or stream' derived from the old words 'hreod' and 'wella'. The development of Rodwell began in the first half of the 19th century, with large houses being built along Longhill Road (today's Rodwell Road).

RODWELL HOTEL, No.35 Rodwell Road was renamed The Mighty Hood for some years in the 1980s.

RODWELL HOUSE, No.34, Rodwell Road, was designed by architect James Hamilton for the Rev. Joseph Addison of Holy Trinity around 1800 and was one of the earliest houses in Rodwell. Later extended, it became a school, run by Addison's son in the 1850s and early 1860s. Now the Rodwell House Hotel.

RODWELL LODGE (sometimes known as Rodwell Villa) A mansion set in extensive grounds on the east side of Rodwell Road, close to its junction with Rodwell Avenue. Owned by Alfred Owen **Swaffield** in the 1920s. In 1973 it was converted to a hotel, but it was demolished later in the 20th century. The present development of apartments on the site has retained the name 'Rodwell Lodge'.

RODWELL PUMP stood on Rodwell Road almost opposite its junction with Rodwell Avenue. It was removed in August 1966 and not preserved.

RODWELL ROAD In 1872 it was decided that the road *'from the bottom of Boot Lane to Clearmount be called Rodwell Road'*. Clearmount is the corner where Rodwell Road joins Buxton Road and the sharp bend here was widened in April 1963, a WW2 bombed house being cleared as part of the work. The following year Rodwell Road between Rodwell Avenue and Clearmount was widened.

RODWELL STATION on the Weymouth and Portland Railway, opened June 1870, closed March, 1952 when the line closed to passengers. Badly damaged in an air raid on 15th April 1941, in which the ticket collector was killed. The station platforms remain, now part of the **'Rodwell Trail'**.

A wintry scene at Rodwell Station on the Weymouth and Portland Railway.

RODWELL TERRACE was the name used in Victorian times for a pair of large houses on the east side of Rodwell Road, at its junction with St Leonard's Road. They were bombed during WW2 and pulled down in 1948. 'Briarswood', an apartment block built on the site in 1964, retains the name of one of the old houses. Rodwell Terrace was the name later used for the houses on Boot Hill between James Street and Franchise Street.

RODWELL TRAIL is a scenic walk from Westham to Wyke Regis following the line of the Weymouth and Portland Railway. Plans for a Portland relief road along the old line were rejected in 1988.

RODWELL VILLA *see* RODWELL LODGE

ROLLER SKATING was tremendously popular in the late 19th and early 20th century. An indoor rink opened in the Burdon Hotel in July 1875, prior to the opening of an outdoor rink in Grange Road later the same month. Others opened at Arcadia (the Jubilee Hall) and at the rear of the Pavilion Theatre in 1909. Many were the complaints in these years about roller skaters whizzing along the Esplanade to the annoyance of those enjoying a leisurely stroll. Later in the 20th century the Sidney Hall was a popular roller skating venue.

ROLLING STONES played at St Thomas Street's Gaumont Cinema on 24th August 1964 (2 houses).

ROLLS COURT is between Nos.60 and 61 St Mary Street. A second Rolls Court was in East Street.

ROMAN SETTLEMENT Roman rule of Dorset began in 43 AD with the capture of Maiden Castle by the Second Roman Legion commanded by Emperor Vespasian. Scattered Roman remains suggest a substantial Roman presence in the Weymouth area. At Preston, on the cliffs overlooking Bowleaze Cove a large Roman coin hoard was found and the remains of a Roman temple are preserved nearby at Jordan Hill (another theory suggests that this may have been a lighthouse). A fine Roman mosaic pavement was also discovered at Preston in 1832 but souvenir hunters damaged it and it was later covered over. In today's Newstead Road, above Weymouth Harbour, part of another tessellated pavement, probably a villa floor, was uncovered in 1902 and although there is no evidence to prove the theory, it is possible that the Romans used the an inlet on the south side of the harbour as a landing place. Other Roman remains have been found at Rodwell, Wyke Regis and Radipole. At Radipole, it is thought, the Romans landed after sailing their cargo-laden galleys from the river mouth up the River Wey to a spot at the top of Radipole Lake. Here their goods would have been unloaded, ready for onward transport by road to the new Roman town of Durnovaria (Dorchester). The Roman galleys would have found a wide and navigable stretch of water as only in the last couple of centuries has infilling claimed large areas of the Backwater, where today's extensive reed growth dates from the construction of Westham Bridge in 1921. A Roman amphora was dredged from the lake in 1889.

ROOPE, Lieutenant Commander Gerald In April 1940 Lt Cdr Roope on board HMS *Glowworm* led an attack against a superior German force off the Norwegian coast. *Glowworm* was sunk and Lt Cdr Roope drowned but he was awarded a posthumous Victoria Cross. He lived at No.75 Rodwell Road.

ROPEWALK There was a ropewalk where Royal Terrace and Frederick Place now stand, which was later moved to where Brunswick Terrace is today.

***RORQUAL*, HMS** Submarine 'adopted' by Weymouth during WW2.

ROSE AND CROWN INN was in Crescent Street.

ROSE TERRACE became Nos.2-36 Granville Road.

ROWES SQUARE was an alternative name for **Babbidge's Square**.

ROWLAND COURT, Greenhill was built in 1965.

ROYAL ADELAIDE HOTEL, Abbotsbury Road (formerly the **Adelaide Arms**) The original Adelaide Arms pub was extended by the purchase of adjoining cottages in 1927 and when it re-opened in 1928 it was renamed the Royal Adelaide Hotel (after the wreck of the *Royal Adelaide* off Chesil Beach in 1872) at the suggestion of brewer Major Herbert Groves. In WW2 the publican was Joe Goddard, long-serving mayor of Weymouth and he was inside when the pub was bombed on 1st November 1941. Rebuilt after the war, the pub closed in 1987 and was converted to apartments known today as Adelaide Court.

ROYAL ARCADE, Esplanade was part of the scheme for the redevelopment of the old Royal Hotel site in the 1890s. Designed by the same architect as the present Royal Hotel, C. Orlando Law, its foundation stone was laid in December 1896 and the building was almost completed when the foundation stone of the present Royal Hotel was laid in April 1897. The Arcade originally contained fourteen shops.

ROYAL BATHS These linked the two main streets at their northern end and occupied a handsome building with Doric columns in St Mary Street and Ionic columns in St Thomas Street. They were erected by the **Johnstone Estate** and opened in 1842. Warm, cold, shower and vapour baths were on offer, supplied with pure sea water piped from the Bay. Charges depended on the season – a sixpenny Hot Sea Bath in winter went up to a shilling in the summer when the visitors were in! In rooms above the baths, meetings of the Literary Institution were held in Victorian times. The Royal Baths were demolished in 1927, and replaced by the **Clinton** building.

ROYAL COUNTIES AGRICULTURAL SHOW This prestigious 4-day show was first held in Weymouth in 1901 at Lodmoor, with grandstand, tents, stalls and show ring. The site was the same in June, 1911 but the occasion was more splendid, this being Coronation Year. Visitors were welcomed into the town by a huge decorated arch on the Esplanade, its banners changed once the show was over to commemorate the forthcoming coronation of King George V and Queen Mary. The Show visited Weymouth once more – from June 5th-8th, 1935, but this time the venue was Chickerell Airfield.

ROYAL CRESCENT, Esplanade is a terrace of 15 houses, now numbered 101-115, The Esplanade. It was probably completed about 1805 and the straight line of houses was originally planned as crescent.

ROYAL DORSET YACHT CLUB was founded in 1875. King Edward VII, then Prince of Wales, and the Duke of Connaught joined as founder members. The Club HQ was No.51 The Esplanade from 1875 until 1981, when the RDYC relocated to the former Sailors' Bethel, No.11 Custom House Quay.

ROYAL ENGINEER INN was in Prospect Place, Chapelhay.

The Royal Counties Agricultural Show at Lodmoor in June 1911.

For those who preferred not to plunge into the sea in the Victorian era, hot and cold salt water baths could be taken at the Royal Baths.

ROYAL ENGINEERS were granted the Freedom of the Borough in 1984, more than 50 years after they first set up camp at Wyke Regis. *See also* BRIDGING CAMP

ROYAL HOSPITAL *see* WEYMOUTH ROYAL HOSPITAL AND DISPENSARY

ROYAL HOTEL (1773-1891) Weymouth's first 'Royal Hotel' was built in the early 1770s on land leased from the Corporation by Andrew Sproule, a speculative Bath developer. It was originally known as 'Stacie's Hotel' after its first proprietor, adopting the 'Royal' name when the Duke of Gloucester built neighbouring **Gloucester Lodge** in 1780. The hotel continued in business until it was demolished in 1891, Weymouth Corporation having decided that the bow-fronted Georgian building was out-of-date and that something on a more palatial scale was required on the seafront. *See also* ROYAL HOTEL (1899 to date)

The bow-fronted Royal Hotel of 1773...

...was demolished in 1891, leaving a gap in the Esplanade buildings...

...until the late 1890s. The present Royal Hotel opened in 1899.

ROYAL HOTEL (1899 to date) Weymouth Corporation pulled down the first Royal Hotel in 1891 -rather prematurely as it turned out, since the expected investment in the site by private enterprise did not materialise for several years. Plans for a 'Grand Hotel' fell through and an unsightly rubble-strewn gap in the middle of the Esplanade remained until the foundation stone of the present Royal Hotel was laid by Mayor Charles Jesty on 22nd April 1897, work being completed in May 1899. The syndicate responsible for the development was led by Lewis Chave and the architect was C.Orlando Law, of London. The hotel opened on 16th May 1899. At the rear is the Queen's Hall ballroom. In 1928 decorative cast iron balconies were added to the front of the building.

ROYAL LODGE *see* GLOUCESTER LODGE

ROYAL NATIONAL LIFEBOAT INSTITUTION *see* LIFEBOATS

ROYAL NAVAL HOTEL, on the corner of Greenhill and Westerhall. *See* PROVINCE OF NATAL HOTEL (its later name)

ROYAL NAVAL SAILORS', HOME *see* SAILORS', HOME

ROYAL OAK INN, Custom House Quay is a mid-19th century rebuild of an earlier inn on the site described in 1858 as *'the Royal Oak of very ancient date, rooms small and low, front portion of the house was gabled and windows latticed. Pulled down recently and a new brick house erected on the site thereof bearing the name of the former and used as an inn'.*

ROYAL OAK PUBLIC HOUSE, Upwey was pulled down to make way for road widening at the foot of Ridgeway in 1965.

The Royal Oak pub at Upwey (on the right of the picture) was pulled down in 1965 in order to widen the road at the foot of Ridgeway.

ROYAL TERRACE is now Nos.68-84 The Esplanade and was built c.1816 on 'The Shrubbery', the former gardens of Gloucester Lodge. It was originally a terrace of eighteen houses, now reduced to seventeen. The end house, at the Esplanade's junction with Westham Road, was demolished in 1929 for road widening, necessary for the increasing traffic going to and from Westham via Westham Bridge. On the rebuilt corner Electric House was opened for the then Council-run electricity office and showroom, with the Electra Hotel next door. Electric House provided accommodation for Weymouth's first public library – a 'reference only' service from 1944 to 1948. The building is currently occupied by a kitchen equipment firm – 'The Cookshop'.

ROYAL VICTORIA HOTEL, Ferrybridge is now known as the Ferry Bridge Inn.

ROYAL VICTORIA PARK *see* PARK DISTRICT

ROYAL VISITORS include the following (excludes royal visits made solely to Portland):-
1343 Edward III landed here when his ships were blown off course in a gale.
1471 **April** Margaret of Anjou landed here with her son Prince Edward.
1506 **January** Philip and Joanna of Castile landed, sheltering from a gale in the Channel.
1665 **September** King Charles II dined with the Corporation.
1789-1805 King George III and Queen Charlotte paid 14 visits to Weymouth accompanied or visited here at various times by all of their 13 surviving children (George, Prince of Wales, born 1762; Frederick, Duke of York and Albany, born 1763; William, Duke of Clarence and St Andrews, born 1765; Princess Charlotte, the Princess Royal, born 1766; Edward, Duke of Kent and Strathearn, born 1767; Princess Augusta, born 1768; Princess Elizabeth, born 1770; Ernest, Duke of Cumberland, born 1771; Augustus, Duke of Sussex, born 1773; Adolphus, Duke of Cambridge, born 1774; Princess Mary, born 1776; Princess Sophia, born 1777; Princess Amelia, born 1783 (Prince Octavius, born 1779 and Prince Alfred, born 1780 both died in 1782, before the Weymouth visits began). The dates of the King's visits are as follows:-
1789 30th June to 14th September (on a tour to Plymouth and the west country 13th -28th August)
1790 no visit
1791 3rd September to 15th October
1792 17th August to 1st October
1793 no visit
1794 15th August to 27th September
1795 17th August to 3rd October
1796 1st August to 17th September
1797 31st July to 18th September
1798 1st September to 22nd October
1799 17th August to 14th October
1800 30th July to 8th October
1801 3rd July to 1st October
1802 3rd July to 1st September
1803 no visit
1804 25th August to 29th October
1805 13th July to 4th October
1814 **September-December** Princess Charlotte of Wales.
1815 **July-January 1816** Princess Charlotte of Wales. After her death in 1817, her husband, Prince Leopold of the Belgians, visited Weymouth in 1818.
1817 **September-November** Duke and Duchess of Gloucester.
1833 **July** Duchess of Kent and Princess Victoria, aged 14 (later Queen Victoria) visited Weymouth on a tour of southern England.
1843 **August** Queen Victoria and Prince Albert anchored in Portland Roads in the royal yacht *Victoria and Albert,* whilst sailing in the Channel. The Queen did not leave the yacht, but Prince Albert visited Portland.
1846 **August** Queen Victoria and Prince Albert made an unintentional visit to Weymouth when the Royal Yacht *Victoria and*

Albert put into Portland Roads during a spell of boisterous weather. The royal pair landed at Weymouth and proceeded straight to Abbotsbury where they visited the Earl of Ilchester and inspected the Swannery.

1849 **July** Prince Albert arrived at Weymouth en route to lay the first stone of Portland Breakwater.

1872 **August** Prince of Wales (later King Edward VII) accompanied by the Duke of Edinburgh and the Duke of Connaught arrived in the royal yacht *Victoria and Albert* when the Prince laid the final stone marking the completion of the Portland Breakwaters.

1880 **August** Prince of Wales (later King Edward VII) arrived in the royal yacht *Victoria and Albert* to visit Portland Prison, afterwards landing at Weymouth to visit the Royal Dorset Yacht Club.

1898 **October** Prince and Princess Louis of Battenberg, she to open the Seamen's Reading Room.

1902 **April** King Edward VII visited Whitehead Torpedo works.

1902 **October** Princess Henry of Battenberg to unveil Queen Victoria statue.

1905 **June** Queen Alexandra was on board royal yacht anchored in Weymouth Bay on both the outward and homeward legs of a voyage to Spain. She did not land.

1905 **September** Duke of Connaught at Portland. Returned to London by train from Weymouth.

1906 **May** Queen Alexandra and her daughter Princess Victoria visited Weymouth in the royal yacht. Princess Victoria came ashore.

1906 King Edward VII Channel Fleet inspection at Portland.

1908 **August** King Edward VII reviewed Channel Fleet.

1910 **November** Princess Henry of Battenberg to open a Naval Bazaar and Nelson 'Victory' Exhibition.

1912 **May** King George V accompanied by the Duke of York (later King George VI). Home Fleet inspection in Weymouth Bay and watched flights by naval and civilian aviators.

1914 Duke of York (later King George VI) served in the Grand Fleet at Portland.

1923 **July** Prince of Wales (later King Edward VIII) took tea at the Gloucester Hotel following a tour of Duchy of Cornwall properties.

1928 **April** King Amanullah of Afghanistan arrived by train to visit the naval fleet at Portland (part of a state visit).

1930 **July** Duke of York (later King George VI) opened Weymouth Town Bridge.

1932 **July** King George V inspected the Home Fleet in Weymouth Bay accompanied by the Prince of Wales (later King Edward VIII) and Prince George.

1933 **July** Prince of Wales (later King Edward VIII) opened the new Weymouth Pier and Harbour works. First flight by a member of the royal family, and bad weather caused the pilot to make a forced landing in a Swanage field. The Prince made the remainder of the journey by car, arriving at Weymouth two hours late and somewhat muddy.

1936 **November** King Edward VIII passed through Weymouth on his way to inspect the Fleet at Portland. He arrived in the early hours of Thursday 12th and slept in the royal train, unaware that he was marooned in a flooded siding as gales lashed the island.

1938 **July** King George VI and the Duke of Kent sailed on exercises with the Home Fleet after arriving at Weymouth in the Royal Train and motoring to the Pier to be taken out to the Royal Yacht *Victoria and Albert.*

1939 **July** King George VI, Queen Elizabeth, Princess Elizabeth and Princess Margaret arrived at Weymouth on the Royal Train to embark on the royal yacht *Victoria and Albert* (a private visit).

1939 **August** King George VI reviewed the Reserve Fleet in Weymouth Bay.

1949 **June** Princess Elizabeth and the Duke of Edinburgh passed through the town on their way to the Channel Islands.

1959 **April** Queen Elizabeth II and (unexpectedly) Prince Charles, aged 10, to visit aircraft carrier HMS *Eagle* in Weymouth Bay.

1964 **June** Duke of Edinburgh landed by aircraft on deck of guided missile destroyer HMS *London* in Weymouth Bay, which took part in anti-submarine exercises the next day.

1971 **June** Princess Anne opened the new Municipal Offices on North Quay on the 400th anniversary of the Union of the towns of Weymouth and Melcombe Regis.

1973 **December** Prince Charles on navy training was in a car on the A353 at Preston which crashed into the back of

King George V and Prince Albert (later King George VI) visited the Fleet in May 1912

another vehicle which had been hit by an oncoming police car. No injuries.
1975 Duke of Edinburgh visited the Swimming Pool and Weymouth Grammar School where he met youngsters on his award scheme.
1978 **March** Duchess of Kent to open Law Courts.
1981 **July** Duke of Gloucester visited Welsh Territorials at Wyke Regis.
1981 **August** Queen Elizabeth II and the Duke of Edinburgh arrived by train to visit the Royal Fleet Auxiliary vessel *Fort Austin* at Portland.
1981 (Winter) Prince Charles arrived by train and was driven to Portland Air Station.
1984 March Princess Anne to visit Olympic Sailing Week and meet disabled people on holiday at Pontin's Riviera.
1984 **May** Princess Anne to visit Olympic training hopefuls.
1984 **May** Princess Alexandra to inaugurate the £35 million pound main drainage scheme for Weymouth and Portland.
1986 **June** Prince Andrew and Sarah Ferguson to attend a charity gala at Weymouth Pavilion.
1986 Princess Anne to visit Olympic Sailing Week.
1988 **June and October** Princess Anne (now Princess Royal) for sailing events.
1989 **June** Princess Anne to the Pavilion Gala Music Hall.
1990 **January** Duke and Duchess of York.
1990 **November** Princess Royal to open Weymouth Library.
1995 **March** Duke of York to open St John Ambulance Brigade Hall.
1996 **September** Duke of York to open the sea defence scheme, Preston Beach Road.
1998 **December** Duke of Kent to visit DEK printing machines on the Granby Industrial Estate.
2002 **February** Princess Anne to open the new Police HQ off Radipole Lane.
2002 **October** Prince Charles to visit Tecan Components on Granby Industrial Estate.
2006 **April** Princess Anne to visit Westhaven House and Buxton House in Radipole Lane.

ROYAL WEDDING CASCADE was opened in September 1982 in the Nothe Gardens to commemorate the wedding of Prince Charles and Lady Diana Spencer.

'ROYAL WEYMOUTH' compiled by Alexander Meyrick Broadley is a unique and important 4-volume work comprising original documents, letters, illustrations , maps etc. relating to the period of King George III's visits to Weymouth, 1789-1805. It is in Weymouth Reference Library's Local Studies Collection.

ROYAL YEOMAN see GLEED'S SHIPYARD

ROYAL YORK TERRACE became Nos.1-5 Lennox Street.

RUSSELL, John, 1st Earl of Bedford *see* PHILIP and JOANNA

RUSSELL, Robert Art master at Weymouth Grammar School in the 1940s who also taught elsewhere in Dorset and had a studio in Swanage. Lived in Lyndhurst Road with his wife Russian-born wife Natalia, a former ballet dancer. Water colour and oil painter best remembered for landscape and architectural studies. Died, aged 82, in December 1984.

RUSSIAN GUN Captured weapons were available following the ending of the Crimean War and Weymouth Council requested two. The government granted the town one large gun on a carriage. It arrived in November 1857 and was placed opposite Pulteney Buildings. It seems to have been moved around, finally being placed on the Pier. Its eventual fate remains to be discovered.

RYLANDS LANE was still being referred to as Rylands Drove in the 1890s. This is an ancient place name dating back to the 14th century.

RYME, Old Castle Road This private house was used as a WWI Red Cross Hospital from July 1915 until January 1919.

In July 1939 the Royal Family, King George VI, Queen Elizabeth and the Princesses Elizabeth and Margaret arrived in Weymouth on the Royal Train to embark on the royal yacht Victoria and Albert. Seen here outside the Pavilion Theatre.

King George VI and Weymouth's wartime mayor Joe Goddard. The King had arrived in Weymouth to review the Reserve Fleet in August 1939, shortly before the outbreak of World War II.

SDT (South Dorset Trades) Mineral Water Company Limited

S

SDT (South Dorset Trades) Mineral Water Company Limited, 31-33 Holly Road Formed in 1903 by local licensees who decided to produce their own mineral water, and later, soft drinks. Originally in Edward Street, moved to Nos.31-33 Holly Road in 1922. Celebrated 50th anniversary in 1953 by which time they were also dealing in sweets, chocolates, crisps etc.

SAILORS' BETHEL, Custom House Quay The society founded in Weymouth in 1834 as the Weymouth Seaman's Friend Society, provided bibles and religious books to ships and held religious services on board. In the 1840s a store on the Quay was rented as a Bethel, until Sir Frederic Johnstone gave a new site on the Quay in 1865, formerly hot and cold sea water baths. The newly built Sailors' Bethel and Reading Room opened 6th June 1866, intended mainly for the use of local sailors. Later there was a decline in sailing ships owned by and using the port and steamers came and went so quickly that the Bethel was not used. In 1908 it was taken over by the British and Foreign Sailors Society, enlarged and refurbished to provide a 'home from home' for Royal Navy and mercantile marine sailors, with beds, recreational facilities and religious services. Renamed 'The Sailors' Rest and Institute', but to locals it was always the 'Sailors' Bethel'. It closed in September 1950 and the premises were sold in 1951, becoming a youth club, later being converted to a restaurant- 'The Spinnaker', and currently the HQ of the Royal Dorset Yacht Club.

SAILORS' HOME, St Nicholas Street When the Fleet was in Portland Harbour thousands of sailors thronged the streets of Weymouth on shore leave- sometimes for several days- and recreational facilities were inadequate. The **Sailors' Bethel** was not enlarged until 1908 and the Temperance Association could only provide basic facilities. But there were plenty of public houses! A much larger establishment was required and in St Nicholas Street Sir Frederic Johnstone donated a garden then on the site and adjoining cottages were purchased. The Weymouth Royal Sailors' Home, a Crickmay design, was opened by Lord Tweedmouth, First Lord of the Admiralty, on 28th February 1907, a day of great celebration and ceremony. The exterior of the building was appropriately decorated with stonework dolphins, anchors and decorative rope work. It provided beds, washing facilities, billiards, reading room, dance floor, restaurant, beer, tea and coffee. Although temperance was very much an issue of the day, it was decided not to make the Home teetotal. Later known as the White Ensign Club, the diminishing naval presence in the area saw it being little used by the early 1960s and it closed in December 1965. It was demolished in July/August 1970 and a supermarket was built on the site, later replaced by the present cinema.

SAILORS' HOME INN, Chapelhay

SAILORS' REST AND INSTITUTE Sailors Rests in the 19th century were usually run on religious lines, intent on keeping the men off drink and other attractions in the port. One, run by the British Women's Temperance Association had been at the entrance to the Jubilee Hall (Weymouth Sailors' Rest) later moving to larger premises in St Thomas Street in 1899. Another was The East Memorial Sailors and Soldiers' Home (after Weymouth resident Rear Admiral East, whose daughter started the home in 1901) in King Street.This one closed in 1929, due to a falling-off in visits from the Atlantic Fleet. *See also* SAILORS' BETHEL; SAILORS' HOME

ST ALBAN TERRACE became Nos.1-8 Lower St Alban Street. Demolished in April 1963 when the present telephone exchange and sorting office were built.

ST ALBANS, Duke of In July 1790 the Duke asked the Corporation if he might, at his own expense, erect a seat on the Esplanade and steps leading down from the Esplanade to the

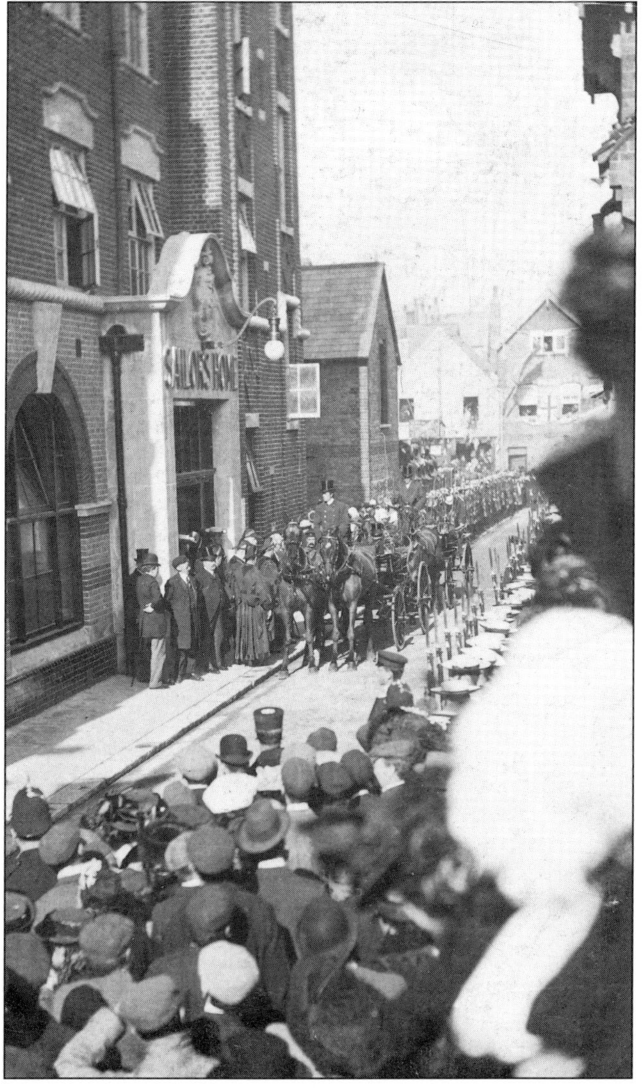

The Sailors' Home, St Nicholas Street on opening day 28th February 1907.

sands opposite his house. Permission was granted. His house was in Clarence Buildings, on the corner of St Alban Street.

ST ALBANS COTTAGES were on the east side of West Street.

ST ALBANS ROW was the name once used for Upper St Alban Street.

ST ALDHELM'S CHURCH, Spa Road, Radipole was consecrated in 1940. Sister church to St Ann's Radipole and built to serve the extensive housing developments in the Dorchester Road area. The building incorporates pews from **Christchurch** and organ and stained glass from **Weymouth College** (the boys' public school) as well as the College's Roll of Honour. The church was considerably altered in the late 1960s.

ST ANDREW'S CHURCH, Preston dates from the mediaeval period, with traces of Norman work.

ST ANDREW'S SQUARE is a place name no longer used. It is the area where East Street opens onto The Esplanade between the northern end of Grosvenor Place (No.34 The Esplanade) and the southern end of Augusta Place (No.35 The Esplanade).

ST ANN'S CHURCH, Radipole (until 1927 known as St Mary's, Radipole) Dating from the 13th century, this was once the parish church for Melcombe as well as Radipole. Being some two miles from Melcombe, on Sundays and Feast Days the inhabitants of the town were away from their homes for some considerable time, an absence which French privateers and pirates made good use of, looting, burning and causing much havoc. These raids were one of the arguments put forward by the people of Melcombe when they petitioned for and were granted a church of their own in 1606. Until 1927, St Ann's, Radipole was dedicated to St Mary but it was decided to change the dedication owing to confusion with the parish church of Melcombe, which was also dedicated to St Mary.

ST AUGUSTINE'S ROMAN CATHOLIC CHURCH, Dorchester Road In the 1700s and early 1800s, in the days before catholic emancipation there was no resident Catholic priest in Weymouth and no church building. Visiting priests ministered to those of the faith. St Augustine's RC church and presbytery opened on 22nd October 1835 on Dorchester Road at Lodmoor Hill, the first Roman Catholic Church to be built in Weymouth since the Reformation. The church was enlarged and a new presbytery built towards the end of the 19th century.

ST AUGUSTINE'S SCHOOL, Walpole Street opened in 1906, having previously been in rented accommodation in the Park District. The present school in Hardy Avenue opened in September 1964.

ST BOTOLPH'S FAIR was granted in a Charter of 1280, confirmed in 1318, and was held in the first week of June.

ST CHARLES' ROMAN CATHOLIC CHURCH, Sunnyside Road, Wyke Regis opened 10th May 1956. It was built with money left in the will of Mr Charles Wilson, a Gloucestershire man who had also played a large part in the building of St Joseph's Church at Westham. Now closed.

ST EDMUND STREET Its western end was renamed Lower St Edmund Street in 1872.

ST EDMUND'S CHURCH, Lanehouse Rocks Road St Edmund's (in temporary accommodation) became a separate parish in July 1950. The present church was consecrated on 16th October 1954.

ST FRANCIS OF ASSISI CHURCH, Littlemoor was dedicated in 1986.

ST GABRIEL'S HOME was a home for unmarried mothers. It was founded in Great George Street as St Gabriel's Mission Home in the 1880s, moving to Abbotsbury Road in 1937 and to larger premises at No.18 Dorchester Road in January 1952,

St Ann's Church and School, Radipole. A miniature engraving of 1868.

where it was opened by the Bishop of Sherborne. Inter-denominational and open to all classes and creeds, St Gabriel's was a registered adoption society but assistance was given to girls who wanted to keep their babies. It closed in 1973.

ST JOHN AMBULANCE BRIGADE HALL opened in Westwey Road on 12th April 1939. In 1994 the building was demolished as structurally unsafe and a new hall on the same site was opened by the Duke of York on 17th March 1995.

Further reading : *Bandages and benevolence: the history of Weymouth through the eyes of Weymouth St John Ambulance Brigade*, by Andrew Bryant (White Cross Publishing, Weymouth, 1995)

ST JOHN'S CHURCH Designed by Talbot Bury and built by Philip Dodson, the church was consecrated on 19th October 1854 and its vicarage was built in 1859. In the early 1900s extensive remedial work was required to underpin the foundations.

St John's Church, consecrated in 1854.

ST JOHN'S GARDENS opened on 20th July 1904 on land given by Sir Frederic Johnstone.

ST JOHN'S HOSPITAL was a temporary WWI Red Cross Hospital in **St John's Mission House**. The hospital opened in October 1914, and in January 1916 moved to a house in Glendinning Avenue, finally closing in January 1919.

ST JOHN'S MISSION HOUSE, Chelmsford Street opened in December 1892. During WW1 it was a temporary hospital and in WW2 it was used as a canteen and recreation rooms for HM Forces run by the redoubtable Mrs Dorothy B. King, of the Weymouth Branch of the National British Women's Total Abstinence Union.

ST JOHN'S SCHOOLS The first school, on the corner of Dorchester Road and William Street, opened on 28th December 1864. It closed in 1974 and the site has been redeveloped as apartments known as St John's Court. St John's Church of England VA Primary School relocated to Coombe Avenue in 1974.

ST JOHN'S TERRACE is now Nos.3-35, Dorchester Road.

ST JOSEPH'S ROMAN CATHOLIC CHURCH, Westham Road was dedicated on 18th April 1934. It was built on the site of a former nursery garden run by E. Mills. The church hall opened in October 1951.

ST LAWRENCE CHURCH, Upwey probably evolved from a little chantry founded by John Bayouse in 1244. At this time Upwey was still known as Waia Bayouse; the place name Wey (from the river) plus the family name of Bayouse.

ST LEONARD'S MAISONETTES became Nos.104-126 St Leonard's Road.

ST LEONARD'S ROAD was originally a country lane known at various times as Bazell's Lane, Dixon's Lane and Butts Lane and then as Union Road and Union Place. In 1872 it was decided *'that Union Road and Place from Mr Groves house to Hope Square be called St Leonard's Road'.* It is likely that the street's name derives from that of Sir Edward Burtenshaw Sugden who was created 1st Baron St Leonards in 1852. An eminent lawyer, he had served as an MP for Weymouth from 1826-31, being appointed Solicitor General during that period and later Lord Chancellor. The street was re-numbered in the 1930s.

ST MARTIN'S CHURCH, Chickerell Road Part of Holy Trinity parish, the church was consecrated on 30th October 1908. Services had previously been held in the nearby St Martin's Mission Rooms (once **Snook's Candle Factory**). At the time of its opening, the intention was to enlarge the church at some future date, but it was never completed as originally planned. In the post-WW2 years congregations dwindled and the Salisbury Diocesan Association for the Deaf and Hard of Hearing used the church for their services and as a club. The church was refurbished in 1961 and later became HQ for the Weymouth and Portland Branch of the Dorset Association for the Disabled before being converted to housing – 'St Martin's Court' – in the 1980s.

ST MARY STREET was pedestrianised in 1986.

Now pedestrianised, St Mary Street in 1900 saw two-way horse-bus traffic.

ST MARY'S CHURCH is the parish church of Melcombe Regis. Designed by James Hamilton, its foundation stone was laid in 1815 and the church was consecrated on 21st March 1817. It replaced an earlier church on the same site. Until the 1600s Melcombe's parish church was at Radipole, its location much resented by the people of the town who complained that not only was Radipole Church too small, but that in time of pestilence danger might arise from *'carrying of the contagious dead bodyes soe farr'*, along with the fear of raids by French pirates while they were absent at worship. In 1603 Melcombe people were authorised to build a church where an old chapel had stood and enclose waste ground either side to make a churchyard. As 'Christchurch' it was consecrated on 14th September 1606 and later renamed St Mary's. It was to this modest building that Sir James Thornhill presented his fine altarpiece painting *'The Last Supper'* in 1721. The 1606 church served Melcombe until 1815 by which time it had become rather dilapidated and sections of its plaster ceiling were apt to descend on the congregation during services. The present church replaced it on the same site and the Thornhill painting, which once filled the entire end wall of the old church, can be seen above the altar.

The first St Mary's Church of 1606...

...and the present St Mary's Church which replaced it in 1817.

ST MARY'S MISSION HALL, West Street was built in 1883.

ST MARY'S SCHOOLS, School Street/Great George Street Also known as Melcombe Regis National Schools. Thought to date in some form from 1813, known to have been a school for boys in 1824, girls being admitted in 1826. Rebuilt and enlarged over the years, the school closed in 1982 and was demolished in 1988. On the site now stands Weymouth Library, opened 8th November 1990. A plaque from exterior wall of the school bearing King George III's words *'It is my wish that every poor child in my Dominions should be taught to read the Bible'* has been preserved in Weymouth Library. *See also* LANCASTER, Joseph

Left: *Weymouth Library now stands on the site of St Mary's School. The plaque bearing King George III's words can be seen on the school's front wall and it is now on the main staircase in Weymouth Library.*

ST NICHOLAS AND ST LAURENCE SCHOOL, Broadwey opened in 1972 to accommodate pupils from the closed St Nicholas village school which stood almost opposite the church at Broadwey and has since been converted to housing. In 1976 the new school also took pupils from St Laurence School, Upwey when it closed, hence the dual name.

ST NICHOLAS CHAPEL, Chapelhay The towns of Weymouth and Melcombe Regis had no churches of their own in their early history – parishioners of Melcombe had to journey to Radipole to attend church and those of Weymouth went to the parish church at Wyke Regis. Raids on the town by French pirates and privateers during the times the local people were attending church led to Weymouth petitioning for a church of its own and in 1377 permission was granted to build a chapel which gave the name 'Chapelhay' to the area on which it stood. The chapel was converted to use as a fort during the English Civil War and was too badly damaged in the fighting to be used again as a place of worship. It was not until Holy Trinity Church opened in 1836 that Weymouthians once again had their own place of worship. A pillar from the original chapel, once displayed in the wall of **Holy Trinity Schools**, which were built on the site in 1853, is now in Weymouth Museum.

ST NICHOLAS CHURCH, Broadwey was originally dedicated to St Michael, the name being changed early in the 15th century. The building was extensively altered in the 19th and early 20th centuries.

ST NICHOLAS CHURCH, Buxton Road was erected in 1894 as a chapel of ease for the increasing population of Holy Trinity parish in the Rodwell area. It was originally a corrugated iron building which had already seen some years service in Salisbury when it was purchased 'second-hand'. It became known locally as the 'Tin Tabernacle'and remained in use until 1964. When the present St Nicholas Church (dedicated March 1964) was completed on an adjacent part of the same site, the iron building was dismantled.

ST NICHOLAS STREET There were once streets of this name on both sides of the harbour (St Nicholas being the patron saint of sailors). In Melcombe the street name is still in use. In Weymouth, the old mediaeval chapel on Chapelhay was dedicated to St Nicholas and St Nicholas Street led to it. It was renamed Chapelhay Street in 1872 to avoid confusion with Melcombe's street of the same name.

ST PAUL'S CHURCH, Abbotsbury Road The Reverend Pigou of Wyke Regis purchased a site on Abbotsbury Road to provide a church for the inhabitants of the growing suburb of Westham. It was dedicated in May,1880 and served as a church until 1896, becoming the Parish Room when the first part of St Paul's Church was completed on the opposite side of the road. The foundation stone of St Paul's Church had been laid on 9th May 1894 by Alice, Countess Hoyos, daughter of Robert Whitehead. The architect was George H. Fellowes Prynne of London. The new parish of Westham was formed in 1901 and the church was finally completed in 1913. The Parish Room was demolished in 1974 and houses now fill the site, the parish having gained a new Parish Room on the closure of St Paul's School in 1973. The school building was also demolished when a new hall was erected at the rear of the church.

ST PAUL'S SCHOOL, Abbotsbury Road opened in 1880 and closed in 1973, when the building was converted to a Parish Room, replacing the old chapel which had served this purpose since 1896. It has since been demolished , a new hall having been built at the rear of the church.

ST PAUL'S TERRACE became Nos.156-174 Abbotsbury Road

ST PHILOMENA'S CONVENT SCHOOL, No.74 Wyke Road was established in 1939. It closed in 1981. Attached to the **Convent of Mercy**.

ST THOMAS STREET was partially pedestrianised in 1989, between School Street and St Alban Street. At its southern end a large building was taken down in 1937 for road widening – a scheme which was not implemented. A temporary single-storey structure stood here until 2006 when it was replaced by a new building – an apartment block with shop at street level which blends well in the street scene.

Strong and Williams, a large ironmonger's shop was pulled down in 1937 for road widening...

...which was never carried out. A one-storey building was erected on the site...

...which lasted until 2006 when this building, very like the original one which stood here, replaced it.

SALEM PLACE became Nos.61-67 Franchise Street. Demolished following WW2 air raid damage.

SALISBURY TERRACE became Nos.25-31 Derby Street.

SALLENOVE *see* DE SELLA NOVA

SALLY LUNNE BAKERY, St Alban Street is named after an 18th century Bath pastry cook who had a tea cake named after her, but in the 1890s the bakery here in Weymouth was actually run by M. and A. Lunn.

SALTPANS were anciently thought to be either in the Marsh or Radipole Lake area.

SALVATION ARMY began meeting in Weymouth in 1888 in a disused warehouse in Maiden Street, moving to the **Jubilee Hall** and then to the former **Methodist Chapel in Caroline Place** until 1903 when the Citadel opened in Westham Road. In 1921 the Salvation Army took over the former **Royal Hospital** in School Street, which opened as the Red Shield Forces Club, this later becoming a hostel for the homeless known as **Colwell House**. It closed in 1981 and was demolished, making way for a small shopping complex on the site, known as the Colwell Centre. *See also* BOOTH, General William

SAMSON, Lieutenant Charles, RN Made the first flight from the deck of a moving warship, HMS *Hibernia,* in Weymouth Bay on 9th May 1912. He landed at **Lodmoor Airfield** following the flight.

Further reading : *Wings over Weymouth*, by Colin Pomeroy (Dovecote Press, 2005)

SAN SALVADOR Captured Spanish Armada vessel. *See* **SPANISH ARMADA 1588**

SANATORIUM *see* WEYMOUTH SANATORIUM, Clarence Buildings

SAND HOPPERS Two were erected on the Weymouth side of the harbour in April 1963 for a ready-mix concrete factory at Chickerell.

SAND MODELLERS In the early years of the 20th century there were a number of sand modellers of varying artistic merit on the beach, and in the early 1920s the local council introduced a bye-law to regulate their numbers. For those in more recent years *see* ANDERSON, Mark; DARRINGTON, Fred; HAYWARD, Jack

SANDCASTLE COMPETITIONS were a popular feature on the beach in the early years of the twentieth century. They often had commercial sponsors which brought firms good publicity, such as the Bovril Sand Competition entries which had to feature the word 'Bovril' or depict the 'Bovril Bottle'.

A magnificent Seaside Villa and surely deserving of a prize in the sandcastle competition.

SANDERS COAL STORE was adjacent to the George Inn on Custom House Quay. Now part of Vaughn's restaurant.

SANDERSON-WELLS, Dr Thomas Henry (1871-1958) was senior surgeon at Weymouth and District Hospital for many years and son in law of **Dr James Macpherson Lawrie**. Published poetry and set up an essay prize fund in 1942 known as the Sanderson Wells Competition, open to South Dorset schoolchildren.

SANDSFOOT CASTLE was built in 1539. It was one of a series of defence works erected along the south coast by King Henry VIII, uneasy lest the rulers of the Catholic nations of Europe should unite against him following the Dissolution of the Monasteries. It is thought that stone for the building came from the closed Bindon Abbey at Wool. Sandsfoot Castle was intended, with Portland Castle of the same period, to defend Portland Roads. Although manned during the time of the Spanish Armada and English Civil War there is no record of any shots being fired in anger. Upkeep was always a problem as the sea has undermined the soft cliffs on which the castle stands from the time it was built. After 1665 no attempt was made to preserve it and by the early 18th century Sandsfoot had begun to fall into ruin, its decline hastened by the permission granted to local people to remove stone for building purposes. The Royal Arms carved in stone were removed from the Castle to Wyke Regis Church. In 1902 Weymouth Corporation purchased the ruin from the Department of Woods and Forests for £150. Chunks of masonry fell down the cliffs at intervals, the last big fall being in 1952. Tudor-style gardens were laid out in front of the castle in 1931 and a shelter added in 1964. A short novel, *The Poisoned Cup*, by Joseph Drew has a Sandsfoot Castle setting and ran to many editions.

This 1772 engraving shows the Tudor Sandsfoot Castle already in ruins.

SANDSFOOT CASTLE HALT on the Weymouth and Portland Railway. Opened 1932, closed in March 1952, when the line closed to passengers. A few traces can be found along the 'Rodwell Trail'.

SANDSFORD PLACE *see* THORNLOW SCHOOL

SARGEANT'S PAWN SHOP stood on the corner of St Mary Street and Blockhouse Lane and extended back to New Street, the business being founded in the late 1870s. Mr Sargeant was also a jeweller but the three brass balls hanging outside his shop were quite a landmark and it was as a pawnshop that most locals remember the premises. The three balls ended up on naval warship in Portland Harbour in 1948 but were retrieved just slightly the worse for wear. F.W.Woolworth, then in St Mary Street and separated from Sergeants by Blockhouse Lane, bought the pawnbroker's shop in 1960, hoping to build across the lane and extend their store, but planning permission was refused and Blockhouse Lane remains a thoroughfare. Sargeant's shop, No.9, St Mary Street was completely rebuilt in the 1970s and is now a building society.

SAWYERS ARMS was in Great George Street.

SAXON PERIOD King Athelstan in 934 conveyed *'all the water within the shore of Waimouie (Weymouth) and half the stream of Waymouie out to sea'* to Weymouth and the fact that only half the water was granted to the town may suggest some form of settlement on the Melcombe side of the river. *See also* CULLIFORD TREE HUNDRED

SCHNEIDER TROPHY RACES *see* MOORHEAD, Paul; STAINFORTH, Wing Commander George Hedley

SCHOOL STREET takes its name from the early 19th century National School (St Mary's Schools) which stood on the site of the present Weymouth Library.

SCHOOLS are listed by individual names and these include state schools and long- established private schools. Over several centuries numerous small private schools came and went and no study has been made of these. A glance at the advertisement columns of just one issue of the Southern Times, dated 14th May 1898 reveals eight educational establishments- Weymouth Commercial School (boarders and day pupils received), The French Convent, Carlton Road (boarding school for young ladies, day pupils received), Netherton House School (Principals The Misses Tizard assisted by Professors and Qualified Governesses and with a Preparatory Class for Little Girls), Weymouth Collegiate School for Girls (a few boarders received), The Misses Collett's Boarding and Day School for Girls, 10 Frederick Place (pupils prepared for local examinations. A preparatory class for little boys), Mons. and Madame Marinier, Fairholme, Glendinning Avenue (prepared to give pupils lessons at their own or pupils' residences), Mons. B Probst, 11 Dorchester Road, (who received and visited pupils for French, German, Latin, Greek, English, Junior Mathematics, Drawing and Book-Keeping) and Miss A Batt who gave lessons in wood carving.

SCOUT HUT, Rylands Lane opened October 1963 for the 3rd Wyke Regis Sea Scouts.

SCRAMBRIDGE HILL is a local name for the lower part of St Leonard's Road which leads down to Hope Square. Sometimes called Scribbage Hill.

SCRIBBAGE HILL *see* SCRAMBRIDGE HILL

SEA BATHING The benefits to be gained from taking sea water both externally and internally were being extolled in the late 17th century but it was in the 1700s that physicians of the day began recommending sea bathing as a cure for practically every ailment, from deafness and madness to rheumatism and consumption. Many small coastal ports began to look to their beaches as a new source of income and Weymouth, despite its distance from the major towns, could offer fine sands gently sloping to a broad, safe bay. Weymouth's sea water was also bottled in gallon containers, to be drunk a pint at a time and it was 'exported' to London by stage coach for those unable to make the journey to the coast. Georgian sea bathing was an elaborate ritual which had to be undertaken early in the morning *'as to Bathe late in the Day (more especially in hot Weather) will occasion great Depression of the Spirits, particularly in debilitated or paralytic Persons'. See also* BATH, KING'S; BATHING MACHINES; BATHS ON THE QUAY; MIXED BATHING; ROYAL BATHS.

SEA CADETS' HQ *see BOSCAWEN*

SEA LIFE CENTRE, Lodmoor opened in May 1983.

SEA VIEW CONCERT PLATFORM was on the beach in the years before WW1.

SEAMEN'S READING ROOM at No.4 Trinity Road was opened on 7th October 1898 by Victoria, Princess Louis of Battenberg, accompanied by her husband. It provided local and visiting merchant seamen with newspapers, books, stationery, games and refreshments and, unlike the Sailors' Bethel, was run on non-religious grounds. Prince Louis of Battenberg, serving in the Royal Navy, eventually became First Sea Lord and he and Princess Victoria were the maternal grandparents of Prince Philip.

SEATON TERRACE became Nos.33-37 Ranelagh Road

SECOND ADVENT CHRISTIANS began their services in 1860, using various premises until 1905 when they began meeting at the Temperance Hall, Park Street.

SECOND WORLD WAR *see* WORLD WAR 2

SEDAN CHAIRS These were the 'taxis' of the Georgian era, upright 'boxes' with hinged roofs in which one passenger was seated, carried on long poles by two men, one at each end, and used to transport visitors around the town for a set fee. (Locals knew their way around and probably walked).

SELOUS, Edmund (1857-1934) Noted naturalist. Lived at Wyke Castle in the 1920s. Brother of the explorer and big game hunter Frederick Selous.

'SEQUAH' or 'THE GREAT SEQUAH' (real name Ernest Osmonde) gave stage shows in Weymouth in the 1890s performing 'miracle cures' to advertise his wonder medicines (available at local chemists).

SERRES, J.T. (1759-1825) Marine Artist. Painted scenes of shipping at Weymouth during the visits of King George III.

SEVEN GATES ROAD was an old local name for Littlemoor Road.

SEWARD, Edwin Henry (1877-1954) Prolific photographer of Weymouth and the surrounding district who published hundreds of picture postcards which provide a superb record of life in the town.

Further reading : *Weymouth and Portland* by Geoff Pritchard and Andy Hutchings (Tempus, 2004) – a collection of more than 200 Seward photographs.

SEWERAGE Problems regarding the disposal of sewage dogged the Town Council throughout the 19th century but there was a marked reluctance to actually take any positive action. George Clark, an inspector from the General Board of Health, visited the borough in 1849, the year of a cholera epidemic during which some 40 local people died. It is a disease commonly spread by contaminated water. He published a damning report on conditions in the town, which had no efficient method of disposing of sewage, Melcombe's few sewers being only intended for rain water. House drainage consisted of a privy over a pit, the contents of which ran into the soil around it, these overflowing cesspools polluting the shingly ground on which Melcombe was built. If there was no pit, the privies' contents were tipped into open street gutters or directly into the Backwater. Some seafront properties discharged sewage directly on to the beach. If Melcombe was smelly, Weymouth was worse. Mr Clark put forward suggestions for the provision of proper sewers, drains and water closets but found in Melcombe a strong disinclination to adopt the Public Health Act largely because landlords were unwilling to put right the appalling conditions of their poor tenants. Architect Talbot Bury prepared some drainage plans shortly after the report was issued but although a Local Board of Health had been formed, no action was taken to implement them. In 1866 the eminent engineer Thomas Hawksley was consulted but his plan was also rejected. By now, complaints about the smell from the Backwater were coming in thick and fast, and even on the seafront people were complaining *'we have to hold our noses on a fine afternoon on the sands'*. Sir John Coode was the next to advise on sewage disposal and his plan was to take sewage away from the Backwater altogether. Coode proposed building a dam to control the flow of water in the Backwater, across which the sewage would be conveyed by pipes to a pumping station and sewage farm on the far side. He also prepared plans for the drainage of the Park district. Building of the dam commenced in October 1872. By December 1874 it needed repair and there were proposals for the addition of a weir to it. Sewage continued to pollute the harbour, the council having considered that the construction of a sewage treatment works might be highly injurious to the interest of the town on the grounds of smells, noise, machinery and expense (!). There was much outspoken comment about Sir John and his failings regarding the dam, but the Corporation had not followed his plans, being again unwilling to contemplate the expense of a pumping station for which land had been purchased at Littlefields in 1872. Only at the very end of the century was something done when the drainage question lent impetus to the inclusion of Westham into the borough in the 1890s. The new suburb had increased by leaps and bounds and the sewage of its houses was draining into the Backwater through a culvert near the Gas Works, adding to the already overloaded and often sluggish water which became ever smellier and more unpleasant. Westham was then in Wyke Regis and its drainage question had not been tackled by the Weymouth Rural District Council. Having failed in its attempts to compel the RDC to take action, the town council decided to include Westham (and part of Radipole) within an extended borough in 1895. Yet another drainage scheme was prepared, this time by Messrs. Bramwell and Harris and at last, on 8th July 1896, tenders were accepted for the new Main Drainage Scheme. By 1904 the long-overdue works were completed and the sewage of the town was being discharged into the sea at a point 1,150 feet beyond the Nothe and 25 feet below the low water level at ordinary spring tides. It was pumped there from a pumping station in the

Corporation Yard, Westwey Road which came into use on 17th July 1897. There were two intercepting sewers to the collecting tank, one for Weymouth, one for Melcombe. Problems in the Park District remained, where sewers and drains were frequently choked (many of the houses did not have flushing cisterns) and the whole area was liable to flooding. Following the enlargement of the borough in 1933 new sewers were laid in Upwey, Broadwey, Radipole and Westham replacing cesspool drainage but it was 1957 before Preston and Sutton Poyntz were connected to main drainage. By 1974 the whole scheme was failing and in need of replacement, responsibility for sewerage that year passing to Wessex Water, the regional water authority. An extensive new scheme was undertaken, involving a major new pumping station at Radipole Lake, with additional pumping stations at Wyke and Portland taking sewage to a major headworks station at Wyke, thence out to sea via a tunnel under Chesil Beach and a 1¾ mile long sea outfall. The completed scheme was officially opened on 8th May 1984 by HRH Princess Alexandra.

SEYMOUR STREET was a terraced street of 12 houses off the north side of Lower St Alban Street. Demolished in the 1930s. Now site of the multi-storey car park.

SHALE WORKS operated from 1848 until 1854 either on the site of, or close to the Brick and Tile Works at Westham. Shale was brought from Kimmeridge by the Bituminous Shale Company and distilled in retorts to produce varnish, lubricating grease, pitch and paraffin wax. It was a smelly industrial process but Westham's green fields remained uninhabited until later in the 19th century.

SHAMBLES LIGHTSHIP The first lightship to warn of the dangers of the Shambles Bank off Portland, formerly marked only by buoys, went on station in 1859. It was replaced in 1883 and again in 1947, but since 1973 high-tech automatic buoys have served instead.

SHAMROCK I and ***SHAMROCK III*** see AMERICA'S CUP

SHELTERS, Esplanade *see* ESPLANADE SHELTERS

SHELTON, Grace Beatrice *see* LODGE, Grace

SHERREN, James (1813-1874) Founder of the local printing firm. *See* SHERREN & SON; SHERREN PAPERS

SHERREN, James (1872-1945) Surgeon and sailor. Born in Weymouth, son of John Angel Sherren. Author of books on medicine and surgery who gave his name to 'Sherren's Triangle', in the abdominal area of the human body.

SHERREN, John Angel (1846-1922) *see* SHERREN & SON

SHERREN, Wilkinson (1875-1953) Born in Weymouth. Journalist and author of *The Wessex of Romance* and many other novels and articles.

SHERREN & SON Printing firm founded in 1837 by James Sherren (1813-1874) and taken over by his son John Angel Sherren in 1874. The business was sold around 1911 although it still retains the family name today. Taken over by Henry Byles and continued by his son Nathaniel 'Nat' Byles until 1976, when the business was sold again.

'SHERREN PAPERS' Today, the collection which became known as the 'Sherren Papers' forms a major part of the town's archives, but, incredibly, these valuable, ancient and irreplaceable documents were almost lost for ever in the 19th century. When the present Guildhall was under construction, the charters and documents housed in the old building on the same site were given into the custody of the then Mayor. They were returned when the new Guildhall opened in 1838, but apparently storage conditions were far from ideal and the papers suffered from damp and decay – to such an extent that some years later they were dumped in a cellar or a stable as rubbish. Mr James Sherren, of the local printing business, spotted them there, probably in the early 1840s. He realised their historical significance, was told they were regarded as rubbish, was given them and attempted some restoration work. When members of The British Archaeological Society visited the town in 1871, they saw the papers and found them of great interest (some dated back to the 14th century). Belatedly, Weymouth Corporation realised their immense significance and attempted to buy them back. Mr Sherren, when questioned about his right to own the papers, felt his integrity was being doubted and withdrew from the negotiations. He died in 1874. In 1876 there was more publicity when the papers were listed and described by the Historical Manuscripts Commission. Sherren's son, who inherited the 'Sherren Papers', put them up for auction in 1879 when, with a reserve price of £300, they were unsold. At last, in a post-auction sale, Weymouth Corporation bought them back for 100 guineas and set about producing a catalogue of them. *See also* ARCHIVES

Further reading : *Descriptive Catalogue of the charters, minute books and other documents of the Borough of Weymouth and Melcombe Regis AD 1252-1800* by H.J.Moule (Sherren & Son, Weymouth, 1883)

SHIP AGROUND PUB was in East Street.

SHIP INN, Maiden Street An ancient building, possibly 17th century. Its modern extension stands on the site of the old **Red Warehouse**.

SHIPBUILDING YARDS *see* AYLES FAMILY; BESANT'S SHIPYARD; GLEED'S SHIPYARD. There were other known yards (owner's names untraced) in the Cove (possibly William Puckett's); on North Quay and on the Backwater shore, close to West Street.

SHIPS It has not been possible to list all the many vessels associated with the port but details of some of the best-known ships can be found in books listed in the 'Further reading' suggestions which accompany the entries for COSENS AND COMPANY and the GREAT WESTERN RAILWAY.

SHIPWRECKS A few well-known local shipwrecks have been included in this work but there have been too many to list individually. A number of books have been published on the subject. *See EARL OF ABERGAVENNY; FOYLEBANK; HARTLEPOOL; SIDON*

Further reading: *Dive Dorset* by John Hinchcliffe (Underwater World Publications Ltd., 1984); *Shipwreck index of the British Isles. Volume 1, Isles of Scilly, Cornwall, Devon, Dorset*, by Richard & Bridget Larn (Lloyd's Register of Shipping, 1995)

SHIPWRIGHT'S ARMS public house was in **Salem Place**, Franchise Street, Chapelhay.

SHIRLEY TERRACE was at the beginning of Cromwell Road, east side, at its junction with Old Parish Lane.

SHOREY, 'Sugar-'em' One of Weymouth's best known characters. Mr Shorey lived in a disused toll house which had been the family home for around 100 years. It stood on the Lodmoor side of Preston Beach Road, about 150 yards north of the present entrance to the waste disposal site. His father, Albert Shorey, ran a horse-drawn cab and charabanc service, continued by Sugar-'em. In the winter months he took to supplying and delivering logs. His nickname, Mr Shorey once explained, derived from a phrase his father Albert used – 'We sugared 'em!'- when he'd beaten another cabbie or done a good business deal. It was a bitter blow for 73-year old 'Sugar-em' and his sister when they had to leave the dilapidated tollhouse, entirely devoid of mod cons such as electricity, running water and main drainage, prior to its demolition in 1959. The Shoreys were moved to a prefab in Littlemoor Crescent, where they grappled unhappily with 20th century living. *See also* PRESTON TOLL HOUSE

SHOWNIGHT (of the late 19th/early 20th century) A tremendous occasion in Weymouth when, five or six days before Christmas, all the shops 'dressed up' for the crowds who turned out to feast their eyes on the festive wares displayed outside and in the shop windows. Shopkeepers stayed open until midnight. Butchers hung up sides of beef, lamb and mutton, sucking pigs and bladders of lard, boars heads and pigs trotters, fat geese and ducks; grocers displayed Dorset's Blue Vinny cheese; fish on fishmongers' slabs had to be constantly doused with water; confectioners showed huge iced Christmas cakes; clockwork toys tumbled and performed their automated routines in toyshops and everywhere oil lamps, holly, paper chains and mistletoe added to the atmosphere. WW1 saw the decline of the tradition but there was a revival of a Christmas shopping night in the 1980s. (*See* next entry)

SHOWNIGHT (modern) in Weymouth is a Christmas event. Started in the 1980s it is a late-night shopping event based on the 'Shownight' Christmas shop-dressing of the late 1890s/early 1900s. Shops in the town centre and Brewer's Quay stay open late on one day, usually a Thursday, staff and shoppers dress in Victorian costume (for a few years it was known as 'Victorian Shownight'), there are street entertainments and stalls selling seasonal fare such as mulled wine and roast chestnuts. Now run by Weymouth Community Volunteers, the event also raises funds for charity. On 24th November 2005 the town's ceremony of switching on the Christmas lights was held the same evening when the event was renamed 'Festival of Light'.

SHRUBBERY, The This was the name of the extensive gardens belonging to **Gloucester Lodge** when it was a royal residence. They occupied the ground on which Royal Terrace and Frederick Place have since been built.

SIDNEY HALL stood at the bottom of Boot Hill. It was built by Sir John Groves, the local brewer, in memory of his son Sidney who died of pleurisy in 1895, aged 26. Designed by Crickmay, the foundation stone was laid in 1897 and the hall was opened on 18th April, 1900, by Lord Chelmsford,

On Shownight, close to Christmas in the 1890s and early 1900s, local businesses stayed open until midnight and crowds thronged the streets to see displays like this one at Andrews the butcher, No.6 St Mary Street.

Governor Commandant of the Church Lads Brigade. The Hall was a gift to Holy Trinity parish, and was primarily intended for use by the Brigade, of which Sidney Groves had been a member. A smaller adjacent drill hall at the rear of the main building later became known as the 'Small Sidney Hall'. During WW1 the Sidney Hall was used as a military hospital and in WW2 it was a temporary school for children bombed out of Holy Trinity Schools at Chapelhay. Later use in the 20th century included exhibitions, roller skating etc. A Scout Hut at the rear (9th Weymouth (Holy Trinity) Scout Group) opened in February 1955 and there was also a Red Cross hut on the site. The Sidney Hall was demolished in 1987 to make way (along with Weymouth Football Club's ground and the two huts) for the Gateway supermarket and its car park, since taken over by Asda. The borough's Coat of Arms from high above the Hall's front door is now prominently displayed in Asda's car park, along with the foundation stone.

Today shoppers park here in Asda's car park at the bottom of Boot Hill. The Sidney Hall, opened in 1900, was demolished in 1987.

***SIDON*, HM submarine** Sank in Portland Harbour on the morning of 16th June 1955 after a terrific explosion on board, caused by the premature activation of propellant fuel in a torpedo still in the torpedo tube. Thirteen of her crew died. A big celebrity concert was held at the Alexandra Gardens Theatre the following month to raise funds for their dependants. Sidon was raised on 23rd June 1955. She was later sunk off Portland to be used by the Navy as a target on the sea bed.

SILVER STREET once known as Silver Lane ran below and parallel with High West Street in the area known as the 'Plains of Weymouth'. Silver Street Court was on its north side. All the houses were removed in the 1930s under slum clearance orders. Now the site of Weymouth Fire Station, completed in 1939.

SIMMONS, Edward George *see* STEPHENS, Hettie (he was found guilty of her murder in 1902)

SIMONDS LANE is described as being at the top of Butts Lane (today's St Leonard's Road) in the 17th century.

SKATING RINKS *see* ROLLER SKATING

SKEE BALL A game that originated in the 1920s. A ball was thrown along an alley in the centre of which was a bump which caused the ball to leap high in the air and enter a target. Weymouth's Skee Ball Pavilion, a hut built on piles at the southern end of the Esplanade, was erected in 1926. It closed during the war years and was removed shortly afterwards.

SKEW BRIDGE takes Dorchester Road over the railway line at the Spa, Radipole.

SKIMMINGTON RIDING is an old custom aimed at ridiculing anyone the local population felt deserved public humiliation.

SLAUGHTERHOUSES According to the Medical Officer of Health's report of 1902, there were eleven slaughterhouses within the borough! By 1924 only four remained and in the late 1960s Weymouth lost its last slaughterhouse – Hurdle's, in St Nicholas Street.

SLAVE TRADE Although ships embarked from Weymouth on occasional voyages to the plantations, Weymouth merchants do not appear to have directly participated in the slave trade to any great extent, compared with other Dorset ports such as Lyme and Poole.

SLUICE GARDENS, Greenhill The drain at the Sluice Gardens was the main outfall for Lodmoor. The Gardens stand on land given by Sir Frederic Johnstone and were redesigned with chalets, paddling pool and sandpit in 1961. Sometimes known as the Spoon Gardens.

The walks, flowerbed and rustic shelter in the Sluice Gardens were replaced by chalets, sand pit and paddling pool in 1961.

SLUM CLEARANCE ORDERS Under Housing Acts in the 1930s, local authorities were obliged to draw up plans for slum clearance. Properties had to be brought up to a required standard within three months; if not, demolition orders were served. Overcrowded areas of the town such as **Silver Street** and **Jockey's Row**, which today would no doubt be thought quaint and picturesque, were lost to the town under these orders and WW2 bombing was to account for many more.

SMALLMAN, Percy Town Clerk from 1926 until 1956. Granted Freedom of the Borough 14th March 1956.

SMALLMOUTH is where the waters of The Fleet flow into what is now Portland Harbour. *See* FERRY, SMALLMOUTH; FERRYBRIDGE; PASSAGE HOUSE

SMALLPOX Weymouth's last and most serious smallpox outbreak occurred in 1871 and lasted some four months, being declared over by late September. More than sixty people died in the town, with a few more deaths in the villages. *See* ISOLATION HOSPITAL, Rocks Terrace

SMART, Hawley Novelist. Published *Broken Bonds* in 1874, and used for the first time the name 'Upwey Wishing Well' as a descriptive term for the springs at Upwey – the name being soon afterwards adopted by the proprietors of the springs.

SMART, Robert J (1877-1953) Artist. Started his career as an engineer but began full-time teaching at the age of 32. Art Master at Weymouth Grammar School in the 1920s and 1930s. Produced many paintings and sketches of Weymouth, six of which were produced as a set of black and white postcards. Lived at No.18 Kirtleton Avenue.

SMITH, Right Rev. Aloysius J. Born in Weymouth. First Abbot of Bodmin and author of theological works.

SMITH, George Joseph The notorious 'Brides in the Bath' murderer, who married three women and drowned each one in the bath to get hold of their money. He wed the first of these, Bessie Mundy from Warminster, at Weymouth Register Office on 26th August 1910 – he was already married, so used the alias Henry Williams. The couple settled in Rodwell Avenue, but by the end of the year, having pocketed some of his wife's inheritance, he left her and returned to an old girlfriend in Bristol. Unfortunately for Bessie, she met up with him again in 1912 and even made a will in his favour. They moved to Herne Bay, where Smith drowned her in the bath, convincingly acted the distraught husband and got away with it, the coroner recording a verdict of accidental death. Two more brides suffered the same fate – in 1913, the verdict was 'death by misadventure', in 1914 'accidental death'. These deaths were reported in the newspapers, suspicions were aroused, exhumations took place and Smith was found guilty of murder. He was hanged at Maidstone in August 1915.

SMITH, W.H. Booksellers The firm built up its trade in the late 19th century as proprietors of railway station bookstalls. Contract difficulties with the railway companies in the early 1900s led W.H. Smith to open some 140 shops in towns in Wales and the west of England in 1905. One of these was in Weymouth, opening in December 1905 in the Georgian roundhouse behind the King's Statue, with entrances in St Thomas Street and St Mary Street. The old small-paned windows were replaced by plate glass in 1960. The firm remained in these premises until 1998, moving then to a more central location at No.88 St Mary Street, still with entrances in both main streets, this having been John Menzies store until the two companies amalgamated.

SMUGGLER'S TOMBSTONE *see* LEWIS, William

SMUGGLING Smuggling was rife in the local area and continued well into the 19th century. As with all illegal activities our knowledge of it is based only on those runs which were intercepted and the preventive men faced an almost impossible task as most of the population considered it was quite in order to profit from the 'runned goods' once they were ashore. Clashes between smugglers and officers of the law were often violent. Captured smugglers faced heavy fines, the forfeit of their vessels and impressment on a man of war so were far more likely to fight their way out of trouble than surrender. *See also* KNIGHT, Lt. Thomas; LEWIS, William

Further reading : *Dorset smugglers*, by Roger Guttridge (Dorset Publishing Company, 2nd ed. 1987)

SNAILS 17th century traveller Peter Mundy reported that it was 'raining snails' in Weymouth. *See* MUNDY, Peter, for his account of this odd phenomenon

SNOOK, Dr Samuel Penny- (died 1949) Well-known old Weymouth family, the Pennys were at one time owners of Netherton House and Dr Penny-Snook was living there at the time of his death. The family owned **Snook's Candle Factory** at Pye Hill and were leaseholders of the Marsh for many years. *See also* NETHERTON HOUSE; PENNY FAMILY

SNOOK'S CANDLE FACTORY was *'near Marsh Road by the side of the Recreation Ground which was afterwards put to political uses and later still became a mission hall'*. The 'mission hall' was the forerunner of **St Martin's Church** and is thought to have been at the entrance to Weston Road, close to its junction with Boot Hill.

SNOW The winter of 1962-63 was described as the worst since 1947 and recalled memories of the great blizzard of January 1881 and snowstorms of March 1891 and 1896. Snow fell at the end of December 1962 and snowfalls continued into February 1963. The worst incident occurred on Ridgeway Hill where the five occupants of a snowbound car attempted to keep warm by running the car engine and two died from carbon monoxide poisoning.

SNUG CORNER was a terrace of 5 houses which once stood behind No.14 St Mary Street.

SOCIETY OF FRIENDS Appear to have had a meeting house in Melcombe, at the southern end of St Thomas Street (probably No.45, long since demolished) from the late 17th century until the 1830s. The Quakers Burial Ground of 1713 on the Nothe, also known as Quakers Grove, still exists although the gravestones have been moved to the outer walls. Other non-conformists were also buried here.

SOMERSET PLACE, Greenhill is now Nos. 8-16 Greenhill.

SOPHIA, Princess (1777-1848) Daughter of King George III and frequent visitor to Weymouth. Unmarried, she was the subject of a scandal in 1800 when she gave birth to a son in Weymouth, the father of whom is unknown to this day. The King kept his daughters so strictly controlled that opportunities for romance were few and far between. Sophia is rumoured to have had an affair with an equerry of the king, a much older man called General Thomas Garth, of Ilsington House, Puddletown near Dorchester. The boy was brought up at Ilsington and was known as Tommy Garth, although his paternity was never acknowledged. He turned out to be an unpleasant character in adult life, a drinker, frequently in debt and an unsuccessful blackmailer of the Royal Family when he claimed to be able to prove the truth about his background. Some said he was the outcome of an incestuous union between Princess Sophia and her elder brother Ernest, Duke of Cumberland.

SOPHIA, PRINCESS (1773-1844) Daughter of the Duke of Gloucester. A view of Wyke Regis which appears in the collection of prints published by **John Love** is believed to have been painted by her, the collection being dedicated to her father.

SOUTH AFRICAN WAR (BOER WAR) Local men who served in the South African War 1899-1902 were granted the **Freedom of the Borough.**

SOUTH DORSET TECHNICAL COLLEGE, Newstead Road was built and first used in 1938, being officially completed and opened on 26th October 1940. For its history *see* WEYMOUTH COLLEGE (present day), Cranford Avenue

SOUTH VIEW was the name of No.44 Abbotsbury Road and No.91 Newstead Road.

SOUTHAMPTON ROW was off the north side of St Leonard's Road. It was cleared in 1955 following WW2 air raid damage, some properties having been demolished pre-war.

SOUTHDOWN FARM is situated on the slope of the hill overlooking Lodmoor and prior to the 1920s the farm was the only building on this now heavily developed residential area of Preston. A serious fire in June 1907 destroyed much of the farm property, its inaccessible position some mile and a half off the road and a lack of water hampering the local fire brigade's efforts to contain the blaze. The farmhouse was saved, but all the buildings around it were lost.

SOUTHDOWN VIEW became part of Knightsdale Road, probably Nos.10-16.

SOUTHERN TIMES *see* NEWSPAPERS

SOUTHILL Southill Garden Village was built by Messrs. George Calverley and Sons (Contractors) Ltd. of Leicester. The show house of the new estate opened in March 1960. Southill Shopping Centre was built 1974-5 and the Community Centre opened in December 1974, replacing an older centre.

SOUTHVIEW ESTATE at Westham. First portion of building land was offered for sale in July 1898.

SOUTHWICK TERRACE became Nos.24-31 Ranelagh Road.

SOWTER HALL, No.8 North Quay was a club for young people run by Holy Trinity parish in the years following WW2, in premises formerly occupied by the Girls' Friendly Society. The building took its name from Rev. Francis Briggs Sowter, M.A. vicar of Holy Trinity from 1884-1890. In 1961 Sowter Hall (by then a guest house) was demolished in the clearance of the High Street/North Quay area.

SPA HOTEL, Radipole was built in 1899.

SPANISH ARMADA 1588 Local defences were reviewed and three vessels, the *John*, the *Reprisal* and a pinnace sailed from Weymouth to join Sir Francis Drake's fleet at Plymouth when the threat of war with Spain became a certainty. Weymouth also supplied 185 men and six supply ships to the victorious English fleet : *Golden Lion/Ryall, Galleon, Sutton, Bond, Heath Hen and Catherine*, vessels of between 60 and 120 tons. The town must have been prospering more than other Dorset ports at this time as Lyme supplied only 2 vessels and Poole, pleading poverty, none at all. There were no enemy landings but sea battles were fought off Portland and Purbeck before Philip of Spain's fleet sailed on up the Channel to eventual defeat. One Portuguese carrack was brought into Weymouth, badly damaged by fire. The *San Salvador* was too big to bring into the harbour and anchored out in the Bay. As soon as a town official was sent on his way to find out from the Admiralty in London what should be done with this prize, the locals descended on the ship and stripped it of everything of value. There was reputed to be treasure on board the vessel. If there was, it had certainly been removed before her final voyage, for when the San Salvador set sail for Portsmouth she was by then so light in the water that she turned turtle and sank off Studland. On the 300th anniversary of the Armada celebrations were held in Weymouth and Portland which included beacon lighting, torchlight processions and fireworks. *See also* ARMADA CHEST; BEACONS

Further reading : *Dorset Elizabethans at home and abroad*, by Maureen Weinstock (John Murray, 1967)

SPAS *see* NOTTINGTON SPA; RADIPOLE SPA

SPEEDWAY started at the newly opened Wessex Stadium on 4th August 1954. Local team was the 'Scorchers'. Closed May 1955, due to poor gates, bad weather and heavy taxation. Revived in 1974 as the 'Weymouth Wildcats' but moved to Poole in 1985 when there were doubts over the future of the Wessex Stadium. The Stadium was replaced by the present Wessex Stadium when Weymouth Football Club moved here from their previous ground in Newstead Road in 1987. Speedway returned in 2006.

SPETCH, 'Pop' ran the billiards saloon above No.62/62a St Mary Street from 1940 until his death in February 1961.

SPIES The two local people found guilty in the naval secrets case of 1961 were Harry Houghton and Ethel Gee. Both worked at the Admiralty Underwater Weapons Establishment at Portland. Houghton lived at No.8 Meadow View Road, Broadwey, 'Bunty' Gee at Portland. They were sentenced to 15 years apiece and married soon after their release in 1970.

Further reading : *Spy ring*, by John Bulloch and Henry Miller (Secker & Warburg, 1961); *Operation Portland* by Harry Houghton (Hart Davis, 1972)

SPINNAKER VIEW Art-deco style flats at the bottom of Boot Hill fronting onto Weston Road. Completed in 2005. The site was formerly occupied by Broadwey Motors garage and Weymouth Snooker Club.

SPRING GARDENS The original Spring Gardens no longer exists. It was a street of terraced houses with long front gardens, which ran between St Leonard's Road and Rodwell Avenue. Some houses suffered WW2 air raid damage, and in post-war years the decision was taken to demolish the whole street and rebuild. The present cul-de-sac of the same name dates from the 1950s.

SPRINGFIELD, Rodwell Road The house's lodge and entrance drive stood almost opposite St Leonard's Road and the gate pillars and lodge can still be seen. It was built for the Devenish brewery family in 1879 and its last occupant was Major J.H.C. Devenish. Taken over by the military in WW2, the house subsequently suffered air raid damage and remained unoccupied from 1945 until it was sold in 1959, too damaged and neglected to convert to old people's housing as originally planned, although land within its grounds was set aside for this purpose (*See* Devenish Homes). The houses of Portwey Close were built on the remaining land.

SPRINGHEAD HOTEL, Sutton Poyntz was built and opened in 1898.

SPYGLASS INN *see* EMBASSY HOTEL

STACIE'S HOTEL *see* ROYAL HOTEL (1773-1891)

STAG PUBLIC HOUSE was at No.29 Lennox Street

STAGG, Mr One of Westham's early residents, probably its second inhabitant, the tenant of Goldcroft Farm being the first in 1865. Stagg was foreman of a firm engaged in restoring West Lulworth church tower. He built himself a house on wheels and had it horse-towed to Westham. Known as The Bungalow, it had a garden and greenhouse and stood on the site of the present St Paul's Church vicarage.

STAINER'S ROW was a terrace of houses leading off the west side of West Street.

STAINFORTH, Wing Commander George Hedley Setter of world air-speed records and a member of the Schneider Trophy seaplane racing team in 1931. The trophy was won for Great Britain, but Stainforth (then a Flight Lieutenant) was determined to be the first to fly at more than 400mph and on 29th September he flew six circuits of a set course in a Supermarine S6B and broke his previous two world records with a speed of 407.5 mph – a record not broken until 1934, when an Italian aviator set a new record of 440.68mph, which still stands today. Stainforth was an old boy of Weymouth College, the boys' public school, and in 1932 he presented the College with a wind vane, in the form of the S6B. When Weymouth College closed shortly after the outbreak of WW2, the vane was stored until 1952, when it was re-erected in Greenhill Gardens with an appropriate descriptive plaque. Stainforth was killed when night flying out of Aboucir in 1942, and is buried in Egypt. The houses of Stainforth Close, built on the former Chickerell Airfield, commemorate the air ace.

STANDISH-SWEENEY, Robert (1917-1995) Artist. Presented many of his works to Weymouth Library and other public buildings in the town.

STANLEY STREET The name is probably derived from Edward Stanley, Earl of Derby and Prime Minister in the Tory governments of the 1850s and 1860s. The Park District was developed by the **Conservative Land Society**.

STANLEY TERRACE became Nos.3-10 Stanley Street.

STANTON COURT, No.11 Greenhill A mansion built for Colonel Pickard Cambridge in the late-19th century which later became the home of some of the town's leading citizens. The house is now divided into flats.

STAPLE PORTS An attempt to share the trade between the squabbling ports came in 1310 with the granting of staples – Weymouth became a staple port for the import of French, Gascon and Anjou wine and Melcombe a staple port for the export of wool, providing the towns with exclusive rights in dealing with these commodities. The wool trade was extremely important in the mediaeval period and Dorset was famed for its sheep, although Melcombe, during a downturn in its fortunes, lost the wool staple to Poole in 1433.

STAR AND GARTER PUBLIC HOUSE/HOTEL, Crescent Street, has now been converted to a chemist's shop.

STATUE HOUSE and its companion at the entrance to the town's main streets were built to plans Sir William Pulteney had put forward in 1802. His death in 1805 probably delayed the project and Johnstone Row was not built until 1812, finished with its round house which has been little altered. This was once known as 'Croyden's Corner', as Victorian shop proprietor R.H. Croyden's name was emblazoned in large letters high up on the building. More recently, it will be remembered as a model railway emporium. Statue House dates from a little later and in 1815 paupers living in the almshouses on the site (built but not endowed by Sir James Thornhill) were evicted so the old buildings could be pulled down. This action was questioned by some who wanted to know how Pulteney and subsequently the Johnstone Estate had acquired the property. Nevertheless Coburg Place was built with its rounded end, now known as Statue House, much altered with shop fronts at ground-floor level.

STAVORDALE ROAD, Westham takes its name from one of the family names of the Earls of Ilchester, ground landlords of much of the land on which Westham is built. These larger Westham properties were built in the 1890s with 18th century bricks taken from the demolished first Royal Hotel (1773-1891) on the Esplanade.

STAVORDALE VILLAS, Abbotsbury Road were demolished in the late 1980s when Lloyds built a short-lived out-of-town banking facility. The building is now occupied by Betterment Properties.

STEAM PACKET INN, Custom House Quay became the Steam Packet Café and is now Floods's Seafood Restaurant.

STEPHENS, Hettie An attractive and popular 24-year old from Cornwall, Hettie was employed in Graham's Bar, where she became too friendly with Edward George Simmons, the 37-year old steward of the Royal Dorset Yacht Club – and paid with her life. The RDYC on the Esplanade backed onto Graham's Bar in New Street, where Simmons, newly arrived in Weymouth with his wife and young adopted child, was a frequent visitor. He gave Hettie small gifts and appears to have become infatuated with her. Things changed, however, and by late March 1902 Simmons was warning her employer Percy Graham that Hettie was a thief and a drunk, allegations that Graham repeatedly refused to accept. Simmons (having purchased a revolver locally) asked Hettie to meet him on 27th March and they returned to the bar together. As she prepared to leave for her break, Simmons approached her again, but she walked away, telling him she had no more to say to him. Three shots rang out, and Hettie Stephens died as Simmons unsuccessfully attempted to turn the gun on himself. At his trial he pleaded Not Guilty, and the defence spoke at length about his mental state, citing, among other conditions, delusions and paranoia which had led him to kill Hettie. The verdict on Simmons was that he was guilty but insane and he was sent to Broadmoor. Hettie was buried in Melcombe Regis Cemetery.

STEPHENSON, George Robert A frequent visitor to Weymouth with his family in the mid-19th century aboard his fine steam yacht *Northumbria.* Mainly remembered for his gift to the town in 1867 of the purchase money for 'The Rings', the land on which the Alexandra Gardens were later laid out.

STEVENS, Harold Charles Gilbard Born in Weymouth. Worked in the theatre. Publicity manager for the original London production of *Journey's End.* Wrote plays, children's books and lyrics and music for revues.

STEWARD, Gabriel (1731-1792) Of the influential Tucker/Steward dynasty, important in 18th century local politics. Made his money in the 1760s as Captain of the *Neptune,* an East India Company ship trading in China, after which he settled in Weymouth. The Steward family seat was at **Nottington House**. Inherited property from his uncle, John Tucker, who had inherited it from George Bubb Dodington and thus Gabriel Steward had an important parliamentary interest in the town. He was the town's MP from 1778-1786 and 1788-1790 and its Mayor in 1769, 1779 and 1791 (dying in office). He sold his Weymouth property in 1790 to **Sir William Pulteney** for £30,000, the latter's local 'property empire' later becoming part of as the **Johnstone Estate**.

STEWARD, Gabriel Tucker (c.1768-1836) Son of Gabriel Steward. A banker. Disapproved of his father's sale of Weymouth property to Sir William Pulteney and managed to get himself elected as MP from 1794-1810, after which he tried to curry favour with the Johnstone interest, but failed to get re-elected. His bank failed in 1824, following a fraud by one of the partners.

STEWARD'S COURT was a little alley of houses off Governor's Lane. The houses were demolished, along with most of the other buildings on the north side of Governor's Lane, in the late 1950s and this is now the site of Governor's Lane car park.

STOCK CAR RACING was first held at the Wessex Stadium on 19th September 1954.

STONE PIER The short stone jetty shown on 18th century maps has been extended over the years. It had to be reconstructed after damage caused by the 'Great Gale' of 1824 and at one time the date '1826' cut into a stone bollard marked this rebuilding. In 1876-78 the pier was extended, aided by financial assistance from Sir Henry Edwards. The additional 250 feet was intended to act as a breakwater, giving protection to vessels and also to the Pile Pier which was being damaged by the sea's action. It was lengthened again during WW1 when a decorative navigation light support structure was added at the seaward end. Storms in the 1970s and early 1980s caused considerable damage and large blocks of Portland stone were used to strengthen the pier's centre section until major reconstruction work took place between 1985 and 1988. At the same time, stone seats were added and the elegant light support structure and observation platform was refurbished. The Stone Pier is sometimes claimed to be the oldest pier in England but this claim is impossible to substantiate.

STORMOUNT, Nos.76 and 78 Buxton Road This large house near Foord's Corner was built in the mid-19th century by the Reverend. H.C. Pigou, Rector of Wyke Regis, for his sisters, the Misses Pigou. Extended by its next owner, Oliver Warner, but had to be much rebuilt after being gutted by fire in 1911. After his death in 1929, Dorset County Council bought the property for use as a Children's Home which remained in use until the early 1950s. At the time of its demolition in 1997, the house was let as flats. Houses since built on the site are known as Swaffield Gardens, after one of the prominent Wyke families.

STOTTINGWAY, Upwey was anciently a manor in its own right and the name dates back to the 13th century. A large sale of land and property known as the Stottingway Estate took place in November 1918.

STREET NAMES The following appear in 17th century documents but the locations are so far unidentied : Hynes Lane; Hodges Corner; Knight's Corner; Little Lane; Meechers Lane; New Key Street; Rosemarie Lane; Roger's Lane; Stephen Street (which had a house called The Shambles in it).

STRONG & WILLIAMS, No.46 St Thomas Street Ironmongers. The shop was demolished in 1937 for planned street widening which did not take place. A single storey building stood on the site until 2006 (then occupied by the Car Shop) when it was demolished and a block of apartments was built on the site with a shop at ground floor level. The Car Shop, which relocated until rebuilding was completed, moved back in. Illus. p.122.

STUCKEY'S BANK opened a branch in a new building in Charlotte Row at the Esplanade's junction with Bond Street in 1884. This most unusual seafront building – a 'chateau' of pinkish brick and stone, was described by its architects (Paull and Bonella of London) as being in the Burgundian style. The bank eventually became the Westminster, which moved to No.69 St Thomas Street in 1957, leaving the seafront building to be converted into a stylish public convenience soon afterwards.

STURMEY, Henry (John James Henry Sturmey) (1857- 1930) Cycling and motoring pioneer. Perhaps not a true son of Weymouth, as he was born in Somerset, but his father, a Master Mariner, was from the town and it was to Weymouth that the family came when Captain Sturmey was drowned at sea in 1859. The young Sturmey attended Weymouth Middle School and went on to become a schoolmaster, eventually moving to Coventry when he was about 20 years old. The acquisition of a penny-farthing bicycle in his teens began a life-long interest in cycling (the local newspaper *Southern Times* reported that he had *'knocked down a lady'* whilst cycling, fortunately without injury to either party). By the 1870s, having left Weymouth, he was designing bicycles and was the inventor of the Sturmey-Archer 3-speed gear. He published *The Indispensable Bicyclist's Handbook* in 1878, along with numerous articles in *The Cyclist* magazine, which he edited. Motoring was added to his interests in the 1890s; he became the first editor of *The Autocar* magazine, and in 1897 completed a 14-day John O' Groat's to Land's End tour in a Daimler car. Calling at Weymouth on the return journey *'where considerable excitement was occasioned by the appearance of a motor car running through the streets'* he took passengers on short excursions so that they could experience travel in a horseless carriage. Sturmey was hugely influential in many spheres – engineering, journalism, cycling, motoring, photography and he was a founder member of the Aero Club, in the early days of flying when motor car engines were being considered as a means of controlling balloons in flight. He died in 1930, and is buried in Coventry.

STYLES COURT was between Nos. 14 and 15 East Street.

SUBWAY, Esplanade This large and controversial subterranean walkway under the Esplanade opened in May 1988 but although it was intended to take pedestrians safely from one side of King Street to the other, most people were surprised and disappointed to discover that it did not also lead to the beach.

SUBWAY, Westham The town's first subway opened soon after the end of WW1. It took pedestrians beneath the Weymouth and Portland Railway at Littlefield Level Crossing, Westham and no longer exists. The current subways at Westham date from the construction of Weymouth Way and Swannery Bridge in the 1980s.

***SUCCESS* Convict ship** More correctly, a convict hulk, as she was not used for the transportation of prisoners. Built originally for the tea trade in 1790, in the 1850s she was converted to become one of five prison ships moored off Williamstown, Victoria, Australia. Conditions on board were grim and the hulks were phased out by the end of the decade, the *Success* being the only one not broken up. In the 1870s she was converted to a floating museum exhibition as a reminder of the bad old days. She was brought to Britain in the 1890s and went on show in various ports until she was taken to America in 1912. Her visits to Weymouth were in 1904 and 1905.

The convict ship Success, *a tourist attraction in Weymouth in 1904 and 1905, where for a small fee it was possible to tour the vessel and witness the grim conditions endured by prisoners on an Australian convict hulk in the 1850s.*

SUFFRAGETTES Meetings of supporters of the women's suffrage movement in Weymouth were addressed by a number of eminent speakers in 1913 and in 1914 the National Union of Women's Suffrage Societies held a week-long tented camp at Lodmoor. These non-militant, non-party suffragettes were anxious to disassociate themselves from the violent acts of the more extreme members of the movement. The Lodmoor camp held lectures and entertainments as well as sending speakers out to open-air meetings in the town and villages round about. Dress rules were strict – the suffragettes camp uniform was a long green skirt and jacket, white blouse and tie plus green felt hat. No jewellery, no frills and no tight skirts were allowed- probably just as well since conditions at Lodmoor were fairly spartan.

Suffragettes at their camp at Lodmoor in 1914.

SUN INN on the north side of King Street at its junction with Crescent Street was rebuilt by Devenish in 1903. The Devenish initials/logo can be seen in the brickwork at first floor level. In 1986 the pub underwent a name change and became Kings Wine and Ale House but it has since reverted to the original Sun Inn name. (An earlier Sun Inn stood on the Weymouth side of the harbour in the 18th century.)

SUNNY TERRACE became Nos.1-21 Granville Road.

SUNNY VIEW became Nos.4-6 Longcroft Road.

SUNNYBANK was the name of the house and grounds belonging to John B. Cole in Stavordale Road which he agreed to sell to the Borough Council in 1901 to make way for Weymouth Electricity Generating Station. *See also* ELECTRICITY SUPPLY

SUNNYSIDE COTTAGES are adjacent to No.23 Hope Street.

SURREY TERRACE became Nos.66-98 Newstead Road. Also the original name of Nos.23-42 Charles Street.

SURREY VILLAS became Nos.83-84 Walpole Street.

SUTTON MILL, SUTTON POYNTZ Watermill rebuilt in the early 19th century. It remained in use until the 1960s and was converted to a private dwelling in the 1980s.

Left: *Suffragettes on Weymouth seafront.*

SUTTON POYNTZ The first part of the name is derived from the Old English words 'sud'(south) and tun (farm). The manor here was held by the Poyntz family from the 13th century. On 18th April 1908 a serious fire broke out in the village and by the time the Weymouth Fire Brigade arrived almost a quarter of a mile of buildings was on fire. It was contained to one side of the street, but several buildings including the Court House were completely gutted. In the years following the end of WW2 Sutton Poyntz was in rather a run-down state. Formerly picturesque thatched cottages of Northdown Farm were crumbling and dilapidated, overlooking a dried-up duckpond. Work on restoration and rebuilding began in spring 1962 and Sutton Poyntz today is picture-postcard-pretty.

SUTTON POYNTZ WATER WORKS *see* WATER SUPPLY

SWAFFIELD FAMILY The Swaffields of **Wyke House** were local landowners. John Swaffield purchased the house in 1811 and several generations of the family lived there. Joseph Swaffield was Mayor of Weymouth in 1745-6, 1752-3 and 1764-5 and Town Clerk in the 1740s. The Swaffields left Wyke House in the 1920s, one branch of the family moving to Markham House. Alfred Owen Swaffield lived at Rodwell Villa (renamed Rodwell Lodge) and a map handed down though the family indicates that Robert Hassell Swaffield owned **Belfield House** and a considerable amount of land around it in the mid-19th century.

SWAFFIELD GARDENS built in 1998, is named after the **Swaffield Family.**

SWAINE, Hume Artist. Author and illustrator of *An Artist's Rambles around Weymouth and Portland* published in 1898.

SWALLOW COURT *see* LAUNDRY, No.77 Abbotsbury Road

SWAN INN, St Thomas Street The present pub, a Wetherspoons house, takes its name from the old Swan Inn of c.1870 which stood on the site. Prior to that it was Reynolds Brewery, a small brewery. The original pub building and adjacent shops were knocked down in 1975 and made way for a large store, occupied by Centre News and then John Menzies. Menzies moved out on the firm's amalgamation with W.H. Smith, and the empty building was converted to the present Swan pub in 1999.

SWANNERY It seems that the first swans were presented to the town by the Earl of Ilchester in May 1859. Swans from his Swannery at Abbotsbury were colonising the Backwater and the best solution was for him to make a present of them to Weymouth, with the Corporation taking responsibility for their care. In 1874 a man was to be engaged to look after them and work was carried out on the Swannery that year. It was officially named the Weymouth Swannery in 1889.

SWANNERY BRIDGE opened in May 1987.

SWANNERY COURT is an apartment block built in the 2001 opposite Weymouth Bus Station. It stands on the site of the former **Melcombe Regis Station**.

SWATRIDGE'S FLOUR MILL, Helen Lane was established in 1892, and originally owned by a partnership of John Swatridge and Thomas John Templeman. It was renamed Templeman's Flour Mills when Swatridge died, but was also known as Crown Flour Mills and Weymouth Flour Mills. *See* TEMPLEMAN, Thomas John

SWIMMING POOL, Knightsdale Road was completed in December 1974 and officially opened 26th February 1975.

'SWINDON WEEKS' were usually at the beginning of July when the GWR railway works at Swindon closed for the annual holiday. The workers and their families, although not paid for the time off, received a free railway warrant enabling them to travel to a GWR destination, or they could opt for reduced rates on other lines. Many elected to visit the seaside, Weymouth and Weston super Mare being favoured by the majority. In the GWR's heyday over 6000 workers came to Weymouth in special trains which arrived throughout the morning on 'Trip Day'. Some stayed just for the day, others, if they could afford it, lodged for the week, usually in one of the hundreds of family 'B&B's' in the Park District and Westham, where families accepted it as normal practice that they shared a bedroom to make room for the Swindon visitors. This heralded the beginning of the 'summer season' as 'Trip' took place before the commencement of school holidays. Swindon Week, which had probably begun in the 1880s, later became Swindon Fortnight. Seaside holidays were suspended for the duration of WW2, and although Swindon Trip recommenced in the late 1940s, Swindon visitor numbers were to be much reduced in the Fifties as more and more people chose to travel by coach and car and a wider choice of railway destinations became available.
Further reading : *TRIP : the annual holiday of GWR's Swindon Works*, by Rosa Matheson (Tempus, 2006).

SWISS COTTAGE *see* MARQUIS OF GRANBY PUBLIC HOUSE

SYDENHAM Thomas (1624-1689) Eminent Dorset physician whose medical treatments succeeded in an age of superstition. He fought in the English Civil War on the side of Parliament and was wounded at Weymouth. An unsuccessful Parliamentary candidate for Weymouth in 1659, he returned to medicine.

SYDNEY TERRACE became Nos.4-12 Charles Street.

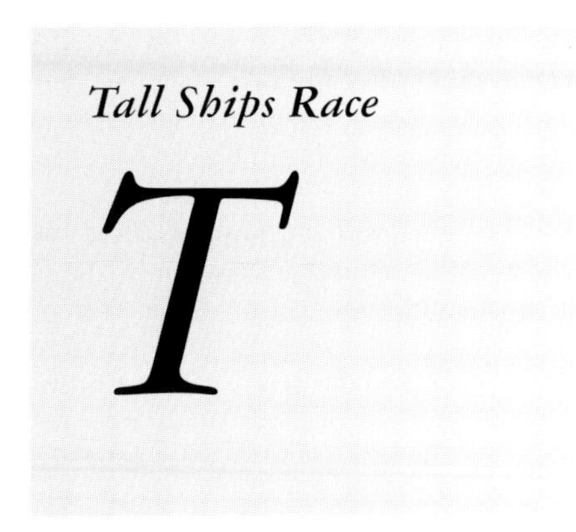

TALL SHIPS RACE Weymouth has hosted the start of the Cutty Sark Tall Ships Race on three occasions – 1983, 1987 and 1994.

TANNER, Reverend Edward Victor (1886-1977) Chaplain and Housemaster of **Weymouth College**, the boys' public school. Historian and keen photographer. A member of the Dorset Natural History and Archaeological Society from 1921 until his death. His collection of Dorset photographs is now in the Dorset County Museum and his Weymouth College memorabilia is in Weymouth Museum.

TAVER FAMILY were brewers at least from the early eighteenth century onwards. Charles Taver and his son John were both Mayors in the 1700s. Related to the **Arbuthnot** and **Penny** families.

TAYLOR CHARITY Jonathan Taylor in his will of 1753 left £70, the interest on which was to be spent on the education of two poor boys and their instruction in the art of navigation.

TEA CABIN, Esplanade Opened early in 1878 as the Cabmen's Shelter, a refreshment kiosk for the horse and carriage cabmen who waited for fares in the vicinity of the King's Statue. Since enlarged, it now serves light refreshments and ice creams to holidaymakers and locals.

TEA GARDENS occupied a strip of land behind the shipyards on Hope Quay in the mid-19th century.

TEACHERS TRAINING COLLEGE *see* WEYMOUTH TEACHERS' TRAINING COLLEGE

TECHNICAL SCHOOL was founded in the early 20th century in today's Arts Centre building formerly occupied by the Middle School. Known from 1918 as 'The Weymouth Engineering and Junior Technical School', it was the forerunner of the present Weymouth College. *See also* SOUTH DORSET TECHNICAL COLLEGE

TEDDY BEAR WOODS *see* HORSE LYNCH PLANTATION

TEDDY BOYS in drape jackets, drainpipe trousers and 'brothel-creeper' shoes were an occasional nuisance in the 1950s and caused considerable damage on the seafront in 1956. (Some towns banned the showing of the film 'Rock Around The Clock' that summer, but it was screened in Weymouth without incident).

TELEPHONE EXCHANGE The automatic telephone exchange behind the Post Office was opened on 14th December 1966.

TELEVISION MAST, Wyke Road, Wyke Regis was erected in 1973.

TEMPERANCE MOVEMENT Drunkenness was a great concern in the Victorian period and temperance movements flourished in the late 19th and early 20th centuries. Temperance meetings were held (2000 people attended a Weymouth temperance meeting in 1908), Temperance Hotels and Coffee Taverns opened and many of the charitable institutions for sailors were run on temperance lines. Weymouth had a disproportionate number of public houses and it is obvious from reading the descriptions of them in the minutes of the Licensing Justices that the management of some of them left a lot to be desired! *See* COFFEE TAVERN, Melcombe Regis; COFFEE TAVERN, Weymouth; GOOD TEMPLARS HALL

TEMPLEMAN, Thomas John (1848-1919) Five times Mayor of Weymouth (1891-2, 1892-3, 1904-4, 1905-6, 1906-7). Leading figure in the local business world as a Corn and Coal merchant. He built the Weymouth Flour Mills (originally Swatridge's Flour Mills, also known as the Crown Flour Mills and more often as Templeman's Flour Mills) in Helen Lane, in partnership with miller John Swatridge in 1892, continuing the business after Swatridge's death. The cargoes of the largest grain ships coming into the port were for Templeman's; some were too big for Weymouth Harbour and had to first be unloaded onto lighters in Portland Harbour. On the Quay a loop line along the quay wall on the Weymouth Harbour Tramway served the mill and was known as Templeman's Siding. Disaster struck on 3rd December 1917 when fire raged spectacularly through Templeman's Mill, causing its closure and the voluntary liquidation of the company. The building shell was later converted to stores and flats by Weymouth Waterworks Company. Alderman Templeman lived for many years at Stanton Court, Greenhill.

TEMPLEMAN'S COURT was on the north side of Lower St Edmund Street.

TEMPLEMAN'S FLOUR MILLS *see* TEMPLEMAN, Thomas John

TEMPLEMAN'S SIDING *see* TEMPLEMAN, Thomas John

TEMPORARY TRAIN FERRY TERMINAL WW2 (Weymouth Harbour) Alongside the cargo stage at the end of a short wooden pier built out from the quay, the temporary train ferry terminal was constructed in Weymouth Harbour by the Royal Engineers in the run up to D-Day. It was intended for use by Southern Railways train ferries, but was never used and was dismantled in 1945. No photographs are known to exist of it.

TEMS WELL A place name dating back at least to the 16th century. It was the Greenhill/Preston Beach area.

TERMINUS HOTEL, Queen Street is now known as the Giant Pot Public House.

TERRACE COURT was between Nos.16 and 17 Great George Street.

TERRACE STREET was adjacent to No.12 Commercial Road and was demolished when the present **Bus Station** was built. *See also* BUS STATION

'TERRAS' is the name of Weymouth Football Club (the team strip was originally terracotta and blue, now described as claret and blue)

TERRITORIAL ARMY Freedom of the Borough was granted to R' Battery of the 250 (Queen's Own Dorset and West Somerset Yeomanry) Medium Regiment, Royal Artillery on 22nd October 1966.

THATCH was banned in the town as a building material from 1st January 1784 due to the risk of fire and previously thatched buildings had to be re-roofed.

THEATRE ROYAL, Esplanade This was the theatre patronised by King George III and the royal family during their visits to Weymouth 1789-1805, when some noted actors appeared on its stage, including Sarah Siddons and Robert William Elliston. Joe Grimaldi the clown also entertained here, and Fanny Kemble at a later date. The theatre was built in 1771, and largely rebuilt by James Hamilton in the 1780s. Although the theatre's entrance was in a building in Augusta Place, the theatre itself was behind the building and extended into Bond Street. It went out of use probably at the end of 1859 and was partially pulled down and rebuilt in the 1880s. For many years in the 20th century this was the site of the Weymouth Hotel, No.44 The Esplanade, since converted to a nightclub.

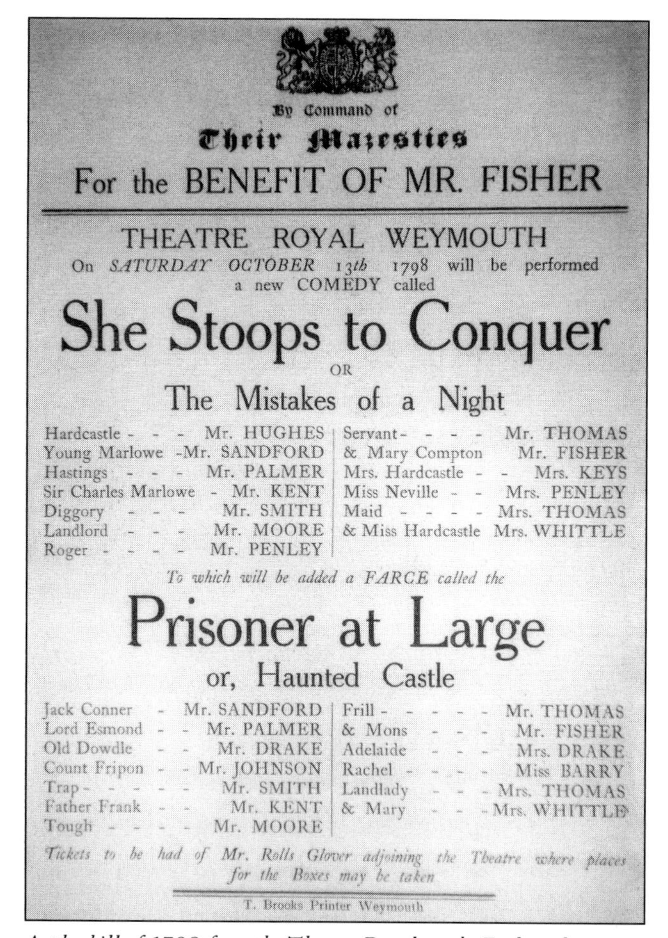

By Command of

Their Majesties

For the BENEFIT OF MR. FISHER

THEATRE ROYAL WEYMOUTH

On *SATURDAY OCTOBER 13th* 1798 will be performed a new COMEDY called

She Stoops to Conquer

OR

The Mistakes of a Night

Hardcastle	Mr. HUGHES	Servant	Mr. THOMAS
Young Marlowe	Mr. SANDFORD	& Mary Compton	Mr. FISHER
Hastings	Mr. PALMER	Mrs. Hardcastle	Mrs. KEYS
Sir Charles Marlowe	Mr. KENT	Miss Neville	Mrs. PENLEY
Diggory	Mr. SMITH	Maid	Mrs. THOMAS
Landlord	Mr. MOORE	& Miss Hardcastle	Mrs. WHITTLE
Roger	Mr. PENLEY		

To which will be added a FARCE called the

Prisoner at Large

or, Haunted Castle

Jack Conner	Mr. SANDFORD	Frill	Mr. THOMAS
Lord Esmond	Mr. PALMER	& Mons	Mr. FISHER
Old Dowdle	Mr. DRAKE	Adelaide	Mrs. DRAKE
Count Fripon	Mr. JOHNSON	Rachel	Miss BARRY
Trap	Mr. SMITH	Landlady	Mrs. THOMAS
Father Frank	Mr. KENT	& Mary	Mrs. WHITTLE
Tough	Mr. MOORE		

Tickets to be had of Mr. Rolls Glover adjoining the Theatre where places for the Boxes may be taken

T. Brooks Printer Weymouth

A playbill of 1798 from the Theatre Royal on the Esplanade.

THEATRE ROYAL, St Nicholas Street opened in 1865 and was initially known as the 'New Concert Hall' or 'New Music Hall'. The building had begun life as a Congregational Chapel in 1804 and was purchased by Captain Cosens when the congregation moved to a new church in Gloucester Street. Under a new manager it was renamed The Theatre Royal and Concert Hall, before being sold to Joseph Drew in 1875. It continued in use as a theatre until 1893, having been extensively remodelled in 1884, and was then bought back by Cosens and converted to a foundry. It next saw use in 1924 as Cosens' cold store which went out of use in the late 1960s with the widespread use of commercial and domestic refrigeration. In 1968 Weymouth Corporation purchased the building and demolished it to make a car park – although the theatre's entrance arch in St Nicholas Street remained until 1985. Today, apartment blocks fill the site.

THISTLE AND CROWN public house of the 18th century, location unknown.

THOMPSON, William (1822-1879) Born in Hamworthy, moved to Weymouth soon after his marriage in 1847. He was a solicitor, and the couple lived at No.11 Frederick Place, later moving to Gloucester Row. He was elected to Weymouth Town Council but his civic duties and his profession took second place to his other interests. These included fishing and sailing (he was a founder member of the Royal Dorset Yacht Club) and he was a noted naturalist. His identification and conservation of the wealth of marine flora and fauna along the coast was an interest shared with naturalist **Philip Henry Gosse**. Thompson's real claim to fame is in the world of photography. He took some of the earliest known photographs of Weymouth, but it was a stormy day in 1856 which put his name in the annals of photography. While considering the effects of the storm on the underwater timbers of Ferrybridge he decided to attempt an underwater photograph. Having designed a waterproof box in which to install a camera, he prepared a tent on Weymouth beach in which to develop the hoped-for photograph, and rowed out to 'a nook in Weymouth Bay' where he lowered the apparatus. Several attempts later he was able to discern faint outlines of boulders and seaweed on what has gone down in history as the first known underwater photograph. William Thompson died on 15th April 1879 at No.3 Gloucester Row (this building has since completely changed its appearance, *see* Gloucester Row). He is buried in the Thompson family tomb at Wyke Regis (this is the largest memorial in the churchyard opposite All Saints Church, close to Portland Road). A plaque on his former house No.11, Frederick Place, St Thomas Street records his pioneering achievement in underwater photography.

THORNE, Reverend George One of the first leaders of Dorset non-conformism. Appointed as minister at Radipole Church in 1648, he was ejected when the 1662 Act of Uniformity required all ministers to publicly consent to everything contained in the Book of Common Prayer. Having refused to do so, Thorne had to practise his ministry in secret, moving from place to place and eventually fleeing to Holland. He later returned, but was prohibited by the Five Mile Act of 1665 from living nearer than that to the place where he had previously practised his ministry. In 1672 the Declaration of Indulgence granted religious liberty to Romanists and Dissenters but it was later withdrawn and Thorne was once more persecuted, dying, impoverished, in August 1679. Only after the passing of the 1689 Toleration Act, were the scattered nonconformists able to gather as a congregation in three cottages which were converted into a Meeting House in West Street. The following centuries saw a strong tradition of non-conformity in the town, many of its leading citizens being 'chapel' rather than CofE. *See* CONGREGATIONAL CHURCH, West Street; NON-CONFORMITY.

THORNE, Guy (pseudonym) Novelist. *See* GULL, Cyril Arthur Edward Range

THORNELOE SCHOOL *see* THORNLOW SCHOOL

THORNHILL, Sir James (c.1675-1734) English painter with strong Weymouth connections, but of whose personal life very little is known. He became court painter to King George I, was knighted in 1720 and his many famous works on a grand scale include the interior of the dome of St Paul's Cathedral and a series of wall and ceiling paintings at Greenwich Palace. Of a Dorset family, he was probably born in Melcombe Regis but, rather oddly, his entry in the Baptism Register appears to have been inserted at a later date, faintly and in a different hand. Traditionally, his place of birth is thought to be the building now the **White Hart Inn**. He was related to the Sydenhams and lived with his uncle **Dr Thomas Sydenham** when as a 14-year old he left to train in London. It was in the 1720s that he appears to have renewed his links with Weymouth, where he owned a considerable amount of property, possibly acquired as a means of obtaining votes. He was a close friend of **George Bubb Dodington**, the notorious 'wheeler-dealer' of 18th century local politics and it is quite likely that Dodington engineered Thornhill's election as one of the borough's MPs in 1722 and he remained in Parliament until his death in 1734. Thornhill painted the interiors of Eastbury Park, Dodington's enormous and extravagant Dorset country seat, and bought back for himself land at Stalbridge, where his profligate father had once had an estate. Here he built Thornhill House. In 1721 he had promised to build an almshouse for the 'decayed seamen' of Weymouth, but unfortunately he failed to endow the building, which stood at the northern end of St Thomas Street and it was subsequently pulled down. The town does have two examples of Sir James Thornhill's work – his painting 'The Last Supper' can be seen in St Mary's Church and a Coat of Arms of King George I now in Weymouth Guildhall is also attributed to him. A commemorative stone found in Royal Terrace and inscribed 'I.Thornhill Eqs/Fundr Mar 30/MDCCXXII/Ed. Tucker Mayor' is thought to have come from the almshouses.

THORNLOW SCHOOL was first established in Bridport, probably in the 1890s. Moved to Weymouth in 1912 as Thorneloe Girls School, Rodwell run by Miss K. Bussell, one of the joint principals with Miss James. The School changed hands after WW2. Today it is Thornlow Preparatory School in Connaught Road. The Senior School at Sandesfort House, on the corner of Buxton Road and Rylands Lane, closed in July 1998 and the houses and flats of Sandsford Place and Thornlow Close now fill the site.

***THRASHER* Army Balloon** Took off from Aldershot on an exhibition flight on 28th May 1907, in the presence of King Edward VII and Prince Fushimi of Japan, who was on a state visit. *Thrasher* was expected to land a few hours later but was blown off course and crashed in the Channel after passing over Weymouth. Both the aeronauts on board, Lieut. W.T. M'Clintock Caulfeild and Lieut. T.E. Martin-Leake were drowned. Lt. Caulfeild's body was recovered off Wyke Regis by the crew of the lerret *Agnes* the following month; that of his fellow officer was washed up later off Burton Bradstock.

THREE CROWNS INN was in **Babbidge's Square**, close to the harbour at the lower end of St Thomas Street and St Mary Street.

THREE TUNS INN was on the east side of Maiden Street at its junction with Governor's Lane.

'TIDAL WAVE' HOAX A prophesy was made that Weymouth would be destroyed by a huge tidal wave on Tuesday May 29th 1928. The story made front-page news in the nationals and everyone feared the adverse publicity would ruin Weymouth as a resort. It had quite the opposite effect and thousands of people turned up on the day, during which not a ripple disturbed the blue waters of the Bay. Yet there was a tragedy that afternoon, when an airman performing stunts over the water crashed to his death in the Bay, although his companion was saved.

TILLEYS GARAGE Victoria Street Built in 1907 and demolished in February 1982, by which time it was owned by Wadham Stringer. The flats of Nightingale Court, built in 1984, fill the site.

TIMBER PONDS Park Street car park is an infilled timber pond belonging in the mid-19th century to builder Philip Dodson. Commercial Road car park behind the Marina was the timber pond of another 19th century builder, George Welsford.

TIMEWALK, Brewer's Quay This atmospheric walk through Weymouth's history with the sights and sounds of past events opened on 30th June 1990.

'TIN TABERNACLE' *see* ST NICHOLAS CHURCH, Buxton Road

TIVOLI GARDENS This was a public house built in Victorian times, and rarely referred to by its full name -'Tivoli Gardens Inn'. It stood at the lower end of Franchise Street, between No.6 and the first house of Hartlebury Terrace. Closed in the mid-1960s, the building has since been converted to a private dwelling. The 1864 Ordnance Survey map shows extensive gardens laid out on this area and these may well have been the inspiration for the 'Tivoli Gardens' of the pub's name, popularised in the 19th century by the famous Tivoli amusement parks in Paris and Copenhagen, which in turn had derived their names from the spectacular gardens of Tivoli, near Rome.

TIZARD, Thomas Henry Naval captain born in Weymouth. Navigating officer of HMS *Challenger* during her epoch-making round the world expedition of 1872-1876.

'TOAST RACK' BUSES these open buses ran between the Pavilion Theatre and Bowleaze Cove and to the Nothe and Sandsfoot Gardens in the late 1920s and 1930s.

TOKENS *see* TRADE TOKENS

TOLL HOUSES *see* PIER TOLL HOUSE; PRESTON TOLL HOUSE; RADIPOLE TOLL HOUSE

TORRINGTON DIARIES *see* BYNG, Colonel John

TOURIST INFORMATION CENTRE, Esplanade opened in 1984.

TOWN BRIDGE The name we are so familiar with today is of comparatively recent origin, the bridge having usually been known in the past as Harbour Bridge, and sometimes, after the Church was built, as Trinity Bridge. Although the two separate towns of Weymouth and Melcombe Regis became one borough on the passing of the Act of Union in 1571, the inhabitants continued to cross the harbour by way of a tethered ferryboat and showed no great enthusiasm for replacing it with a bridge. Eventually work on constructing the first 'Town Bridge' began in the early 1590s. According to **Bond's Chronology** it had 17 arches and a drawbridge in the middle to allow ships to pass up harbour. Severely damaged in Civil War fighting, this bridge, much patched up, appears to have survived until the early 18th century (although in 1669 a treasurer and surveyor was appointed for building a new bridge and Bullen Reymes, MP was prevailed upon to obtain a grant of stone for its construction). It was replaced in 1712 or thereabouts, but because this was a privately financed venture, there are no references to it in the Council Minutes of the period. Another bridge of 1741, also said to have been privately sponsored, is similarly undocumented. It is difficult to ascertain whether references to a 'new bridge' mean a totally new construction or the extensive overhaul of an existing one. The 1741 bridge was replaced in 1770, and this, the last of the wooden structures, was the only one to cross the harbour from the end of St Nicholas Street, all other Town Bridges before and since having been built opposite St Thomas Street. It was intended to enlarge the harbour but many locals objected to its new position. It lasted 50 years, but when replaced in the 1820s the bridge reverted to its original position. 10th September 1821 saw the ceremonial laying of the foundation stone of the harbour's first stone bridge with a central iron swing section, which opened on 1st January 1824. During excavation of the foundations a pot containing a large quantity of silver coins was found dating from the reigns of Charles I and James I and when old properties at the bottom of St Thomas Street were demolished to make way for the bridge an inscription of Elizabethan date was uncovered. The 1824 bridge was extensively remodelled in 1880 after it was discovered to be in a poor state, and a new swing section was installed, which hung out over the water to allow the passage of ships, although the opening was quite narrow. While the work went on, a temporary wooden bridge was put up just to the west of the bridge until the reconstructed bridge reopened in May 1881. The works had to be paid for and until 1889 tolls were charged on traffic using the bridge, as they had been in earlier centuries. Increasing 20th century traffic, both shipping and road, led to the decision to completely remove the bridge, and demolition commenced in 1928, a temporary bridge for foot passengers once again crossing the harbour during building work. The new bridge, our present Town Bridge, with hydraulically operated lifting sections, was declared open with great ceremony by the Duke of York (later King George VI) on 4th July 1930 who, under the direction of Mayor Percy Boyle, operated the electric control raising the two massive bascules and allowing Cosens paddle steamer *Empress*, laden with local schoolchildren to pass through. Today the Town Bridge is raised on a two-hourly timetable in the summer months to allow pleasure craft in and out of the Marina. Until the late 1960s Cosens paddle steamers passed through the bridge on their way to berth alongside the firm's workshops in Commercial Road, but few large vessels use the bridge today. *See also* WEYMOUTH, Massachusetts

Above: *The Town Bridge of 1824, much reconstructed in 1880, was to last until 1928.*

Left: *Its successor, the Town Bridge of today, is seen here nearing completion in 1930, ready for a Royal opening by the Duke of York (later King George VI).*

TOWN BRIDGE HOUSE of 1959 and 2005. In 1959 an uninteresting brick building with no architectural features of note was erected on the corner of Lower St Edmund Street, initially to house local and central government offices. The building, No.50 St Thomas Street, was partially demolished in 2004, its concrete and girder 'skeleton' being retained as the basis for new apartments with a restaurant at street level. These, completed in 2005, have a stone façade in keeping with adjacent former warehouses. The new building kept the name 'Townbridge House'. *See* also BRIDGE BUILDINGS, Town Bridge (an earlier building on the site)

TOWN FIRE 18th September 1666 A great fire which nearly destroyed the town. At the time King Charles II was in Weymouth dining with the Corporation and he later granted a brief for collecting £3000 towards the rebuilding of some of the houses. 37 were destroyed in or near the east side of St Mary Street, north of Blockhouse Lane. Many had been thatched and were not rebuilt for years.

TOWN HALL, MELCOMBE REGIS *see* GUILDHALL

TOWN HALL, WEYMOUTH *see* OLD TOWN HALL, High Street

TOWN LANE was the old name for Chickerell Road, still in use in the mid-19th century.

TOWN WALK was a paved area in front of the **Guildhall**.

TOWNEND FIELDS descriptions of this area of the town vary, as do the spellings and origin of the name. It seems to have been land 'at the end of the town' described as being immediately behind the ground on which Frederick Place and Royal Terrace stand, once part of the royal 'Shrubbery' attached to Gloucester Lodge, extending northwards onto the Coneygar and also known as Town's End, Townsend's Ground and Townsend's Fields. G.A. Ellis interprets the name differently and suggests it took its name from the Townson family whose property it became – the name Townson does appear in town deeds.

TOWNSEND, Joe Window cleaner who was Weymouth's 'memory man' of sport.

TOWNSEND & SONS Fairground proprietors since the mid-19th century. Richard and Kate Townsend came to Weymouth in the early 1900s and set up their first rides and stalls on an area off Commercial Road. The family travelled all over Dorset and neighbouring counties with their travelling fair and ran the swings and roundabouts on Weymouth sands since 1918.

Further reading : *Townsends : a showman's story*, by Kay Townsend (Kay Townsend, 2006)

TRADE TOKENS Tradesmen's tokens were coined in the 16th and 17th centuries by local tradesmen who found that too few coins of low value were being minted. Although strictly illegal, they were tolerated as they filled the gap in legal currency. They were usually a farthing or halfpenny in value and bore the date or trader's name or emblem or all three. Their use was banned in 1672 when King Charles II minted sufficient quantities of 'small change' for the country's needs.

TRADES UNION CONGRESS was held in Weymouth in 1934, honouring the centenary of the Tolpuddle Martyrs, the men who began the movement to resist wage cuts and were sentenced to transportation in 1834.

TRAFALGAR, BATTLE OF, 1805 Weymouth men known to have served in Nelson's fleet are:- HMS *Victory*-Edward Grey, Festing Horatio Grindall, Richard Heaver; HMS *Royal Sovereign*-John Loman; HMS *Britannia*-Captain Charles Bullen, John Smith, John Green; HMS *Temeraire*-Edward Posher; HMS *Neptune*-James Green; HMS *Dreadnought*-John Russell; HMS *Prince*-Captain Richard Grindall, Lt Abel Ferris, John Marshalsea; HMS *Defiance*- Robert Smith; HMS *Minotaur* William Jones, William Manning; HMS *Conqueror*- Samuel Dennis; HMS *Swiftsure*- William Gray; HMS *Thunderer*-Christopher Deamon, John Richards; HMS *Agamemnon*- Peter Patience. *See also* BULLEN, Charles; FERRIS, Abel; GREEN, Peter; GRINDALL, Richard.

TRAFFIC LIGHTS The first set of traffic lights in Weymouth were installed in October 1964 at the junction of Lennox Street and Victoria Street.

TRAMS Proposals for the provision of a tram service in Weymouth were put forward in a fairly modest scheme in the early 1880s but it was the early 1900s before more serious discussions took place, including a possible service between Portland and Upwey. The opening of Weymouth's electricity generating station in 1904 brought forward more proposals but no action. The possible introduction of a tram system was a concern for the GWR railway company and its solution was to open more halts along the railway and introduce a motorbus service, although this finished in 1909. Some locals were unhappy about trams running along the seafront. In 1908 the Railless Traction Company was approached about the advantages of its new system (these were to become known as trolleybuses) but this was seen as untried at the time and not adopted. In 1911 the idea of having trams in Weymouth was abandoned. In 1996 the possible use of the redundant Weymouth Harbour Tramway as a tram route was trialed, but proceeded no further.

TRAMWAY *see* WEYMOUTH HARBOUR TRAMWAY

TRAWLER RACE DAY This event, held on the Spring Bank Holiday Monday at the end of May, began in 1977.

TRIMAR HOSPICE *see* MASSANDRA, No.9, Greenhill

TRINITY COTTAGES were in Chapelhay Street, a pair of cottages almost opposite the present Trinity Court and now the site of the gardens adjacent to Chapelhay Steps.

TRINITY PLACE is now known as Trinity Terrace.

TRINITY ROAD until 1872 was part of High Street.

TRINITY STREET until February 1873 was part of High Street.

TRINITY STREET COTTAGES, Nos.2 & 3 Trinity Street Known as the Tudor Cottages and dating from the late 16th century, these would have been demolished under slum clearance orders but for an appeal by a specially formed local conservation group in 1937. A trust was established to preserve them, but in 1939, a day after an order was given for a builder to commence work, war broke out and conservation had to be abandoned. The cottages were damaged during an air raid and after the war they became dilapidated and it was not until April 1959 that a grant was awarded towards the cost of repairs. By this time the only survivor of the original trustees was local architect Ernest Wamsley Lewis and he was largely responsible for preserving this historic piece of old Weymouth which is now managed by Weymouth Civic Society. The restoration was completed and the two premises converted into one early in 1961. The cottages are furnished and can be visited at stated times.

TROCADERO CAFÉ, No.71 St Mary Street (now occupied by Bakers Dolphin Travel). Dating back to the WW1 years, the 'Troc' was taken over by Maynards in 1936 and given an art deco frontage with the latest in neon signs. Although this has now given way to modern plate glass, look upwards, for the building boasts an elaborately detailed façade to the first floor.

TUCKER FAMILY Powerful merchants in the 18th century, much involved in the Portland stone trade. Virtually ran the town and wielded great influence in local and national politics in the days when the borough sent four MPs to Parliament. Edward Tucker and his son John both represented Weymouth in Parliament and Tuckers were frequently Mayors in the 18th century. In parliamentary affairs they were first associated with William Betts, a London merchant and MP for Weymouth in the early years of the 18th century and then with George Bubb Dodington, whose uncle had assisted Betts in making his fortune. *See also* PARLIAMENTARY REPRESENTATION; STEWARD, Gabriel; STEWARD, Gabriel Tucker

TUDOR COTTAGES, Nos.2 & 3 Trinity Street *see* TRINITY STREET COTTAGES

TUDOR HOUSE No 4, North Quay Thought to have been the harbourmaster's house in Tudor times. Moves to preserve it began as early as 1951 when the redevelopment of this bomb-damaged area of the harbourside was being considered. Despite strenuous efforts to keep the old building, the decision following a Public Inquiry held in 1959 was that no preservation order should be made. It was demolished in 1961. A staircase from the house was installed in St Ann's Church, Radipole.

TUNBRIDGE WARE James Medhurst from Tunbridge Wells owned a Tunbridge Ware Manufactory in Weymouth and was one of the few producers of mosaic Tunbridge Ware working away from Kent and Sussex. He came to Weymouth in the 1840s and his 'Tunbridge Warehouse' was at No.11 Maiden Street. Interested in antiquities, he set up a Museum at his next address, No.9 Chesterfield Place, where he also produced Tunbridge Ware boxes made from the wood of two local shipwrecks – the *Earl of Abergavenny* (1805) and the *Columbine* (1838). *See also* MEDHURST, James

A decorative box from James Medhurst's Tunbridge Ware Manufactory, Chesterfield Place. Its label states that it is 'Made from the Columbine, wrecked on Portland Beach, November 28th 1838' and is 'an interesting and superb, as well as a most choice Present from Weymouth'.

TURK'S HEAD INN was on the east side of East Street, just south of its junction with Belle Vue. Now No.19 East Street.

TURNER, Joseph Mallord William (1775-1851) Artist. Turner toured Dorset and the West Country in 1811, making preliminary sketches for his *Picturesque Views on the Southern Coast of England*, engravings being made for the book from his watercolours by George and William Bernard Cooke. His painting 'Weymouth, Dorsetshire' was produced as an engraving by W.B. Cooke in 1814.

TURNPIKE TRUSTS After centuries of very poor or almost non-existent road maintenance the turnpike trusts were set up in the 18th century and empowered to levy charges, or tolls, for the upkeep and improvement of stretches of highway. Weymouth's date from 1760. The principal road from the north came via Sherborne to Dorchester, then via Winterborne Monckton to Upwey and Melcombe Regis. One problem initially was the steep road over Ridgeway known now as the 'Old Roman Road'. In 1824 a new road was cut – the present A354, with lesser gradients and a hairpin bend. It

Left: *Weymouth's Tudor house, No.4 North Quay, demolished in 1961.*

was considerably widened in the 20th century. The road from the east was via Osmington and Jordan Hill but in 1812 this was re-routed via Chalbury Corner. From the west a road came in via Martinstown, Stottingway and Broadwey. A fourth road ran from Weymouth to Chickerell. Perhaps the most interesting of the turnpike roads was that which took travellers from Weymouth to the ferry at Smallmouth. It followed today's Rodwell Road but then took Castle Lane (today's Old Castle Road) down to the sands which became the 'road' to the ferry until 1811 when it was re-routed via Wyke Church and then southwards to Smallmouth. During the latter half of the 19th century the trusts were gradually extinguished, responsibility for public highways passing to local authorities and county councils.

TURTLE STONES This is a local name for Septaria, the large and beautiful stones found in the Oxford Clay of Weymouth. Veins of these Septaria are filled with yellow semi-transparent calcareous spar, often passing into a deep brown colour. Many were collected from the shores of Radipole Lake. Their beauty when polished caused them to be manufactured into slabs and table tops, and fine specimens could be purchased in the town in the nineteenth century.

TURTON, Dr John (1735-1806) Physician at the court of King George III from about 1770, then mainly concerned with the health of Queen Charlotte and her children. He was appointed physician to Queen Charlotte in 1782 and to King George III in 1797. He may have accompanied the royal family to Weymouth on some of their visits, this being one of the theories for the naming of Turton Street. (but *see also* W. Turton) He was wealthy, having estates in Yorkshire and Kent, where he is buried.

TURTON, W. In June 1856, the Southern Times reported the death of W.Turton *'liberal supporter of the various charitable institutes in the town'* so perhaps he was the source of Turton Street's name. To add to the mystery, 'Turton Villa' in Turton Street bears a plaque dated 1771, yet the building is not shown on large-scale maps of the 19th century.

'TWELVE APOSTLES' this was a popular name for a court or some houses in the Chapelhay district, but those who could pinpoint its location are no longer living. Wellington Place at the lower end of Franchise Street seems to be a likely spot, although there were 15 properties here, not the 12 of the name. It no longer exists, a victim of slum clearance in the 1930s.

TWENTY TWELVE BAR *see* LONDON HOTEL

TWIN TOWNS Weymouth is twinned with Louviers in Normandy, France and Holzewickede in Germany's Westphalia.

In the days of the Turnpike Trusts, the way from Weymouth to Portland was via Rodwell Road and Castle Lane (today's Old Castle Road) along the beach to Smallmouth where a ferry took foot passengers across the water John Upham's engraving of the early 19th century shows the way down to the beach with Sandsfoot Castle in the background.

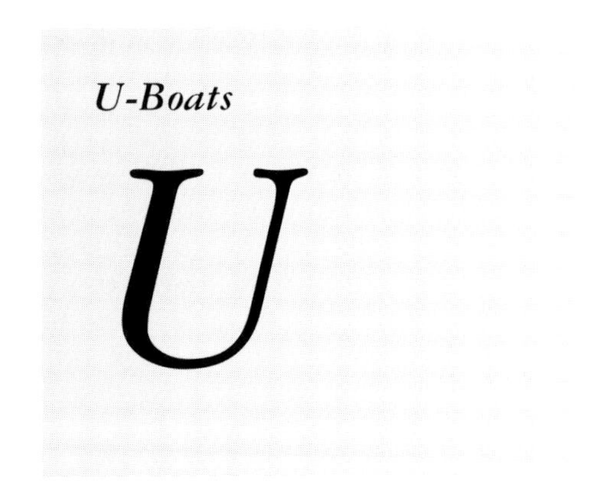

U-BOATS Soon after the end of WW1 a captured German U-Boat was moored in Hope Cove, during a tour of British ports. On 10th May 1945, U-249, the first German U-Boat to surrender at the end of WW2, arrived in Weymouth escorted by frigates HMS *Magpie* and HMS *Amethyst.* U-1023 followed later the same day and U-776 the next week.

ULLSWATER CRESCENT was known as **Abbot's Court** Road prior to houses being built along it in the 1920s. It had previously led only to the mansion of the same name.

UNDERBARN WALK A popular walk along the cliffs from Sandsfoot Cove to The Nothe with fine views of Portland Harbour, but frequently closed due to serious landslips in the area, and closed at the time of writing. *See also* CLOVELLY, Belle Vue Road

UNION (of Weymouth & Melcombe Regis) *see* ACT OF UNION 1571

UNION (Poor Law) *see* BOARD OF GUARDIANS; WORKHOUSE

UNION ARMS PUBLIC HOUSE was at Chapelhay. There was also a Union Arms at Radipole, on the site of which **Lodmoor House** was built.

UNION COTTAGES were at the back of No.117 Dorchester Road.

UNION COURT *see* PORTWEY HOSPITAL; WORKHOUSE

UNION PLACE was a terrace of houses on the south side of St Leonard's Road. Cleared following WW2 air raid damage and rebuilt as Nos.33-47. There was also a Union Place at Radipole.

UNION ROAD was the original name of St Leonard's Road, so named because Union Place was one of the first terraces built there. In 1872 it was decided *'That Union Road and Place from Mr Groves house to Hope Square be called St Leonard's Road'. See also* ST LEONARD'S ROAD

UNITED FREE METHODIST CHAPEL, Caroline Place *see* METHODIST CHAPEL, Caroline Place

UNITED REFORMED CHURCH, Trinity Street *see* CONGREGATIONAL CHURCH, Trinity Street

UNITED REFORMED CHURCH, Roman Road, Radipole *see* CONGREGATIONAL CHURCH, Roman Road, Radipole.

UPHAM, John William (1772-1828) Artist. Born near Honiton, Devon in 1772, later moving to Weymouth, where between 1801 and 1825 he produced many water colours, pen and wash drawings and engravings of the local area. His *'1825 Series'* of eighteen views in and near Weymouth is well known. Upham, who lived at South Parade, taught at Weymouth and Melcombe Regis National Schools (St Mary's Schools) in Great George Street (now the site of Weymouth Library). He died on 5th January 1828 and is buried in the churchyard of All Saints', Wyke Regis.

UPPER MILL, SUTTON POYNTZ was purchased by the Weymouth Waterworks Company in the 1850s and demolished to make way for the pumping station at Sutton Poyntz.

UPTON FORT lies between Osmington Mills and Ringstead. Was one of the defences built to protect Weymouth and Portland in the latter half of the nineteenth century, although it was not completed until 1902. It saw service in WW2 when it fired on German E-boats off Weymouth and was de-commissioned in 1956. It is now a private dwelling.

UPWEY The village takes its name from its location at the head of the River Wey. This is now the generally accepted spelling, although the older 'Upway' was still used as an alternative well into the twentieth century and 'Upway Street' appears as a street name in the town. Mediaeval documents sometimes refer to Upwey as Weybayouse, and the family of Baieux once dwelt here.

UPWEY AND BROADWEY MEMORIAL HALL was opened 24th November 1956. It commemorates the fallen of the parishes in two World Wars.

UPWEY AND BROADWEY STATION *see* UPWEY JUNCTION STATION

UPWEY JUNCTION STATION Opened in April 1886 on the Dorchester-Weymouth section of the Wilts Somerset and Weymouth Railway. Originally a junction for the Abbotsbury branch. When the branch line closed in 1952 the station was renamed Upwey and Broadwey.

UPWEY MILL, Church Street, Upwey Watermill. Rebuilt in 1802 on the site of an earlier mill. It was restored and brought back into use in 1987 but the mill and its mill house are now in private ownership.

UPWEY STATION Opened in June 1871 on the Dorchester-Weymouth section of the Wilts, Somerset & Weymouth Railway. Closed in April 1886. It was sited at Broadwey, hence 'Old Station Road' which led to it. No traces are left now. It was replaced by Upwey Junction Station.

UPWEY STATION Opened in November 1885 on the Abbotsbury Branch Railway when it was known as Broadwey Station. It was renamed Upwey in 1913. Closed to passengers in December,1952 (after which it was renamed Upwey Goods) and to goods in January, 1962. The station building can still be found, now within a small industrial/commercial site off Dorchester Road.

Further reading : *The Abbotsbury Branch*, by B.L.Jackson (Wild Swan,1989)

UPWEY WISHING WELL HALT Opened in 1905 on the Dorchester-Weymouth section of the Wilts, Somerset and Weymouth Railway. Closed January 1957. Its name was probably chosen to distinguish it from the other Upwey stations, although it was a long, long walk from the village Wishing Well. No traces remain today apart from steps alongside the railway bridge over the A354.

UPWEY WISHING WELL was originally known as 'The Springs' at Upwey. The Wishing Well name came into use when Hawley Smart used the term to describe the springs when he used them as a setting in his popular novel *Broken Bonds* published in 1874. The name was soon afterwards adopted by the proprietor of the springs.

Above: *Early visitors to Upwey Wishing Well found a wooden shelter beside the well, where they were able to ponder before they made their wish.*

Right: *About 1905 a stone shelter was erected at the Wishing Well by the Gould family of Upwey, the owners of the well and much else in the village. The initials C.T.I.G.above the arched stonework are those of Captain Gould.*

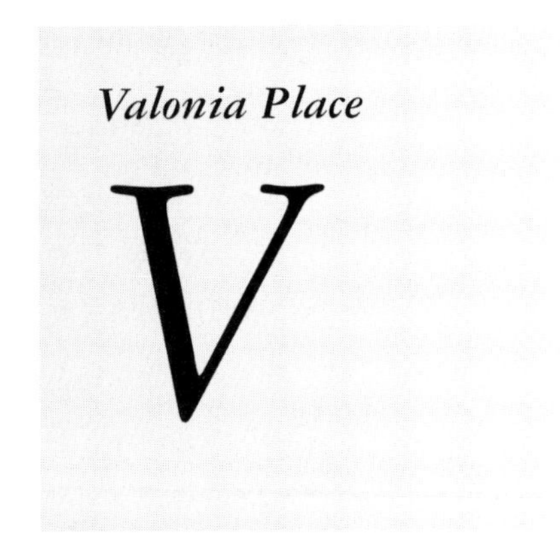

VALONIA PLACE became Nos.6-8 Weston Road.

VAUX, Val (William Valentine Whitehouse-Vaux) (died 1960) Concert party leader and repertory actor. Val Vaux and the 'Vaudesques' performed between the wars on an outdoor stage on the beach, opposite where M&S stands. His wife, stage name Ruby Lee, performed with the troupe. He later appeared as an actor in plays at the Alexandra Gardens Theatre.

Val Vaux and the Vaudettes entertained audiences on the beach in the summer season.

VICKERS-ARMSTRONG *see* WHITEHEAD TORPEDO WORKS

VICTOR EMANUEL PUBLIC HOUSE was in St Nicholas Street.

VICTOR TERRACE became Nos.42?-57 Brownlow Street.

VICTORIA AND GREAT WESTERN HOTEL, Augusta Place is today known as the Fairhaven Hotel and The New Vic. It is now numbered 41-42 The Esplanade. As a hotel it dates back at least to 1820 and in its early days it was Scriven's Boarding House, later Luce's Hotel. The GWR addition to the name railway appeared when the railway reached Weymouth in 1857. The bust of Queen Victoria on the front of the hotel commemorates her Jubilees of 1887 and 1897.

VICTORIA ARCADE Linked Crescent Street and Queen Street. It was demolished in 2001 and flats were built on the site in 2006.

VICTORIA CROSS *see* MANTLE, Jack; ROOPE, Lieutenant Commander Gerald

VICTORIA HOTEL *see* VICTORIA AND GREAT WESTERN HOTEL

VICTORIA MATERNITY HOME/NURSING HOME, 9-10 Victoria Terrace *see* MATERNITY HOMES

VICTORIA SECONDARY SCHOOL *see* WEYMOUTH GRAMMAR SCHOOL

VICTORIA TERRACE stands on what was described as *'formerly a stagnant morass called the Narrows'*. The terrace comprises 14 houses, 7 each side of the Burdon Hotel (today the Prince Regent Hotel) and is now numbered 132-146, The Esplanade. Leases of the building land were granted to Charles Fooks and Philip Dodson in 1835, and by 1855 Dodson was the sole holder. Building was under way in 1855 but Dodson could not complete it in the time specified in the lease and as it appeared he had also deviated from the original plan he required the Council's approval for the new design. Dodson was accused of changing the plan as originally agreed but councillors were uncertain whose plan they had originally viewed – it was claimed that first plan (approved) was by Talbot Bury, but one councillor said the plan now before them was by Pierse Arthur and the houses on it were not so superior! Only Arthur's plan was produced as evidence and if there was an original it had disappeared. Another Victoria Terrace became Nos.79-85 Abbotsbury Road.

VINCENT, John Beale (1825-1904) Jeweller at No.86 St Mary Street, the business having been founded in the early 19th century, formerly at No.74 St Mary Street. Builder of Faircross House. John Vincent's son, also John, and his wife Mary were drowned when the *Empress of Ireland* foundered in Canada's St Lawrence River on 29th May 1914 with the loss of more than 1000 lives. They were homeward bound after visiting their daughter in Quebec.

VINE COTTAGES became Nos.7-8 William Street

VINING, Robert Local builder/architect. Worked with James Hamilton on the construction of Weymouth Esplanade in 1800. Designed the octagonal spa house at Nottington in 1830. On the passing of an Act of Parliament in 1776 providing amongst other things, for the paving of the town, Robert Vining seems to have taken on the role of unofficial paver. He rebuilt the Esplanade after the **Great Gale** in 1824. Lived at Elwell Manor (since rebuilt), and at one time owned the Rodwell brickyard (Sudan Road).

VON TRAPP FAMILY a local link with the Von Trapps and 'The Sound of Music' dates from 1912 when Frances Whitehead, a granddaughter of Robert Whitehead of the **Whitehead Torpedo Works, Wyke Regis** married Austrian submariner Captain Von Trapp, by whom she had seven children. She died young and Von Trapp engaged a novice nun, Maria Kutschera, to care for the children. Von Trapp later married Maria and she taught the children to sing. As the Von Trapp Singers they became famous in Europe, escaping to America in 1938 after the annexation of Austria by the Germans. In America they found new fame as singers and the famous musical film 'The Sound of Music' tells the Von Trapp story.

VOSS'S BOARDING HOUSE *see* BANK BUILDINGS

VOYLE, Mary Pseudonym. *See* MANNING, Rosemary

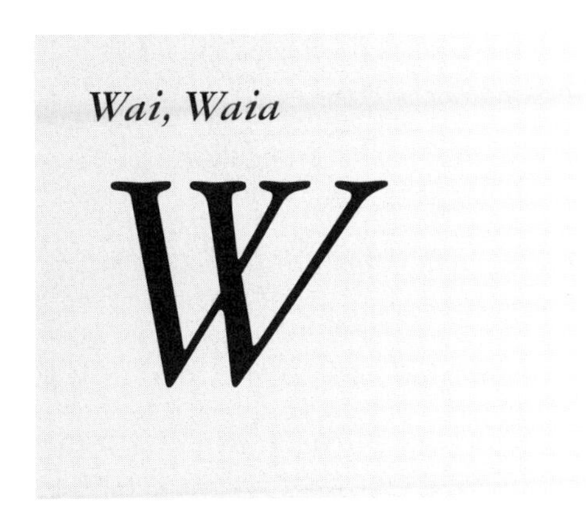

WAI, WAIA A number of settlements of this name are listed in the Domesday Survey, one of which may have been Weymouth, but it cannot be identified with any certainty.

WALKER CRESCENT, Wyke Regis was an Admiralty housing estate. Walker Crescent was named in 1954 after Captain Frederick John Walker CB, DSO, distinguished naval group commander in the offensive against U-Boats, 1939-45, who had lived for some years in Weymouth.

WALLIS, Barnes *see* BOUNCING BOMBS

WALLIS, Thomas Samuel Plucky and hot-headed Weymouth councillor who, as a private individual, challenged the might of the landowning **Johnstone Estate** over its rights to land at the northern end of the town which included the site of St John's Terrace, Greenhill and Melcombe Common. Wallis claimed that this was common land and belonged to the townspeople. On 4th June 1884, he and a local shoemaker named George Mudge led a mob several hundreds strong, which broke down fences, destroyed notices and forced the gates of Greenhill Gardens, threatening to repeat the action if the land was enclosed again. The pair also distributed notices to Johnstone tenants in St John's Terrace, telling them not to pay any more rent. An aggrieved Sir Frederic Johnstone took Wallis and Mudge to court for trespass and the case of Johnstone v. Wallis was heard in July 1886. Mr Wallis, deserted by his counsel and unsupported by his fellow councillors, conducted his own defence in a spirited and unorthodox manner which exasperated the Judge on several occasions. It was a lengthy case, lasting over several weeks. As Wallis tried to prove the disputed land was common land, his succession of witnesses recalled areas of unrestricted open ground years before. There were dark hints of earlier collusion between the Corporation and the Johnstone Estate but there was nothing relevant in the way of documentation which helped the defence case. The judge found for the Johnstone Estate, to which it awarded costs. A plea for these to be waived fell on deaf ears and by the time they were paid Thomas Wallis was in severely straitened circumstances. Many privately agreed with his views and in 1890 Mayor Alfred Dennis made a public appeal for funds to help his fellow townsman. Thomas Wallis died in 1911, in one of Sir Henry Edward's Almshouses.

WALPOLE COTTAGES became Nos.66-70 Walpole Street.

WALPOLE PLACE became Nos.75-82 Walpole Street.

WALPOLE STREET was probably named after Spencer Horatio Walpole, 3 times Home Secretary in Lord Derby's Conservative government in the 1850s and 1860s. The houses were built by the **Conservative Land Society**.

WALPOLE TERRACE became Nos.46-59 Walpole Street

WALTHAM, Baron, of Phillipstown *See* OLMIUS, John

WAR MEMORIAL Weymouth's War Memorial to those service men and women who lost their lives in the two World Wars stands on Weymouth Esplanade, near the Pier Bandstand. Designed by Doyle Jones in Portland Stone, it stands 17' 6" high and was dedicated on Sunday, 6th November 1921. Due to weathering of the stone, the 250 names inscribed on it were transferred to bronze plaques in 1932. Further plaques bearing the names of those killed in WW2 were added in 1997. (Plans for a memorial put forward by V.H. Bennett, Mayor of Weymouth 1918-19 were not adopted and he instead donated the 'Armistice Shelter' in Greenhill Gardens). *See also* AMERICAN MEMORIAL; ANZAC MEMORIAL; BOOK OF REMEMBRANCE, St Mary's Church; WAR MEMORIAL, Wyke Regis.

Weymouth War Memorial, shortly after it was dedicated in November 1921.

WAR MEMORIAL, Wyke Regis The WWI memorial stands in the burial ground opposite the junction of Wyke Road and Portland Road. It was designed by Captain Francis Haigh, of the Whitehead Torpedo Works who lived at Wyke from 1914-1919. The memorial is unusual in that it lists the names of those who died in the conflict, but bears no date. A plaque inside the church commemorates the dead of WW2.

WARD, Albany (1879-1966) was born in London in 1879 and began his career as a film projectionist in the 1890s, the start of a fascination with cinema which continued all his life. In 1908 Ward established his first permanent cinema in Weymouth – the **Palladium** – and went on to build up a huge cinema circuit – the Albany Ward Circuit.

WARD, John MP for Weymouth & Melcombe Regis from 1722 until May 1726, when he was convicted of forgery and expelled from the House of Commons.

WARD'S COURT was between Nos.7 and 8, New Street.

WATCH, Tom has helped train Channel swimmers from the UK and abroad in the waters around Weymouth since 1951.

WATCHMEN *see* POLICE

WATER SUPPLY The town's water supply originally came from wells and springs but as early as 1593 a request was made to the owners of springs on Southdown Common to convey water via pipes to Melcombe, although nothing came of this. It was 1797 when the Company of Proprietors of the Weymouth Waterworks was set up, of which architect **James Hamilton** was one of the founders. The source of the supply was Boiling Rock at Preston and piped water was conveyed only to the Melcombe side of the town. Weymouth relied on wells and a pump erected in the 1770s on open ground below High West Street, supplemented by a second pump at Rodwell in 1854. By the mid-19th century the supply was inadequate for the growing town and in 1855 an Act was obtained to take water from Sutton Poyntz. A new company was formed although its name remained the same. Thomas Hawksley designed the original 1856 waterworks and its buildings, which have been much extended over the years. Water was pumped to the nearby Preston Reservoir (replaced in 1949 by Chalbury Reservoir), from whence it gravitated to Rodwell Reservoir and for the first time piped water was made available to the Weymouth side of the harbour. An additional reservoir was built at Wyke Regis in 1897. The Company's offices moved to a new building at No.77 St Thomas Street around 1900 (since rebuilt and currently the New Look clothing store), relocating to Mitchell Street in the early 1930s. Increasing demand led to the opening of a new borehole at Empool, West Knighton in 1938 and the building of Empool Pumping Station. From here water goes to Northdown Reservoir on the Ridgeway, where a main links it to Sutton Poyntz pumping station and finally to a second reservoir constructed at Wyke Regis. On 1st April 1969 Weymouth Waterworks joined with others to form the Dorset Water Board which in 1974 became part of Wessex Water. The pumping station at Sutton Poyntz is still operational, although now automated. The original water-powered pumps were replaced by steam power which in turn gave way to electricity. The works' tall chimney was taken down in 1979. Wessex Water opened a Museum of Water Supply here in September 1989.

The waterworks at Sutton Poyntz, designed by Thomas Hawksley. The tall chimney was taken down in 1979.

WATERFEST A water festival established in the 1993 which later lapsed. A revival planned for 2005, the 200th anniversary of Trafalgar year, did not materialise.

WATERLOO HOUSE became Nos.48-49 Lennox Street.

WATERLOO PLACE A terrace of 12 houses built in the 1830s at the northern end of the Esplanade.

WATERMILLS *see* MILLS

WAVERLEY Paddle Steamer The last sea-going paddle steamer left in Britain, the *Waverley* has no historic connection with Weymouth but is frequently seen in the port during summer cruises round the coast.

WAVERLEY ARMS public house Westham was rebuilt in 1937 on the site of a late-19th century pub of the same name.

WAYMOUTH the spellings Waymouth and Weymouth were interchangeable from very early times and it was the early 19th century when 'Weymouth' became the generally accepted spelling of the town's name.

WEBB, MAJOR & CO. LTD Established around 1900, the timber and builders' merchants opened new showrooms at No.40a St Thomas Street in October 1955. They had acquired the premises from Hawkes, Freeman, Ltd., and the china, glass and domestic ironmongery showrooms continued to trade under the Hawkes, Freeman name in the same building. Main premises in Commercial Road (formerly Betts) comprised timber yards, sawmill and stores. Also had showrooms and sawmills at Dorchester and a brickyard at Chickerell. Taken over in 1965 by the Devon Trading Company Ltd. The Commercial Road site was cleared in the early 1980s and now forms Park Street car park.

WEINSTOCK, Maureen Local historian, author and lecturer. She was Principal of Weymouth Teachers' Training College for 17 years and published a number books on Dorset's history, which include detailed studies on aspects of Weymouth's history.

Further reading : *Studies in Dorset history*, by Maureen Weinstock (Longmans, Dorchester 1953); *More Dorset Studies* by Maureen Weinstock (Longmans, Dorchester 1960); *Weymouth and Melcombe Regis Minute Book 1625-1660*, edited by Maureen Weinstock (Dorset Record Society, 1964); *Old Dorset*, by M.B. Weinstock (David and Charles, 1967); *Dorset Elizabethans at home and abroad*, by Maureen Weinstock (John Murray, 1967)

WELCOME HOME PUBLIC HOUSE was on the east side of St Nicholas Street.

WELD ESTATE Death duties were the reason behind the sale of a considerable slice of land and property belonging to the Weld Estate which took place in September 1925. As well as Wool and Lulworth, some 2000 acres in the Weymouth area came under the hammer and included much of Preston and Sutton Poyntz and a sizeable portion of Lodmoor.

WELLINGTON COTTAGE was in Lennox Street.

WELLINGTON COURT *see* RED BARRACKS

WELLINGTON PLACE was at the lower end of Franchise Street, linking to St Leonard's Road. Demolished under a slum clearance order in the 1930s. *See also* TWELVE APOSTLES. There was also a Wellington Place at Radipole, which was known as Dorset Place until 1872.

WELLWORTHY LTD. *See* WHITEHEAD TORPEDO WORKS

WESLEY FAMILY Samuel Wesley, father of John Wesley, the founder of Methodism and Charles Wesley the hymn writer, grew up in Preston where his non-conformist minister father settled after being ejected from the living of Winterborne Whitechurch. The family home, Manor Cottage, still stands just off Preston Road. Samuel Wesley had left Preston by the time his sons were born, but John Wesley visited the town and preached in Melcombe in September 1776.

WESSEX STADIUM The original stadium was built on land formerly belonging to East Chickerell Court Farm. The first turf was cut 19 October 1953 and the stadium officially opened on 4th August 1954, when Speedway was held there for the first time. Stock Car Racing took place the same year. In 1955, Pony Racing was tried but abandoned after one meeting due to lack of interest. Greyhound races were held in the early 1960s. In 1987 the Wessex Stadium was rebuilt for Weymouth Football Club following the club's move from its ground in Newstead Road. *See also* WEYMOUTH FOOTBALL CLUB

WEST, Jack (1916-2005) Chief Librarian of Weymouth from 1949 until local government reorganisation in 1974, when he became Curator of Weymouth Museum, which he set up in 1971 in the former Melcombe Regis School, Westham Road, as part of the town's Quatercentenary celebrations. (The Museum moved to Brewer's Quay, Hope Square in 1989, Jack West having retired in 1981). He was a founder member of Weymouth and South Dorset Arts Centre, an authority and lecturer on Weymouth's history and author of books and articles about the town and its past. *See also* WEYMOUTH LIBRARY; WEYMOUTH MUSEUM

Further reading : *Weymouth and Melcombe Regis in the nineteenth century: abstracts from the minute books of the Weymouth Corporation, the Local Board of Health, the Urban Sanitary Authority and the Urban District Council, 1800-1899*, by Henry Wolff and Jack A.C. West (Weymouth Central Library, 1972) and with co-author Maureen Attwooll :- *Weymouth : an illustrated history* (Dovecote Press, 2nd ed, 1995); *Weymouth and Melcombe Regis in old picture postcards*, Volumes 1 and 2 (European Library, 1984 and 1997); *Seaside Weymouth* (Dovecote Press, 1989).

WEST BANK VILLAS became Nos.53-55 Abbotsbury Road.

WEST COTTAGES stood until the late 1950s on the site (approximately) of today's Nos. 172-174 Chickerell Road.

WEST END TERRACE became Nos. 176-182 Abbotsbury Road.

WEST END VILLAS became Nos.161-171 Abbotsbury Road.

WEST MEAD became known as **Radipole Manor.**

WEST PARADE was the original name for part of Park Street, from its junction with Gloucester Street to today's Westham Road.

WEST PLAIN was a row of terraced houses off the north side of High West Street in the area known as the 'Plains of Weymouth'.

WEST QUAY in Melcombe was the part of today's Custom House Quay west of the Town Bridge, which extended round **Ferry's Corner** into what is now the southern end of Commercial Road.

WEST ROW and EAST ROW were terraces on the south side of Chapelhay Street. Lost to 1930s slum clearance and WW2 bombing raids. Two adjacent terraces bearing the same names stood on the north side of St Leonard's Road and suffered the same fate.

WEST STREET on the Weymouth side of the harbour existed in the 17th century but probably due to confusion with a second West Street on Melcombe side, it was renamed High West Street. West Street in Melcombe was much redeveloped in the late 20th century.

WEST TERRACE was part of Commercial Road, and seems to have included the groups of houses south of **Alexandra Terrace**.

WESTBOURNE TERRACE became part of Westbourne Road. Another Westbourne Terrace became part of Cromwell Road.

WESTERHALL takes its name from the family of **Sir Frederick Johnstone** of Westerhall in Dumfriesshire, owner of the land on which the houses in this area were built. Other street names with Scottish connections are Glendinning Avenue, Somerset Place (family name of Johnstones), William Street (Christian name of Sir Frederic's forebears), Gordon Place (family surname).

WESTERN WALK, also known as Western Esplanade, was a lakeside walk along Radipole Lake's eastern side from King Street to Alexander Bridge and beyond. It was lost in the 1920s infilling which provided land for railway sidings and Radipole Park Drive and Gardens.

WESTHAM The development of the suburb of Westham on the farmlands on the western side of the Backwater began in the late 1870s. Prior to this only a handful of inhabitants lived there – a farmer and his family at Goldcroft Farm, and a Mr Stagg whose 'hut on wheels' provided a base whilst he was working locally. The area was far enough from the town for an isolation hospital to be built in 1871 (the year of a smallpox outbreak) and apart from the Gasworks of the 1830s, a cemetery and a pottery there was little else. By 1859 a road bridge spanned the Backwater, but residential development in Westham did not begin for another twenty years – although, once started, it continued apace. A name was needed for the new suburb and 'West Ham' was chosen in 1882 but the two-word spelling was that of the London suburb and it soon became 'Westham'. Rocklands had also been considered and one wag suggested 'Washington' as a Steam Laundry had recently opened in Abbots bury Road. In 1895 Westham, then in Wyke Regis, was brought within the borough boundaries – this area can be thought of as 'old' Westham, ending at today's '**Adelaide Court**' with a rough boundary along its northern edge of Longcroft Road and Longcroft Lane and to the south along the line of Southview Road and The Marsh. 'New' Westham would follow in the wake of the Great War, 1914-18, when council housing schemes spread north and west of the original development, taking in the wartime camps occupied by Australian and New Zealand troops. *Westham's bridges, schools, streets, etc. are listed alphabetically by name in the A-Z sequence.*

WESTHAM BRIDGE (1859-1921) The first Westham Bridge was known as the Backwater Bridge until the 1890s. It pre-dates the development of the suburb of Westham and was built to provide access to the cemetery at Westham, which opened in 1856. Prior to its construction, funeral corteges had to make a long journey along North Quay and Newstead Road. The bridge was built under the powers granted by the Backwater Bridge and Road Act 1857 and opened to the public in 1859. Tolls were charged until 1879 when the highway became a county bridge and road. The lowest toll being one halfpenny, it became known as 'The Ha'penny Bridge'. In the 1880s a considerable sum spent on repairs and the bridge's central drawbridge was removed, having been fixed for some years as few vessels navigated the upper reaches of the Backwater. From then on the bridge seems to have been constantly in need of maintenance, and on occasion was restricted to light traffic only. The bridge was 661 feet long and 16 feet wide, with the later addition of a 7 feet wide footpath. Under the Weymouth and Melcombe Regis Corporation Act 1914 the bridge and its approaches were vested in the Corporation and shortly after the end of WW1 work commenced on the present Westham Bridge, shorter than the original, with considerable infilling at either end. *See* next entry.

The timber bridge to Westham, photographed after the removal of the centre drawbridge. It was longer than the present Westham Bridge, infilling being carried out on both sides in 1921.

WESTHAM BRIDGE (1921- to date) Known during its construction as the Backwater Embankment Road, the present Westham Bridge's reinforced concrete wall provides continuous watertight seal or dam across the Backwater. To get rid of surplus water draining from surrounding land and the discharge of the River Wey into the Backwater, it was necessary to provide a means for drawing off any surplus water which might gather and four culverts are fixed through the dam with automatic discharge flaps, plus four additional ones with hand controlled sluices. The bridge is shorter than its predecessor, with infilling at each end. A footbridge was added to the bridge in 1973-4 and since the introduction of the new road system in 1987, the bridge has carried no traffic, being now used for car parking. (Some photographs show a timber bridge just south of Westham Bridge. This was a temporary structure, with rails carrying a crane, used during the laying of a storm-water sewer across the Backwater in 1936.)

The present Westham Bridge in 1921. The works around it have not been completed. Radipole Park Drive has yet to be built and on the opposite shore the Health Centre was not built until 1930. Westwey Road did not exist – it was not opened until 1932.

WESTHAM CINEMA, Abbotsbury Road was owned by Thomas Moore. When the Australian and New Zealand Forces convalescent camps were set up in the area, he let the cinema to the military. It closed soon after the war ended and has since been used as a church, a garage for Jeanes' motorbuses and vans and was converted to retail units in the 1950s, now Nos.155-159 Abbotsbury Road.

WESTHAM COACH PARK Coaches moved to Lodmoor in the summer of 1971.

WESTHAM COUNTY SECONDARY MODERN SCHOOL *see* CROMWELL ROAD SCHOOLS

WESTHAM HALT on the Weymouth and Portland Railway. Opened July, 1909 and closed in March 1952 when the line closed to passengers. Platform remains, now part of the '**Rodwell Trail**'.

WESTHAM HOUSING ESTATES Compulsory purchase of land for the council estate at Westham was made in September 1919. The first houses were built in 1922.

WESTHAM LAUNDRY *see* LAUNDRY, 77, Abbotsbury Road

WESTHAM ROAD was known as Little George Street until the decision was made to change its name in December 1922. By the beginning of the twentieth century the rapid growth of the suburb of Westham had brought a great increase in the traffic using this route to Westham Bridge (itself replaced in 1921) and the end house of Royal Terrace on the corner of the Esplanade and Westham Road was demolished in 1929 to permit road widening. The road was also widened in 1939 when a row of old shops on south side was demolished and the present shops Nos.1-9 were built.

WESTHAVEN COUNTY INFANTS AND JUNIOR SCHOOLS, Radipole Lane Formally opened 22nd October 1954, although in use since 6th September that year.

WESTHAVEN HOSPITAL, Radipole Lane The hospital, for infectious diseases, opened on 22nd November 1902, replacing the **Port Sanitary Hospital** at Wyke Regis. A small isolation unit nearby, intended for smallpox cases, had opened earlier in the year. Now used as a unit caring for elderly patients, much of the hospital has been rebuilt in recent years.

WESTON, Samuel Four times Mayor of Weymouth in the late 18th and early 19th centuries, he is commemorated by an impressive marble statue in Weymouth Guildhall. In 1804, he was the first Mayor elected after the granting of a new Charter to the town by King George III.

WESTON COTTAGES became Nos.9-18 Weston Road.

WESTON COURT was between Nos.34 and 35 East Street.

WESTON TERRACE is on the north side of Chickerell Road, not far from its junction with Boot Hill.

WESTVILLE TERRACE/WESTVILLE VILLAS became Nos.182-192 Chickerell Road.

WESTWEY HOUSE, Westwey Road was built on the former Gasworks site and opened in 1972. It was much altered in the 1990s.

WESTWEY ROAD A road along the Backwater's western shore linking North Quay to Westham Bridge had been proposed in 1914 but it was 1932 before Westwey Road opened on infilled land bordering the gasworks, which was also extended on reclaimed land at the same time.

WESTWINDS, Bowleaze Coveway was sold in 1986 and demolished; an apartment block built on the site bears the same name.

WEYBAYOUSE (various spellings) is the old alternative name for **Upwey**.

WEYMOUTH Two locomotives have been named Weymouth. The first was a 1907 GWR Bulldog Class

Westham Road in the 1980s. The New Bridge Hotel was replaced by an apartment bock in 2003.

No.3331 (later 3319). Its 'Weymouth' nameplate was removed in the 1930s as it was alleged that locos with town names confused passengers as to the destination of the trains they were hauling!. The second was a West Country Class No. 34091 named on 29th December 1949 by Mayor Percy Burt at Weymouth Station. Withdrawn from service in 1964.

***WEYMOUTH,* HMS** was a light cruiser launched in 1911, the seventh naval vessel to bear the name. The mayor that year, Richard Caines Watts, opened a subscription fund to pay for a magnificent set of silver for the vessel, comprising a large ornate table centrepiece with two side dishes. The vessel saw service in WW1 but was scrapped in 1928. After naval use and display elsewhere, the silver in 1983 went to HMS *Osprey* at Portland, but following the closure of the establishment in 1998, the set was presented to Weymouth and Portland Borough Council on permanent loan. A bronze crest from the ship was presented to the Town Council when she was broken up.

WEYMOUTH derives its name from its situation at the mouth of the River Wey. Although the name is used as a general term for the whole of the modern borough and includes the villages now within its boundary, 'Weymouth' once denoted only a small settlement on the south side of the harbour, opposite the separate settlement of Melcombe Regis. Weymouth is probably the older of the two and a record of it exists in 934. Early spellings of the name vary greatly and 'Weymouth' and 'Waymouth' were both used until the 19th century. In the Domesday Survey of 1086 a number of places called 'Waia' are listed but none can be identified with any certainty as Weymouth. The real growth of the two towns took place after this date (compared with today's definition of a town, these were very small places). Weymouth assumed borough status at some point. In 1578 a Commission from the Lords of the Privy Council could not find that Weymouth had ever been incorporated, but having a common seal and a mace carried before the bailiffs and other like jurisdictions and government, it seemed to be a 'Corporation by prescription'. In 1310 Weymouth was created a staple port for the import of French, Gascon and Anjou wine. Staple ports were given exclusive rights and were authorised to collect the customs duty on the goods passing through their hands. From the late 13th century until their enforced Union in 1571 the two towns quarrelled over harbour dues, shipping and many other contentious matters, Weymouth inhabitants being the more belligerent. When the sea bathing and health and pleasure resort industry grew up, the visitors initially patronized the Weymouth side of the harbour, but the town soon realised that its future prosperity lay in the sands and bay of Melcombe Regis, across the water. *See also* HARBOUR; MELCOMBE REGIS.

WEYMOUTH, Massachusetts In 1926 a delegation from Weymouth, Dorset headed by Mayor Percy A'Court paid an official visit to Weymouth, Massachusetts for the July 4th Independence Day celebrations, taking with them a goodwill message from Thomas Hardy. A return visit by town officials from Weymouth, Mass. attended the opening ceremony of Weymouth Town Bridge in 1930, the American town having presented an inscribed granite slab which can be seen on the Town Bridge today. The American Weymouth was also represented at the unveiling of the Clark and Endicott Memorial in 1914. Weymouth, Mass., on an inlet of Massachusetts Bay, is a manufacturing town about 12 miles SE of Boston and is the second oldest settlement in Massachusetts – only Plymouth is older. Now producing electronics equipment, furniture and sheet metal, it was formerly known for its shoe-making industry.

WEYMOUTH AND CHANNEL ISLANDS STEAM PACKET COMPANY was set up in 1857 with GWR backing, following the opening of the railway to Weymouth. The rival LSWR also ran a steamer service to the Channel Islands, but this finished in 1859 after the company's steamer *Express* was wrecked off Jersey. The GWR maintained its interest in the Weymouth and CI Steam Packet Company, ever mindful of possible future LSWR competition, and took over the company completely in 1889. *See also* GREAT WESTERN RAILWAY; HARBOUR

WEYMOUTH AND DISTRICT HOSPITAL, Melcombe Avenue Took this name in 1921 when the **Weymouth Royal Hospital** (School Street) and the **Princess Christian Hospital** (Melcombe Avenue) amalgamated. Various extensions and departments were added during the 20th century but on the opening of the new Dorset County Hospital at Dorchester in May 1998, the big 1902 building was demolished and only the modern extensions remain as part of Weymouth Community Hospital. Weymouth and District Hospital's ward names are of interest: Annie Lawrie Ward was named after the wife of the hospital's founder, James Macpherson Lawrie; Drake Ward was a name transferred when a ward moved from Portland Hospital (where all the wards were named after famous admirals), and commemorates Sir Francis Drake; Margaret Mitchell Ward was named after the wife of a Portland-born man who made a substantial donation to the hospital in her memory; Maud Alexander Ward was named after another donor of funds, the sister of Rev. Christian Alexander, curate of Holy Trinity in the early 1900s; R.C. Watts Ward took the name of Richard Caines Watts, for many years chairman of the Hospital Committee, and much involved in the 1921 amalgamation.

WEYMOUTH AND DORSET COUNTY ROYAL EYE INFIRMARY was founded in 1836 at surgeon Charles Bridge's house in Bond Street. In 1845 it moved to a new building in St Mary Street (now No.104b) and was granted royal patronage by Queen Victoria. The next move on 18th May 1872 was to purpose-built premises at No.6 King Street and in 1934 the eye hospital transferred to Massandra, No.9 Greenhill, a converted private house. The unit relocated to Dorchester in October 1989.

WEYMOUTH AND MELCOMBE REGIS, BOROUGH OF Existed from the Union of the two towns in 1571 until the formation of the new Borough of Weymouth and Portland in 1974. *See also* BOROUGH STATUS; MELCOMBE REGIS; WEYMOUTH

WEYMOUTH AND MELCOMBE REGIS CENTRAL SCHOOL see CROMWELL ROAD SCHOOLS

WEYMOUTH AND PORTLAND RAILWAY The Railway from Weymouth to Portland opened on 9th October 1865 for goods, 16th October 1865 for passengers. It was extended to Easton for goods on 1st October 1900 and for passengers on 1st September 1902. In its heyday it carried substantial passenger and stone traffic, but by 1952 passengers had dwindled and road traffic was competing for the stone trade. Closed to passengers on 3rd March 1952 and goods on 5th April 1965 (its centenary year).

Further reading : *Isle of Portland Railways*, by B.L.Jackson 4 vols. (Oakwood Press, 1999-2002).

WEYMOUTH AND SOUTH DORSET ARTS CENTRE, Commercial Road opened on 26th October 1955 in the 1860 building originally **Weymouth Middle School**. The building had various educational uses throughout the 19th and 20th centuries, becoming a technical school (forerunner of the South Dorset Technical College) and in post-WW2 years providing temporary accommodation for Holy Trinity School pupils when they were bombed out of their Chapelhay building. As an Arts Centre it brought together various cultural activities in the town and has been used for art exhibitions, music and drama performances, dance, films, lectures etc. In 2005, the Crickmay-designed building was much altered and extended and the ground floor is now used by the government-funded 'Sure Start' scheme. New arts centre facilities are due to open in the building.

The Arts Centre building in its days as a Victorian school.

WEYMOUTH ARMS PUBLIC HOUSE, High Street was demolished in 1961.

WEYMOUTH BARRACKS *see* RED BARRACKS (the name it was known by locally)

WEYMOUTH BAY ESTATE Had this estate been fully developed as originally planned some 600 acres of land would have been filled with houses. Crescents of houses were to have stretched behind today's Brackendown Avenue, enclosing Southdown Farm and with a tract of land east of Horse Lynch Plantation being developed as far as Littlemoor Road. Lodmoor, from Beachdown Way to Overcombe, would also have been built over. East of Preston Road, Jordan Hill and all the ground now taken up with the present caravan parks would have been developed with houses. Building of the estate began in the 1920s, Bowleaze Coveway being the first road of the development, apart from buildings on Preston Road (referred to then as the Weymouth-Bournemouth road).

WEYMOUTH CASTLE is an alternative name for SANDSFOOT CASTLE

WEYMOUTH CEMETERY *see* CEMETERIES

'WEYMOUTH CHIMES' a very successful piece of music for tubular bells, written in the early 1900s. *See* HOWGILL, John Stephen, its composer.

WEYMOUTH COLLEGE (1863-1940) was a boys public school. The College opened in April 1863, occupying the building known to modern Weymouthians as the 'Arts Centre', a Crickmay building in Commercial Road. It was then called 'Weymouth Grammar School'. These premises were soon found to be too small, and a new site was found off Dorchester Road, on land leased from Sir Frederic Johnstone. Once again the architect was Crickmay, and the first buildings opened in 1865. In 1867 a new name was adopted – 'Weymouth Collegiate School', before the school finally became 'Weymouth College'. WW2 brought closure in March 1940 and the boys transferred to Wellingborough, Northants. A carved oak screen and three Books of Remembrance containing the names, accounts and photographs of 180 scholars on the College's roll of honour were dedicated in St Aldhelm's Church, Radipole in 1952. A number of old boys of the school went on to become well-known names – George Stainforth of flying fame, broadcaster Stuart Hibberd and author John Meade Falkner, are a few among many. Following post-WW2 use as a teacher training college and a tertiary college the main buildings on Dorchester Road have now been converted to housing – Cranford House (the main building) with new-build Cavendish Court behind, linked by Ricketts Close. *See also* WEYMOUTH MIDDLE SCHOOL; WEYMOUTH TEACHERS' TRAINING COLLEGE; WEYMOUTH COLLEGE (present-day)

WEYMOUTH COLLEGE (present-day) Cranford Avenue A tertiary (sixth form and further education) college. It began in 1918 as Weymouth Engineering and Technical School in what is now the Arts Centre building in Commercial Road, moving to new buildings in Newstead Road in 1939 as the South Dorset Technical College, which officially opened on 26th October 1940. When the adjacent Weymouth Grammar School moved to a new site at Charlestown in the 1960s, the college took over some of its buildings and added to them. The next development came in 1985 when the expanding college began working on a split site – at Newstead Road and at Cranford Avenue off Dorchester Road, where the buildings which originally housed 'Weymouth College' boys' public school and were latterly used by the Dorset Institute for Higher Education were taken over. In 2001 it was decided to move the entire campus to the Cranford Avenue site where new buildings were erected and the old Victorian Weymouth College buildings were sold and converted to apartments. The Newstead Road site was sold for development as housing, all the former college and school buildings being demolished. As this had once been the site of a pottery long before it was used for educational purposes, the street names chosen for the development are those of famous potteries – Wedgwood, Aynsley, Goss etc.

WEYMOUTH COMMUNITY HOSPITAL, Melcombe Avenue stands on the site of **Weymouth and District Hospital** which was demolished early in 1999. The 1902 building was taken down, but extensions added later still remain in use.

WEYMOUTH CONSUMERS' GAS COMPANY offices were at No.71 St Thomas Street. *See also* GAS SUPPLY

WEYMOUTH COURT was on the east side of Boot Hill, at its junction with High West Street. Now the site of **Edwards Avenue**.

WEYMOUTH ENGINEERING AND TECHNICAL SCHOOL occupied the Arts Centre Building in Commercial Road from 1918-1939. It was the forerunner of the South Dorset Technical College (the present **Weymouth College**).

WEYMOUTH FLOUR MILLS *see* TEMPLEMAN, Thomas John

WEYMOUTH FOOTBALL CLUB was founded in 1890, with **Mark C. Frowde** as the first Honorary Secretary. Matches were first played at Lodmoor, then at a ground at Goldcroft eventually moving to Weymouth Recreation Ground (the 'Rec') in Newstead Road behind the Sidney Hall. The club was admitted to the Western League and in 1924 became a limited company and entered the Southern League with a full professional side. The team's 'Terras' nickname is from their original terracotta and blue strip, now described as claret and blue. The Club moved to a new ground at the new Wessex Stadium in August 1987, following the sale of the 'Rec' for redevelopment as a supermarket.

Further reading : *Weymouth Football Club History*, by Nigel Biddlecombe (2006); *Floodlit dreams : how to save a football club*, by Ian Ridley (Simon and Schuster, 2006)

WEYMOUTH GRAMMAR SCHOOL opened on 8th January 1913 as Victoria Secondary Schools, Alma Road, later known as Weymouth Secondary School, being renamed Weymouth Grammar School in 1927. A new wing was added in the 1930s and huts around the main buildings provided additional classroom space. The school moved to Charlestown, the first section of the new school opening there in 1964 and being completed in 1967. In 1985 on the introduction of comprehensive education, WGS amalgamated with Westham School on an adjacent site and became known as Budmouth School. Much extended since, the school is now known as Budmouth Technology College. All the original buildings in Alma Road were demolished and filled with a housing development known as 'College Heights' (the old school buildings having been occupied by Weymouth College in later years).

WEYMOUTH HARBOUR TRAMWAY The direct link from the railway station to the harbour opened in October 1865, and was horse-drawn in its early years. The first steam loco was used on the line in 1878, but it was two years before engines were in regular service. Goods-only for more than twenty years, it was 1889 before the line carried passengers.

A train on the Weymouth Harbour Tramway. All the water shown in this picture was filled in during the 1920s.

A tank engine prepares to take its passengers to Weymouth railway station in about 1960.

Those travelling on the Channel Islands boat train waited at Weymouth Station for the locomotive that had brought them from London to be uncoupled ; a tank engine was then coupled up to take them onward to the harbour. In its early days the railway line along Commercial Road directly overlooked the water – massive reclamation from the Backwater in the 1920s provided the land on which Melcombe Regis Gardens and Radipole Park Drive now stand. Various improvements to the Tramway have included widening at **Ferry's Corner** and extensions which took the line to the landing stage on the pier. Diesels began to displace steam in 1962 and from the 1970s main line diesels took the boat trains straight to the pier. Electrification of the Weymouth-Waterloo line in 1988 brought about the demise of the Tramway. It was not practicable for passengers to change trains for the last part of their journey and they were bussed between the railway station and the pier. Only a few 'specials' have used the line since then. Weymouth's 'railway through the streets' was unique. Locals became impatient when they were held up by its slow progress (sometimes made even slower by motorists who left cars parked too close to the track : these had to be removed before the train progressed further) and visitors were astonished to see a full-size train pass by as they walked along the pavement. This was the only place in mainland Britain where a train proceeded along the public highway for over a mile. Plans to introduce trams on part of the disused Tramway fell through and it now seems that the lines may be removed.

Further reading: *The Weymouth Harbour Tramway*, by J.H. Lucking (Oxford Publishing Co., 1986) *The Weymouth Harbour Tramway in the steam era*, by Gerry Beale (Wild Swan, 2001)

WEYMOUTH LIBRARY The Public Libraries Acts of 1850 and subsequent years empowered councils to provide free public libraries. Although Weymouth Council resolved in 1893 to establish a free library for the borough nothing was done and in 1903 when philanthropist **Andrew Carnegie** offered £5000 for a library building, the town prevaricated so long over a possible site that the offer was eventually withdrawn. More than forty years would pass before the first public library – a 'Reference Only' service – opened in 1944 in borrowed accommodation, occupying part of the council-owned Electricity Showrooms in Westham Road. One man, Alderman Jennings Attwooll, spent much of his life on the council campaigning for a library in Weymouth and in July 1948 he finally declared open a full reference and lending service in a prefabricated building (supposedly temporary until a more suitable site was found) in Westwey Road. The town's first librarian was Lucie Holman and she was succeeded in 1949 by Jack West, who held the post until 1974. When the present Municipal Offices on North Quay were designed in the 1960s, the original intention was to build a new library in a separate building at its western end, but spending cuts removed it from the plans and the 'temporary' prefab was to serve the town for more than forty years. Extensions to the building included the use of a nearby former wartime decontamination centre which was linked to the main building in 1967. On local government re-organisation in 1974 Dorset County Council took over the service and on the 8th November 1990 the prefab was finally replaced when the Princess Anne opened the present Weymouth Library in Great George Street, built on the site of **St Mary's Schools**.

WEYMOUTH MIDDLE SCHOOL was founded in 1858 and moved in 1860 to a new building in Commercial Road (A Crickmay design, today known as the Arts Centre). Its aim was to provide an education for fee-paying sons of middle class families, and the move for its establishment was led by the Reverend Talbot Greaves, Rector of St Mary's Church. It soon became obvious that the school was not paying its way and in 1862 the trustees decided instead to use the premises to open 'a first-class Grammar School' the following year. It was from this school that Weymouth College, the boys' public school, evolved. The Middle School continued in other premises (probably in Turton Street) but in 1865 the Grammar School found the Commercial Road building too small, a new site was found on Dorchester Road, and the Middle School moved back in. It was still unsuccessful but was 're-launched' in 1869, taking on a new name 'Melcombe Regis School' in 1876.

WEYMOUTH MUSEUM The first 'town museum' (as opposed to small private museums) was set up in 1858 and occupied rooms above the Royal Baths in St Thomas Street. Leading local citizens were on its council, headed by civil engineer John Coode as Chairman with solicitor, naturalist and photographer William Thompson as Hon. Secretary. The Museum aimed to show objects of natural and local history interest. Just how long it lasted is not known but another century would pass before a 'Local History Exhibition' was set up in the former Melcombe Regis School, Westham Road in 1971 as part of the celebrations of the Quatercentenary of the 1571 Union of Weymouth and Melcombe Regis. This Exhibition formed the basis of a new Weymouth Museum, the first Curator being **Jack West**. It was housed in the school until 1989, when the buildings were demolished to provide a site for the new Weymouth Marina headquarters. Weymouth Museum then relocated to Brewer's Quay, Hope Square.

WEYMOUTH OLD BANK *see* ELIOT, PEARCE & CO's BANK

WEYMOUTH PINE is a Northern American tree also known as the White Pine (Pinus strobus). It was introduced into England by **Lord Weymouth** and named by botanists after him.

WEYMOUTH PORT SANITARY HOSPITAL FOR INFECTIOUS DISEASES *see* PORT SANITARY HOSPITAL, Ferrybridge, Wyke Regis

WEYMOUTH POTTERY was started by Leonard Stockley in 1961 in a tiny alley between a pub and a gift shop in Augusta Place.

WEYMOUTH POTTERY COMPANY *see* BRICKYARDS

WEYMOUTH RAILWAY STATION opened 20th January 1857. It was timber built, with an all-over roof, and was a good example of Brunel's designs for the GWR, although the station was shared with the LSWR. GWR plans for a new station in the 1930s were halted on the outbreak of WW2. The glass was removed from the roof in 1939 as an air raid precaution and the timber roof was dismantled in 1951. The pre-war planned expansion began in 1956 when British Railways built two new long platforms but it halted again and there were no further developments after 1958 as

Edwardian travellers at the railway station.

the introduction of diesels was eventually to bring about the end of steam trains and the need for long platforms. The old station building remained until it was demolished in the summer of 1984 and replaced by the present structure which opened on 3rd July 1986. *See also* RAILWAY.

A 1930s view of the railway station with its overall roof. Christchurch is in the background.

WEYMOUTH ROYAL HOSPITAL AND DISPENSARY, School Street opened on 18th May 1872. It had been founded in 1816 as the Weymouth Dispensary under the patronage of Princess Charlotte and Prince Leopold of Saxe Coburg. Its early location is unknown, but it was for the use of the poor and entirely supported by voluntary contributions. In November 1820 the hospital moved to St Mary Street, and again in 1835/6 to No.9 Maiden Street, where it remained until the purpose-built hospital opened in School Street in 1872, enlarged in 1898. Queen Victoria, as Princess Victoria, became a patron of the hospital, hence the 'Royal' prefix. It closed in 1921 on amalgamation with the **Princess Christian Hospital** at Greenhill, being renamed **Weymouth and District Hospital**. The School Street building was acquired by the Salvation Army in September 1921 for use as a hostel, originally primarily for the use of servicemen. This, later known as Colwell House, closed in 1981 and was pulled down. The current building on the site, a small shopping centre, kept the name Colwell Centre and a plaque from the old hospital has been mounted beside its entrance.

The Victorian Weymouth Royal Hospital and Dispensary had closed by the time this picture was taken. The building, sold to the Salvation Army in 1921, was converted to a hostel.

WEYMOUTH ROYAL SAILORS' HOME *see* SAILORS' HOME, St Nicholas Street

WEYMOUTH SANATORIUM, Clarence Buildings Founded by Dr William Smith who also gave free advice to those unable to pay. By 1848 the hospital occupied a small house in Clarence Buildings, but in 1863 he built a larger Sanatorium a few doors away on the corner of Belle Vue, a site obtained from Sir Frederic Johnstone. Not an ideal location due to the constant loading and unloading of cargoes from steamers nearby and the harbour's busy passenger traffic. It was replaced in 1902 by the new **Princess Christian Hospital and Sanatorium** at Greenhill (later to be known as **Weymouth and District Hospital**). From 1904 until 1971 the Clarence Buildings sanatorium was used by Weymouth Corporation as municipal offices.

WEYMOUTH TEACHERS' TRAINING COLLEGE, Dorchester Road Established in the former **Weymouth College** public school buildings in 1946, it was renamed 'Weymouth College of Education' in 1965 and became part of the Dorset Institute for Higher Education in 1976. Closed as a teacher training college in 1985. The next occupant of the buildings was **Weymouth College (present day)**.

WEYMOUTH TELEGRAM was one of the local weekly newspapers in the late 19th and early 20th century. Its printing works until 1905 were in Governor's Lane, after which the paper moved to the disused Methodist Chapel in Caroline Place.

WEYMOUTH WATERWORKS *see* WATER SUPPLY

WEYMOUTH WAY opened in April 1987, part of a scheme to relieve traffic congestion in Weymouth. This included a new road bridge (Swannery Bridge) across the back-water close to where the railway viaduct had formerly crossed the water, with new traffic roundabouts at the end of King Street and Westwey Road. Weymouth Way runs along the Backwater's western shore to Mount Pleasant, crossing the River Wey by means of a bridge and is itself crossed by a bridge at the end of Spa Road.

WHALE In 1752 a huge whale was washed up on the beach. Blubber and spermaceti oil were extracted from it and sold by auction in March 1753, after warnings that no blubber or oil should be boiled within the borough where it might cause a fire or offensive smell.

WHEELER, Harry, 20 and 21 St Mary Street Harry Wheeler was publisher, stationer, photographer (the Van Dyck Portrait Studio), and circulating library proprietor. He was also a theatrical impresario, who took on the running of the Theatre Royal in St Nicholas Street (although this venture did not long survive the opening of the Jubilee Hall in 1887) and the first Pavilion Theatre, where he was succeeded by his son Earnest.

WHETTAM FAMILY The Whettams were prominent builders in Weymouth from the mid-19th century until late in the 20th. The firm was founded by John Thomas Whettam in 1860, and from 1872 operated from Grange Road. Builder of Grange Terrace, Cambridge Terrace (Lennox Street), other houses in the Park District and Grosvenor Road. Other works included the new GWR cargo stage in the 1880s, Town Bridge alterations in 1880 and extensive repairs to the old timber bridge across the Backwater. In 1895 he handed the business to his son John Thomas Whettam, who died in 1913. The business was then run by his son Albert Edward Whettam who did much to repair the ravages of WW2 here and elsewhere. By 1960 the business was supervised by his son, also Albert Edward Whettam whose works included Upwey and Broadwey Memorial Hall, Cosens' new workshops on Commercial Road, and Pickfords' new premises in Lower Bond Street. Albert Edward Whettam formerly of Southdown House, Southdown Avenue died in 1988, having retired to Wimborne.

WHITE ENSIGN CLUB *see* SAILOR'S HOME, St Nicholas Street

WHITE HART INN, Lower Bond Street/New Bond Street The building dates from the 16th or early 17th century and is believed originally to have been the house of Rear Admiral and silk merchant Sir John Browne, although the building has been much altered since. Legend has it that Sir James Thornhill was born here in 1675, although there is no documentary evidence to prove this.

WHITE HORSE, Osmington Hill commemorates King George III's visits to Weymouth 1789-1805 and was completed in 1808. 280 feet long and 323 feet high, it is designed to be viewed to best advantage from the sea and depicts the King riding in the hills around Weymouth, a favourite royal pastime. A local tale suggests that King George III was not at all pleased that the carving showed him riding *away* from his favourite resort and that as a result one of those involved in designing the White Horse committed suicide. Not so, for the King had paid his last visit to Weymouth in 1805; his health and eyesight were failing by 1808 and it is highly unlikely that he was even aware of the planned tribute to his visits. Suggestions that the Osmington White Horse's royal rider was added to a much earlier hill carving are similarly unproven and none of the writers and travellers who described Weymouth prior to 1808 make any mention of an ancient chalk figure in the landscape. John Rainier, brother of retired Admiral Peter Rainier, paid for the work, on land belonging to local bookseller John Wood. The White Horse was cut by soldiers, working under the guid-ance of architect James Hamilton.

WHITE HORSE INN was at No.33, St Mary Street. It closed in 1974.

WHITE HOUSE *see* PILGRIM HOUSE, Hope Square

WHITE LION INN, Melcombe Regis location unknown.

WHITECROSS The house, which stood on Buxton Road near its junction with Cross Road, was once the home of local businessman **Vilat Hackfath Bennett**. It was demolished in 2003, and the apartment block since built on the site has retained the name 'Whitecross'.

WHITEHEAD TORPEDO WORKS, Ferrybridge, Wyke Regis The foundation stone of Robert Whitehead's Torpedo Works was laid in April 1891 by his daughter, Countess Georg Hoyos. The factory provided employment for many and was largely responsible for the growth of 'New Wyke' along Portland Road. First manager of the works was **Captain Payne Gallwey**. In 1907 a controlling interest was purchased jointly by Vickers Ltd and Sir W.G. Armstrong-Whitworth and Co. Production throughout WW1 was followed by a brief period of closure 1921-23 but the factory re-opened and continued under the Whitehead name until 1942 when it was taken over and re-named The Vickers-Armstrong Torpedo Works. An air raid in 1941 temporarily disrupted production and it was deemed advis-able to disperse production to other sites in addition to Wyke. The factory had its own torpedo pier, coming out of the works and continuing under the line of the Weymouth and Portland

Railway, thence out into Portland Harbour. It carried torpedoes which were to be tested from the works along the pier's narrow gauge railway to waiting boats, which took them across to Bincleaves for firing. Post war, the factory diversified into more general engineering work with the last torpedo being fired in 1966. The pier was demolished in 1968. Closure of the works was announced in 1966 and in 1967 it was sold to Wellworthy Ltd., which, as the result of a merger in 1989, became AE Piston Products Ltd. The factory closed for good in 1993 and in 1997 work started on the present housing development on the site – Harbour Point. The Wellworthy name lives on in the nearby Wellworthy Sports and Social Club, opened in October, 1987. *See also* VON TRAPP FAMILY.

Further reading : *The centenary story of the Whitehead Torpedo and Engineering Works, Ferrybridge, Wyke Regis* by Doug Hollings (A Shrubbery Lane Local History Publication, 1991)

WICKHAM, Mabel (1902-1992) Artist. Painted many watercolours of Weymouth. Lived at Rodwell.

WILLIAMS, Thomas H. & Sons General Draper, Milliner and Mantle Maker. No.18 St Mary Street and Nos.9 and 10 Bond Street. Thomas Henry Williams came to Weymouth in 1861. He was the last Mayor of the old Corporation 1894-95 and the first Mayor of the enlarged borough in 1895-96. Boundary stones bearing his name were installed in 1895 to mark the boundary at that time and they can still be found around the town today. HSBC bank stands on the site of the former shop.

WILLIAMS, William (1774-1839) of the Williams family of Bridehead. Barrister and partner in Williams & Co.'s bank at Dorchester. Prominent freemason. MP for Melcombe Regis 1818-1826, and opponent of vote rigging and the controlling interest of the **Johnstone** family. Died at his home Castle Hill, Buckland Newton and is buried at Little Bredy.

WILLIAMS, Winston Williams was a customs official. He and others, including William Freke, 'a gentleman of Upwey', were invited in August 1701 to partake of a drink or two at the home of Thomas Bower in Governor's Lane. There they drank port 'to a greate hight'. Subsequently, Williams and Freke quarrelled and both stormed out of the house to fetch their swords. Other guests appeared not to have noticed anything amiss – or perhaps they had imbibed too much to notice anything at all. Williams stamped about outside, angered still more by being reminded that his choice of language could land him with a fine. Freke, accompanied by a crowd of locals excited by the prospect of a fight, arrived back on the scene. The two rushed at each other with drawn swords, and Williams received a severe stomach wound, from which he died the next morning. Freke took himself off to the Crown Hotel and told the ostler there how very sorry he was. He rode away on horseback but was evidently arrested later as he stood trial at Dorchester in 1702, where he was found not guilty of murder.

WILTON ESTATE *see* JOHNSTONE ESTATE

WILTON TERRACE became Nos.13-23 William Street.

WIMPY BAR Weymouth's first Wimpy Bar opened at No.16 St Edmund Street in June 1960.

WINDERMERE ESTATE off Ullswater Crescent was built in the late 1950s by Ernest Coleman and continued the tradition of 'Lake District' street names. It is believed that he used some of the stone of **Christchurch** (which he demolished) in the estate.

WINDMILLS *see* MILLS

WINDSOR TERRACE became Nos.17-24 Brownlow Street.

WINTERSLOW HOUSE *see* ALLEN, Ralph

WISEMAN, William A barber's apprentice during the time of the **Monmouth Rebellion**, he was ordered to be whipped through all the market towns in the county for having read Monmouth's Proclamation at Weymouth. The 14-year old was whipped at Dorchester but a clergyman complained that the gaoler was not severe enough and Judge Jeffreys ordered the punishment to be repeated the following day. The punishment meted out the second time was so severe it was thought the boy would die. He survived and was subsequently whipped through the town of Melcombe, where the punishment terminated.

WOLCOT, John *see* **PINDAR, Peter**

WOOD, Mrs Henry Her novel *Within the maze* is set partly in Weymouth and Portland. Published in 1902.

WOOLAND GARDENS *see* WYKE HOUSE/WYKE HOUSE HOTEL

WOOLF, Virginia and the Dreadnought Hoax. *See* DREADNOUGHT HOAX

WOOLLEY, Sir Richard van der Riet (1906-1986) Astronomer. Born in Weymouth, he was appointed Astronomer Royal in 1956, a post he held until 1971. Knighted in 1963. Returned to South Africa, where he had spent much of his early life, in 1972.

WOOLWORTH, F.W. The store's first Weymouth shop opened in St Mary Street in August 1923. The acquisition of adjacent properties in the 1930s led to the demolition of the original premises and the building of a superb new art deco

The striking 1930s architecture of F.W Woolworth's St Mary Street store was much missed when the building was altered to provide individual shops with brick façades.

style store which opened on July 28th 1938. The store was modernised in 1972, but closed in 1985. Not being considered worthy of Listed Building status, the building lost its distinctive glazed-tile façade and was converted to a row of individual shops with brick frontages. Woolworths returned to the town in June 2000, its current store being within the New Bond Street shopping development. *See also* BLOCKHOUSE LANE.

WOOPERTON STREET links Commercial Road and Park Street. The street name may have some association with William Wharton Burdon, proprietor of Weymouth Gasworks in the 19th century, who had family connections with Wooperton in Northumberland. The street's main claim to fame is that novelist Thomas Hardy lodged at No.3 during his employment as an architect in Weymouth 1869-1871. Here he worked on his first published novel *Desperate Remedies* and some poems.

WOOTTON, Charlotte was Weymouth's first woman mayor in 1956-57.

WORDSWORTH MEMORIAL HOME OF REST opened 15th October 1895 at No.1 Grosvenor Place on the Esplanade, in premises which were formerly part of the Cutter Hotel. The Home was run by the Girls Friendly Society, an organisation set up in 1875 and dedicated to helping girls who were working away from home and those who were ill or needed recuperation. A similar home had been set up at No.13 St John's Terrace four years earlier. The Society had strong Church of England links, and the Weymouth home was named after its former president, Susan Esther Wordsworth, late wife of the Bishop of Salisbury. The Wordsworth family has another connection with Weymouth – John Wordsworth was commander of the East Indiaman ***Earl of Abergavenny*** which sank with great loss of life off Weymouth in 1805. No.1 Grosvenor Place is now No.31 The Esplanade and is currently occupied by the Bourneville Hotel. The home moved to Swanage in March 1905.

WORDSWORTH TERRACE became Nos.205-227 Chickerell Road.

WORKHOUSE In the 18th century those unable or unwilling to support themselves were confined to workhouses but the rules were later relaxed, allowing them to seek work outside. Those who employed them paid very low wages, knowing that these would be supplemented by parish relief, and the numbers seeking poor relief increased. The Poor Law Amendment Act of 1834 was passed to reduce the amount of outdoor relief and in order to discourage the poor from seeking workhouse accommodation it promoted a harsh regime inside these establishments. Weymouth Union Workhouse on Wyke Road was built in 1836 on the site of an older Poor House. It is square in plan, its long frontage facing onto Wyke Road, and had a Women's Ward and Girls' School on one side and a Men's Ward and Boys' School on the other, with the Master's House between them. Little is known of life inside the workhouse as all the records have been lost, thought to have been handed over in a WW2 waste paper salvage drive. The Workhouse closed in 1929 when workhouses were abolished and the County Council took it over as the Public Assistance Hospital 'Portwey', accommodating the elderly and chronic sick and also providing facilities for unmarried mothers. It was used as an emergency hospital during WW2 and converted to Portwey Maternity Hospital in 1948, closing in 1987. The old workhouse building was converted to housing in 1993 and is now known as Union Court. Prior to 1836 Melcombe had its own Poor House at the junction of Lower St Alban Street and Commercial Road, a building later converted for use by a boatbuilder, but now demolished.

WORKING MEN'S CLUB The present club building in Mitchell Street opened on 12th March 1873. A club founded ten years earlier as a 'Working Men's Reading Room' occupied what was described as *'a very low, damp, musty little room'* in High Street, on the Weymouth side of the harbour, becoming the Weymouth Working-man's Club in 1865. By 1871 it had amalgamated with a second club in Great George Street on Melcombe side, becoming Weymouth and Melcombe Regis Working Men's Club before moving into the new Crickmay-designed building in Mitchell Street, the gift of Mr (later Sir) Henry Edwards on land leased from the Johnstone Estate. Westham Working Men's Club at No.1 Cromwell Road, opened in October 1904, moving to Milton Road in 1909.

WORLD WAR I War was declared on 4th August 1914. Sailors on shore leave in Weymouth had been recalled to their ships days before, when the Battle Squadrons slipped out of Portland Harbour to join the rest of the Fleet. The sudden military takeover of the railways disrupted the holiday industry, local recruiting campaigns intensified, refugees began arriving from Europe and shipwreck victims were landed from vessels sunk by enemy action. Soon the local newspapers began publishing long lists of men killed on active service. Army camps sprang up at Wyke Regis, Westham, Littlemoor, Chickerell and Portland and ambulance trains began to bring in thousands of wounded soldiers for treatment and convalescence. Many of the town's larger buildings were taken over as hospital accommodation. (*See* ANZAC MEMORIAL, ARMISTICE SHELTER; AUSTRALIAN AND NEW ZEALAND TROOPS; HOSPITALS. WORLD WAR I; WAR MEMORIAL).

WORLD WAR 2 War was declared on 3rd September 1939 and the early months, known as the 'Phoney War', were relatively quiet, although survivors from vessels attacked in the Channel were regularly brought into the port and Weymouth's population increased by some six thousand with the arrival of children evacuated from London. Blackout regulations were enforced, rationing began, air raid shelters were distributed and the Home Guard established. Early summer 1940 saw the evacuation of Allied troops from the beaches of Dunkirk and soon thousands of Belgian, Dutch and French refugees and Free French and Moroccan soldiers flooded into the town, followed by 24,000 Channel Islanders, all fleeing the German advance. With the threat of invasion perilously close, Weymouth that summer became a war zone with piers and seafront taken over by the military, the whole area bristling with anti-aircraft guns, anti tank obstacles and barbed wire. The air raids began on 4th July 1940. The town was repeatedly bombed and the air raids are well documented. In 1943 preparations for the Allied invasion of Normandy began and thousands of American troops were encamped in the area training for the amphibious landings on the beaches of France on D-Day, 6th June 1944. *See also* AMERICAN MEMORIAL; CONCRETE ROAD; EDLIN,

US troops loading stores outside the Pavilion Theatre in the run-up to D-Day.

Robert; EVACUEES; *BEE*, HMS; *GRASSHOPPER*, HMS; TEMPORARY TRAIN FERRY TERMINAL WW2; WAR MEMORIAL; WHITEHEAD TORPEDO WORKS.

Further reading : *Brigade in Action : the history of the origin and development of the St John Ambulance Brigade in Weymouth, and its co-operation with the Civil Defence Services during the War 1939-1945* by D.G.F. Acutt (published in Weymouth, 1946); *Weymouth and Portland at War : Countdown to D-Day*, by Maureen Attwooll and Denise Harrison (Dovecote Press, 1994); *Dorset at War: Diary of WW2*, by Rodney Legg (Dorset Publishing Company, 1990); *Dorset at War*, by John Murphy (Dorset Publishing Company, 1979).

WORNHAM TERRACE is now part of James Street.

'WORTH, Patience' Was said to be a spirit who spoke through a Ouija board to an American woman, Pearl Leonore Curran (1883-1937), and apparently described life in 17th century Weymouth in some detail.

WRECKING Wholesale looting of the cargoes of wrecked vessels supplemented the incomes of the local populace in the same way as smuggling. Hundreds descended on the beaches when a vessel was cast ashore, more intent on plunder than saving shipwrecked crew and passengers. It was required of the priests in coastal parishes that they preach a sermon four times a year warning their flocks of the penalties which could be incurred by such behaviour. Such admonition had little effect and it was not until well into the nineteenth century that the saving of life became the priority (although once that was accomplished, the cargo swiftly disappeared into local homes!).

WREN, Sir Christopher (1632-1723) Architect of St Paul's Cathedral, for which many thousands of tons of Portland stone were shipped to London in the late 17th and early 18th centuries. Wren himself visited the Portland quarries on several occasions and in November 1701 he was elected as one of Melcombe's MPs, having previously represented Plympton and Windsor.

WRIGHT'S ENGLISH NAPLES STORES, 49-50, St Mary Street R. J. Wright ran his extensive grocery shop in premises at the lower end of St Mary Street. It was taken over by his son in 1906.

WYKE CASTLE, Pirates Lane, Wyke Regis Not a castle at all, merely a slightly eccentric private house built in the 1850s by Dr Andrew Chadwick Fenoulhet who came to Weymouth as a GP in 1842, and was later appointed medical officer to the Wyke district of the Poor Law Union.

WYKE CHURCH *see* ALL SAINTS' CHURCH, Wyke Regis

WYKE HOTEL, Portland Road was renamed Wyke Smugglers in 1987.

WYKE HOUSE/WYKE HOUSE HOTEL was built about 1805 on the site of an earlier house. It was the home of the landowning Swaffield family for more than a century until it was sold to Henry Collingwood who converted the mansion into a residential hotel in the 1920s. It was demolished in 1974 and the houses of Wooland Gardens were built on the site.

WYKE LODGE *see* DOWMAN, Catherine

WYKE OLIVER FARM/ROAD, Preston Wyke in this instance is thought to be a modern variation of the Old English 'wic', a dairy farm. 'Oliver' dates from its ownership in the 17th century by John Oliver.

WYKE RECTORY beside the church was sold in 1954 when the present rectory on the opposite side of Portland Road replaced it.

WYKE REGIS takes its name from the old word 'wic' or even 'ic', and there are various opinions as to its meaning – it may be 'dairy farm', dependent farm (of Portland?) or harbour/fishery (see the entry for Bridge/Brige). The 'Regis' indicates royal ownership dating back to the 13th century, when the village is named as 'Kingeswic' in some documents. Wyke's Charter of 988 is the earliest one in existence locally and describes the boundaries of Wyke, although these are difficult to identify today.

Further reading : *A history of Wyke Regis*, by Doug Hollings (D.F.Hollings, 2nd ed. 2002).

WYKE REGIS COUNTY PRIMARY INFANTS SCHOOL opened in September 1953. Designed by **Ernest Wamsley Lewis**, its bright colour scheme led to it being known as the 'Rainbow School'. Sculptor Eric Morris produced a mural in the dining hall and a sculpture which stands outside the building.

WYKE REGIS HALT on the Weymouth and Portland Railway opened in July 1909. Closed in March 1952 when the line closed to passengers. A long way from Wyke village, the halt was primarily intended to serve the **Whitehead Torpedo Works** at Ferrybridge. Traces of the platform can be found along the **Rodwell Trail.**

WYKE REGIS HEALTH CENTRE, Portland Road opened 1st June 1964.

WYKE REGIS LIBRARY, Portland Road, opened 7th April 1962.

WYKE REGIS MEMORIAL HALL, Chamberlaine Road opened in 1908. It replaced the old Parish Room on the same site and was paid for by a trust set up in memory of Margaret, wife of the Reverend George Chamberlaine, Rector of Wyke 1809-1837.

WYKE ROAD was sometimes referred to as 'the Higher Road', Buxton Road being the 'Lower Road'.

WYKE SMUGGLERS PUBLIC HOUSE was formerly the Wyke Hotel. Renamed in 1987.

WYKEHAM VILLA became No.13 Cromwell Road.

WYVERN SCHOOL for children with learning difficulties opened in Chickerell Road in 1963, becoming a special school in 1971. It relocated to the mainstream school site at Broadwey in the autumn of 2006.

A postcard view from the 1920s, showing Wyke House in its hotel days, its walls covered with Virginia Creeper.

Y

YACHT INN was in Governor's Lane.

YACHT RACING International yacht racing was first held in Weymouth in August 1973.

YEATMAN, Rev Harry Farr Born in Weymouth. Poem *Brent Knoll* appeared in 1817.

YEOMANRY WEEKS The Queen's Own Dorset Yeomanry Cavalry (its name dates from Queen Victoria's reign), was a volunteer force originally founded in 1794. It consisted of various troops which assembled annually for a week's training camp and Weymouth became the favourite venue in the second half of the 19th century. When the Yeomanry cavalry rode into town in May it heralded the start of the summer season and was a great occasion for the town. As well as military events such as shooting, marching, manoeuvres, reviews, exercises, processions and church parades, there were balls, horse and pony races on the sands, and bicycle and boat races. The week-long camps ceased in the early 1900s, but the Yeomanry were still paying shorter visits to Weymouth in the 1930s.

Crowds always turned out when the Yeomanry rode into town.

YORK BUILDINGS, Esplanade Following the construction of the first Royal Hotel in the early 1770s and Gloucester Lodge in 1780, York Buildings, work on which started in 1783, was the first of the Georgian terraces to be built facing the sea. Originally consisting of three houses on either side of a bow-fronted central feature, the northernmost house of the terrace was demolished in the 1950s. Now numbered 52-57 The Esplanade.

YORK VILLA now Nos.24-26 Alexandra Road is a timber framed single storey building formerly part of **Radipole Barracks.**

York Buildings was a very fine terrace before one house was demolished at its northern end. Modern shop fronts and windows have altered the original façade.